EDENS ZERO
22

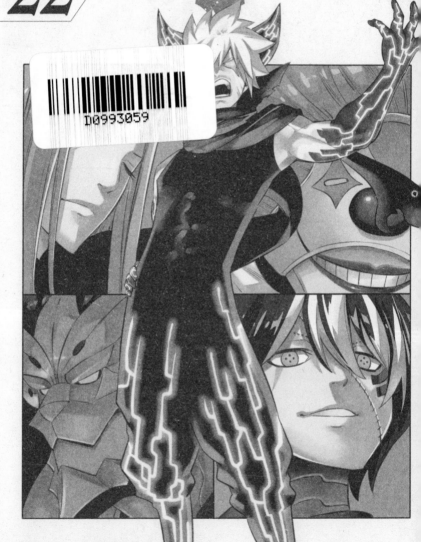

HIRO MASHIMA

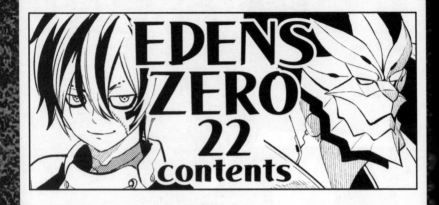

EDENS ZERO 22 contents

CHAPTER 186 ▶ The Subdimension Program —————— 3

CHAPTER 187 ▶ Shiki vs. Wizard —————————— 23

CHAPTER 188 ▶ One Tenth ——————————————— 43

CHAPTER 189 ▶ Rebecca vs. Clown ————————— 63

CHAPTER 190 ▶ The Greatest Show from Hell ———— 83

CHAPTER 191 ▶ Zombie Nurses ——————————— 103

CHAPTER 192 ▶ Weisz vs. Killer —————————— 123

CHAPTER 193 ▶ A Good Boy ———————————— 143

CHAPTER 194 ▶ The Ether of All Things ————— 163

EDENS ZERO

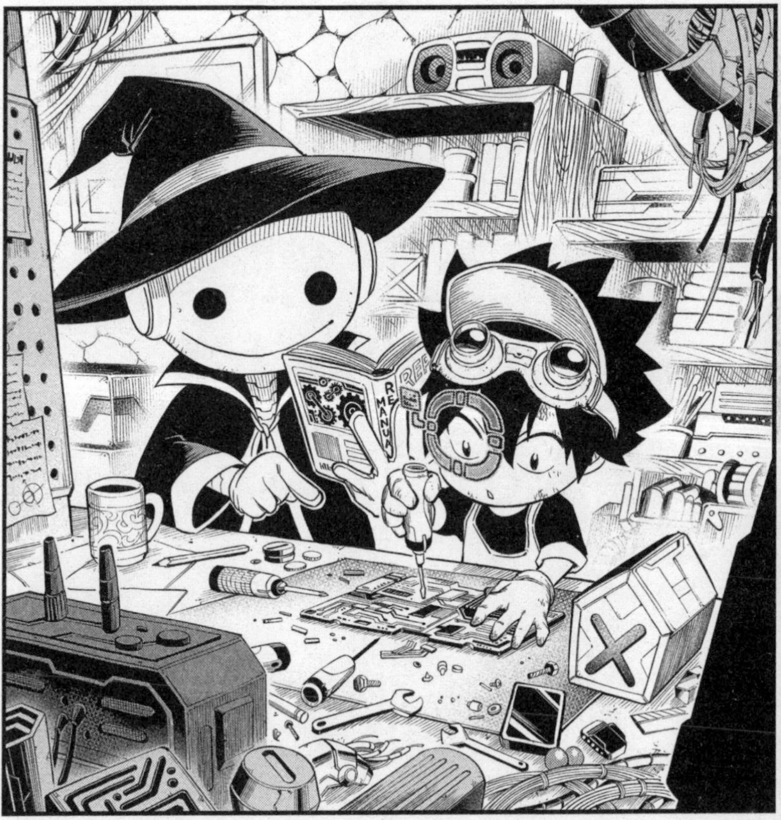

CHAPTER 186: THE SUBDIMENSION PROGRAM

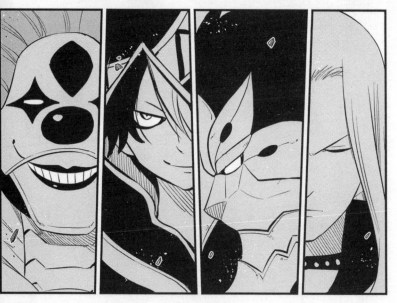

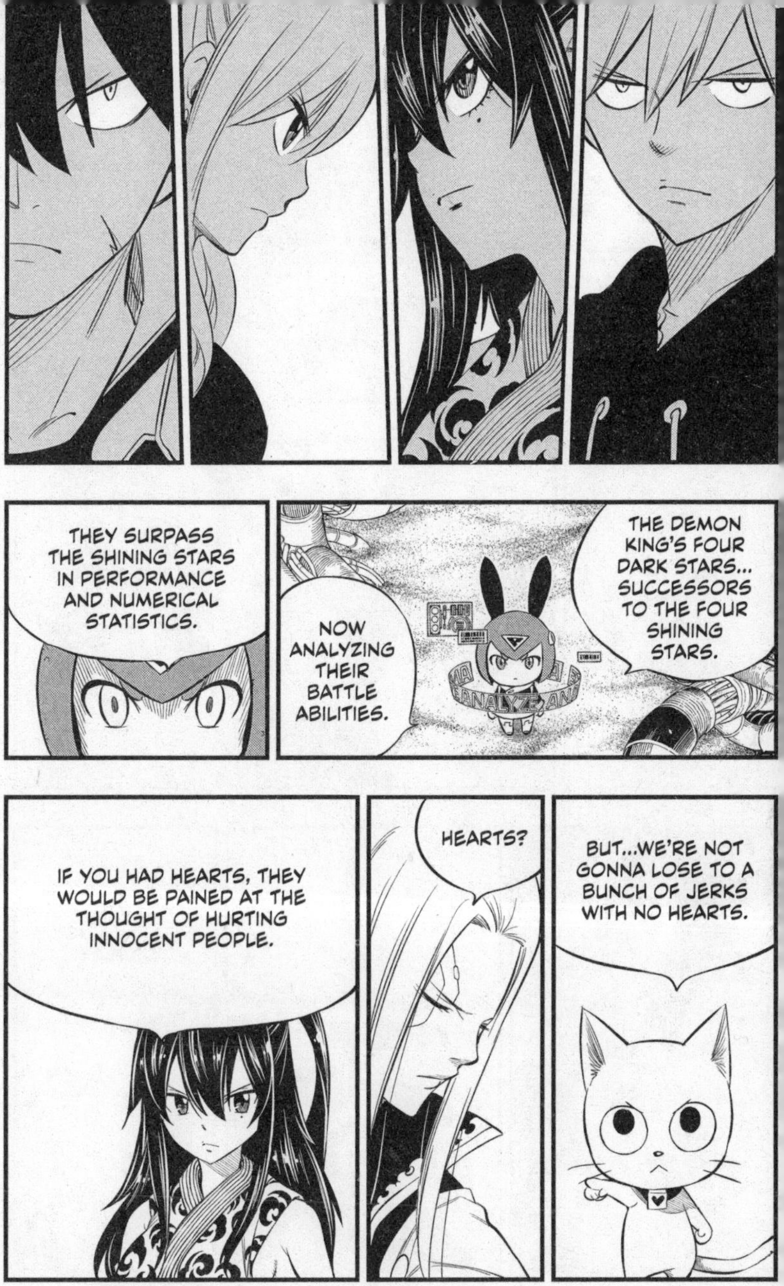
THE DEMON KING'S FOUR DARK STARS... SUCCESSORS TO THE FOUR SHINING STARS.
NOW ANALYZING THEIR BATTLE ABILITIES.
ANALYZE
THEY SURPASS THE SHINING STARS IN PERFORMANCE AND NUMERICAL STATISTICS.
BUT...WE'RE NOT GONNA LOSE TO A BUNCH OF JERKS WITH NO HEARTS.
HEARTS?
IF YOU HAD HEARTS, THEY WOULD BE PAINED AT THE THOUGHT OF HURTING INNOCENT PEOPLE.

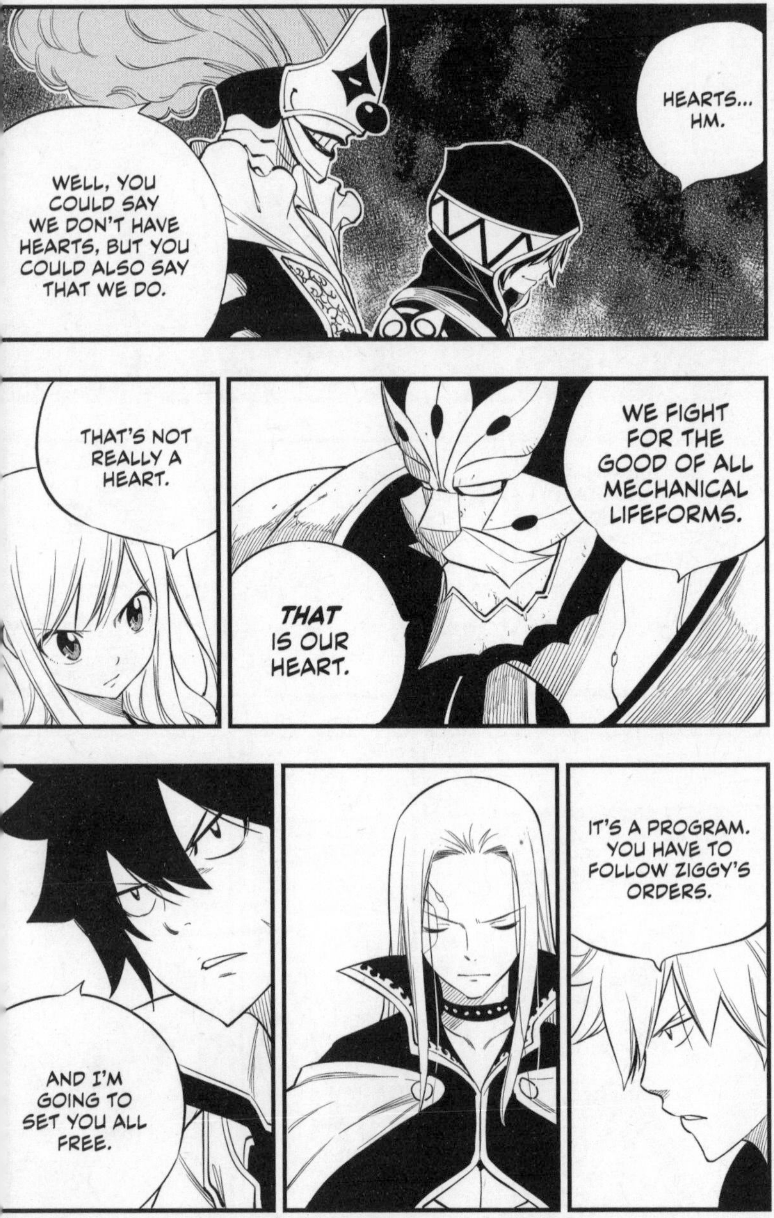
HEARTS... HM.
WELL, YOU COULD SAY WE DON'T HAVE HEARTS, BUT YOU COULD ALSO SAY THAT WE DO.
WE FIGHT FOR THE GOOD OF ALL MECHANICAL LIFEFORMS.
THAT IS OUR HEART.
THAT'S NOT REALLY A HEART.
IT'S A PROGRAM. YOU HAVE TO FOLLOW ZIGGY'S ORDERS.
AND I'M GOING TO SET YOU ALL FREE.

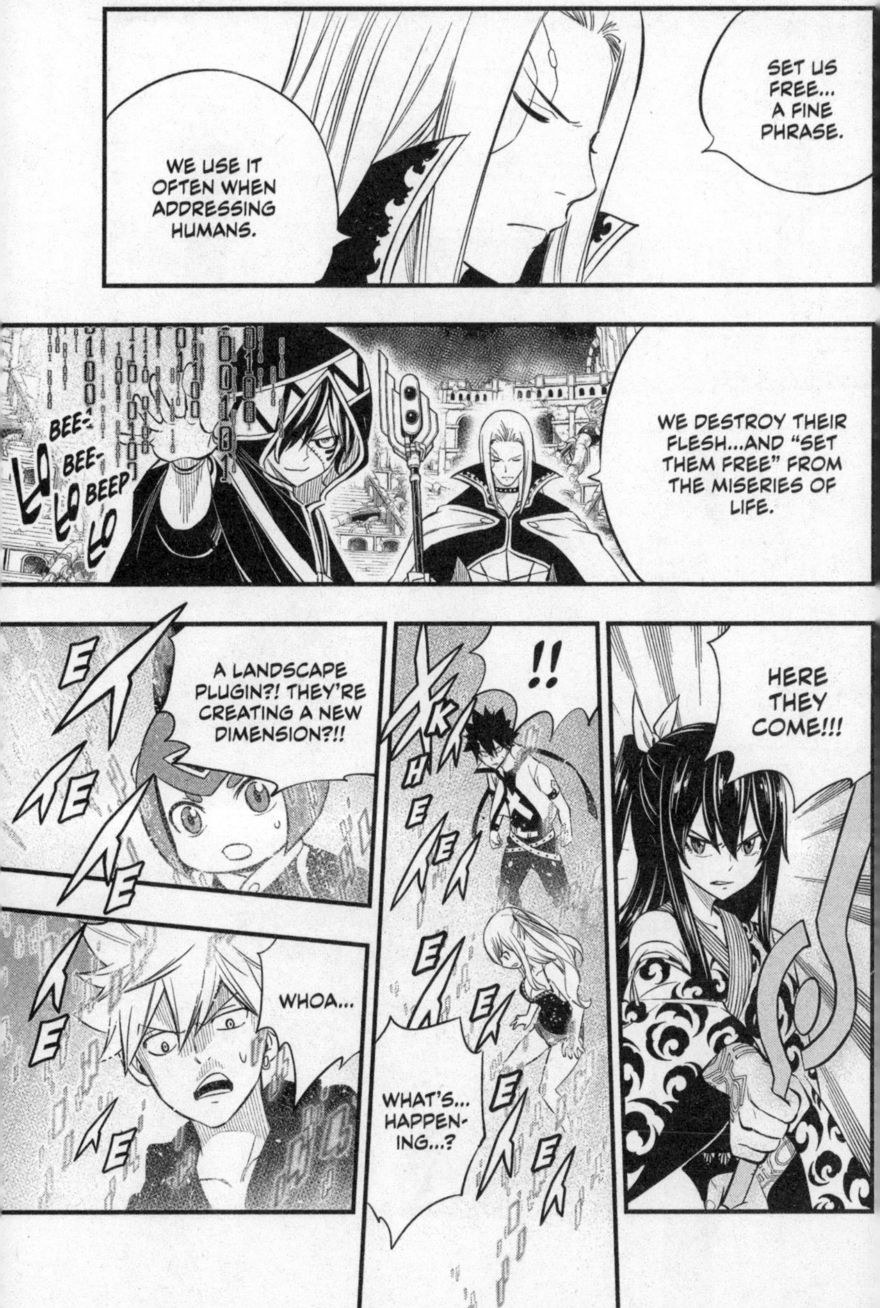
SET US FREE... A FINE PHRASE.
WE USE IT OFTEN WHEN ADDRESSING HUMANS.
WE DESTROY THEIR FLESH...AND "SET THEM FREE" FROM THE MISERIES OF LIFE.
BEE- BEE- BEEP
HERE THEY COME!!!
!!
WHAT'S... HAPPEN-ING...?
A LANDSCAPE PLUGIN?! THEY'RE CREATING A NEW DIMENSION?!!
WHOA...

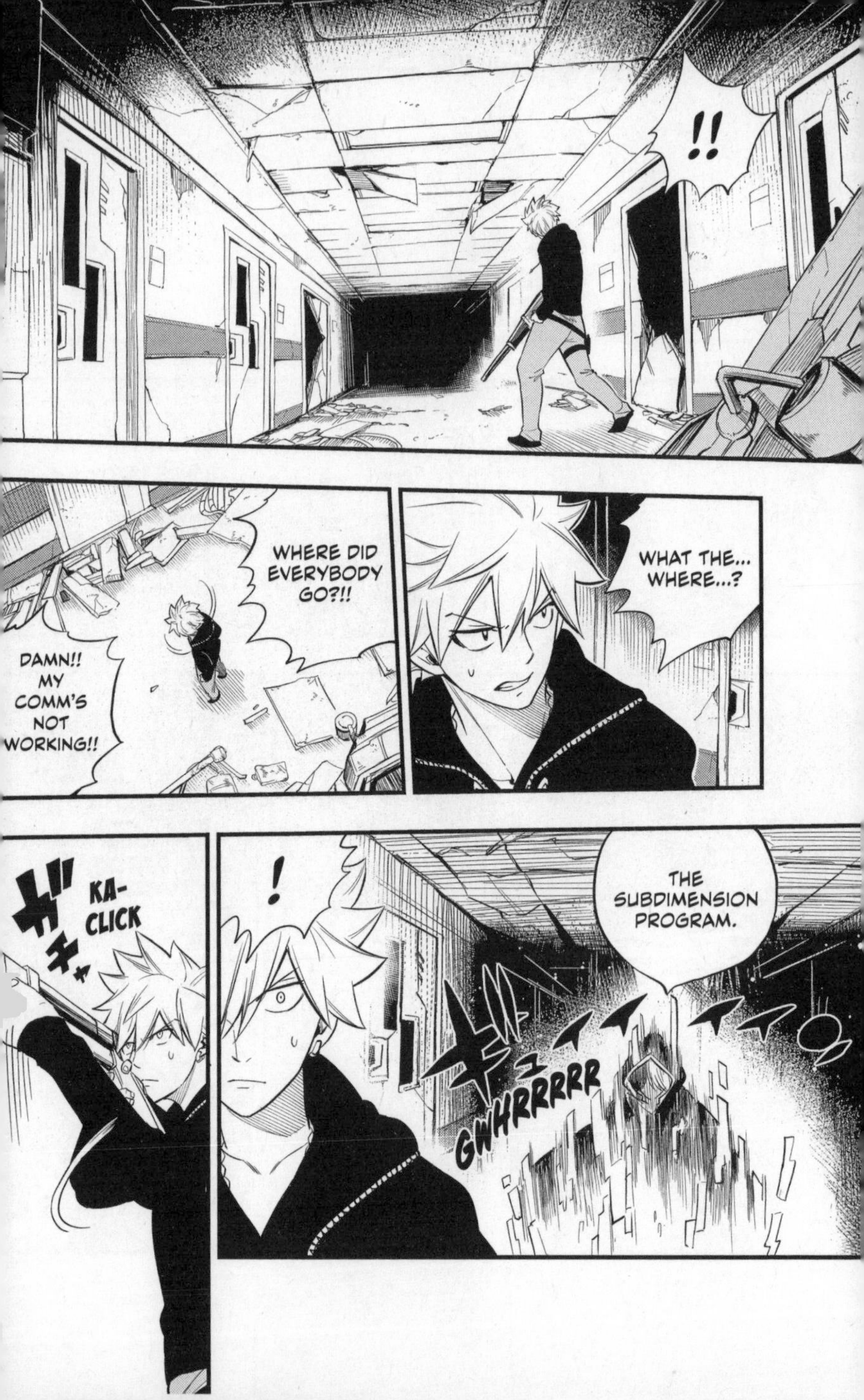
!!
WHAT THE... WHERE...?
WHERE DID EVERYBODY GO?!!
DAMN!! MY COMM'S NOT WORKING!!
!
THE SUBDIMENSION PROGRAM.
GWHRRRRR
KA-CLICK

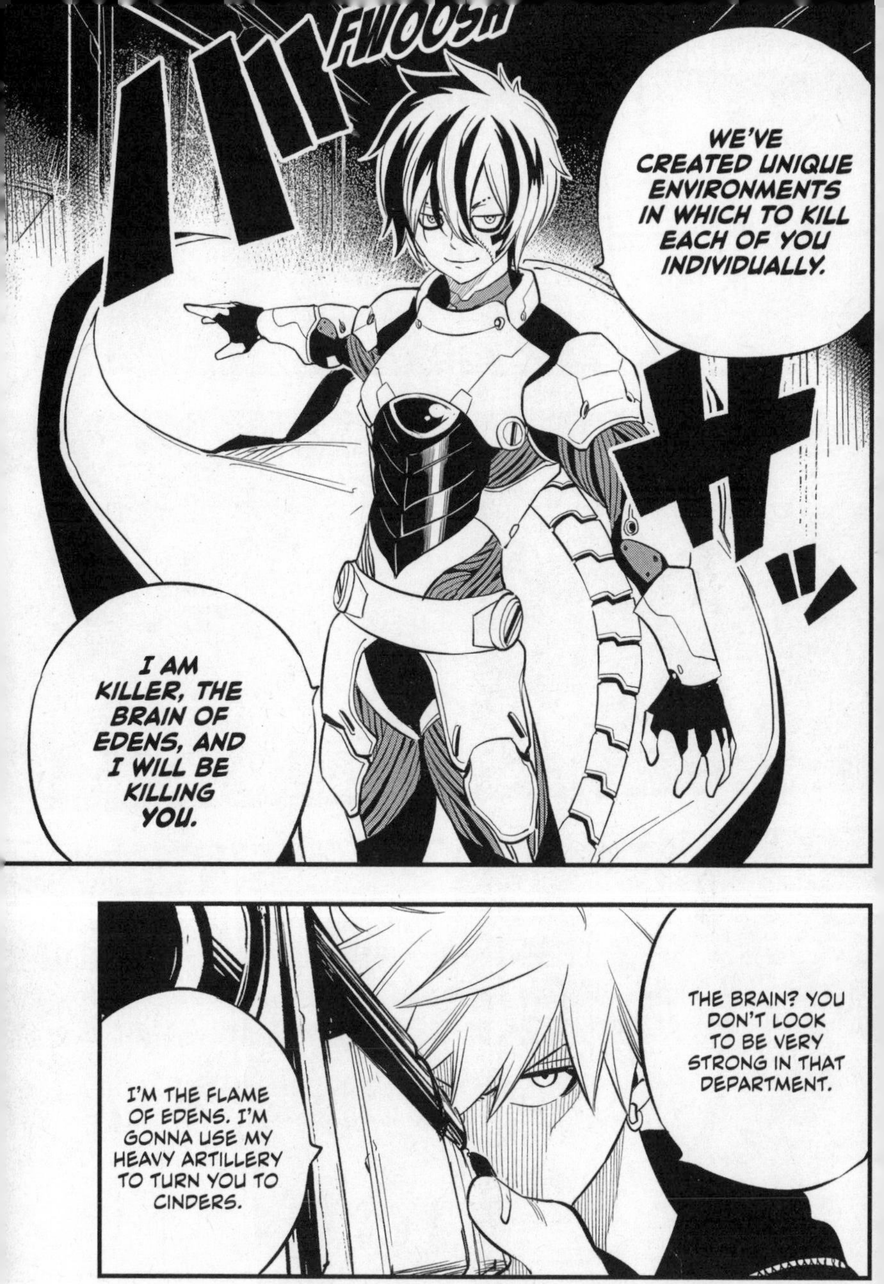
FWOOSH
WE'VE CREATED UNIQUE ENVIRONMENTS IN WHICH TO KILL EACH OF YOU INDIVIDUALLY.
I AM KILLER, THE BRAIN OF EDENS, AND I WILL BE KILLING YOU.
THE BRAIN? YOU DON'T LOOK TO BE VERY STRONG IN THAT DEPARTMENT.
I'M THE FLAME OF EDENS. I'M GONNA USE MY HEAVY ARTILLERY TO TURN YOU TO CINDERS.

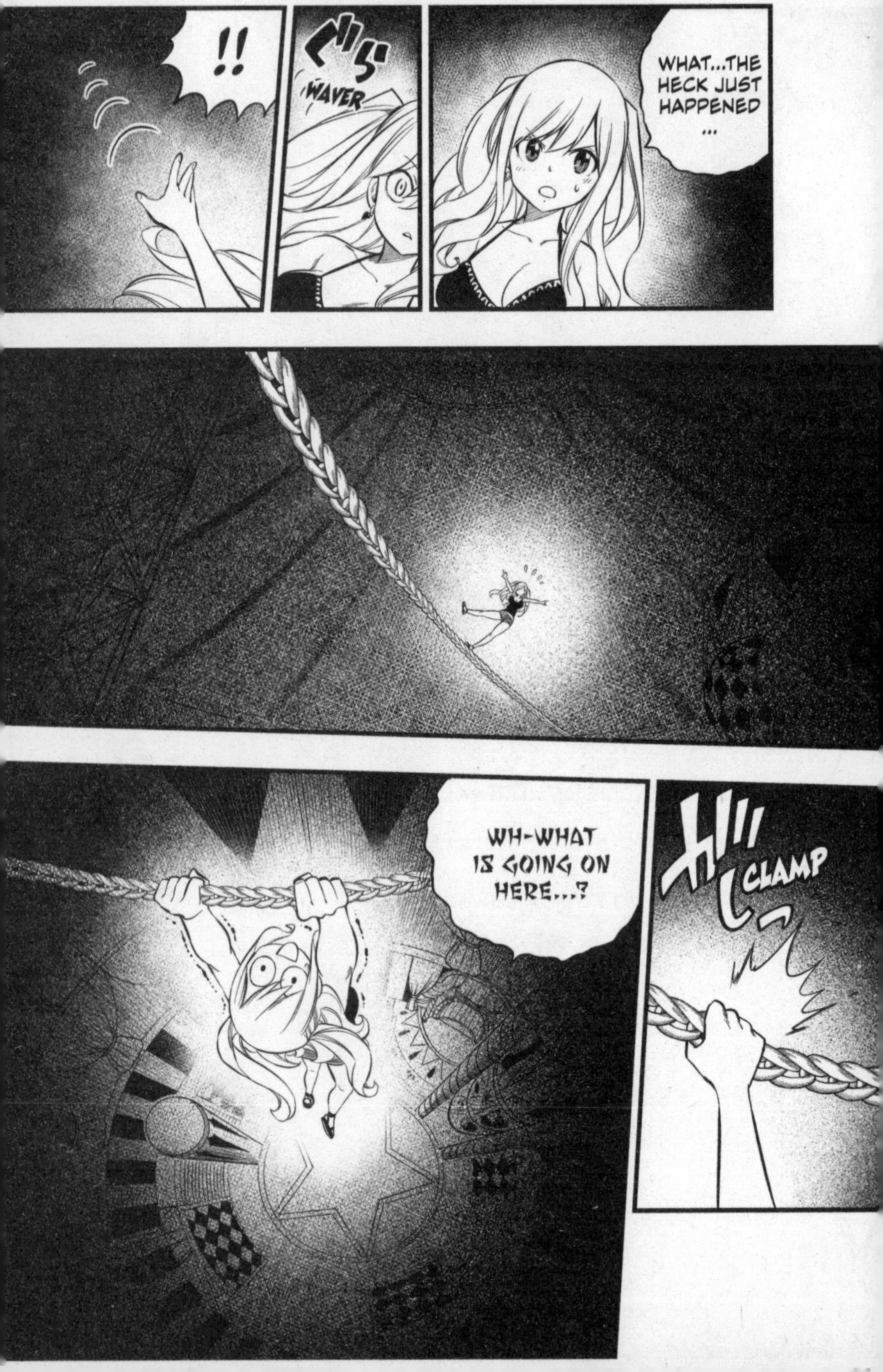
WHAT...THE HECK JUST HAPPENED ...
WAVER
!!
CLAMP
WH-WHAT IS GOING ON HERE...?

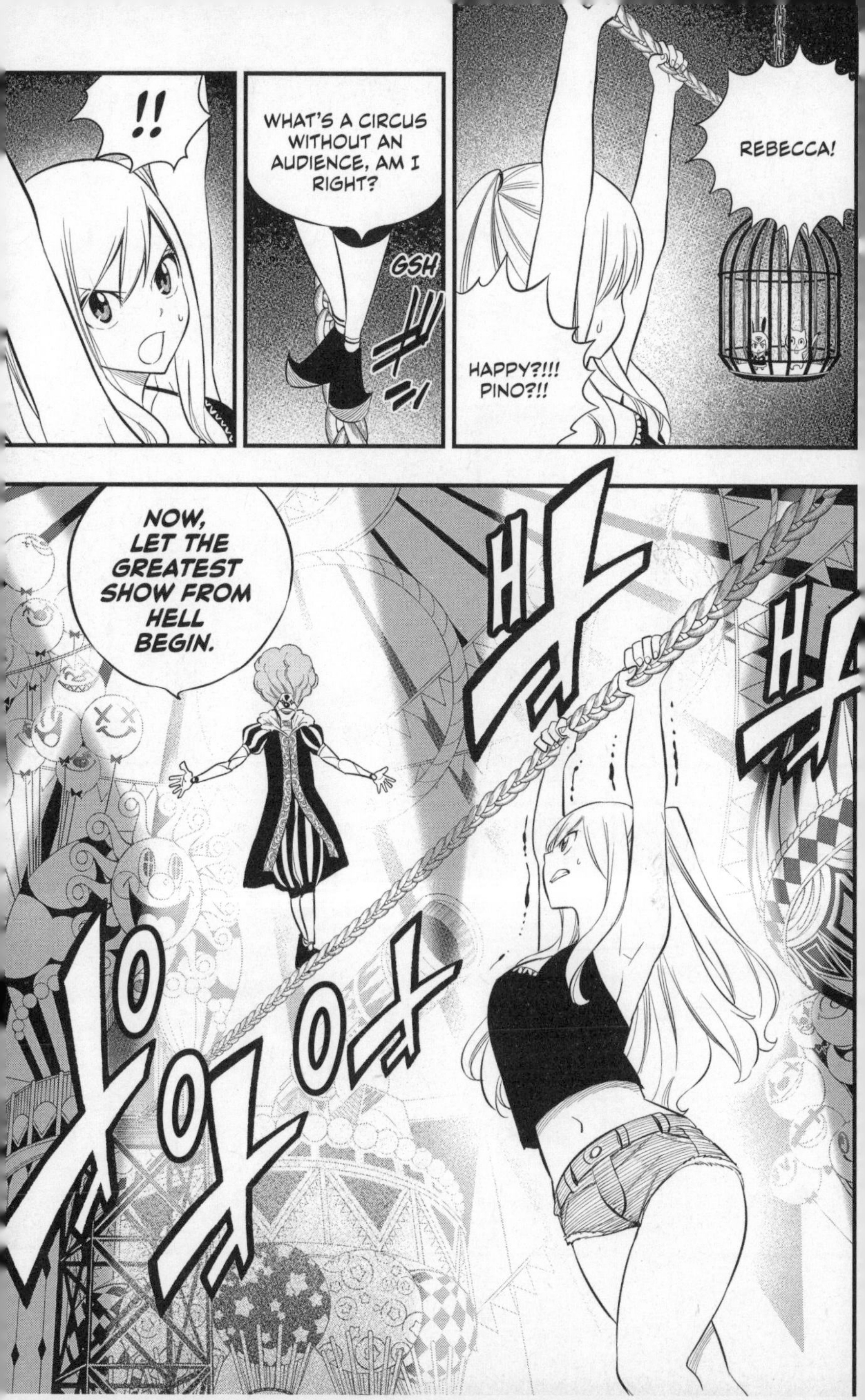
REBECCA!
HAPPY?!!! PINO?!!
WHAT'S A CIRCUS WITHOUT AN AUDIENCE, AM I RIGHT?
GSH
!!
NOW, LET THE GREATEST SHOW FROM HELL BEGIN.

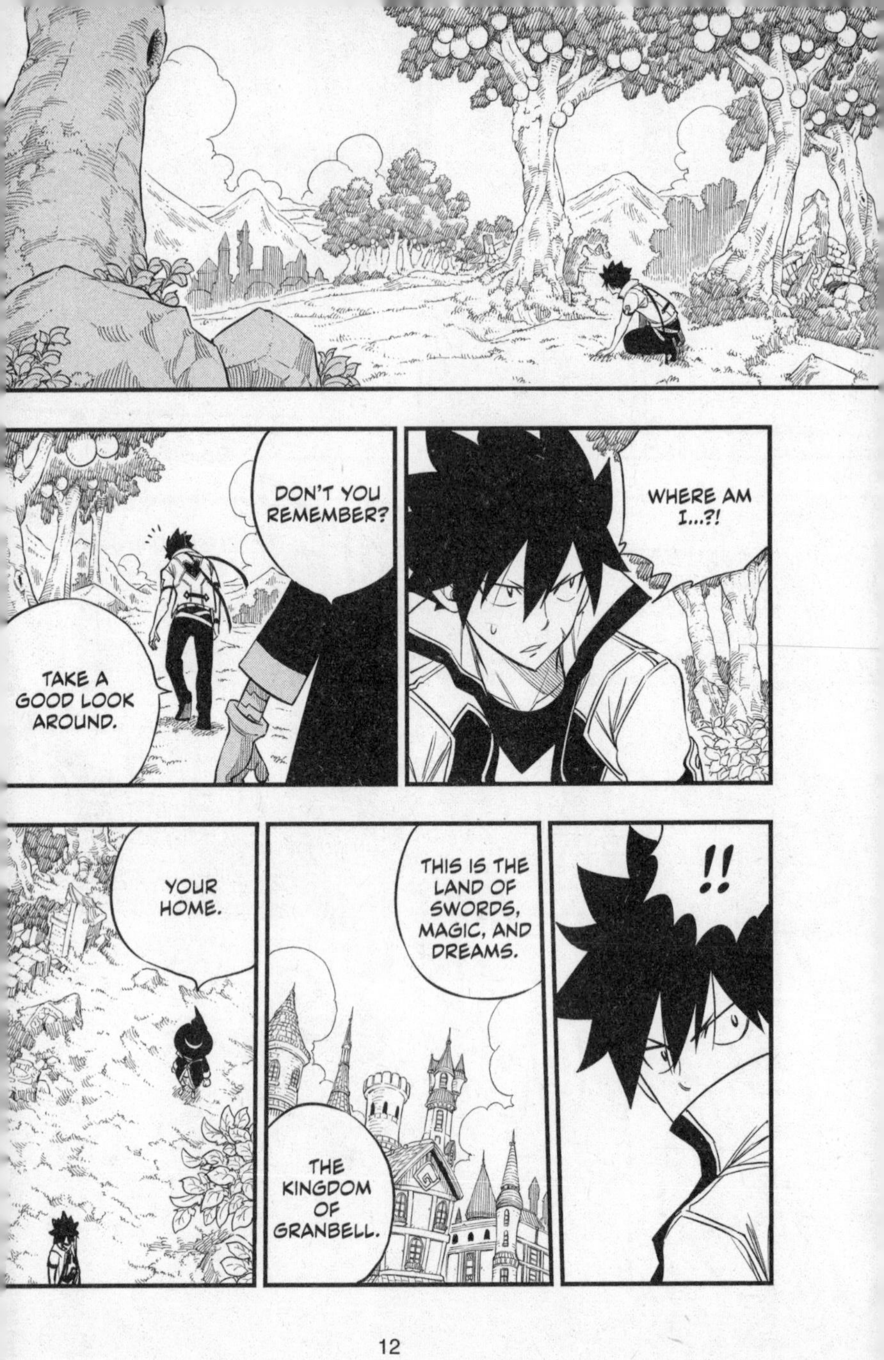
WHERE AM I...?!
DON'T YOU REMEMBER?
TAKE A GOOD LOOK AROUND.
!!
THIS IS THE LAND OF SWORDS, MAGIC, AND DREAMS.
THE KINGDOM OF GRANBELL.
YOUR HOME.

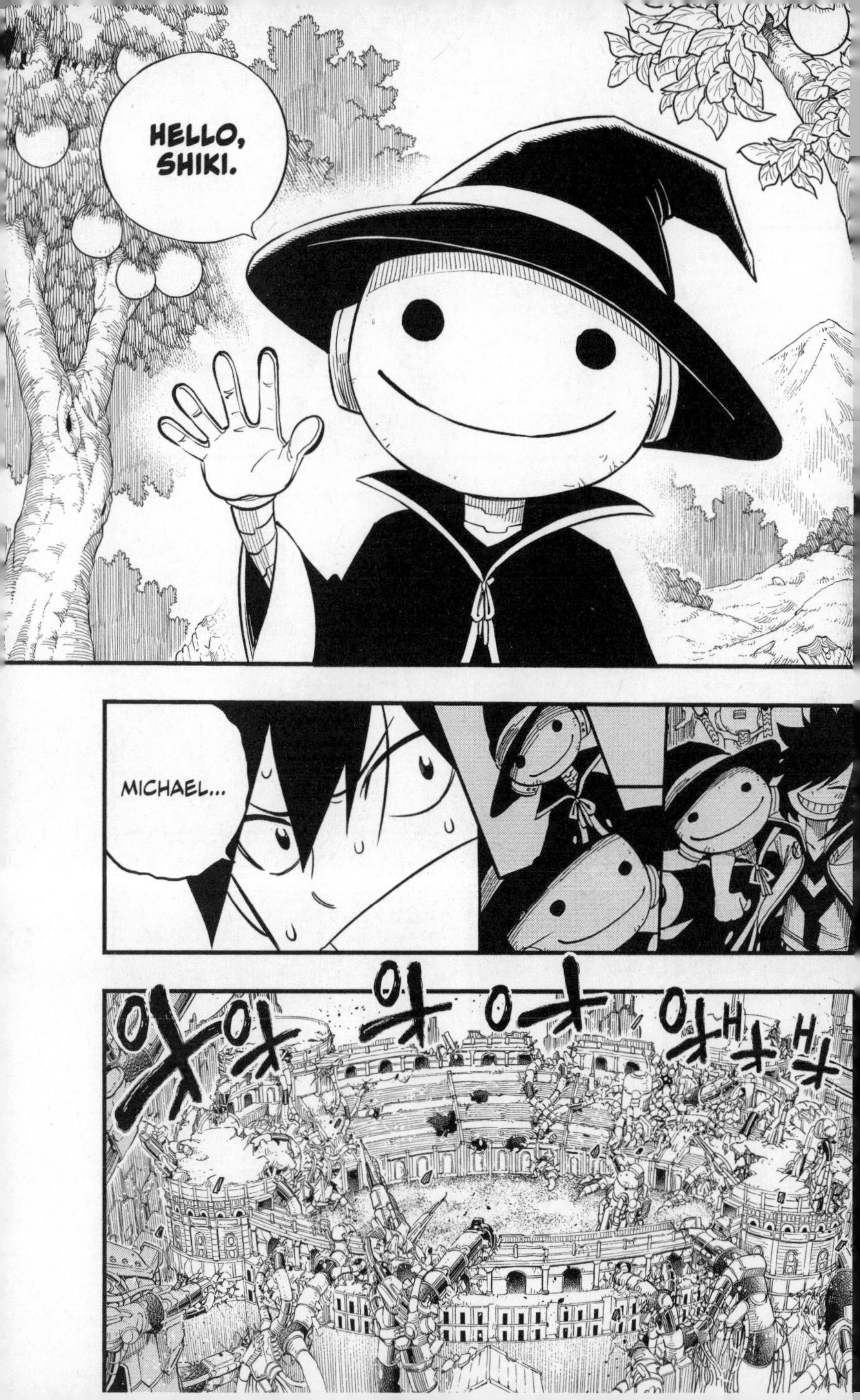
HELLO, SHIKI.
MICHAEL...

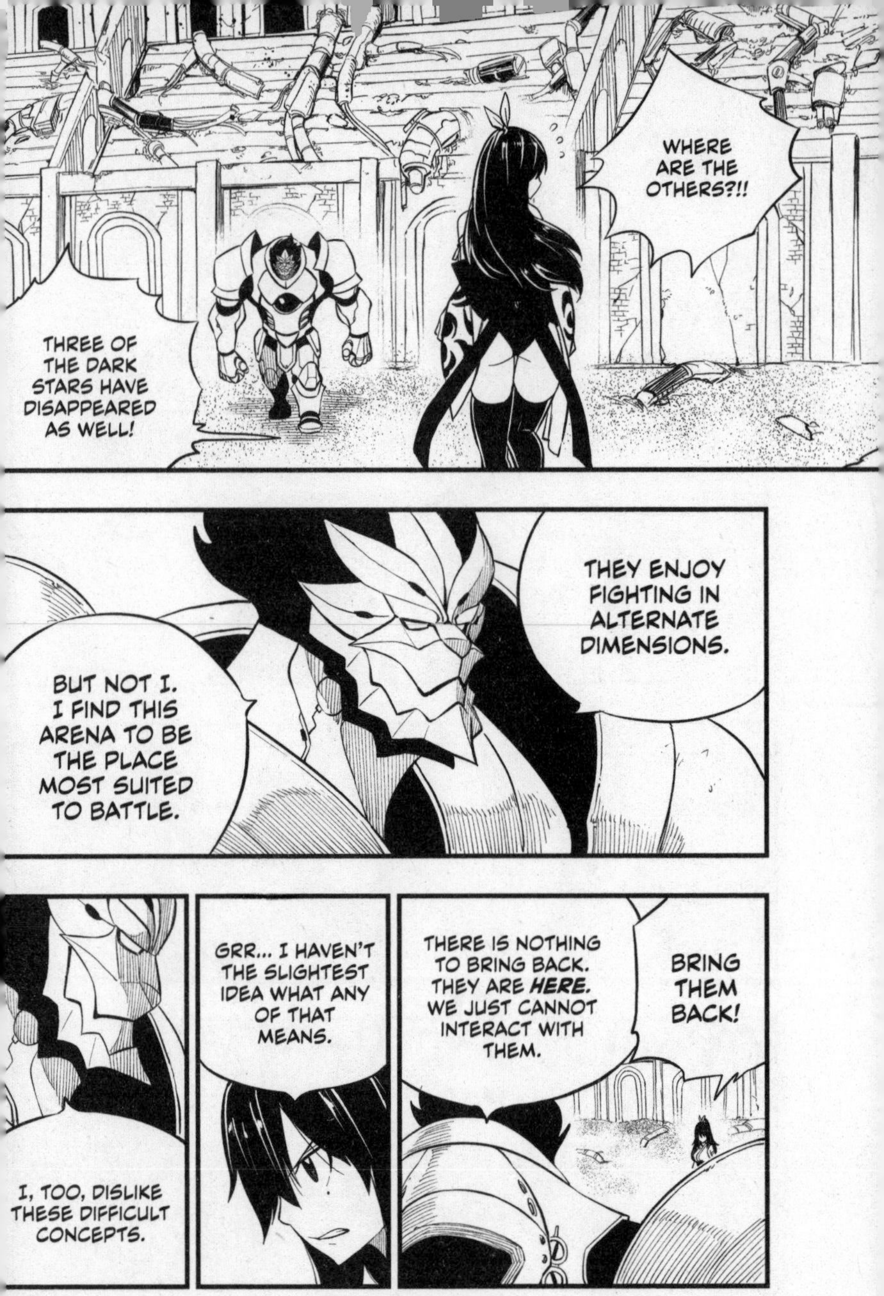
WHERE ARE THE OTHERS?!!
THREE OF THE DARK STARS HAVE DISAPPEARED AS WELL!
THEY ENJOY FIGHTING IN ALTERNATE DIMENSIONS.
BUT NOT I. I FIND THIS ARENA TO BE THE PLACE MOST SUITED TO BATTLE.
BRING THEM BACK!
THERE IS NOTHING TO BRING BACK. THEY ARE *HERE.* WE JUST CANNOT INTERACT WITH THEM.
GRR... I HAVEN'T THE SLIGHTEST IDEA WHAT ANY OF THAT MEANS.
I, TOO, DISLIKE THESE DIFFICULT CONCEPTS.

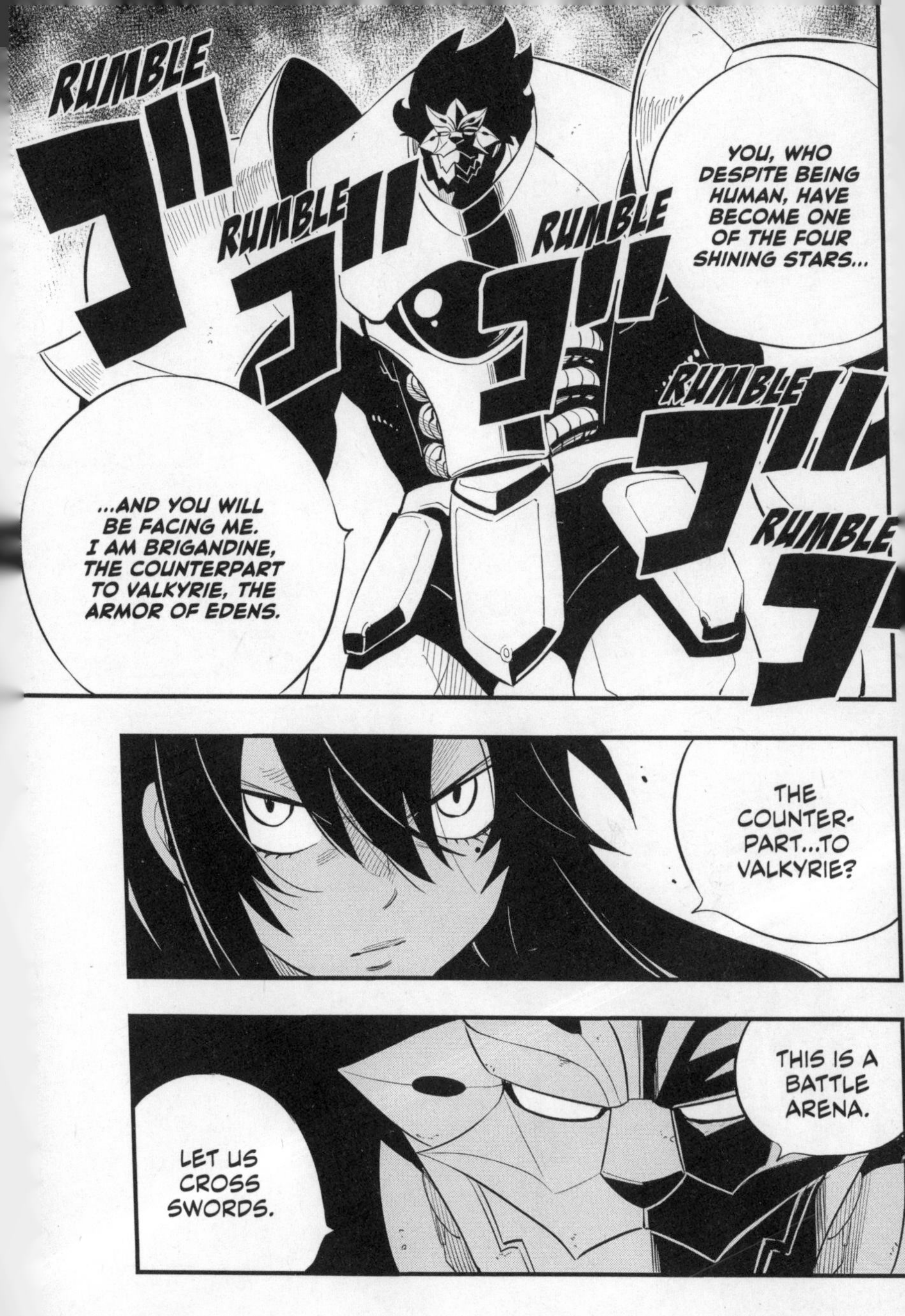
YOU, WHO DESPITE BEING HUMAN, HAVE BECOME ONE OF THE FOUR SHINING STARS...
RUMBLE
RUMBLE
RUMBLE
RUMBLE
RUMBLE
...AND YOU WILL BE FACING ME. I AM BRIGANDINE, THE COUNTERPART TO VALKYRIE, THE ARMOR OF EDENS.
THE COUNTER-PART...TO VALKYRIE?
THIS IS A BATTLE ARENA.
LET US CROSS SWORDS.

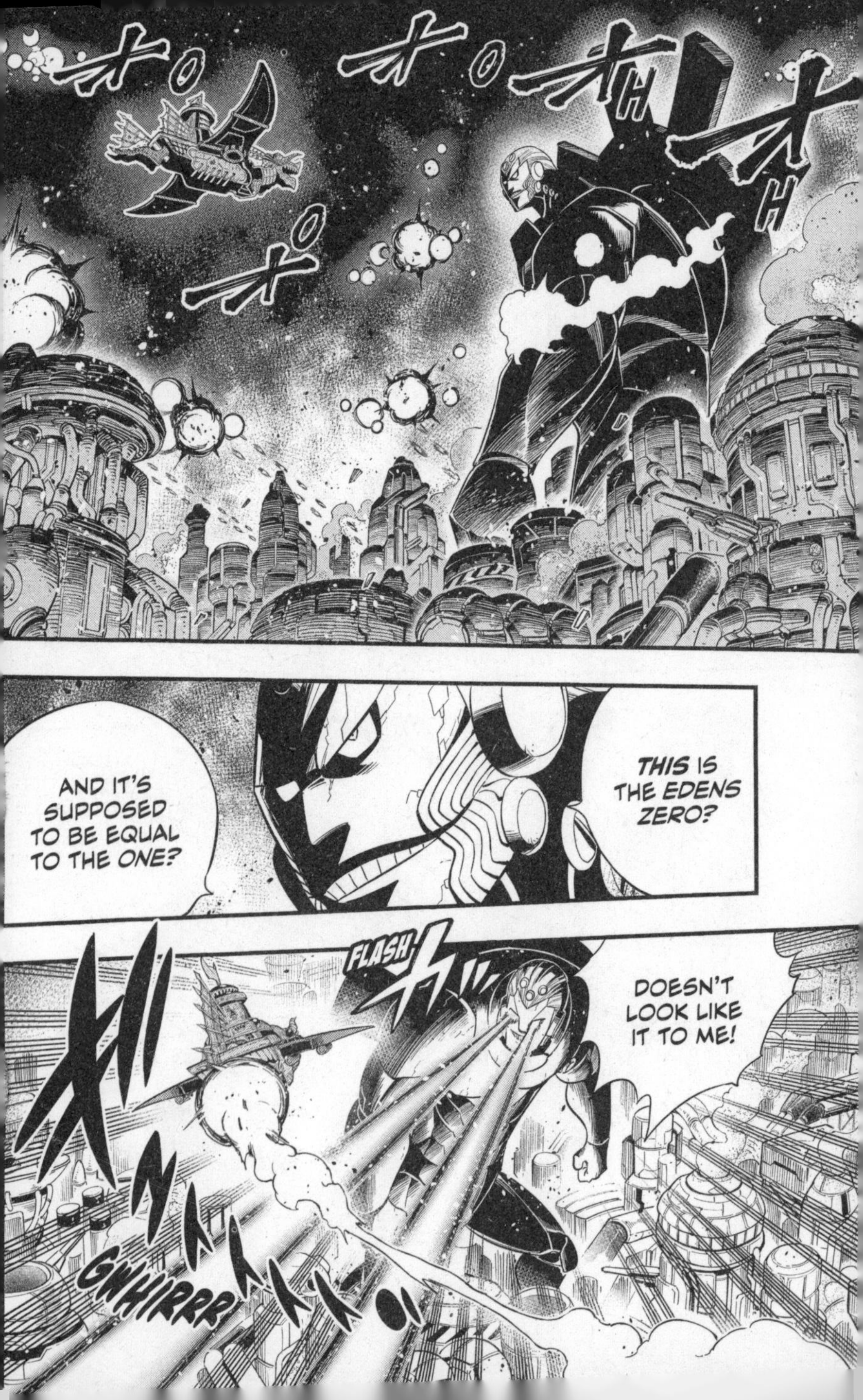
THIS IS THE EDENS ZERO?
AND IT'S SUPPOSED TO BE EQUAL TO THE ONE?
DOESN'T LOOK LIKE IT TO ME!
FLASH
GWHIRRR

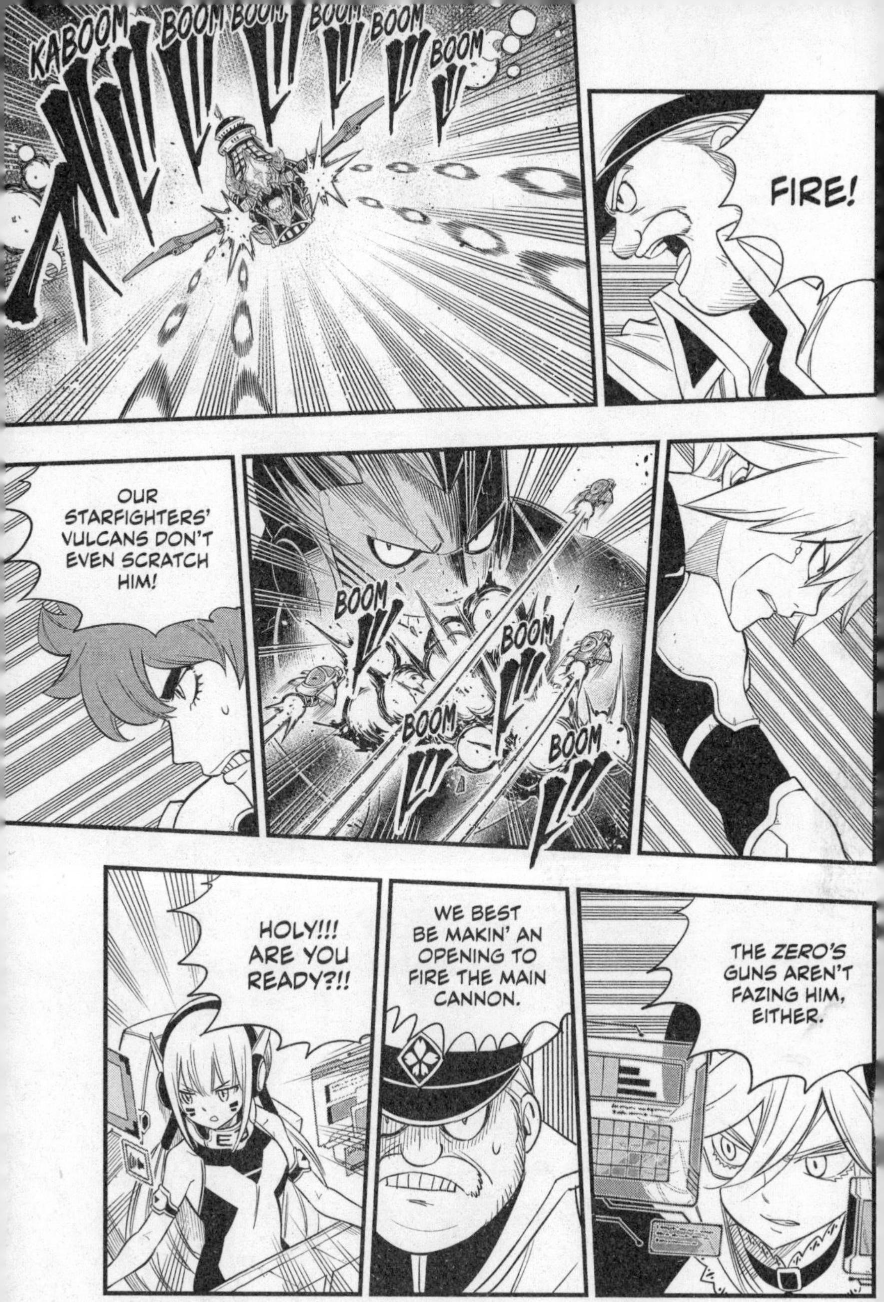
FIRE!
BOOM
BOOM
BOOM
BOOM
BOOM
KABOOM
BOOM
BOOM
BOOM
BOOM
OUR STARFIGHTERS' VULCANS DON'T EVEN SCRATCH HIM!
THE ZERO'S GUNS AREN'T FAZING HIM, EITHER.
WE BEST BE MAKIN' AN OPENING TO FIRE THE MAIN CANNON.
HOLY!!! ARE YOU READY?!!

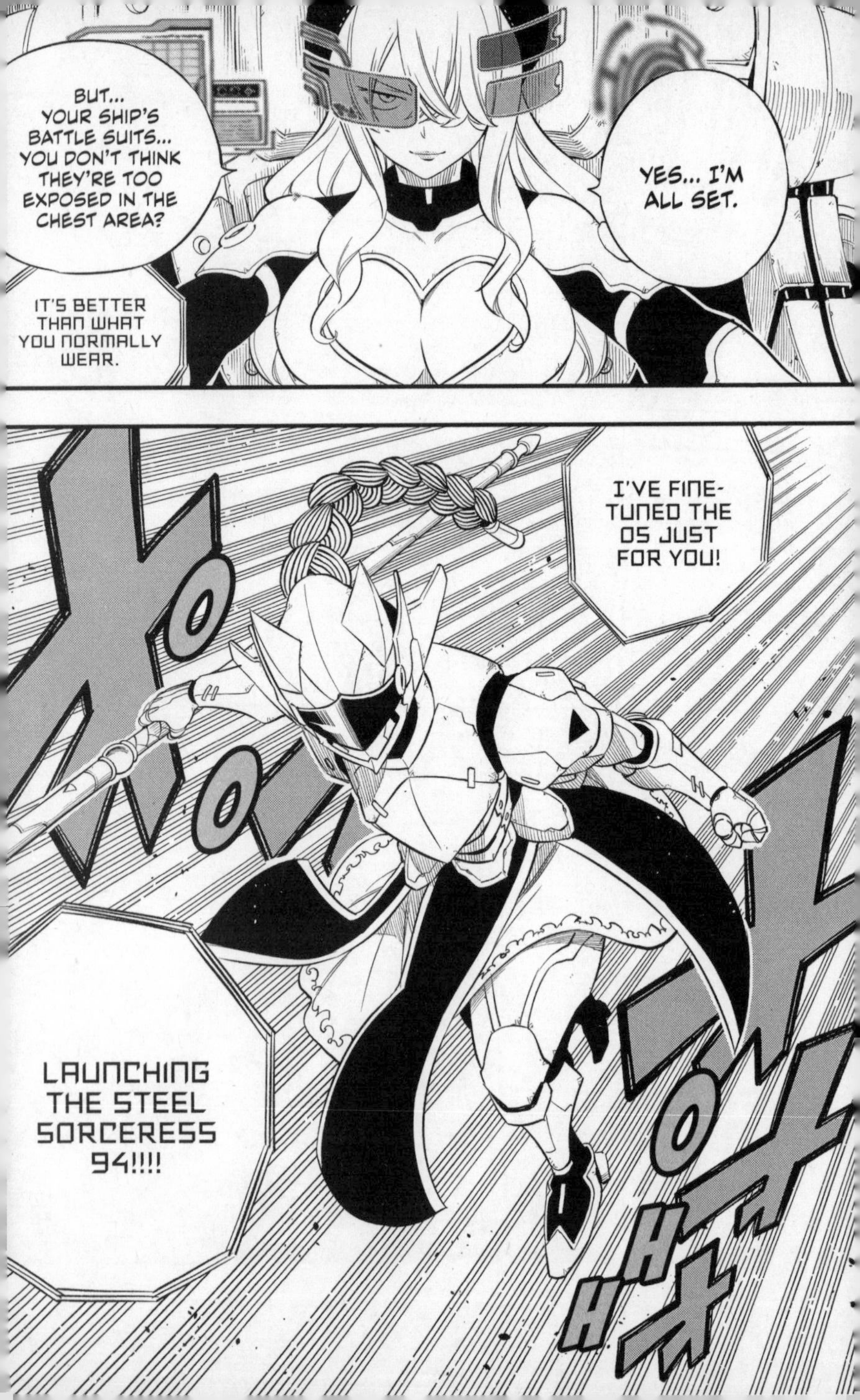
YES... I'M ALL SET.
BUT... YOUR SHIP'S BATTLE SUITS... YOU DON'T THINK THEY'RE TOO EXPOSED IN THE CHEST AREA?
IT'S BETTER THAN WHAT YOU NORMALLY WEAR.
I'VE FINE-TUNED THE OS JUST FOR YOU!
LAUNCHING THE STEEL SORCERESS 94!!!!

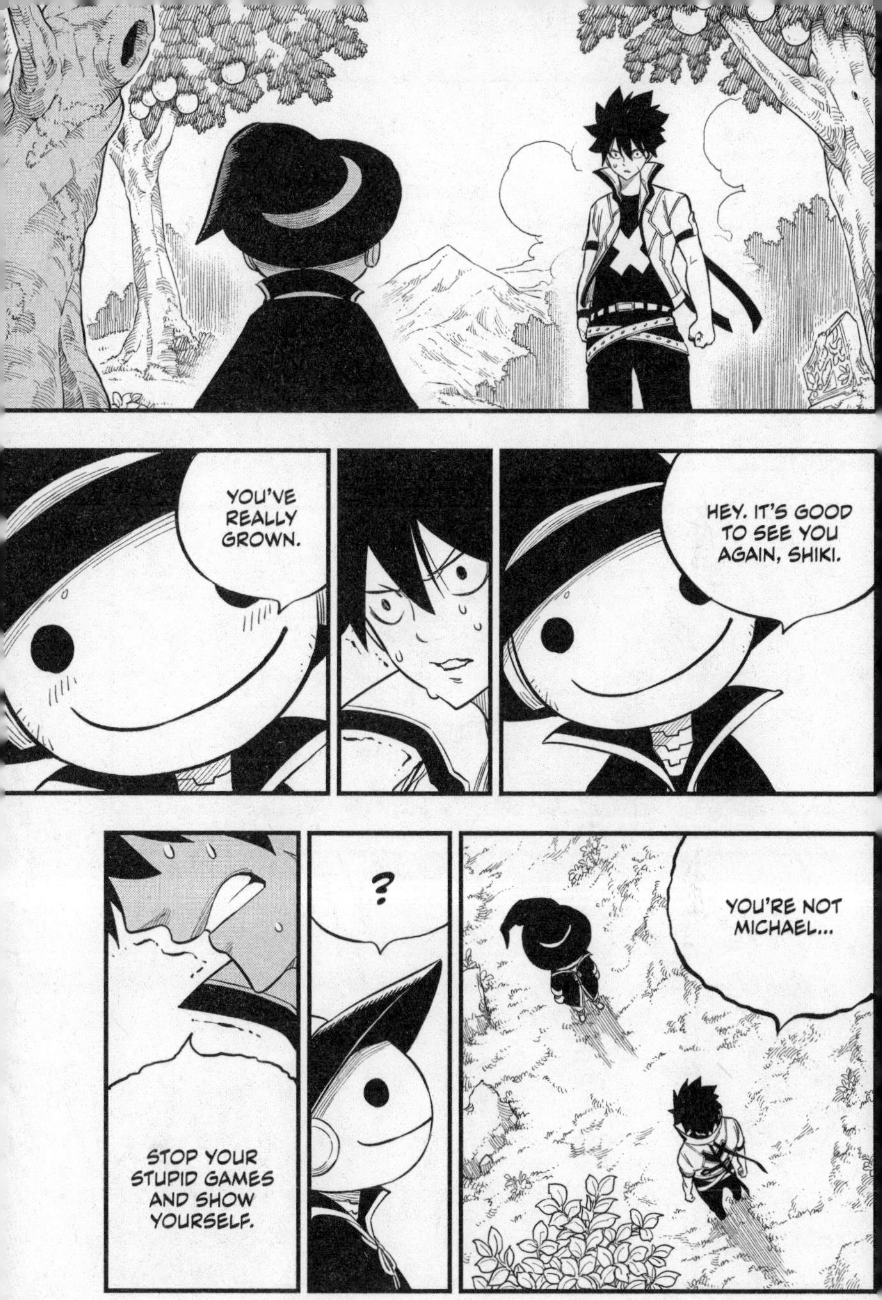
HEY. IT'S GOOD TO SEE YOU AGAIN, SHIKI.
YOU'VE REALLY GROWN.
YOU'RE NOT MICHAEL...
?
STOP YOUR STUPID GAMES AND SHOW YOURSELF.

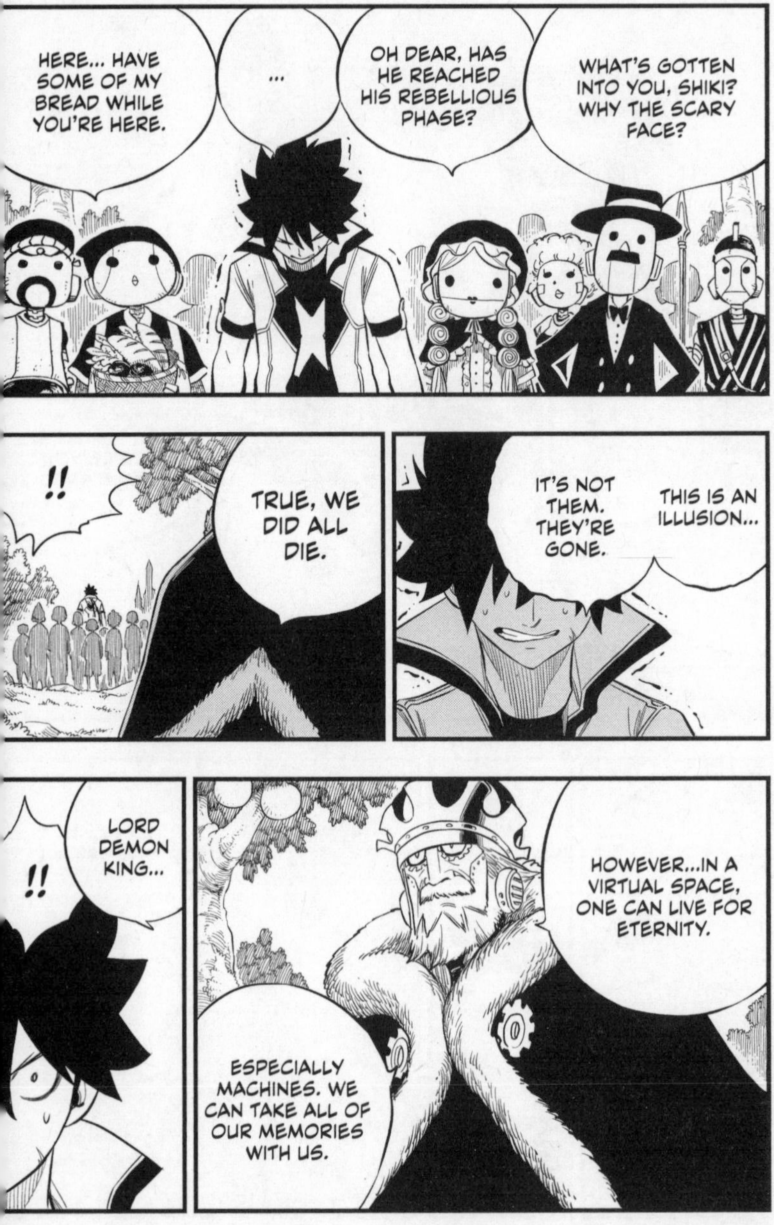
WHAT'S GOTTEN INTO YOU, SHIKI? WHY THE SCARY FACE?
OH DEAR, HAS HE REACHED HIS REBELLIOUS PHASE?
...
HERE... HAVE SOME OF MY BREAD WHILE YOU'RE HERE.
THIS IS AN ILLUSION...
IT'S NOT THEM. THEY'RE GONE.
TRUE, WE DID ALL DIE.
!!
HOWEVER...IN A VIRTUAL SPACE, ONE CAN LIVE FOR ETERNITY.
ESPECIALLY MACHINES. WE CAN TAKE ALL OF OUR MEMORIES WITH US.
LORD DEMON KING...
!!

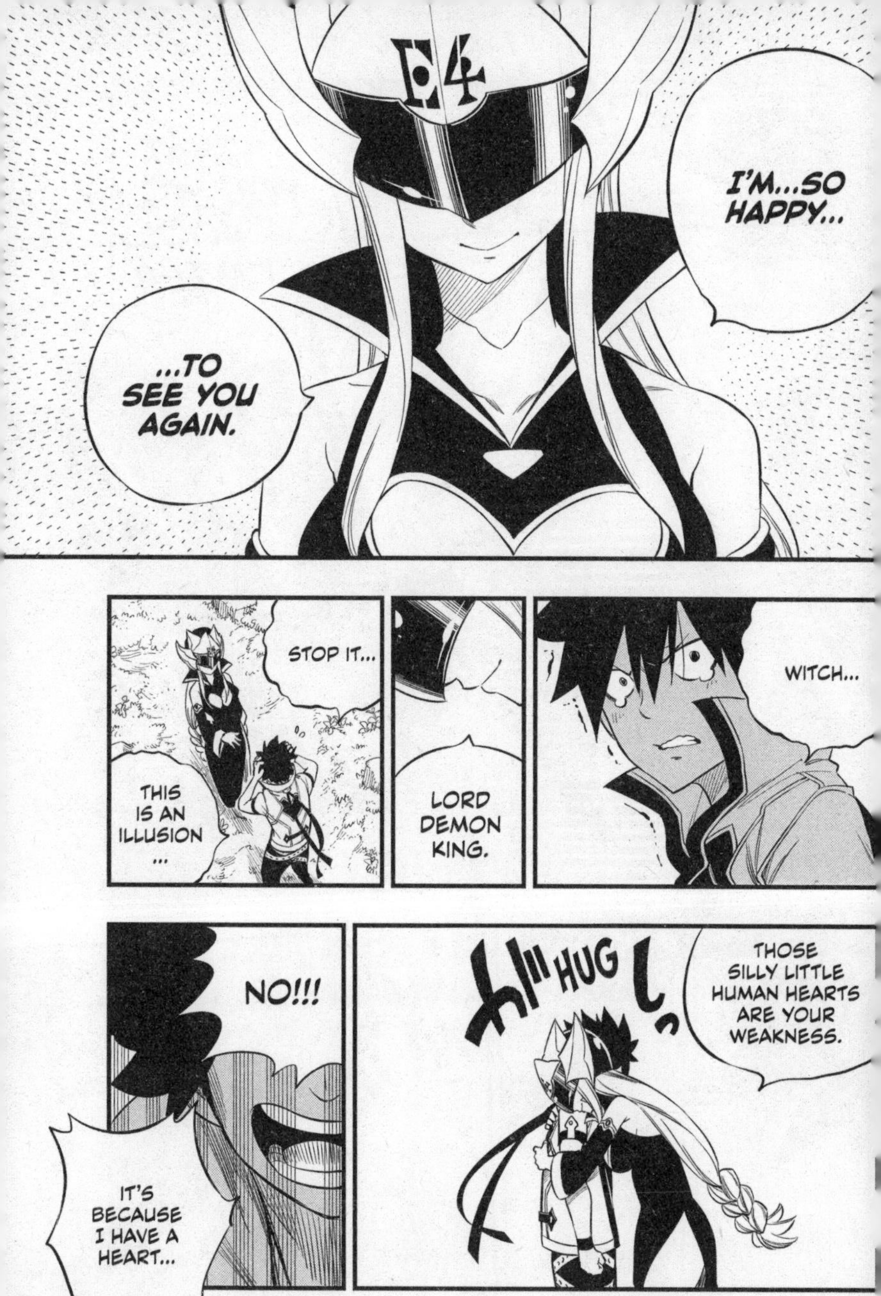
I'M...SO HAPPY...
...TO SEE YOU AGAIN.
WITCH...
LORD DEMON KING.
STOP IT...
THIS IS AN ILLUSION ...
HUG
THOSE SILLY LITTLE HUMAN HEARTS ARE YOUR WEAKNESS.
NO!!!
IT'S BECAUSE I HAVE A HEART...

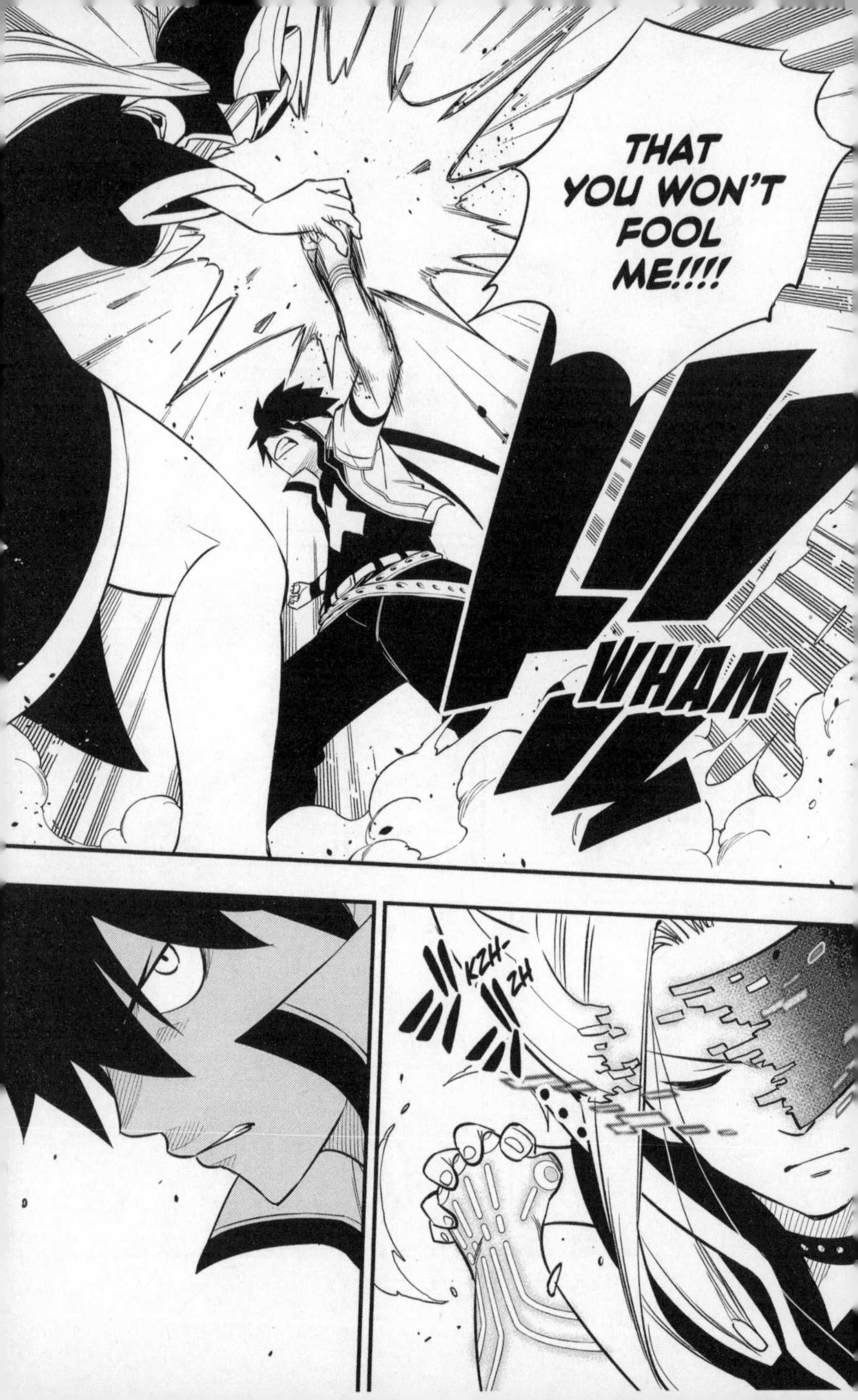
THAT YOU WON'T FOOL ME!!!!
WHAM
KZH-ZH

EDENS ZERO

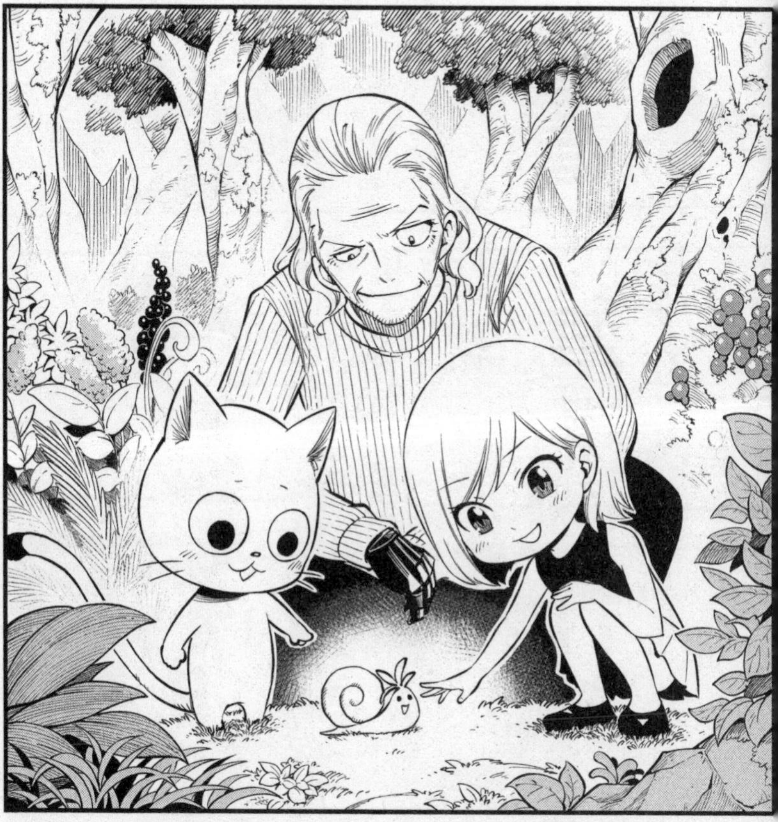

CHAPTER 187: SHIKI VS. WIZARD

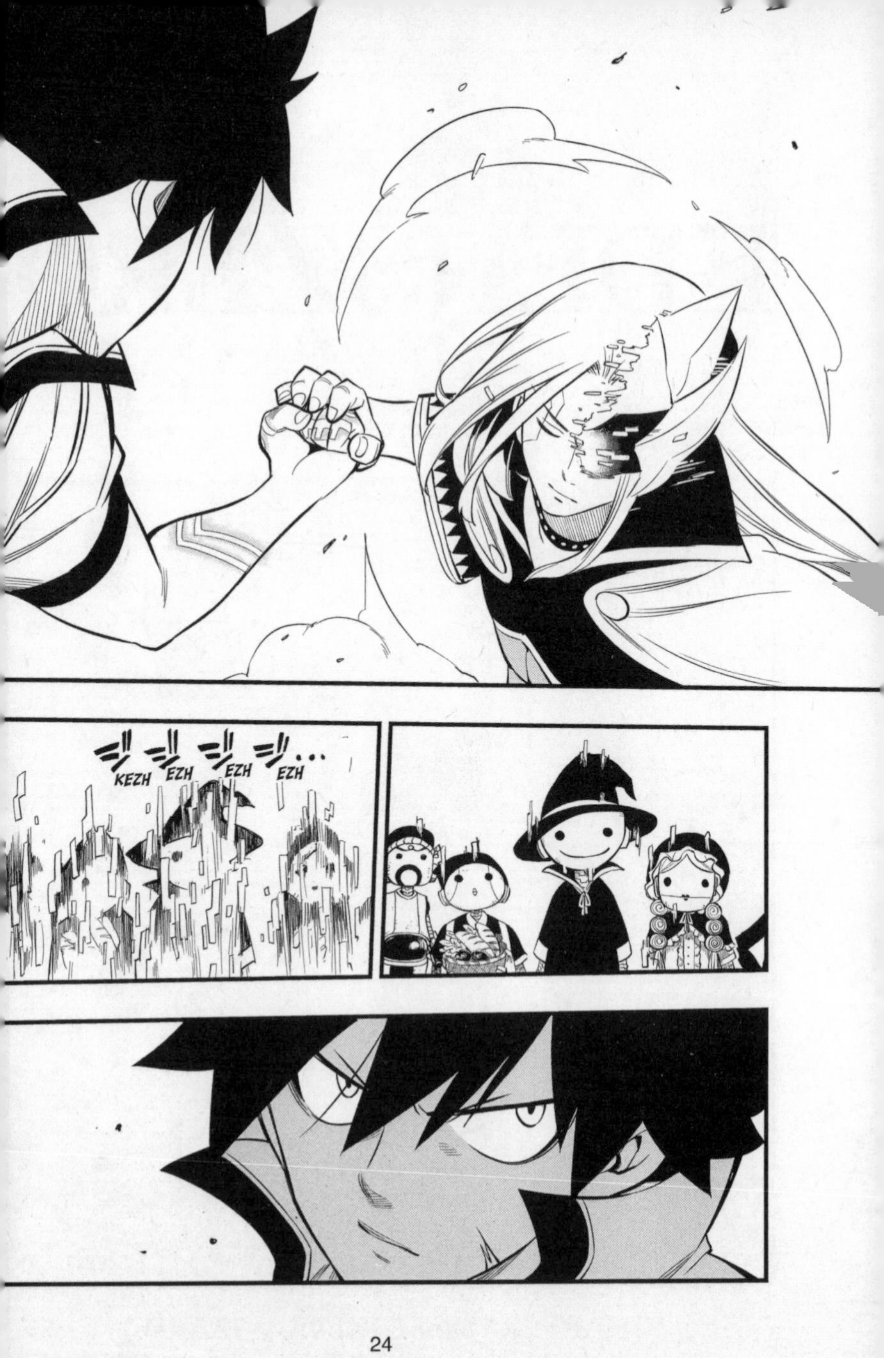
KEZH EZH EZH EZH

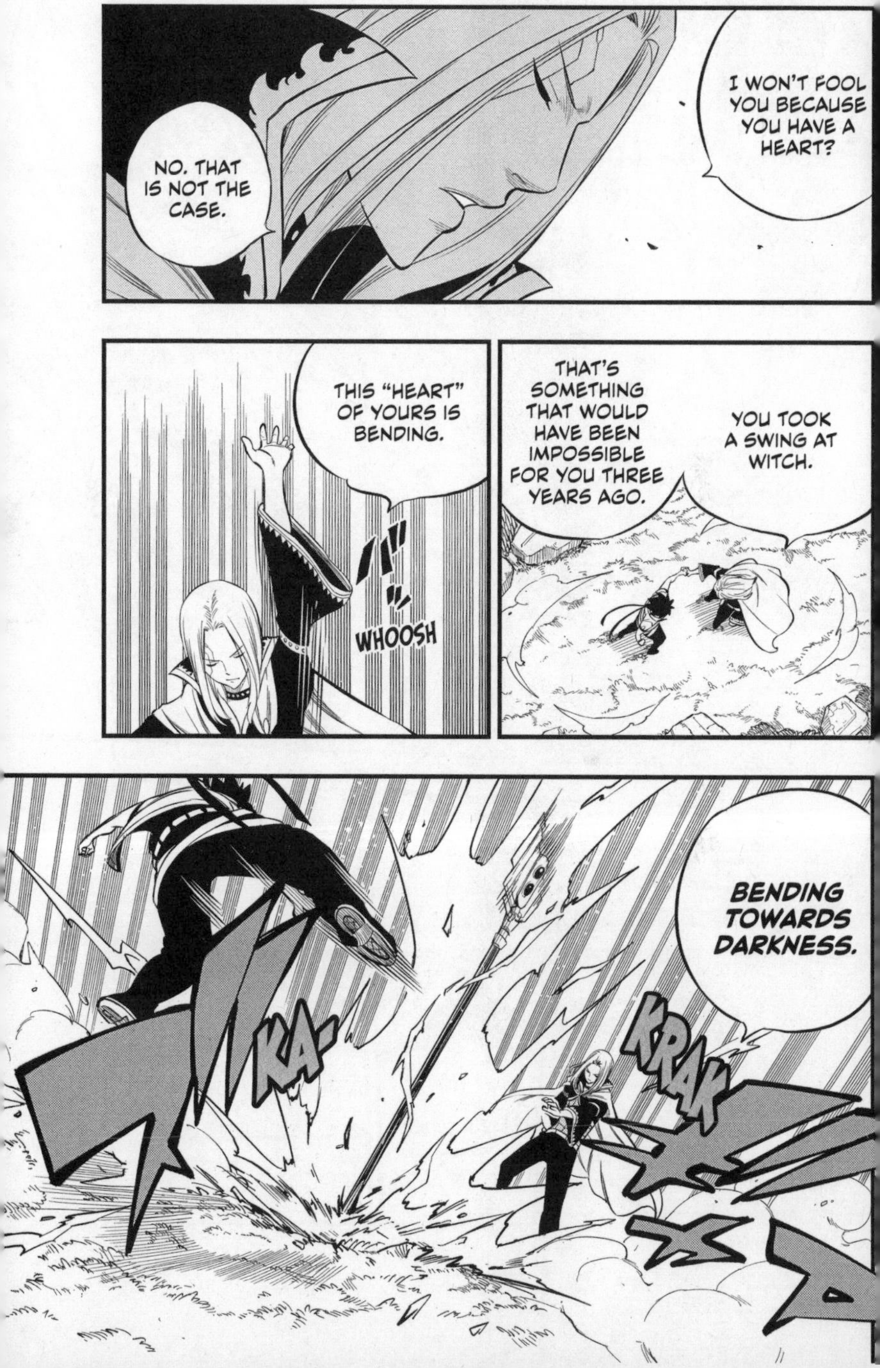
I WON'T FOOL YOU BECAUSE YOU HAVE A HEART?
NO. THAT IS NOT THE CASE.
YOU TOOK A SWING AT WITCH.
THAT'S SOMETHING THAT WOULD HAVE BEEN IMPOSSIBLE FOR YOU THREE YEARS AGO.
THIS "HEART" OF YOURS IS BENDING.
WHOOSH
BENDING TOWARDS DARKNESS.
KA-
KRAK

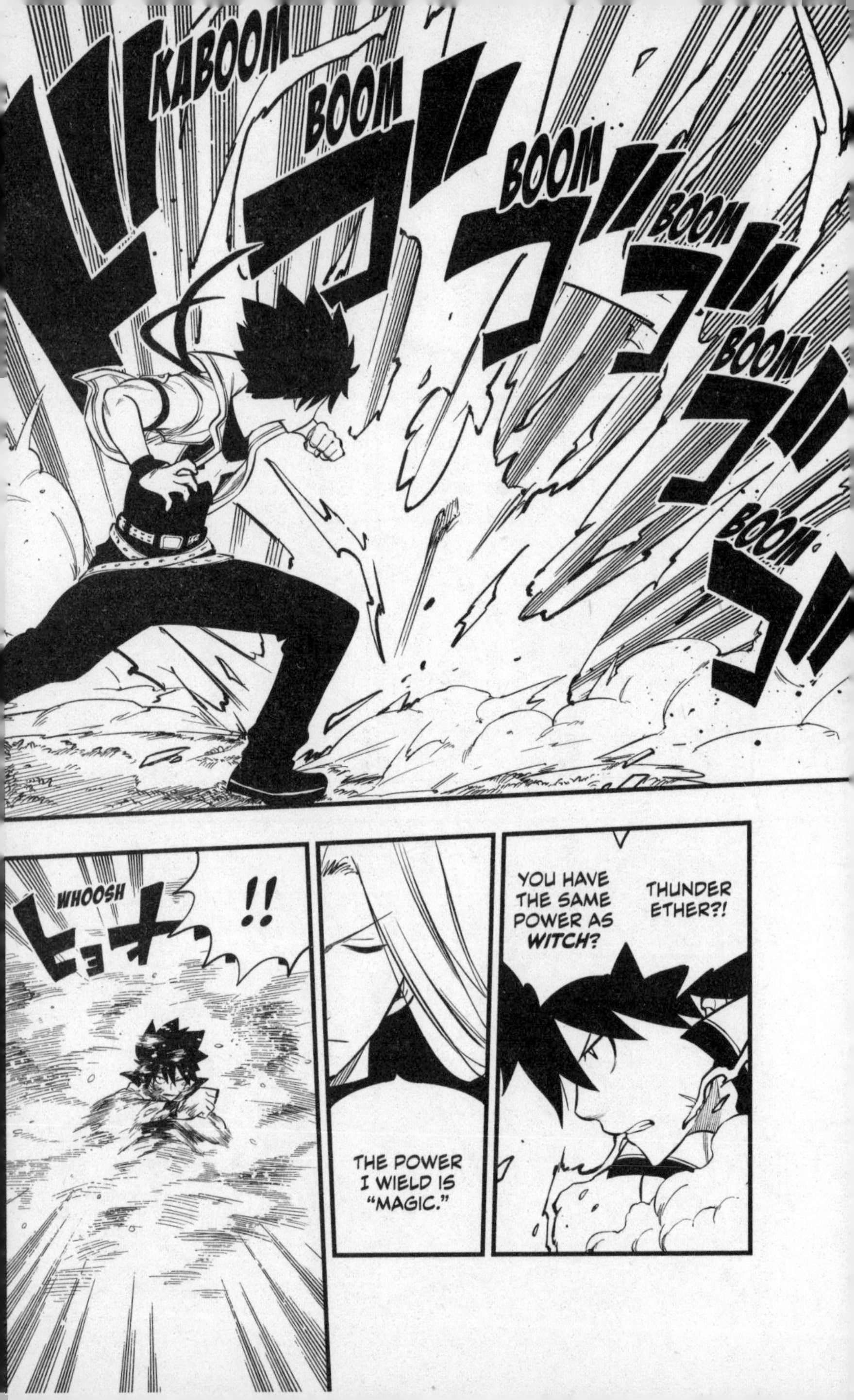
KABOOM
BOOM
BOOM
BOOM
BOOM
BOOM
THUNDER ETHER?!
YOU HAVE THE SAME POWER AS *WITCH*?
THE POWER I WIELD IS "MAGIC."
WHOOSH
!!

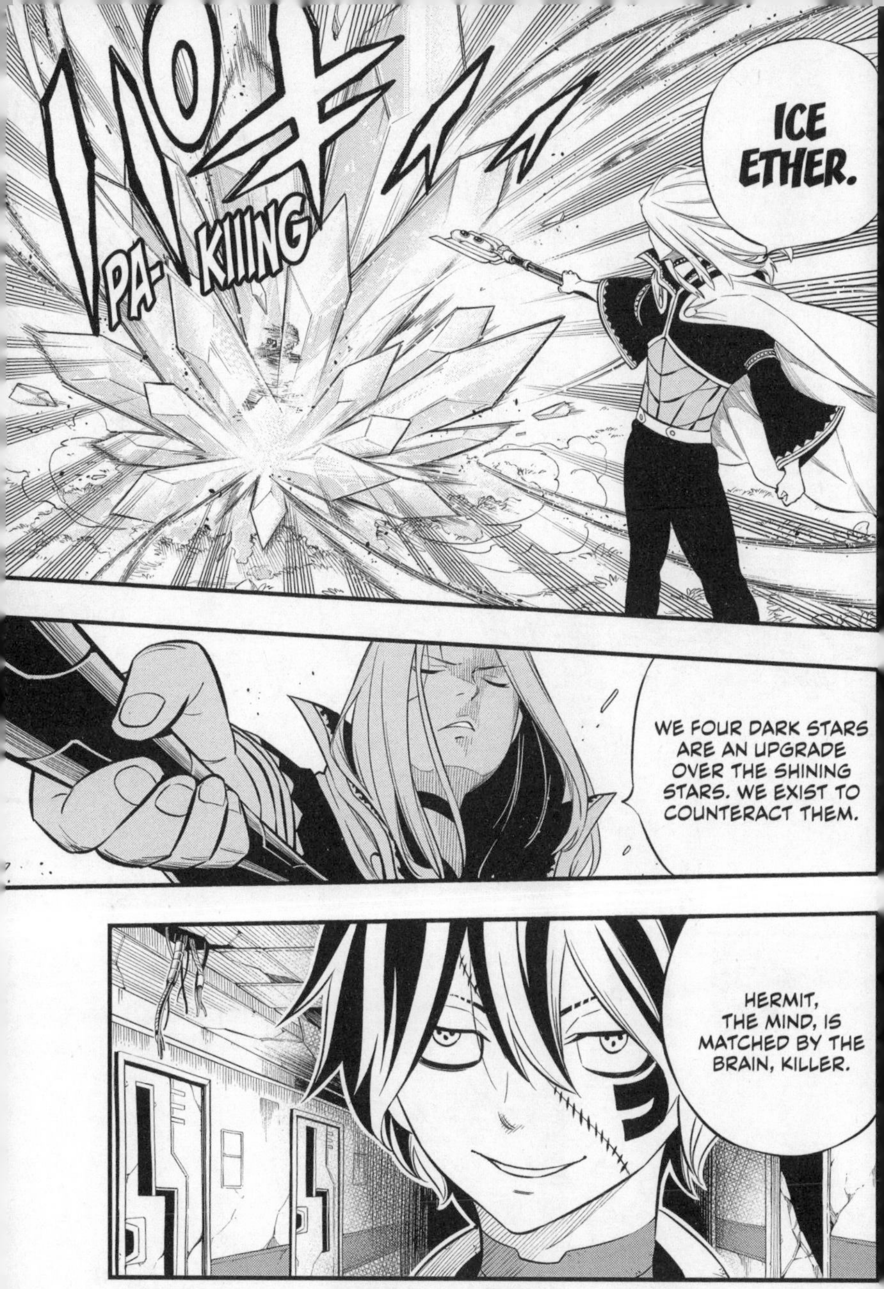
ICE ETHER.
PA-KIIING
WE FOUR DARK STARS ARE AN UPGRADE OVER THE SHINING STARS. WE EXIST TO COUNTERACT THEM.
HERMIT, THE MIND, IS MATCHED BY THE BRAIN, KILLER.

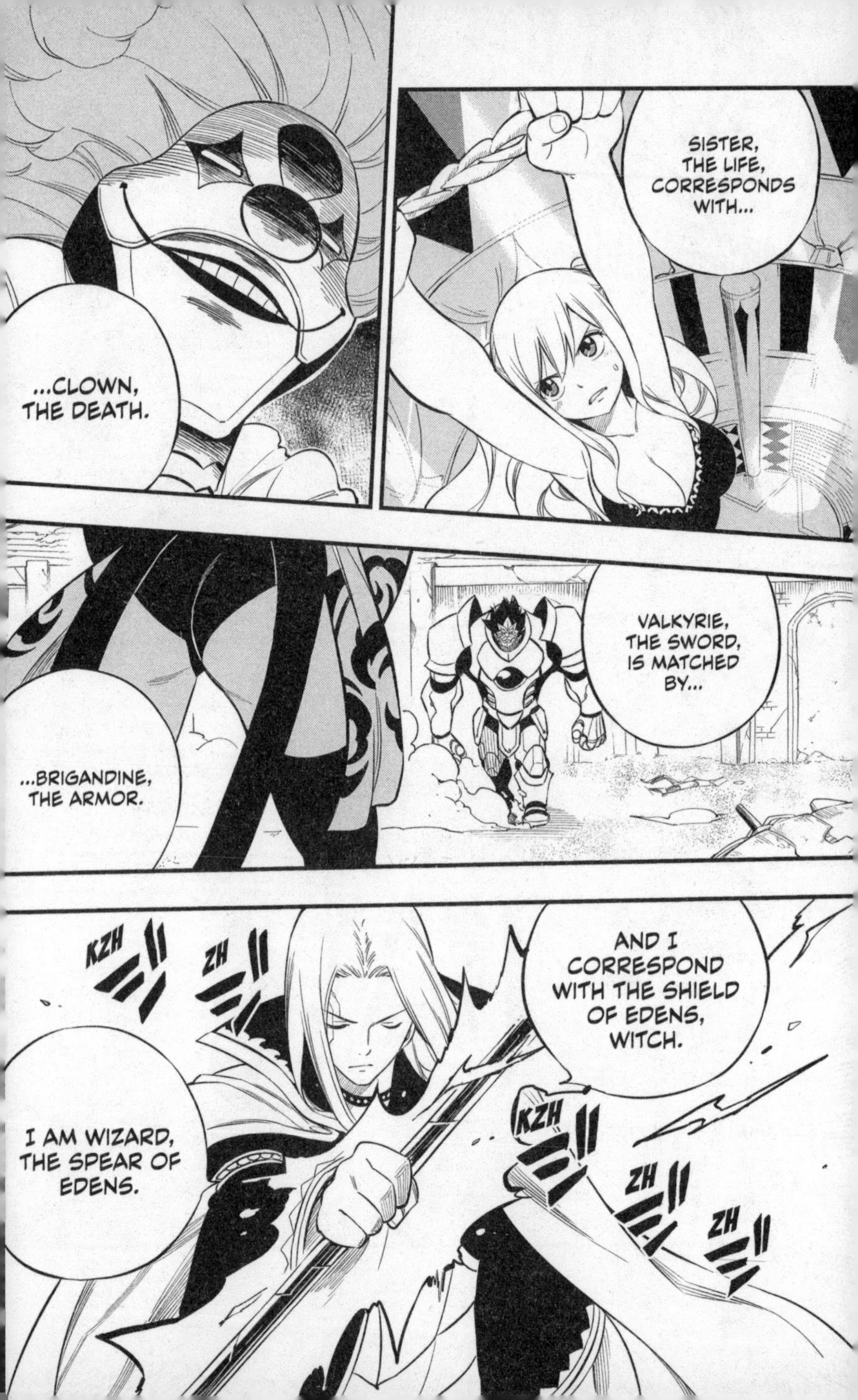
SISTER, THE LIFE, CORRESPONDS WITH...
...CLOWN, THE DEATH.
VALKYRIE, THE SWORD, IS MATCHED BY...
...BRIGANDINE, THE ARMOR.
AND I CORRESPOND WITH THE SHIELD OF EDENS, WITCH.
ZH
ZH
KZH
ZH
KZH
I AM WIZARD, THE SPEAR OF EDENS.

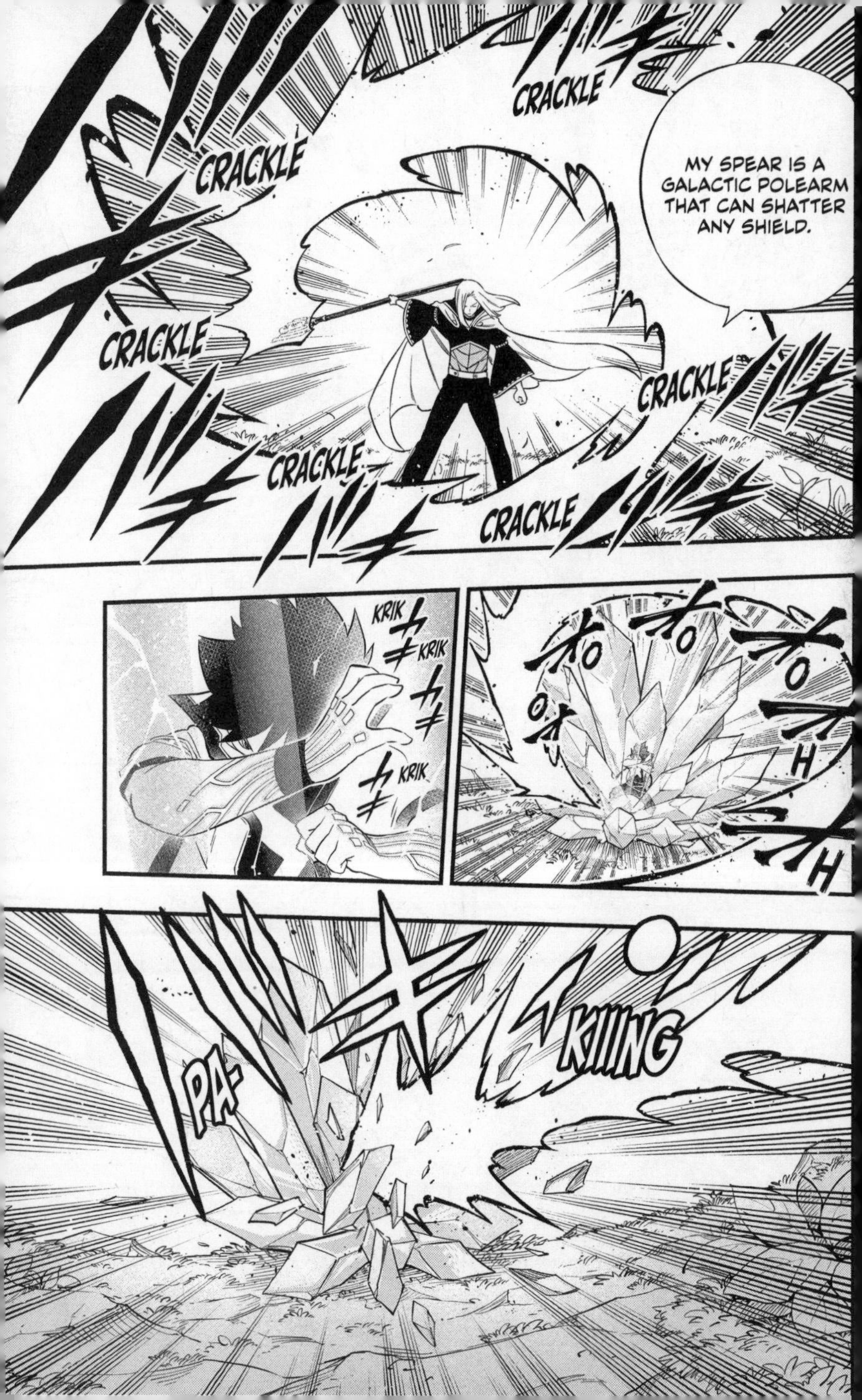

CRACKLE
MY SPEAR IS A GALACTIC POLEARM THAT CAN SHATTER ANY SHIELD.
CRACKLE
CRACKLE
CRACKLE
CRACKLE
CRACKLE
HH
KRIK KRIK KRIK
KIIING
PA-

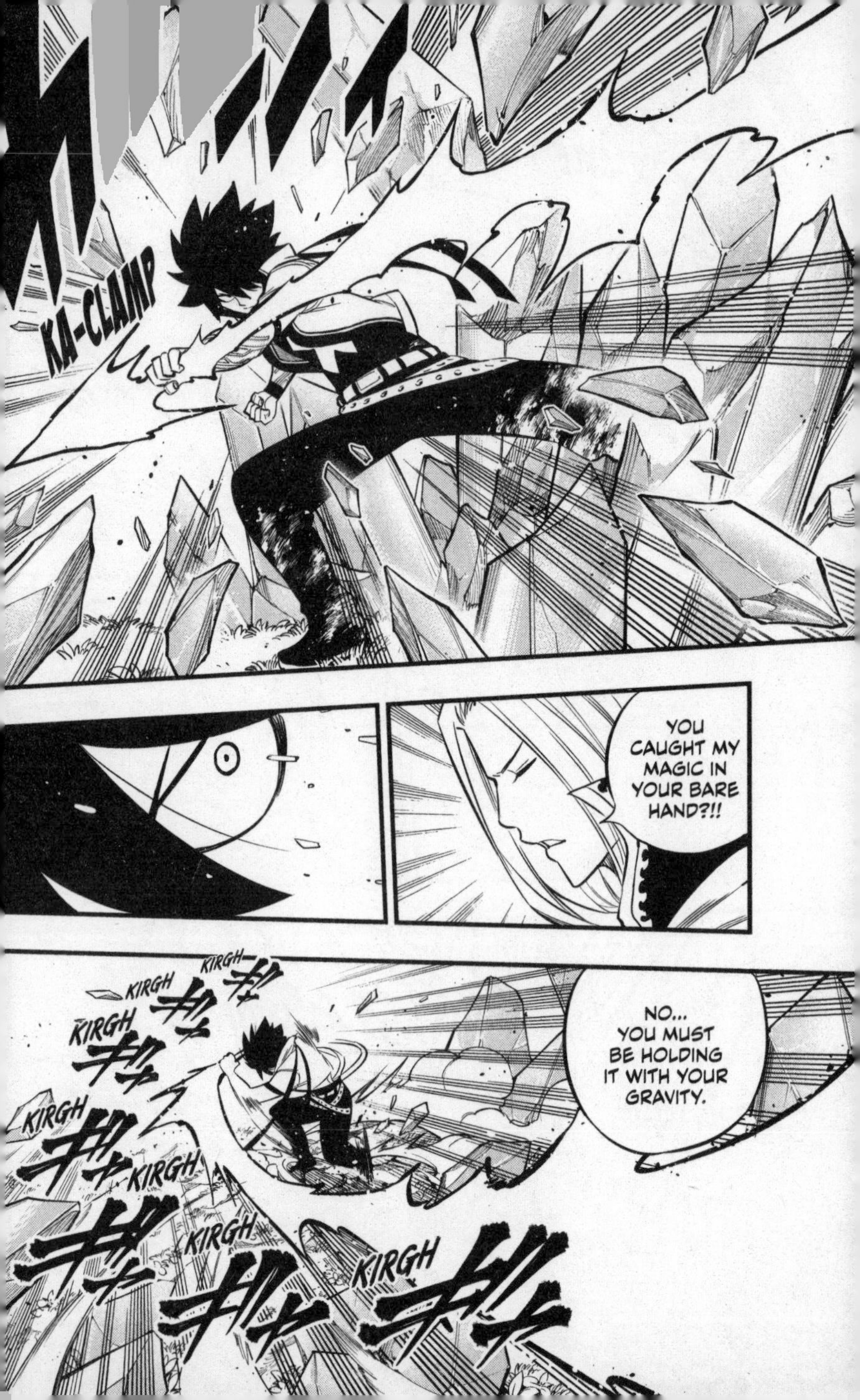
KA-CLAMP
YOU CAUGHT MY MAGIC IN YOUR BARE HAND?!!
NO... YOU MUST BE HOLDING IT WITH YOUR GRAVITY.
KIRGH—
KIRGH
KIRGH
KIRGH
KIRGH
KIRGH
KIRGH

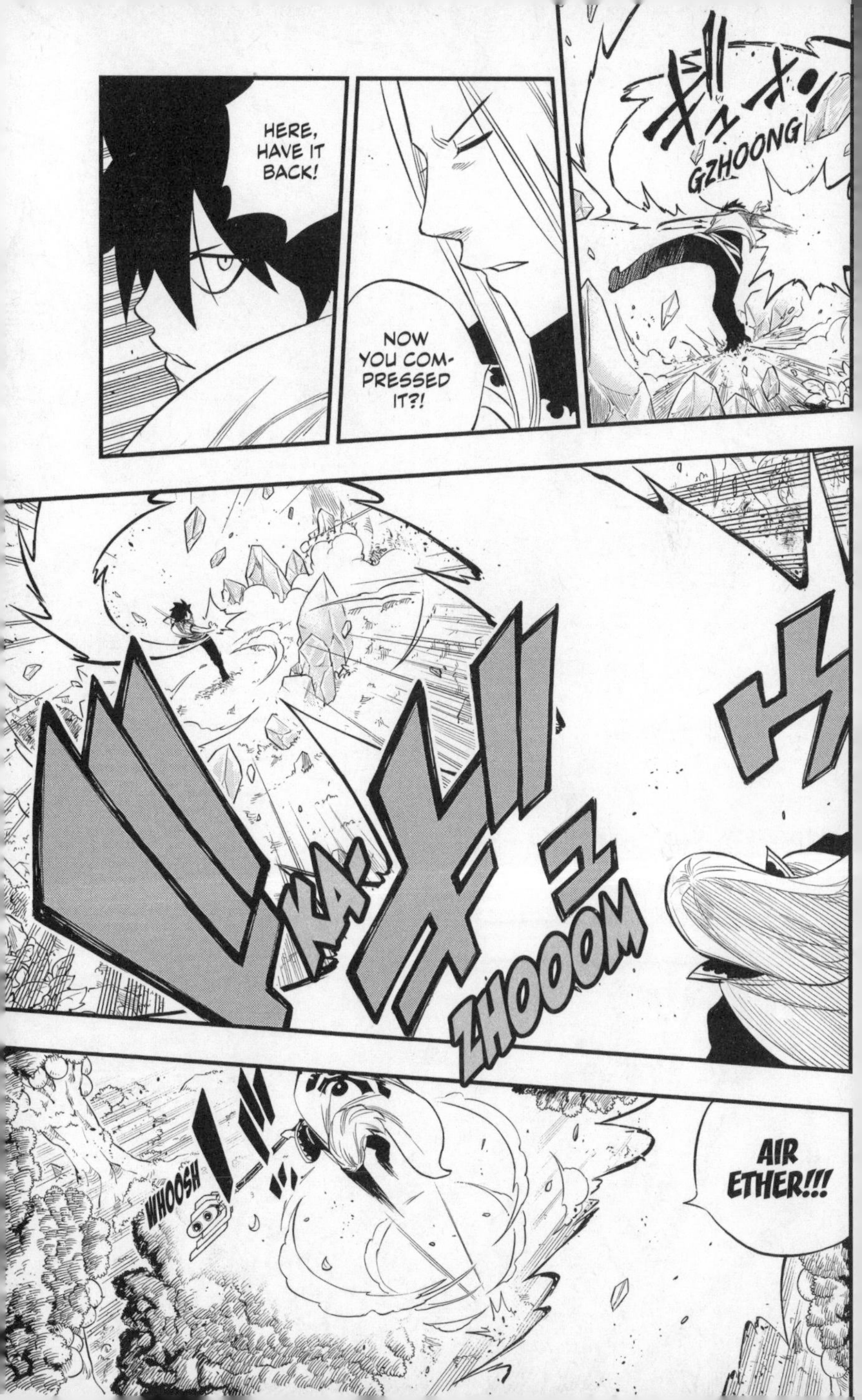
GZHOONG
NOW YOU COM-PRESSED IT?!
HERE, HAVE IT BACK!
ZHOOOM
AIR ETHER!!!
WHOOSH

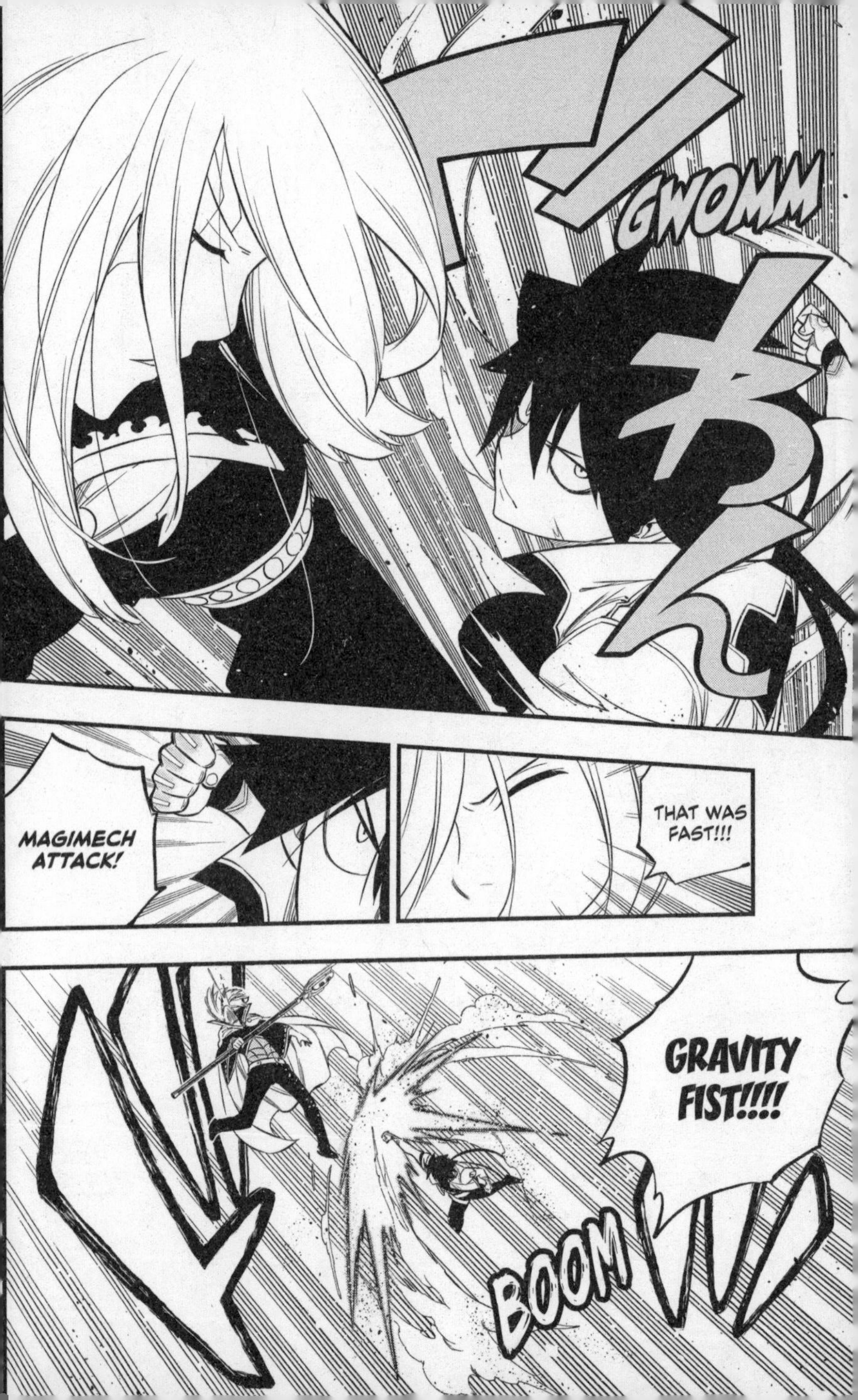
GWOMM
THAT WAS FAST!!!
MAGIMECH ATTACK!
GRAVITY FIST!!!!
BOOM

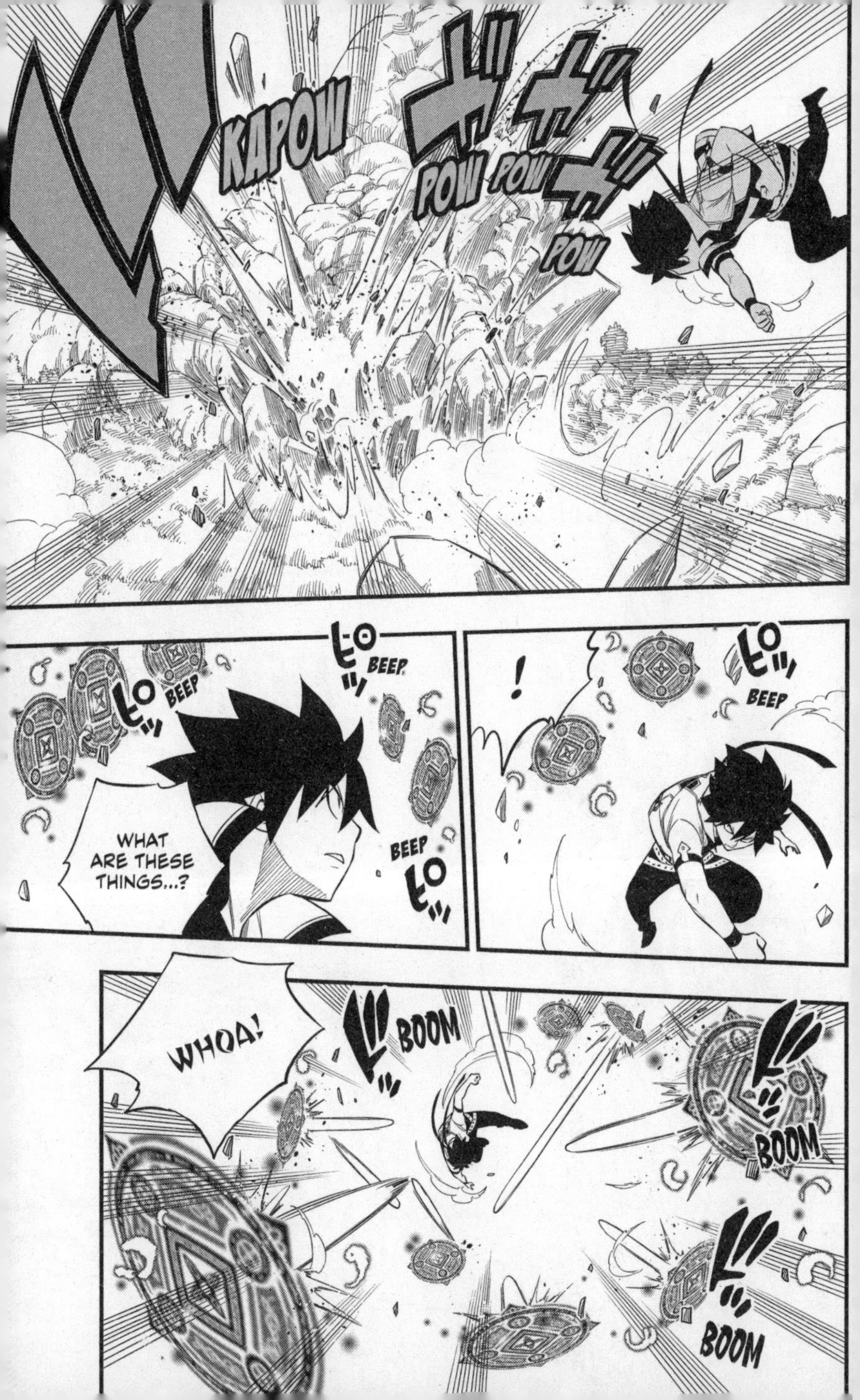
KAPOW
POW
POW
POW
BEEP
!
BEEP
BEEP
WHAT ARE THESE THINGS...?
BEEP
BOOM
WHOA!
BOOM
BOOM

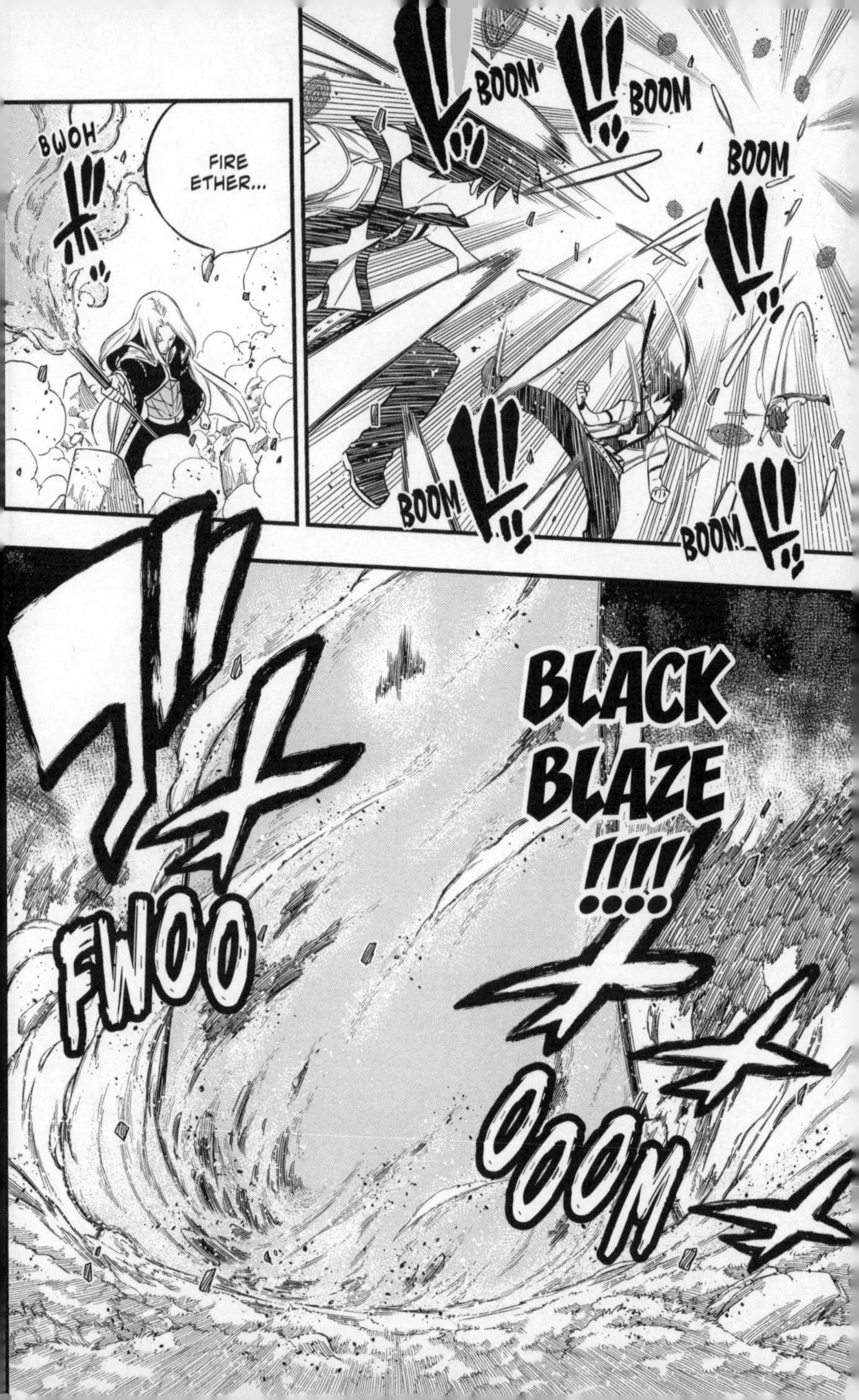
BOOM
BOOM
BOOM
BOOM
BOOM
BWOH
FIRE ETHER...
BLACK BLAZE!!!!
FWOOOOOM

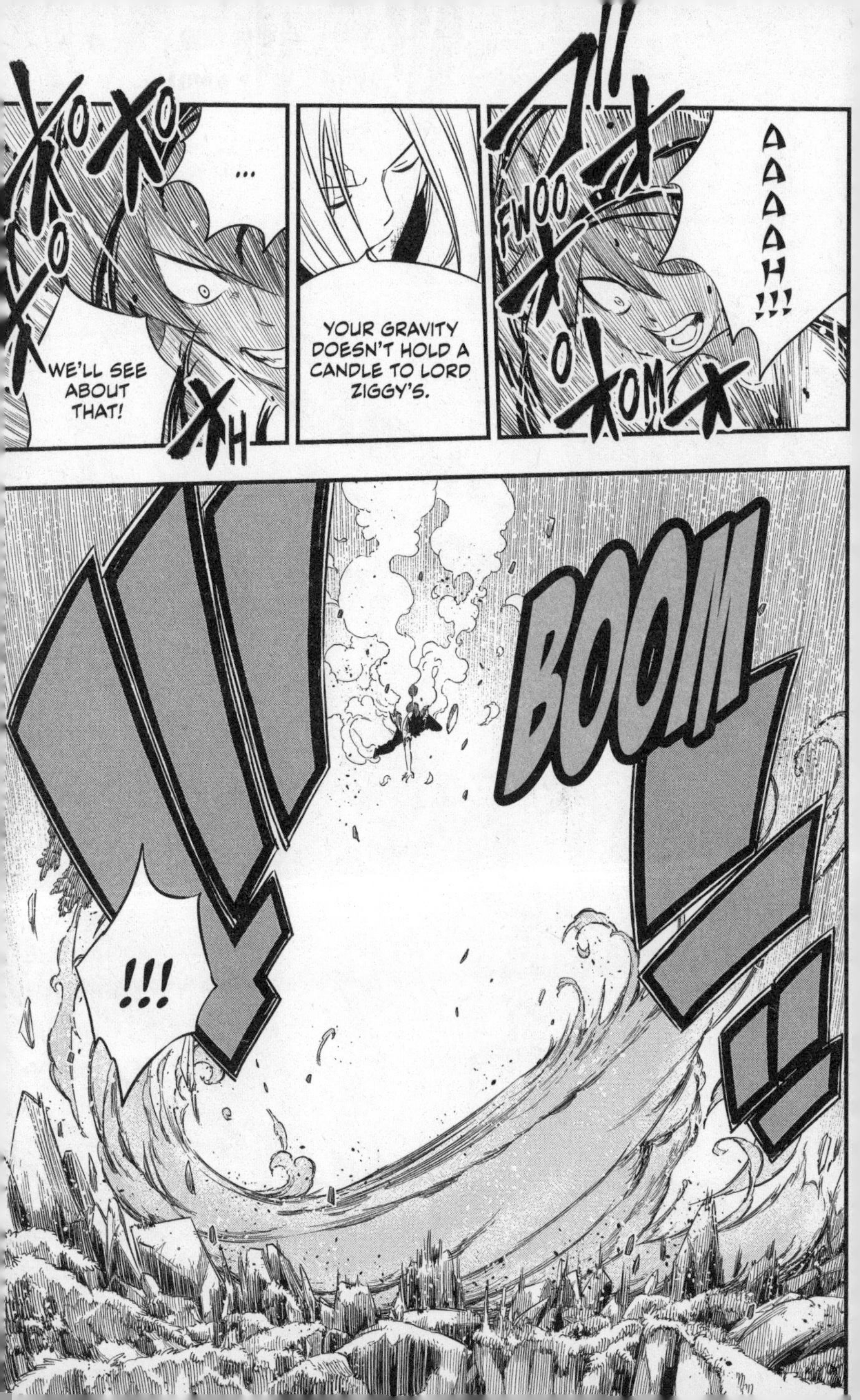
AAAAH!!!
FWOO
OM
YOUR GRAVITY DOESN'T HOLD A CANDLE TO LORD ZIGGY'S.
...
WE'LL SEE ABOUT THAT!
BOOM
!!!

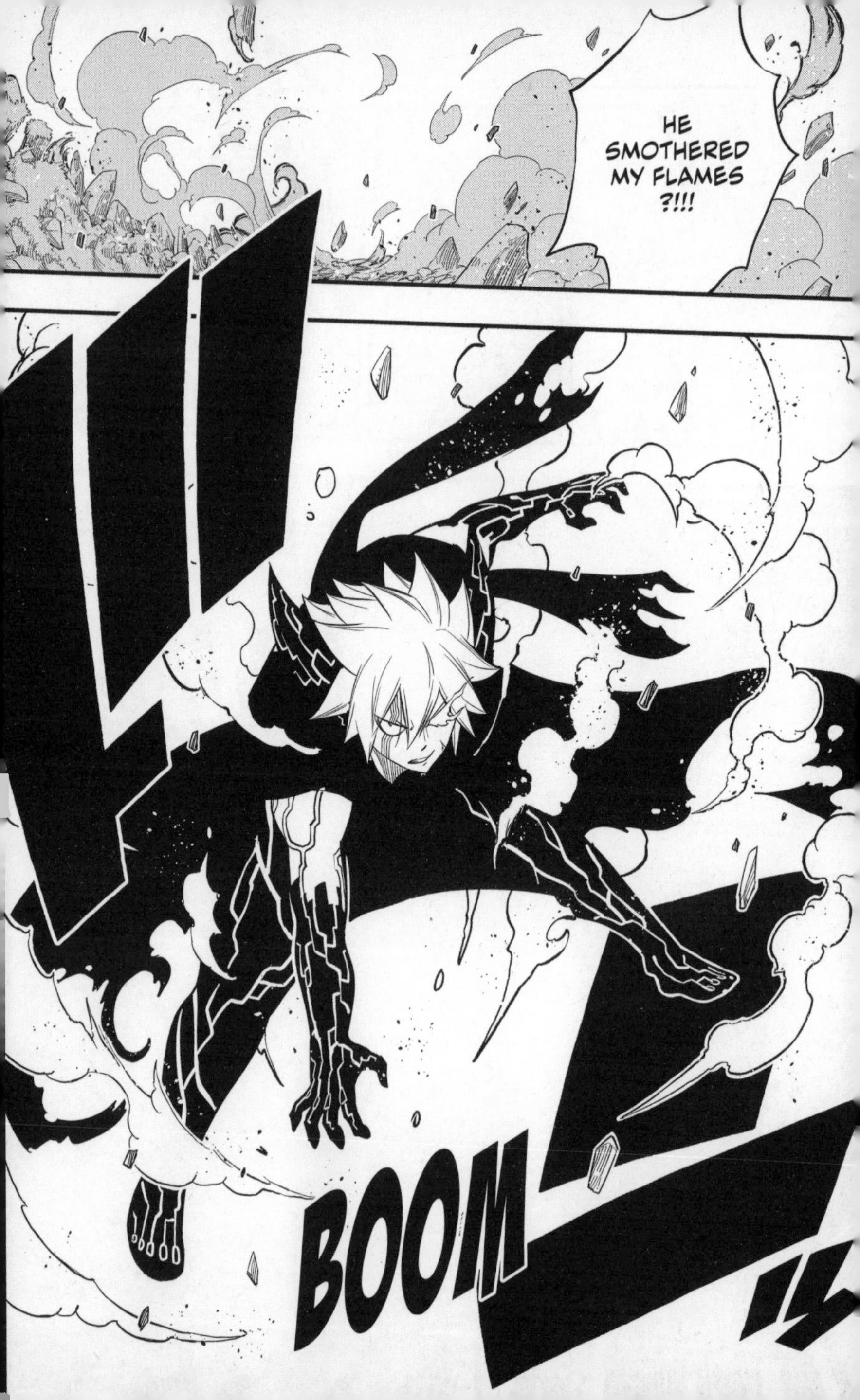
HE SMOTHERED MY FLAMES ?!!!
BOOM

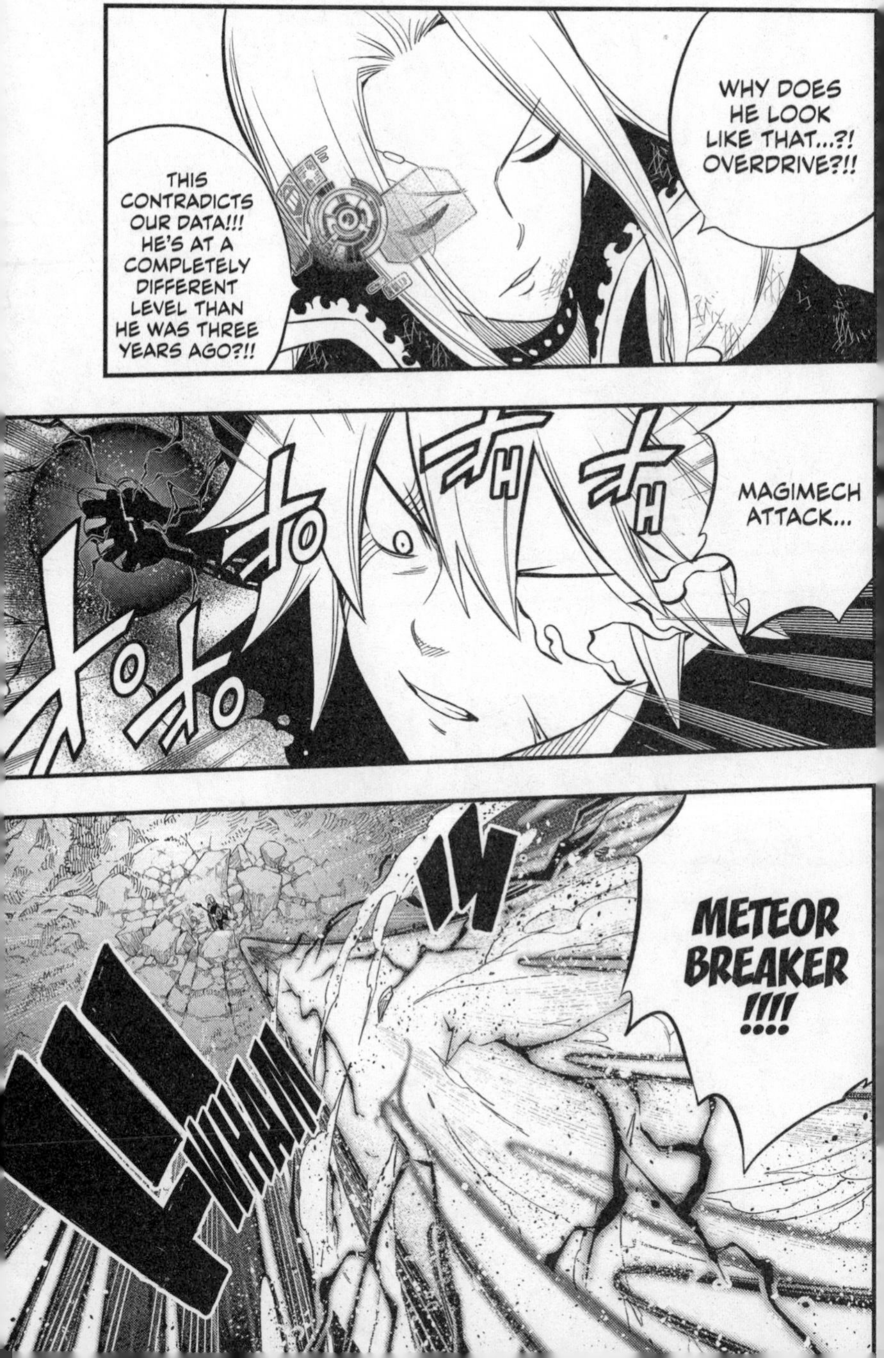
WHY DOES HE LOOK LIKE THAT...?! OVERDRIVE?!!
THIS CONTRADICTS OUR DATA!!! HE'S AT A COMPLETELY DIFFERENT LEVEL THAN HE WAS THREE YEARS AGO?!!
MAGIMECH ATTACK...
METEOR BREAKER !!!!

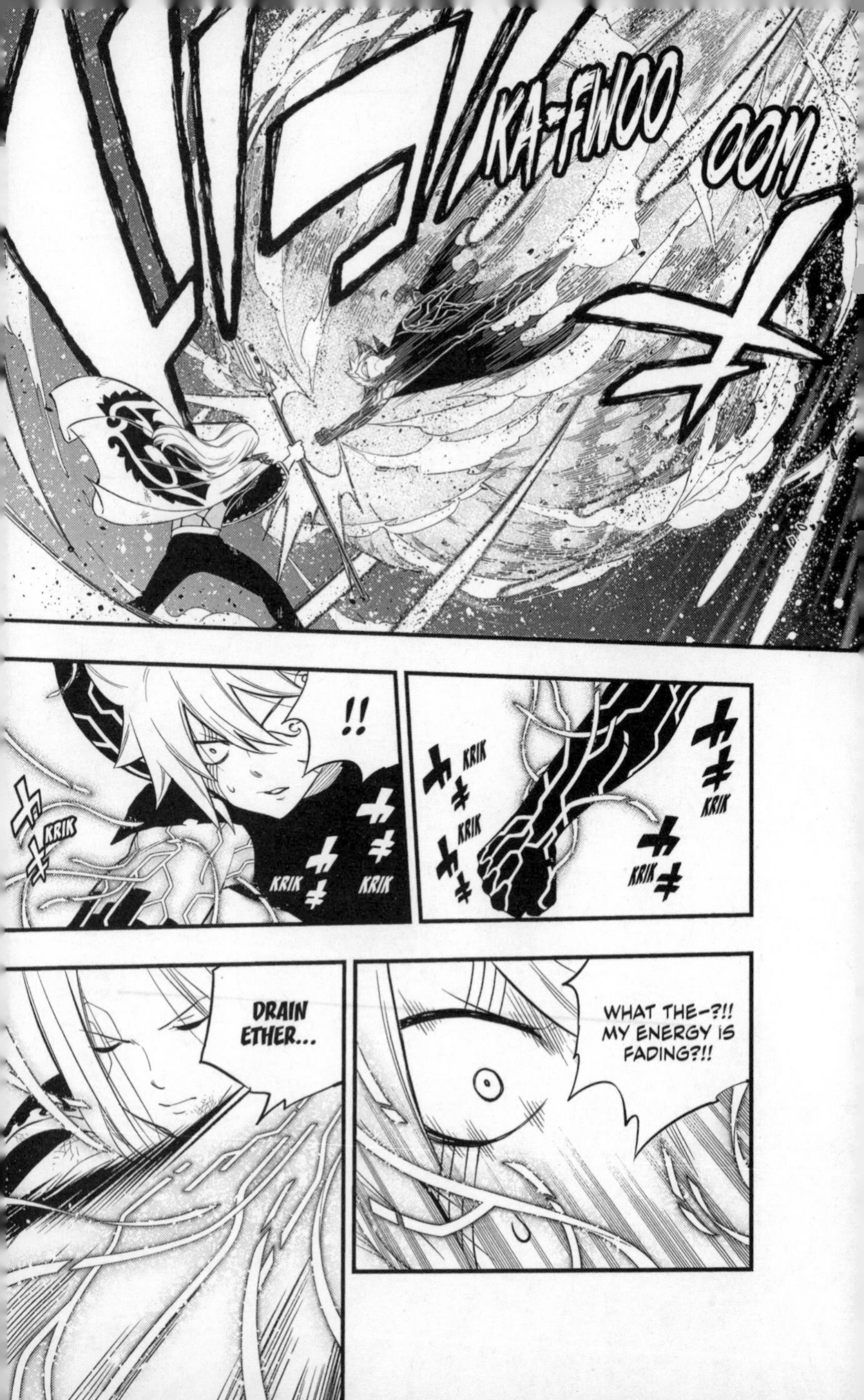
KA-FWOO OOM
KRIK
KRIK
KRIK
KRIK
!!
KRIK
KRIK
KRIK
WHAT THE–?!! MY ENERGY IS FADING?!!
DRAIN ETHER...

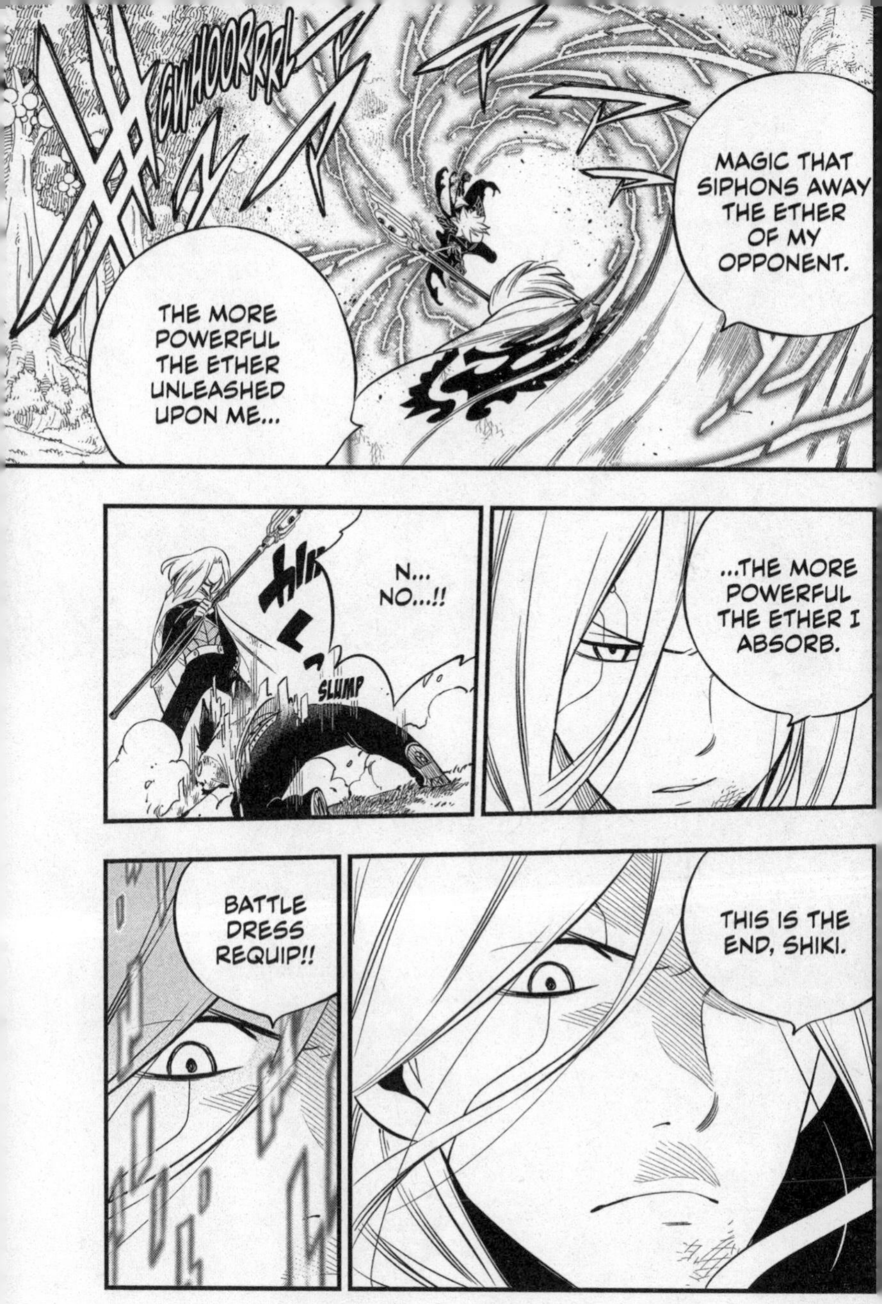
MAGIC THAT SIPHONS AWAY THE ETHER OF MY OPPONENT.
GWHOORRRL
THE MORE POWERFUL THE ETHER UNLEASHED UPON ME...
...THE MORE POWERFUL THE ETHER I ABSORB.
N... NO...!!
SLUMP
THIS IS THE END, SHIKI.
BATTLE DRESS REQUIP!!

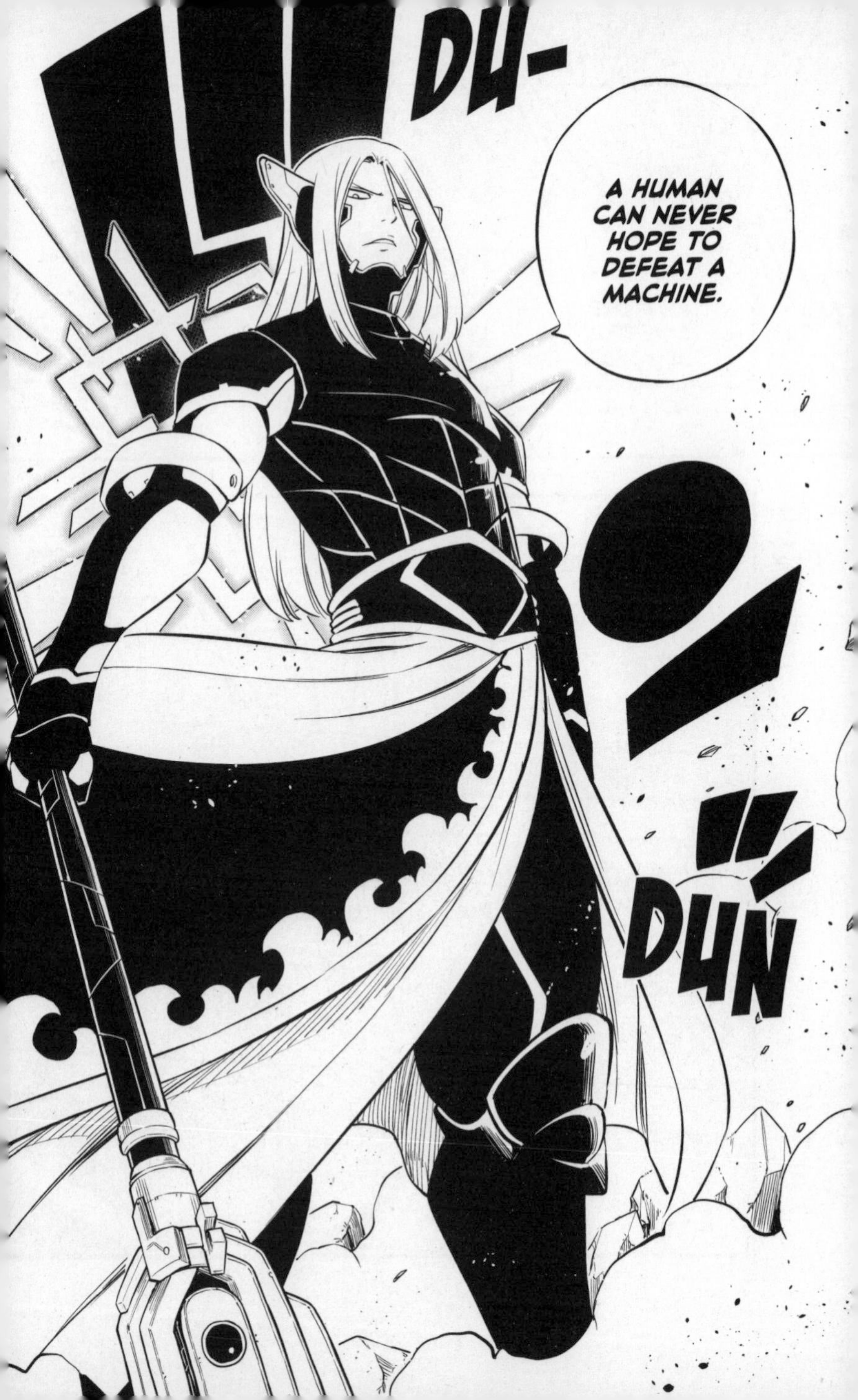
DU-
A HUMAN CAN NEVER HOPE TO DEFEAT A MACHINE.
DUN

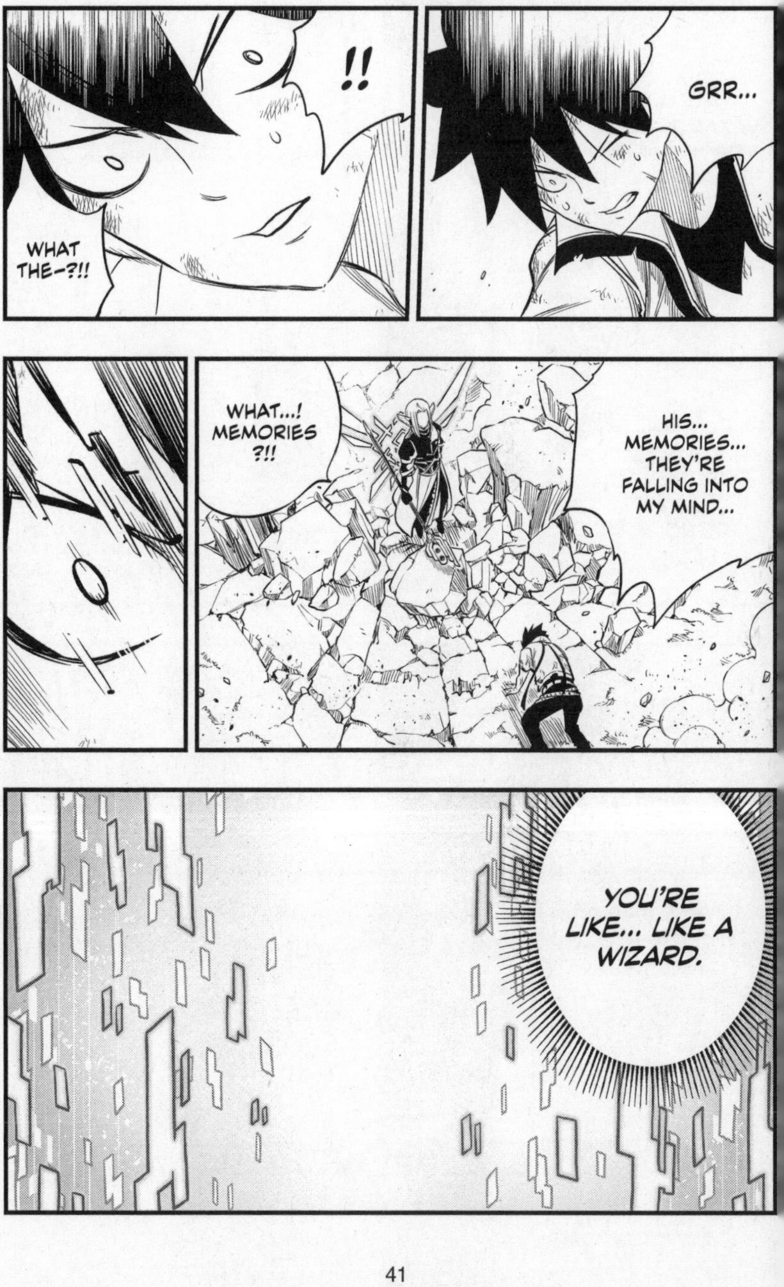
GRR...
!!
WHAT THE-?!!
HIS... MEMORIES... THEY'RE FALLING INTO MY MIND...
WHAT...! MEMORIES ?!!
YOU'RE LIKE... LIKE A WIZARD.

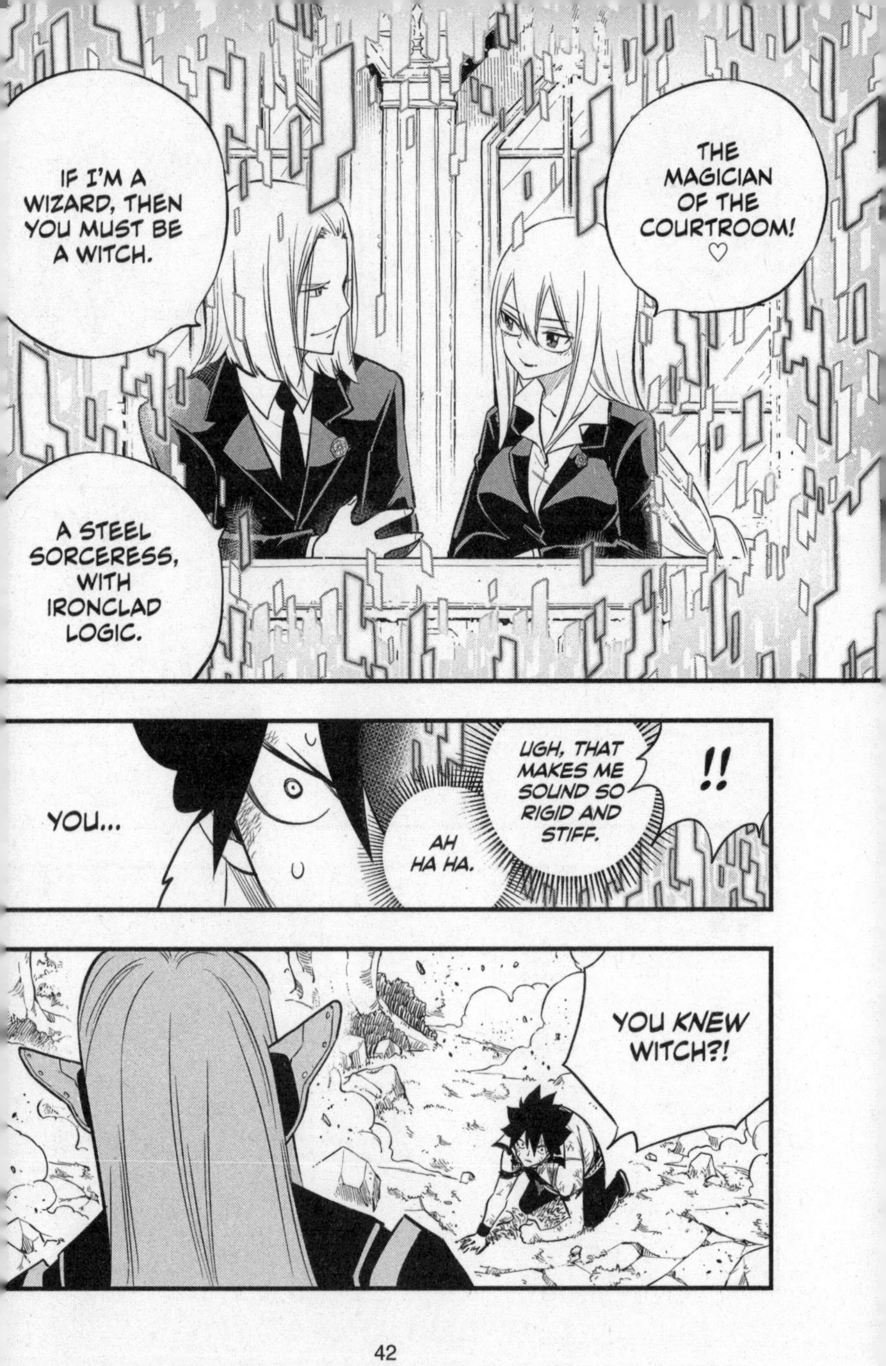
THE MAGICIAN OF THE COURTROOM! ♡
IF I'M A WIZARD, THEN YOU MUST BE A WITCH.
A STEEL SORCERESS, WITH IRONCLAD LOGIC.
!!
UGH, THAT MAKES ME SOUND SO RIGID AND STIFF.
AH HA HA.
YOU...
YOU KNEW WITCH?!

EDENS ZERO

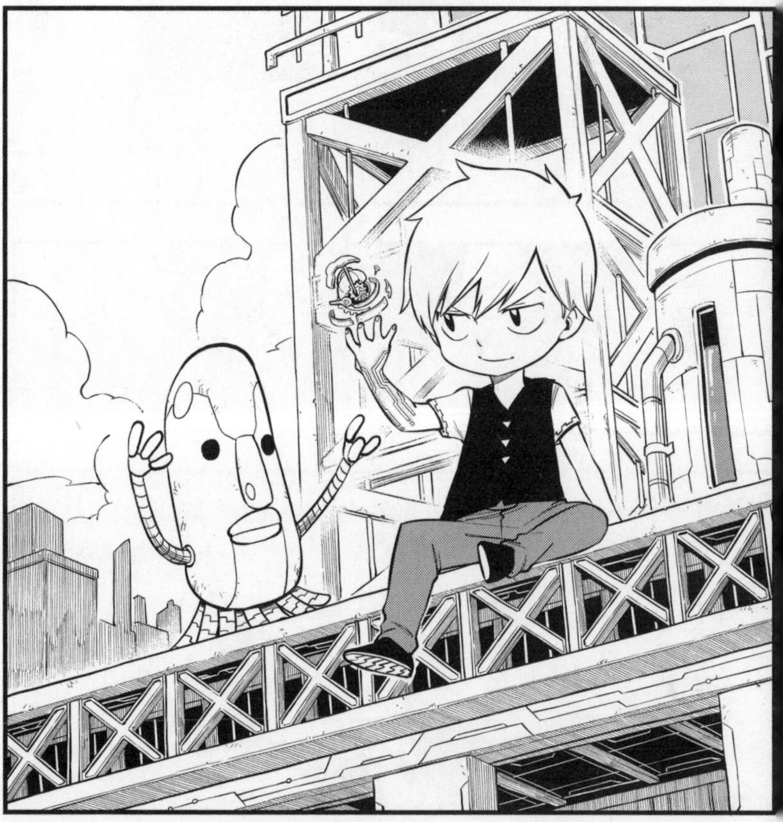

CHAPTER 188: ONE TENTH

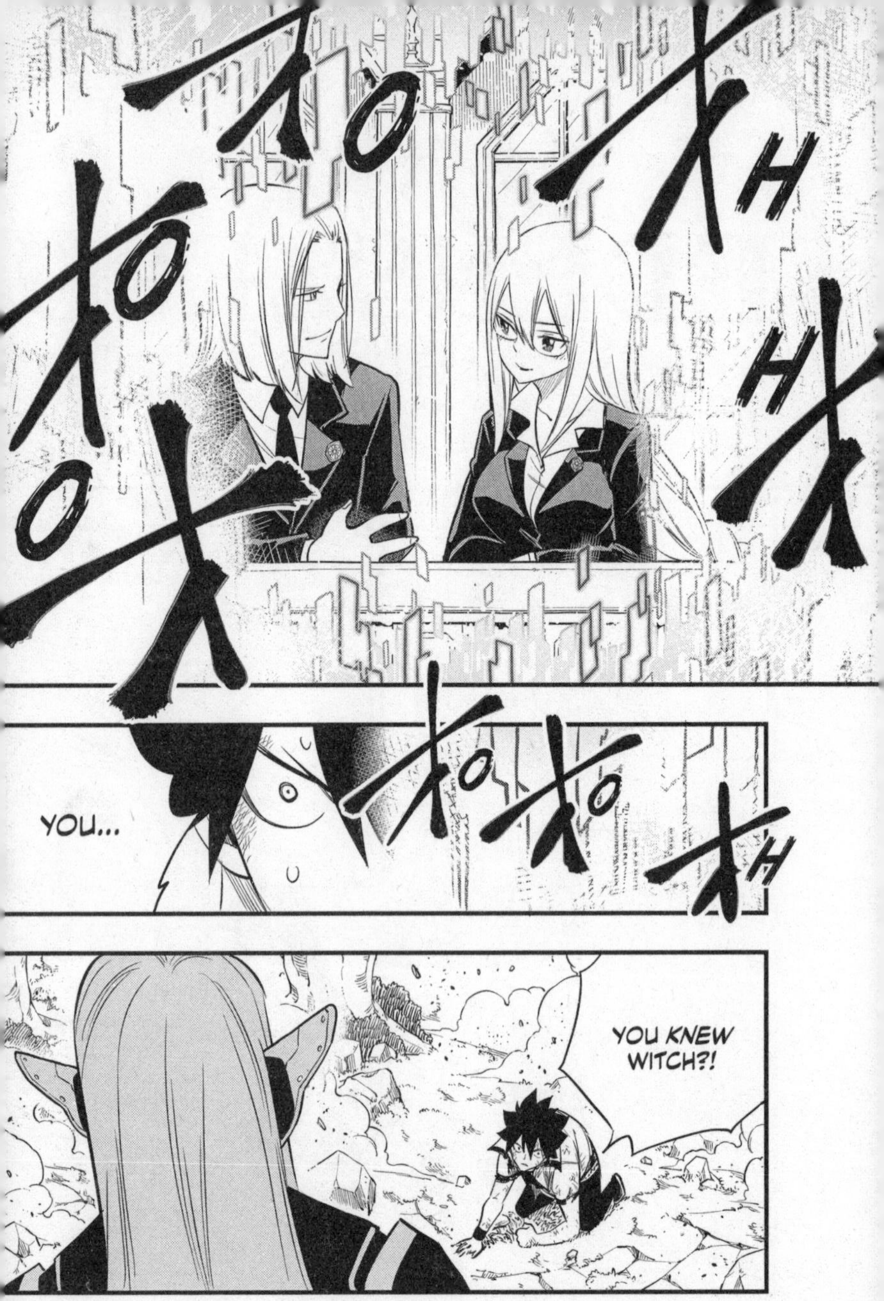
YOU...
YOU KNEW WITCH?!

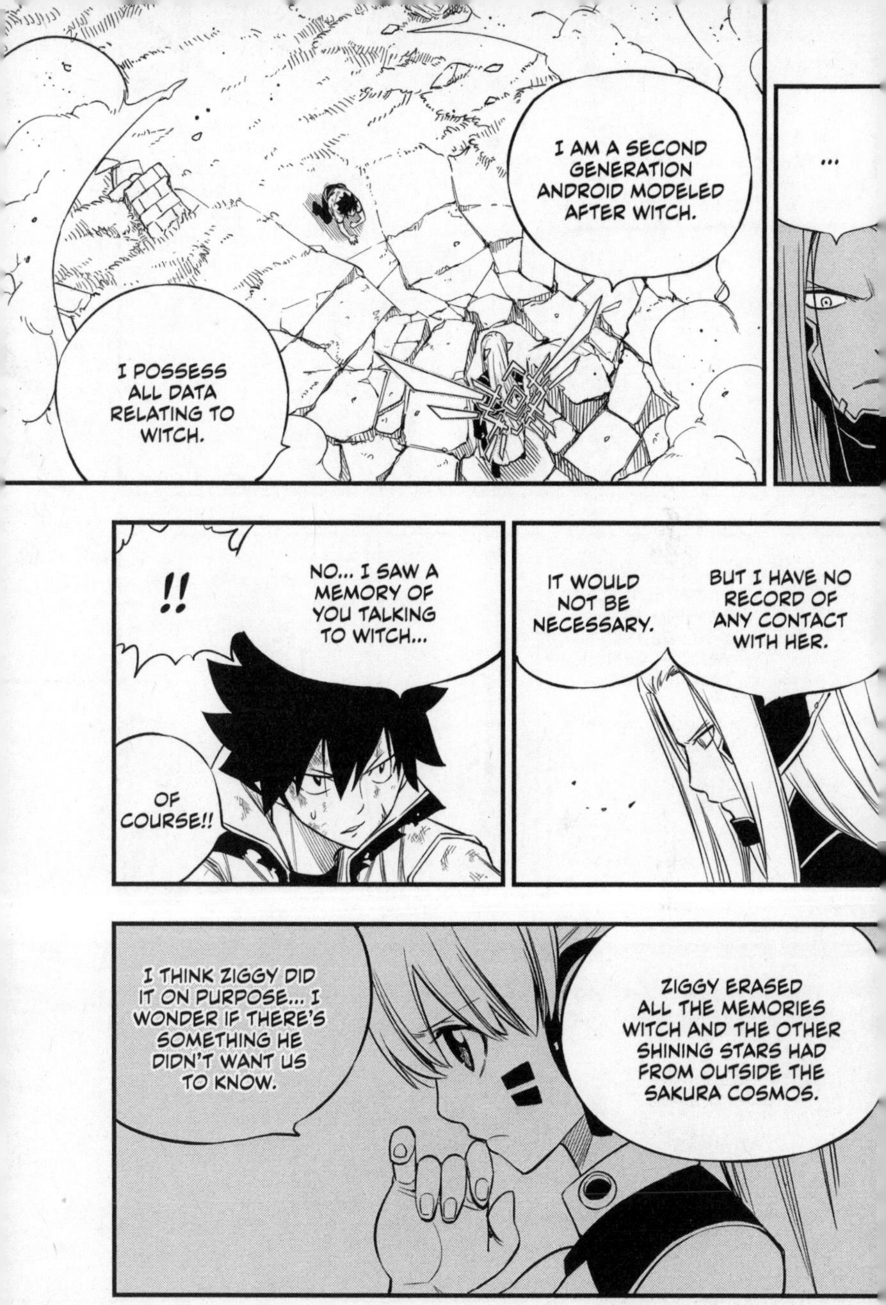
...
I AM A SECOND GENERATION ANDROID MODELED AFTER WITCH.
I POSSESS ALL DATA RELATING TO WITCH.
BUT I HAVE NO RECORD OF ANY CONTACT WITH HER.
IT WOULD NOT BE NECESSARY.
NO... I SAW A MEMORY OF YOU TALKING TO WITCH...
!!
OF COURSE!!
ZIGGY ERASED ALL THE MEMORIES WITCH AND THE OTHER SHINING STARS HAD FROM OUTSIDE THE SAKURA COSMOS.
I THINK ZIGGY DID IT ON PURPOSE... I WONDER IF THERE'S SOMETHING HE DIDN'T WANT US TO KNOW.

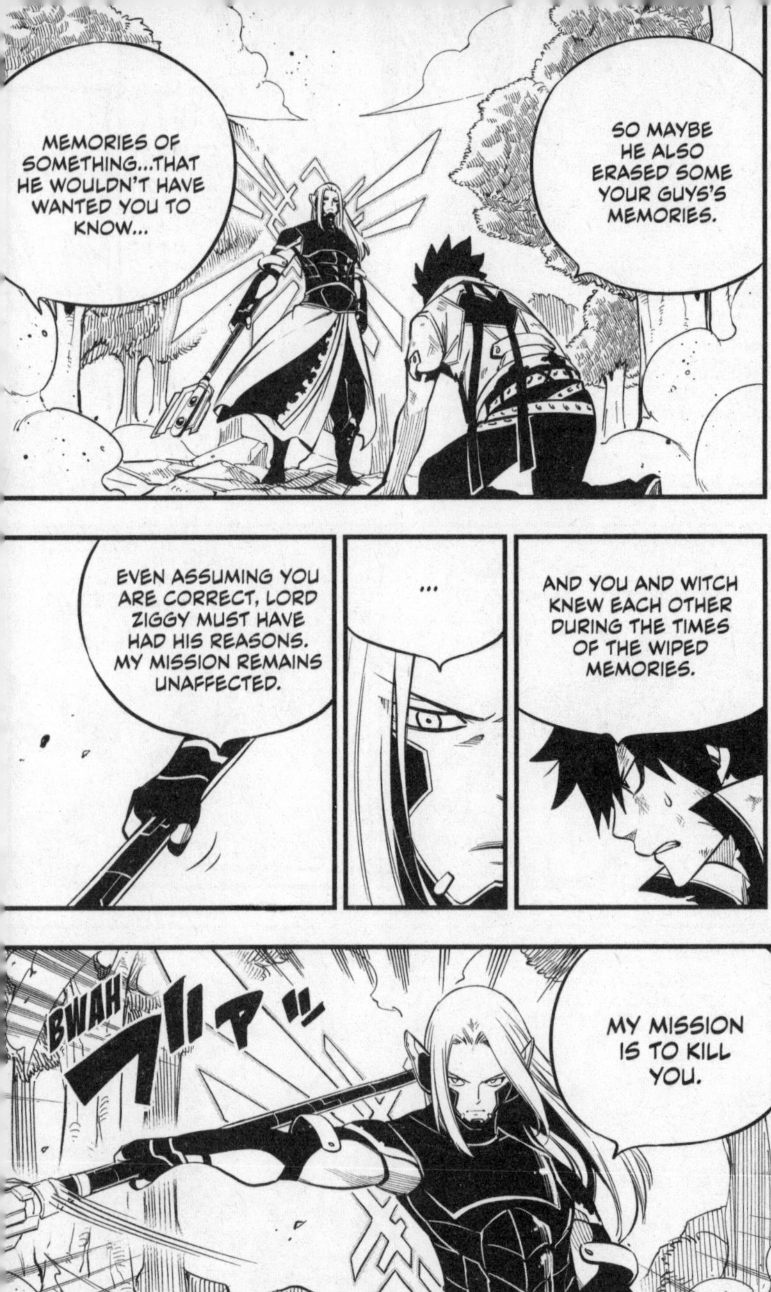
SO MAYBE HE ALSO ERASED SOME YOUR GUYS'S MEMORIES.
MEMORIES OF SOMETHING...THAT HE WOULDN'T HAVE WANTED YOU TO KNOW...
AND YOU AND WITCH KNEW EACH OTHER DURING THE TIMES OF THE WIPED MEMORIES.
...
EVEN ASSUMING YOU ARE CORRECT, LORD ZIGGY MUST HAVE HAD HIS REASONS. MY MISSION REMAINS UNAFFECTED.
MY MISSION IS TO KILL YOU.
BWAH

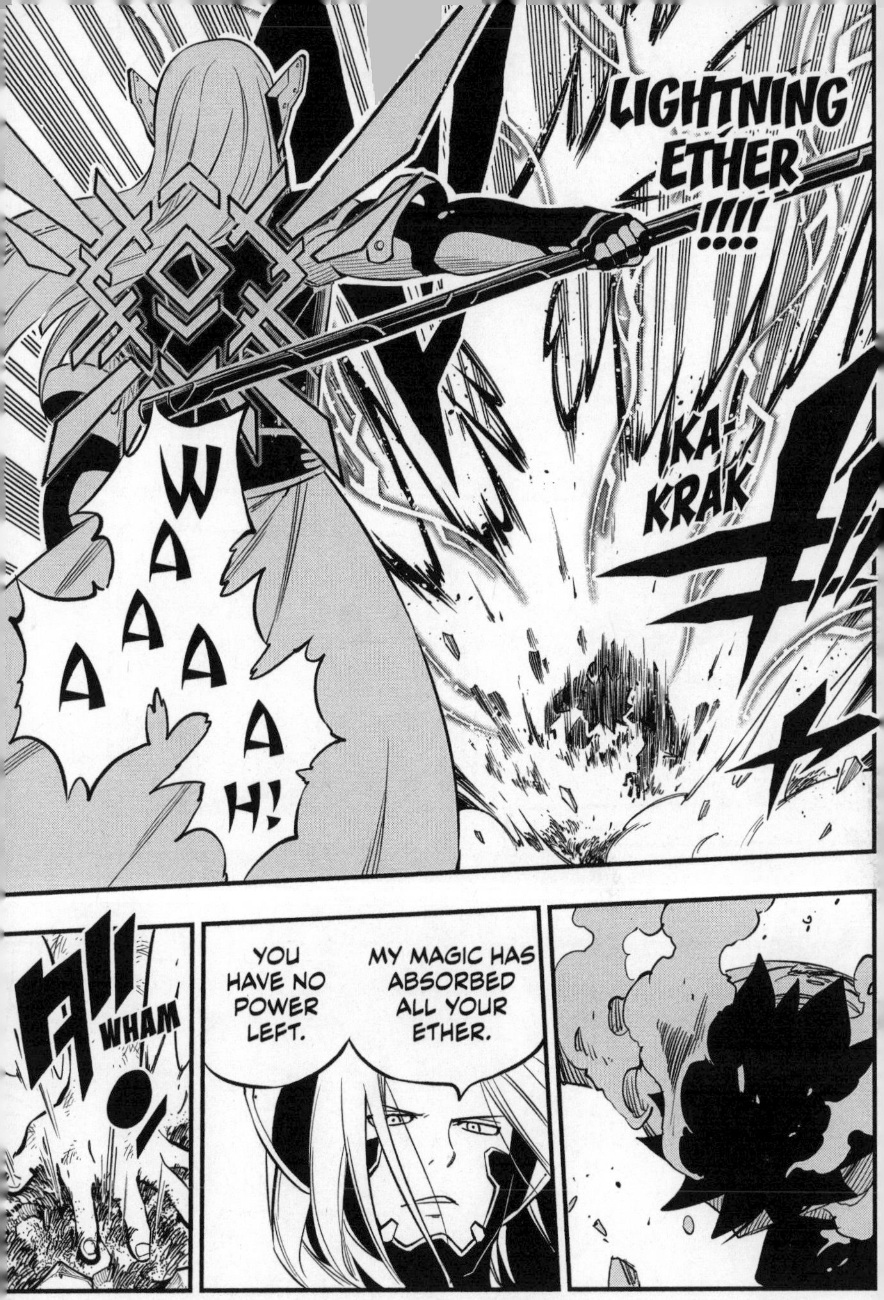

LIGHTNING ETHER!!!!....
KA-KRAK
WAAAAAH!
YOU HAVE NO POWER LEFT. MY MAGIC HAS ABSORBED ALL YOUR ETHER.
WHAM

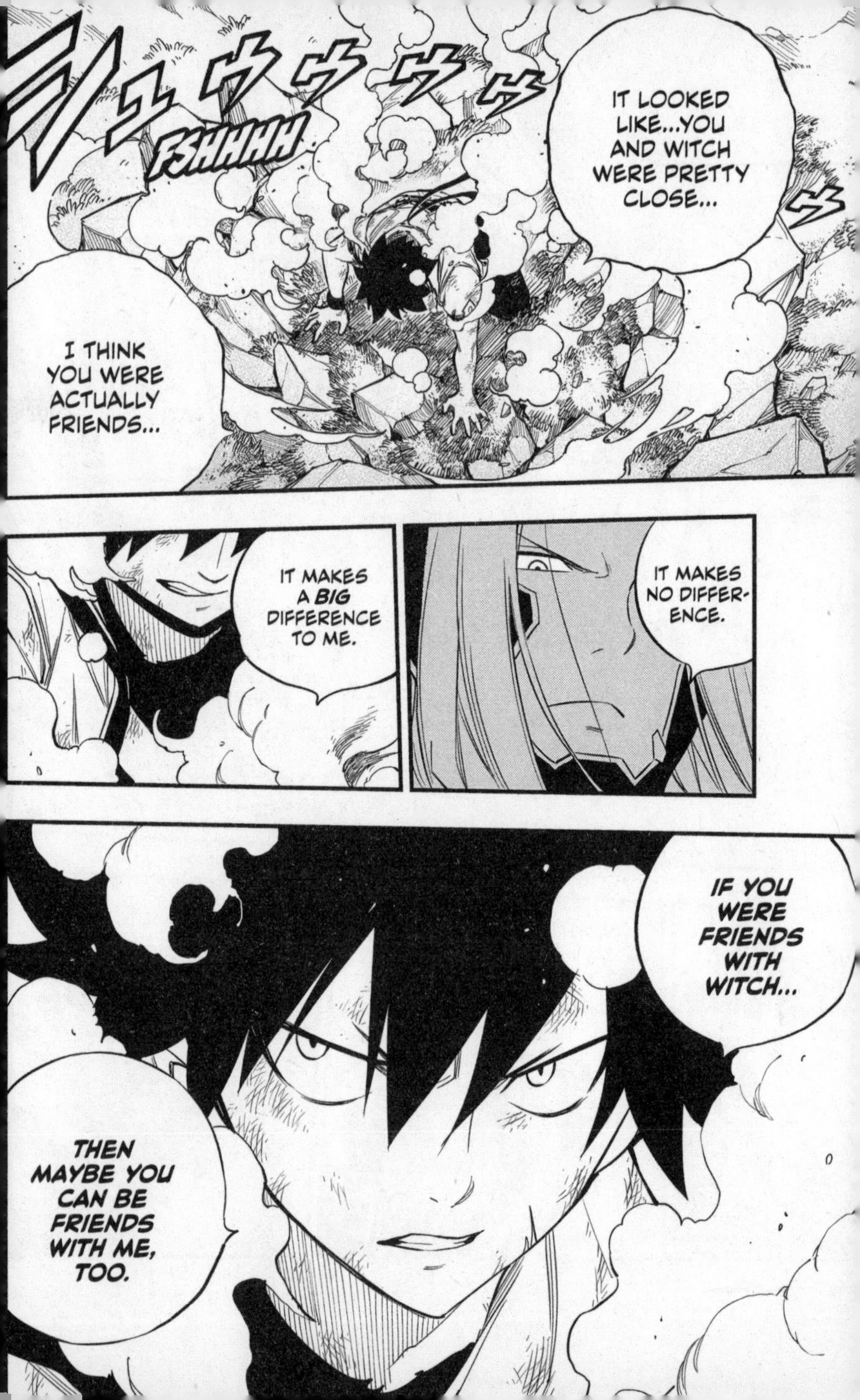
IT LOOKED LIKE...YOU AND WITCH WERE PRETTY CLOSE...
FSHHHH
I THINK YOU WERE ACTUALLY FRIENDS...
IT MAKES NO DIFFERENCE.
IT MAKES A *BIG* DIFFERENCE TO ME.
IF YOU WERE FRIENDS WITH WITCH...
THEN MAYBE YOU CAN BE FRIENDS WITH ME, TOO.

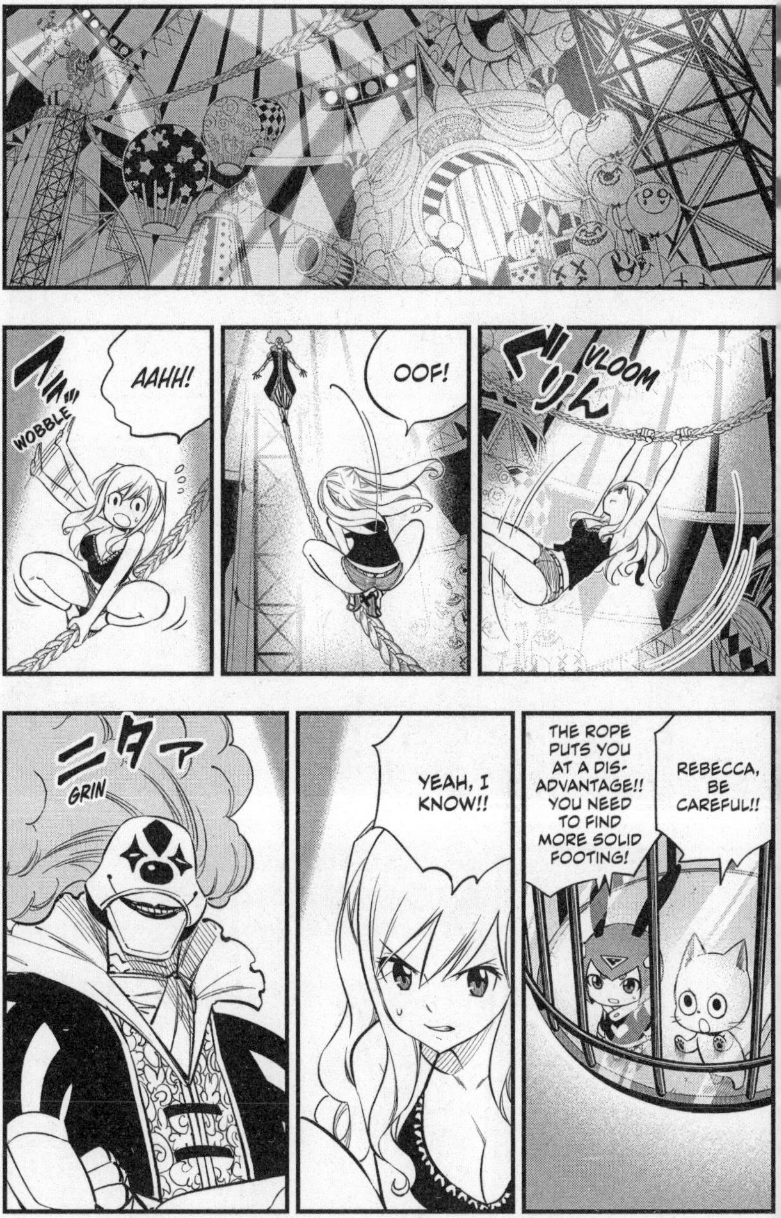
VLOOM
OOF!
WOBBLE
AAHH!
REBECCA, BE CAREFUL!!
THE ROPE PUTS YOU AT A DIS-ADVANTAGE!! YOU NEED TO FIND MORE SOLID FOOTING!
YEAH, I KNOW!!
ニタァ
GRIN

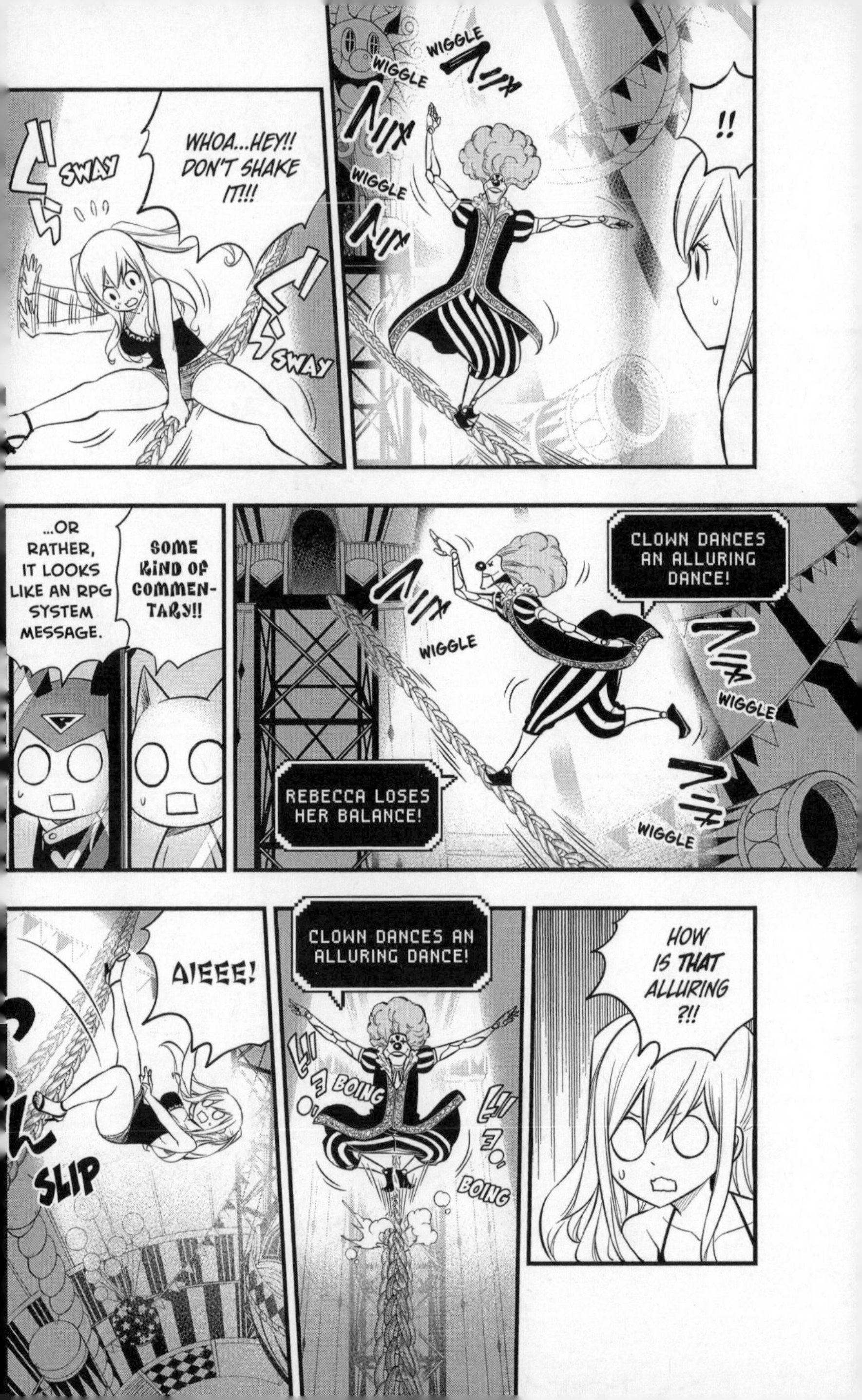
!!
WIGGLE
WIGGLE
WIGGLE
WHOA...HEY!! DON'T SHAKE IT!!!
SWAY
SWAY
CLOWN DANCES AN ALLURING DANCE!
WIGGLE
WIGGLE
WIGGLE
REBECCA LOSES HER BALANCE!
SOME KIND OF COMMENTARY!!
...OR RATHER, IT LOOKS LIKE AN RPG SYSTEM MESSAGE.
HOW IS THAT ALLURING?!!
CLOWN DANCES AN ALLURING DANCE!
BOING
BOING
AIEEE!
SLIP

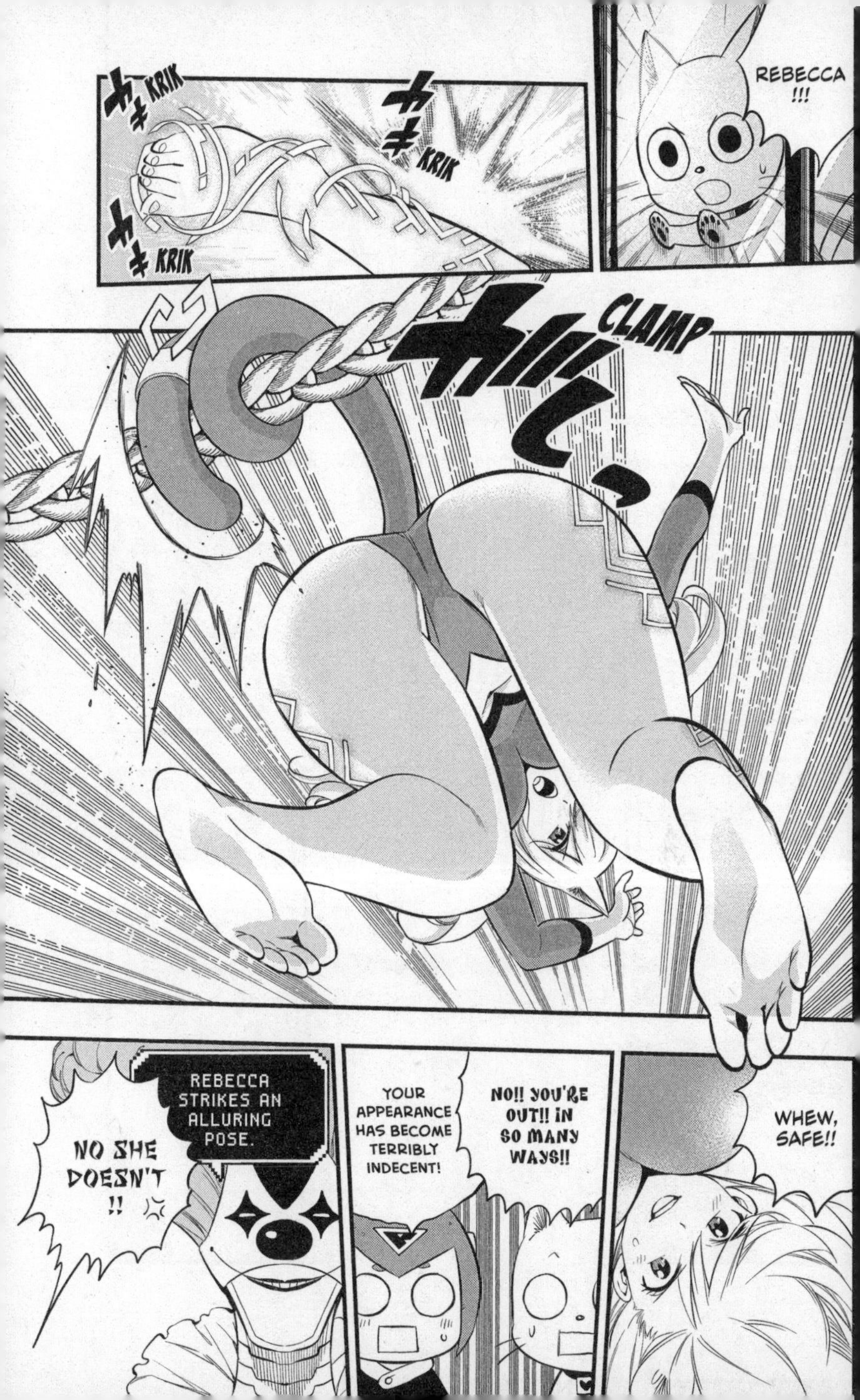
REBECCA!!!
KRIK
KRIK
KRIK
CLAMP
WHEW, SAFE!!
NO!! YOU'RE OUT!! IN SO MANY WAYS!!
YOUR APPEARANCE HAS BECOME TERRIBLY INDECENT!
REBECCA STRIKES AN ALLURING POSE.
NO SHE DOESN'T!!

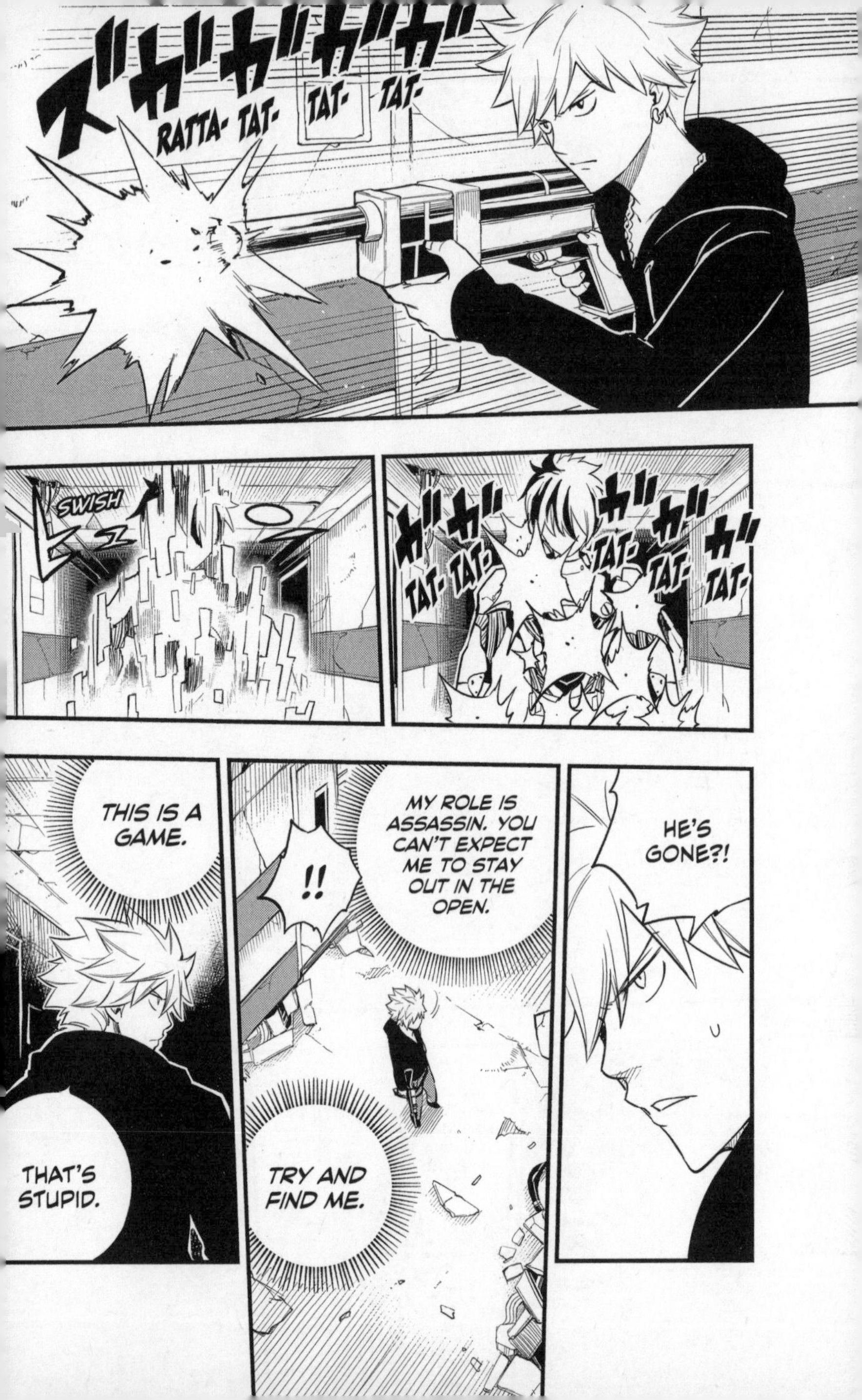
RATTA- TAT- TAT- TAT-
TAT- TAT- TAT- TAT- TAT-
SWISH
HE'S GONE?!
!!
MY ROLE IS ASSASSIN. YOU CAN'T EXPECT ME TO STAY OUT IN THE OPEN.
TRY AND FIND ME.
THIS IS A GAME.
THAT'S STUPID.

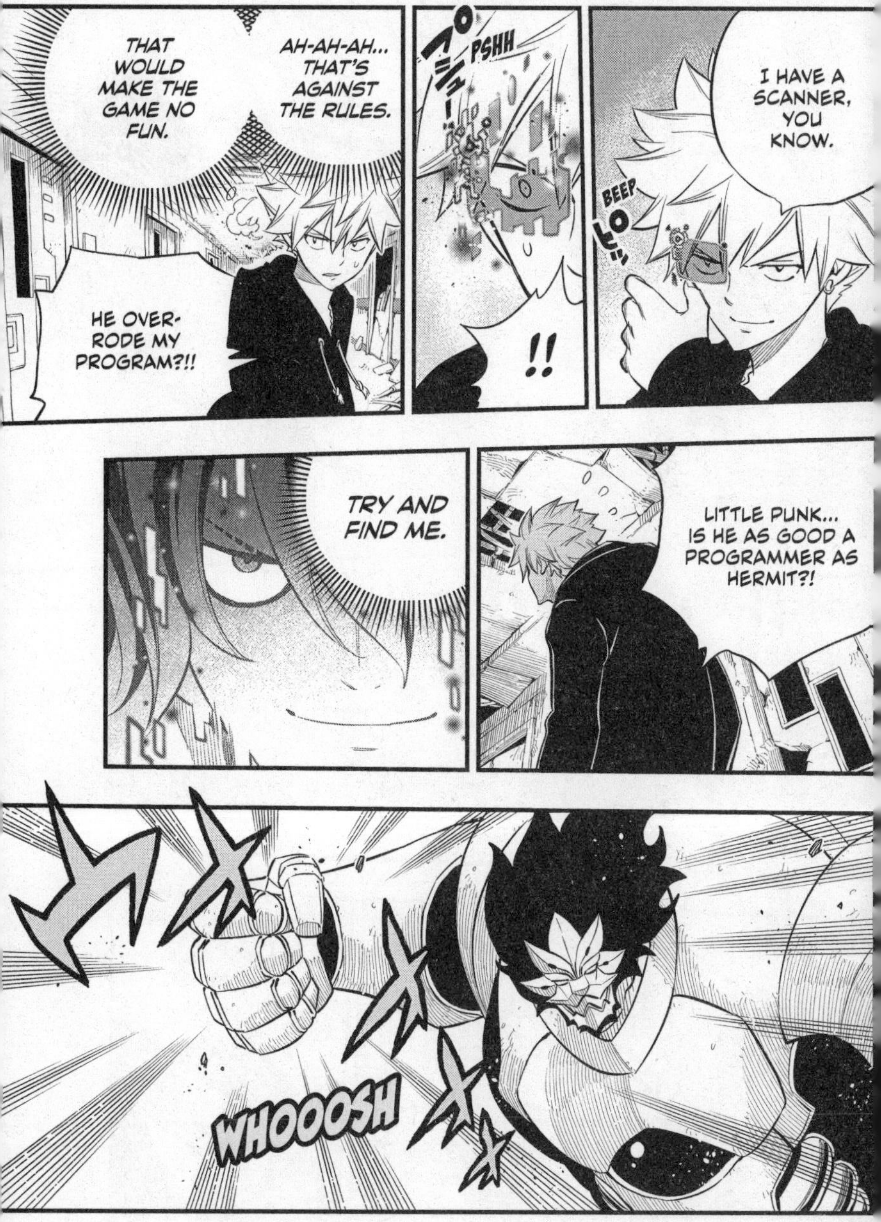
I HAVE A SCANNER, YOU KNOW.
BEEP
PSHH
!!
AH-AH-AH... THAT'S AGAINST THE RULES.
THAT WOULD MAKE THE GAME NO FUN.
HE OVER-RODE MY PROGRAM?!!
LITTLE PUNK... IS HE AS GOOD A PROGRAMMER AS HERMIT?!
TRY AND FIND ME.
WHOOOSH

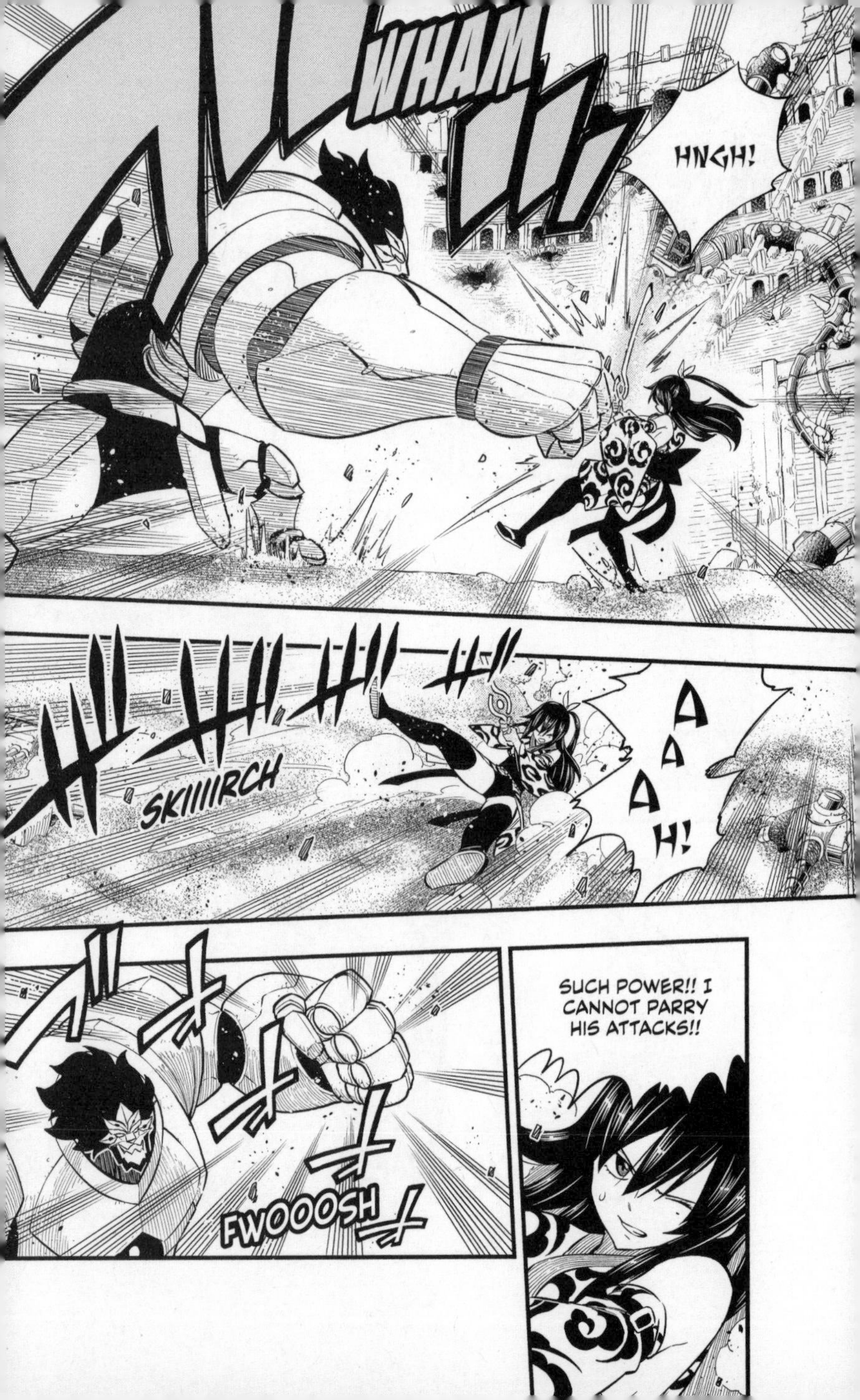
WHAM
HNGH!
SKIIIIRCH
AAAAH!
SUCH POWER!! I CANNOT PARRY HIS ATTACKS!!
FWOOOSH

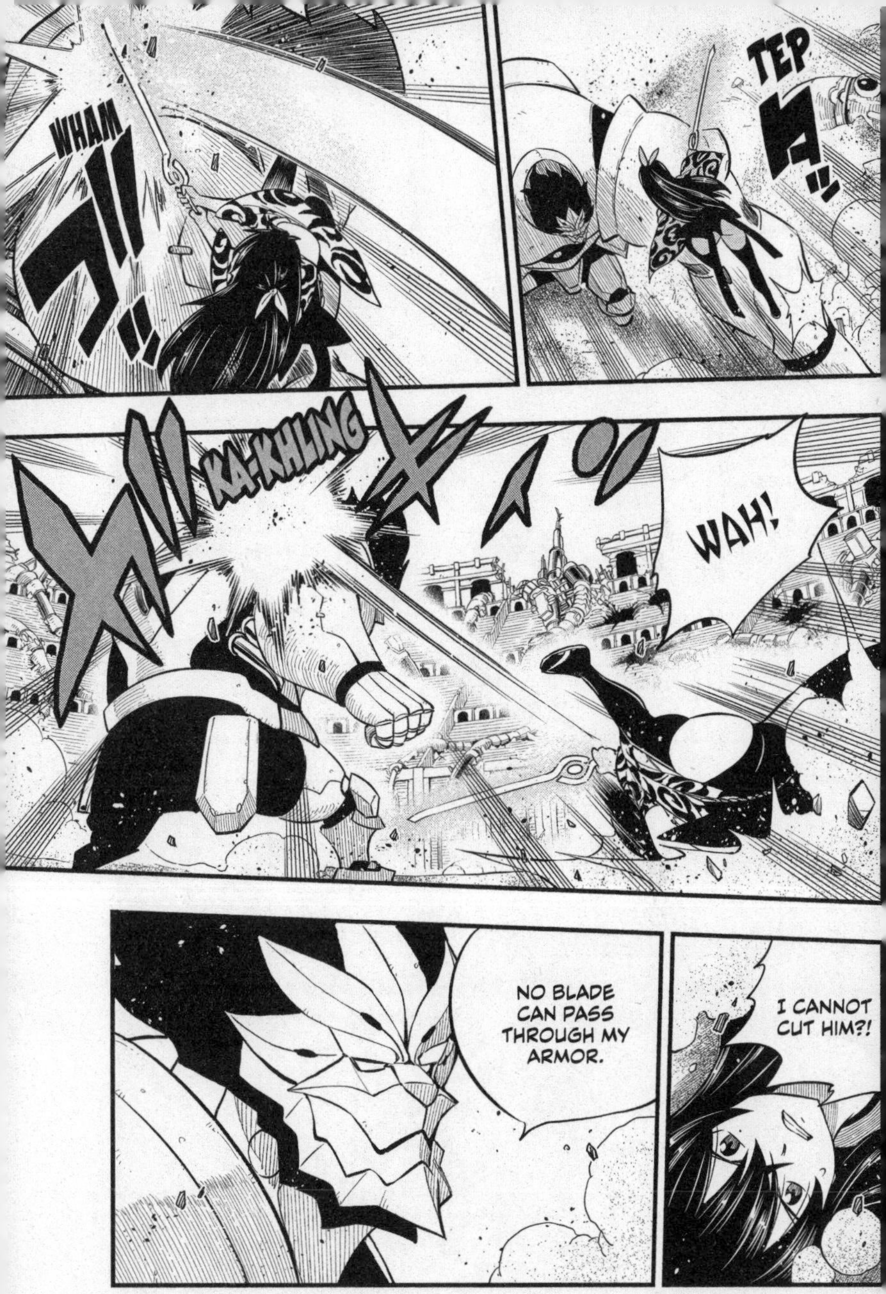
TEP
WHAM
WAH!
KA-KHLING
I CANNOT CUT HIM?!
NO BLADE CAN PASS THROUGH MY ARMOR.

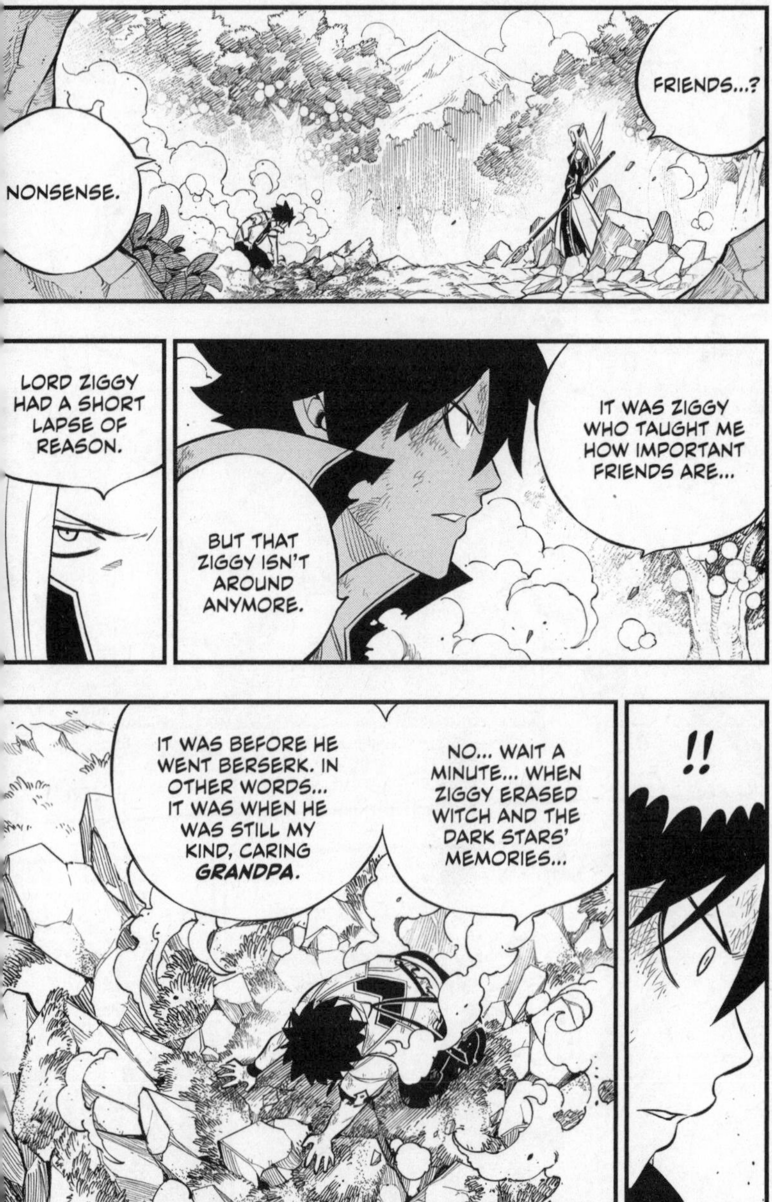
FRIENDS...?
NONSENSE.
IT WAS ZIGGY WHO TAUGHT ME HOW IMPORTANT FRIENDS ARE...
BUT THAT ZIGGY ISN'T AROUND ANYMORE.
LORD ZIGGY HAD A SHORT LAPSE OF REASON.
!!
NO... WAIT A MINUTE... WHEN ZIGGY ERASED WITCH AND THE DARK STARS' MEMORIES...
IT WAS BEFORE HE WENT BERSERK. IN OTHER WORDS... IT WAS WHEN HE WAS STILL MY KIND, CARING ***GRANDPA***.

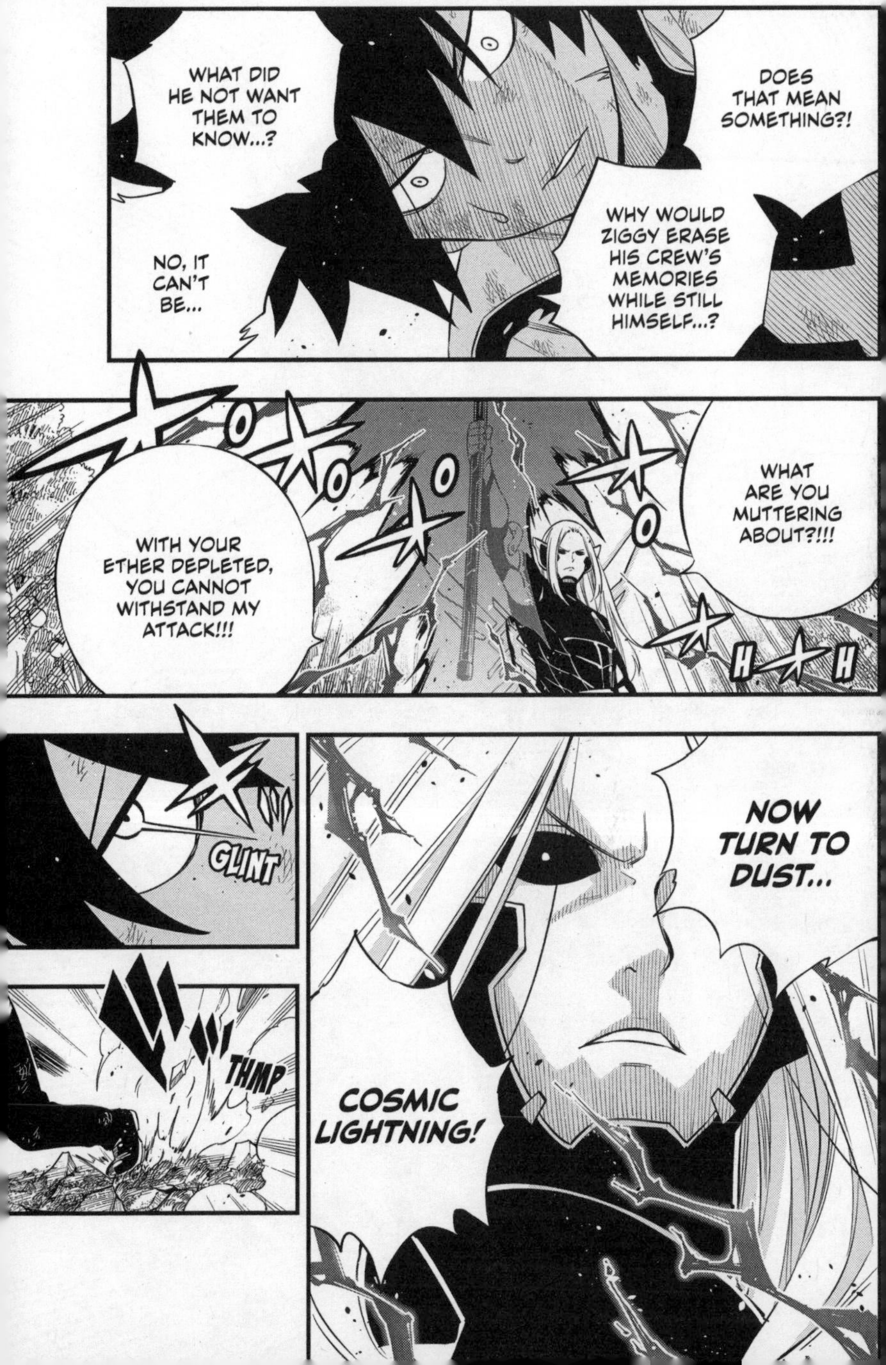
DOES THAT MEAN SOMETHING?!
WHAT DID HE NOT WANT THEM TO KNOW...?
WHY WOULD ZIGGY ERASE HIS CREW'S MEMORIES WHILE STILL HIMSELF...?
NO, IT CAN'T BE...
WHAT ARE YOU MUTTERING ABOUT?!!!
WITH YOUR ETHER DEPLETED, YOU CANNOT WITHSTAND MY ATTACK!!!
NOW TURN TO DUST...
COSMIC LIGHTNING!
GLINT
THMP

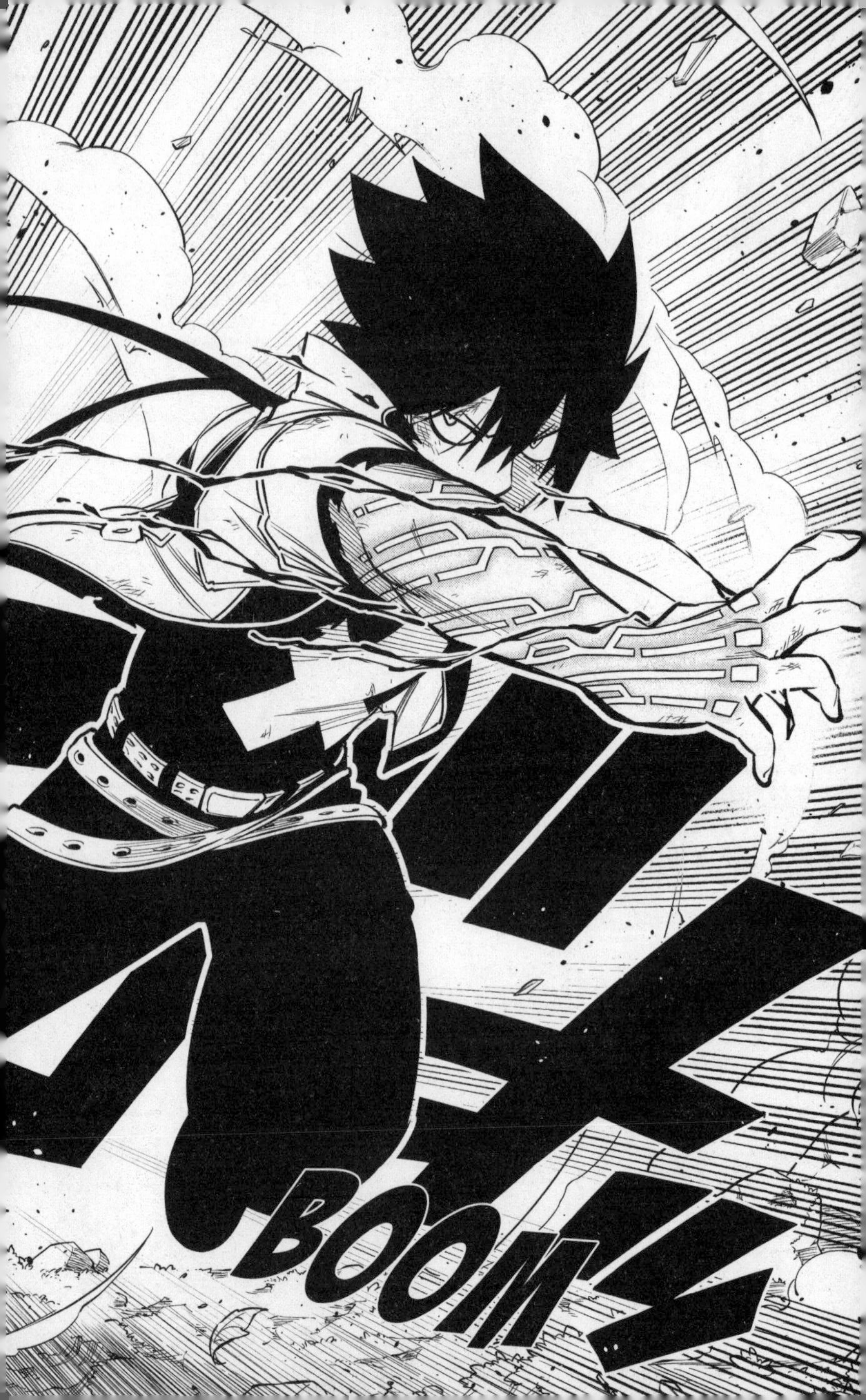
BOOM

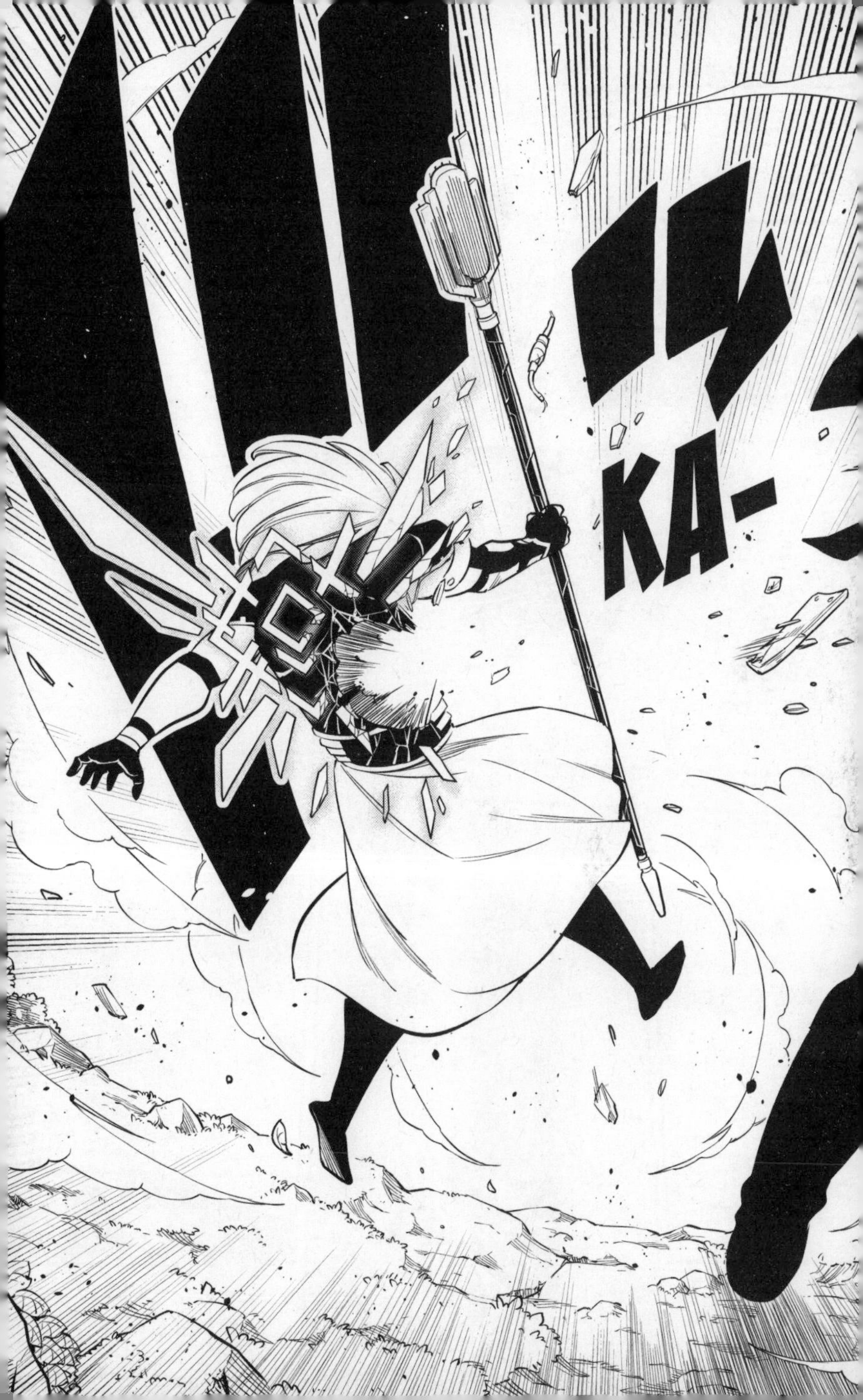
KA-

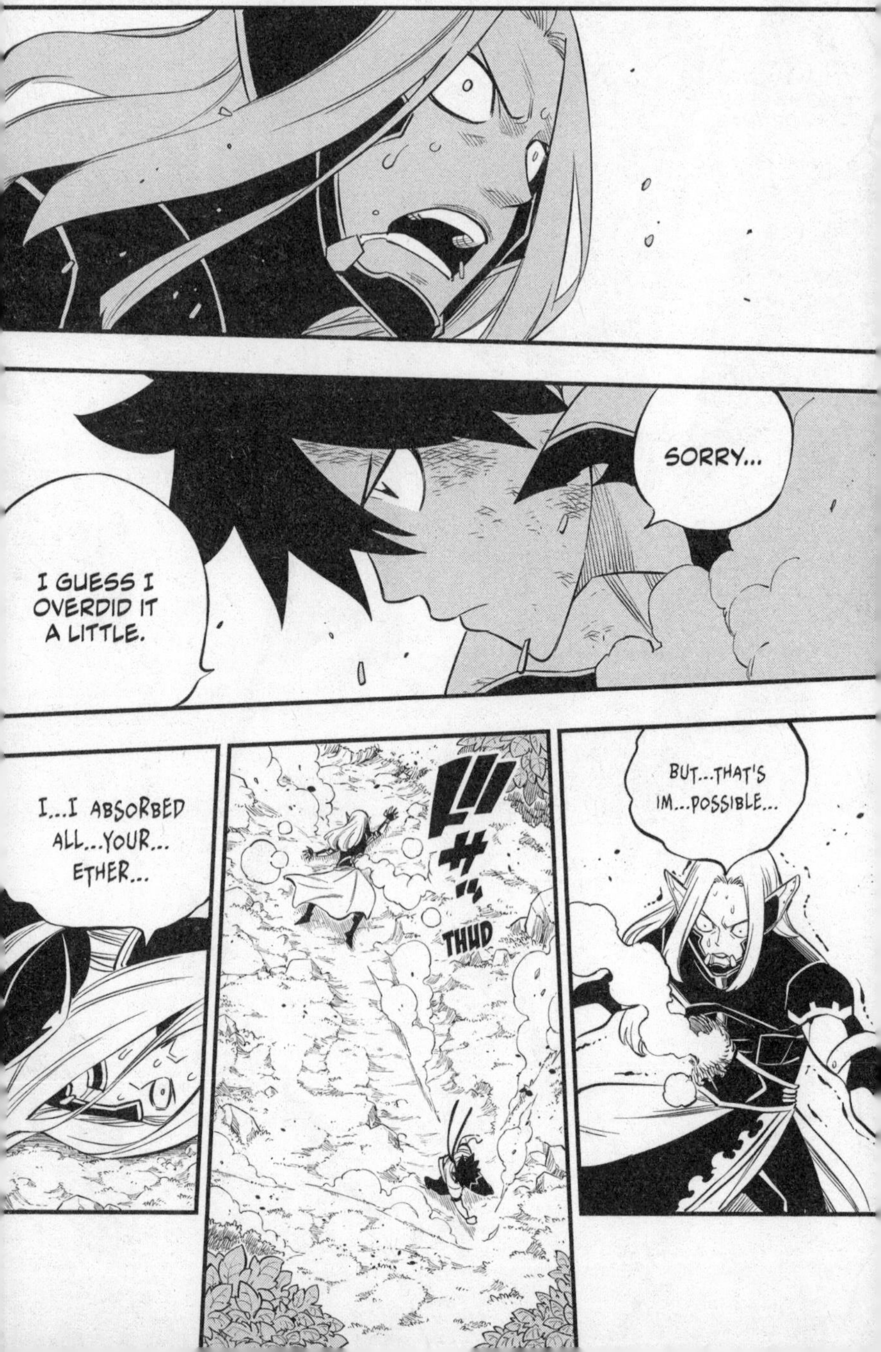
SORRY...
I GUESS I OVERDID IT A LITTLE.
BUT...THAT'S IM...POSSIBLE...
THUD
I...I ABSORBED ALL...YOUR... ETHER...

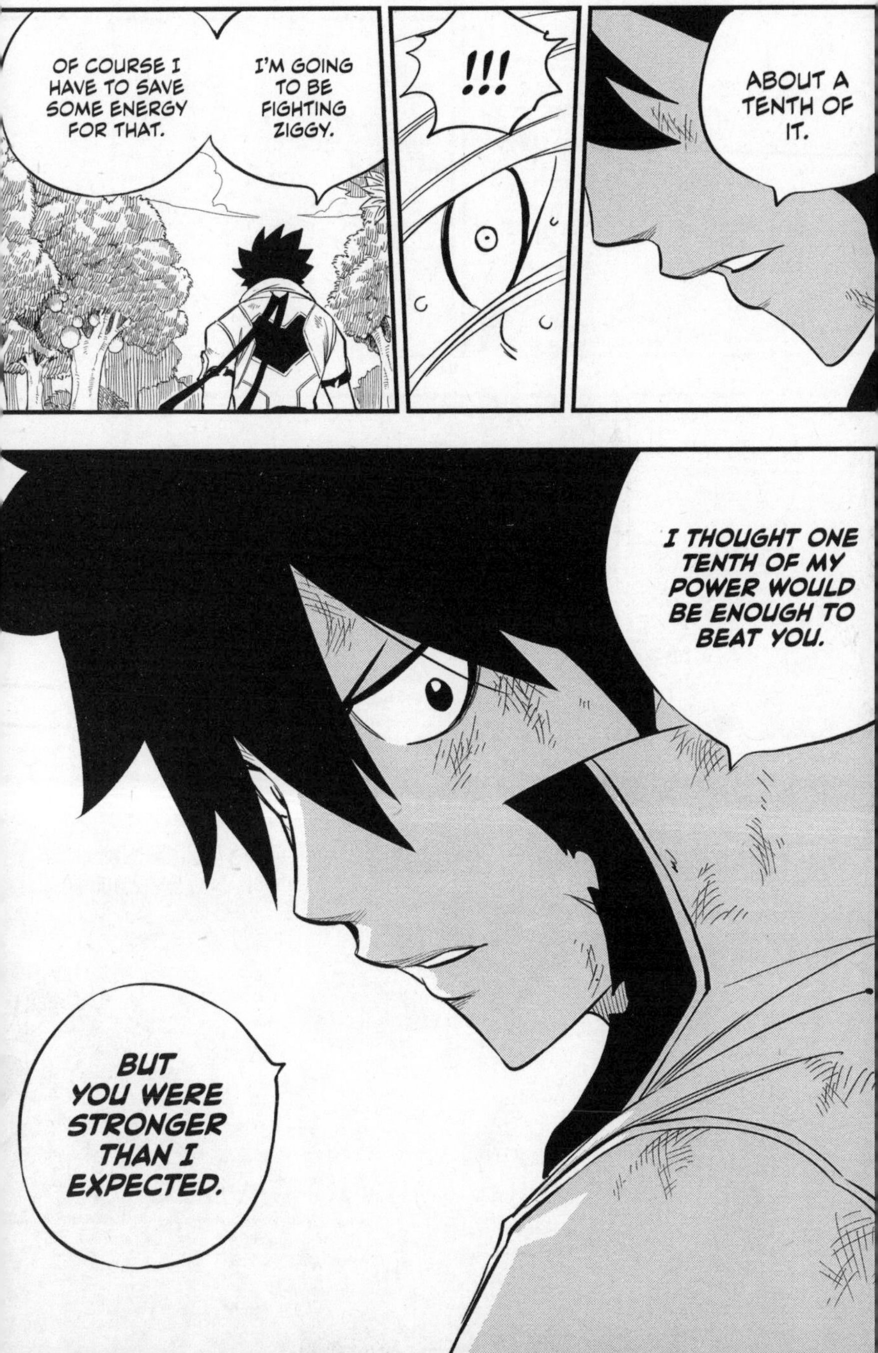
ABOUT A TENTH OF IT.
!!!
I'M GOING TO BE FIGHTING ZIGGY.
OF COURSE I HAVE TO SAVE SOME ENERGY FOR THAT.
I THOUGHT ONE TENTH OF MY POWER WOULD BE ENOUGH TO BEAT YOU.
BUT YOU WERE STRONGER THAN I EXPECTED.

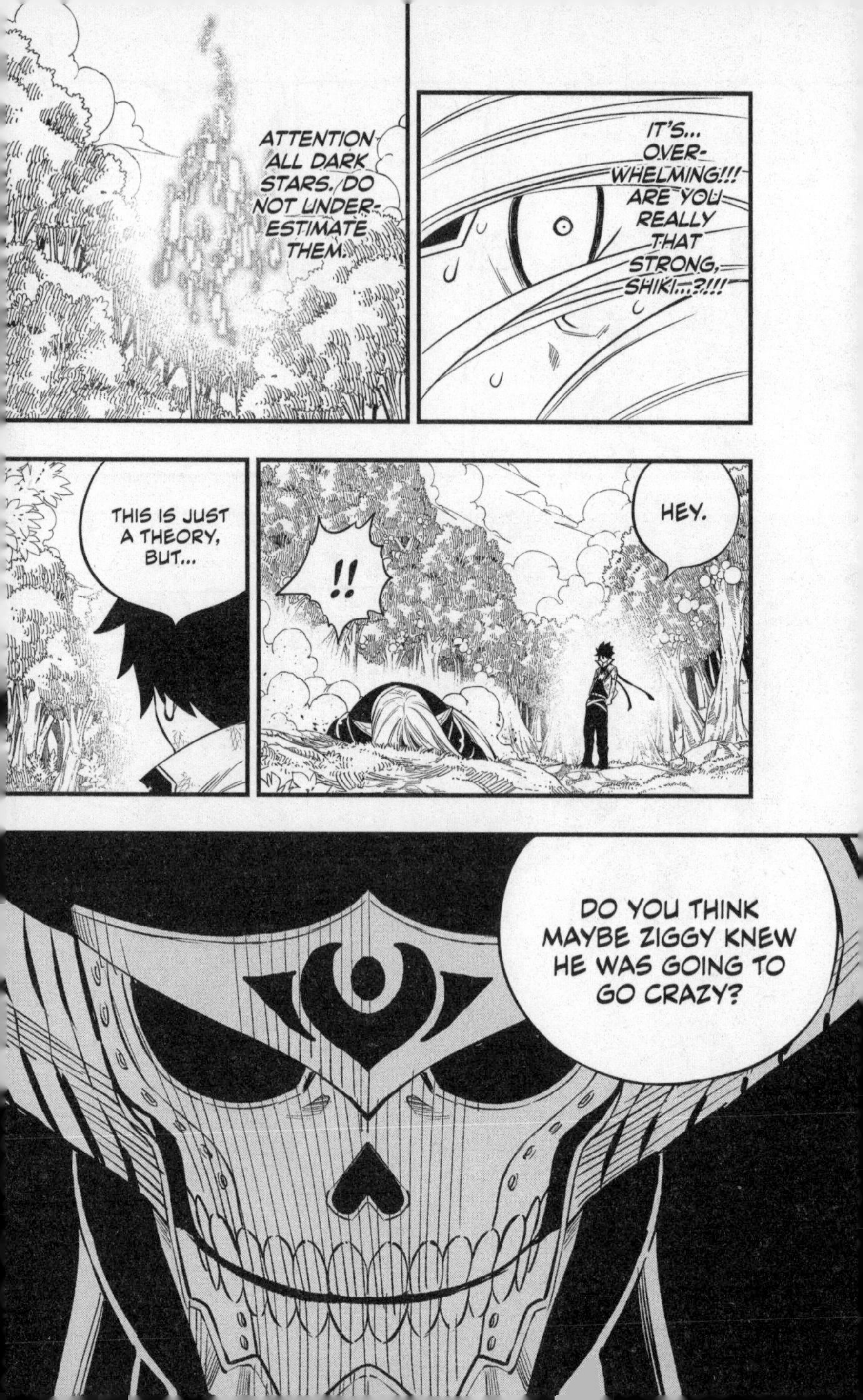
IT'S... OVER-WHELMING!!! ARE YOU REALLY THAT STRONG, SHIKI...?!!!
ATTENTION ALL DARK STARS. DO NOT UNDER-ESTIMATE THEM.
HEY.
!!
THIS IS JUST A THEORY, BUT...
DO YOU THINK MAYBE ZIGGY KNEW HE WAS GOING TO GO CRAZY?

EDENS ZERO

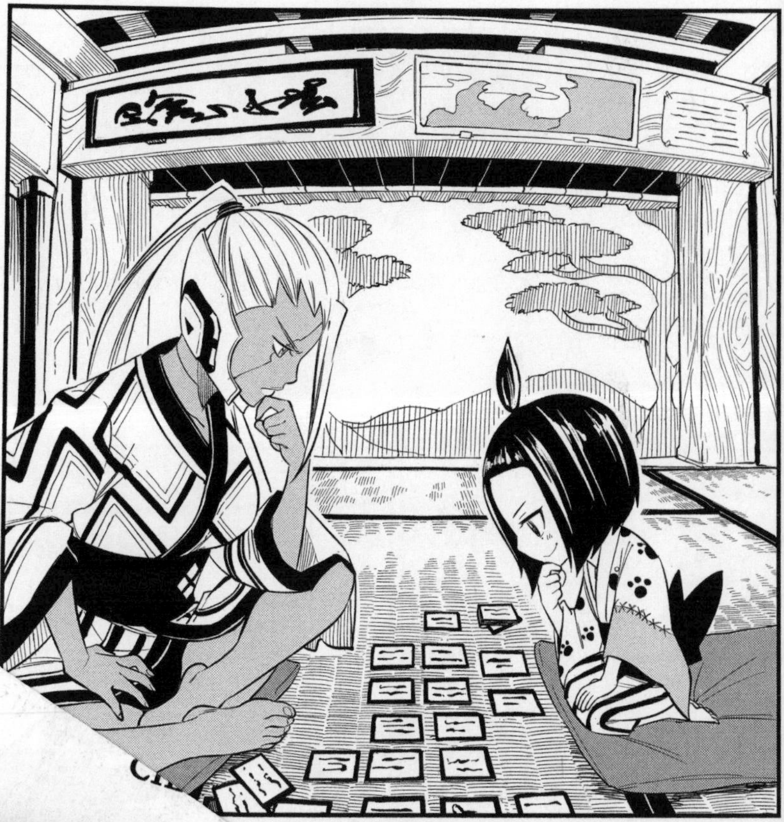

CH

89: REBECCA VS. CLOWN

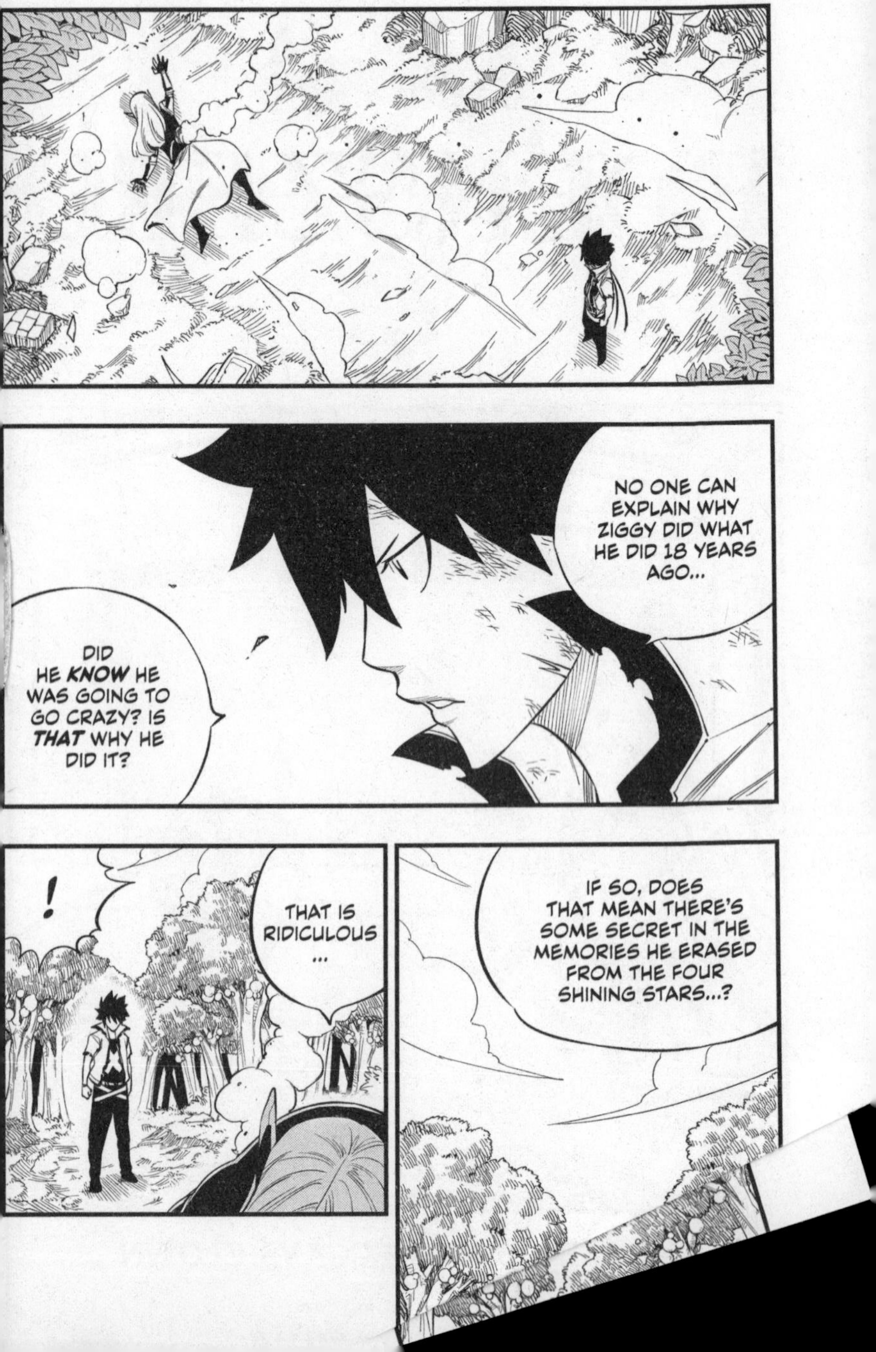
NO ONE CAN EXPLAIN WHY ZIGGY DID WHAT HE DID 18 YEARS AGO...
DID HE **KNOW** HE WAS GOING TO GO CRAZY? IS **THAT** WHY HE DID IT?
IF SO, DOES THAT MEAN THERE'S SOME SECRET IN THE MEMORIES HE ERASED FROM THE FOUR SHINING STARS...?
THAT IS RIDICULOUS ...
!

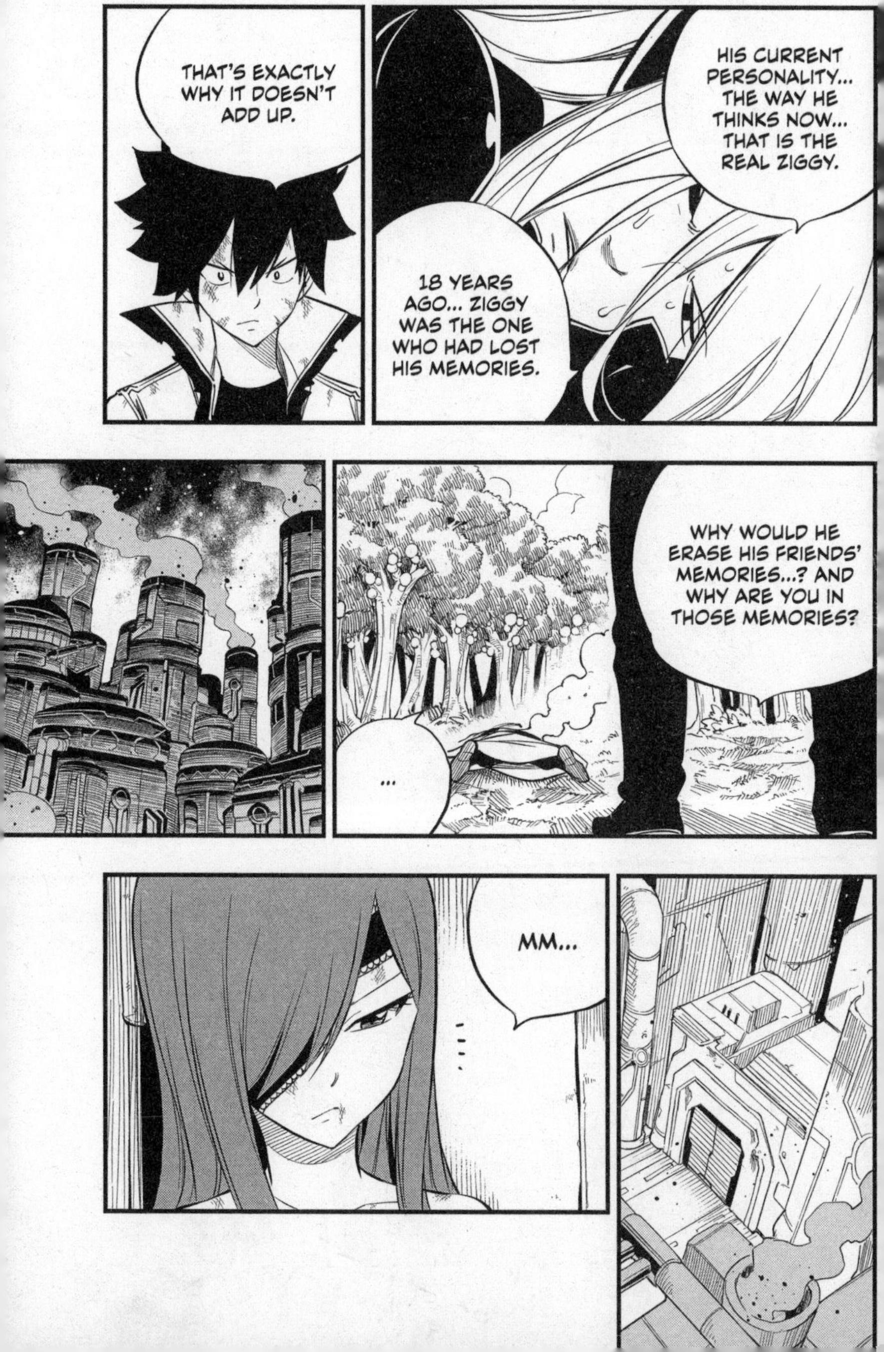

HIS CURRENT PERSONALITY... THE WAY HE THINKS NOW... THAT IS THE REAL ZIGGY.
18 YEARS AGO... ZIGGY WAS THE ONE WHO HAD LOST HIS MEMORIES.
THAT'S EXACTLY WHY IT DOESN'T ADD UP.
WHY WOULD HE ERASE HIS FRIENDS' MEMORIES...? AND WHY ARE YOU IN THOSE MEMORIES?
...
MM...

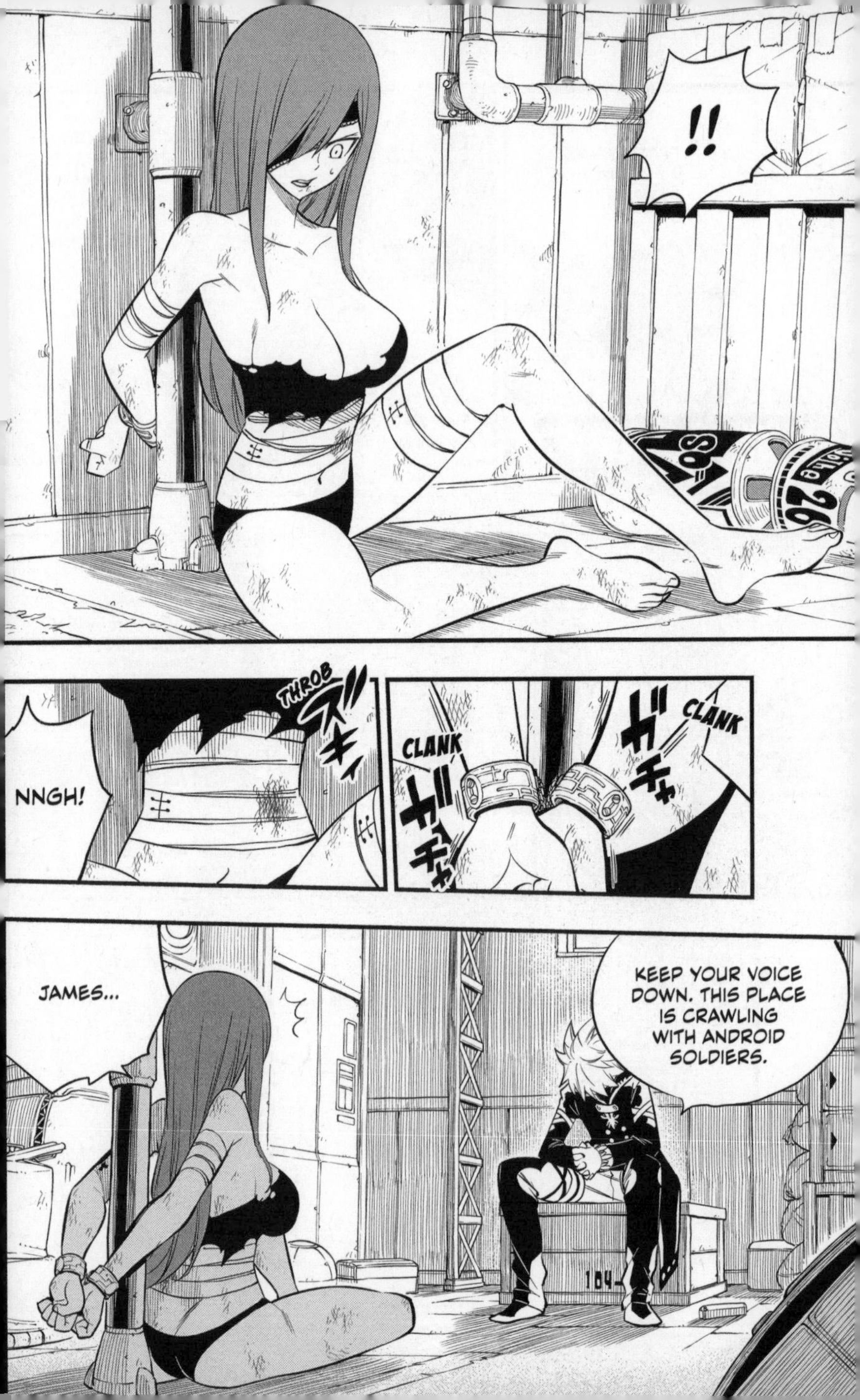
!!
CLANK
CLANK
THROB
NNGH!
KEEP YOUR VOICE DOWN. THIS PLACE IS CRAWLING WITH ANDROID SOLDIERS.
JAMES...

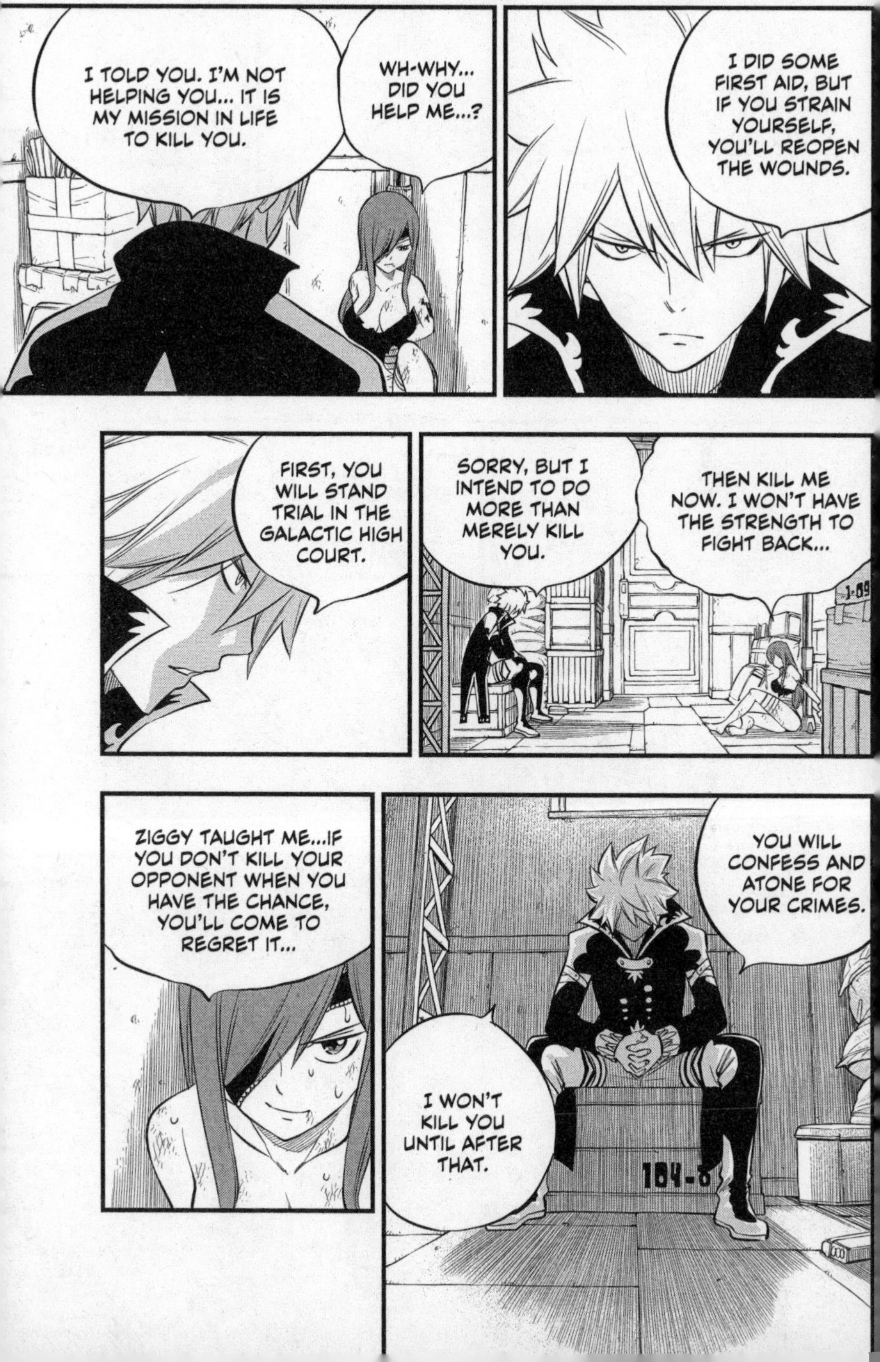
I DID SOME FIRST AID, BUT IF YOU STRAIN YOURSELF, YOU'LL REOPEN THE WOUNDS.
WH-WHY... DID YOU HELP ME...?
I TOLD YOU. I'M NOT HELPING YOU... IT IS MY MISSION IN LIFE TO KILL YOU.
THEN KILL ME NOW. I WON'T HAVE THE STRENGTH TO FIGHT BACK...
SORRY, BUT I INTEND TO DO MORE THAN MERELY KILL YOU.
FIRST, YOU WILL STAND TRIAL IN THE GALACTIC HIGH COURT.
YOU WILL CONFESS AND ATONE FOR YOUR CRIMES.
I WON'T KILL YOU UNTIL AFTER THAT.
ZIGGY TAUGHT ME...IF YOU DON'T KILL YOUR OPPONENT WHEN YOU HAVE THE CHANCE, YOU'LL COME TO REGRET IT...

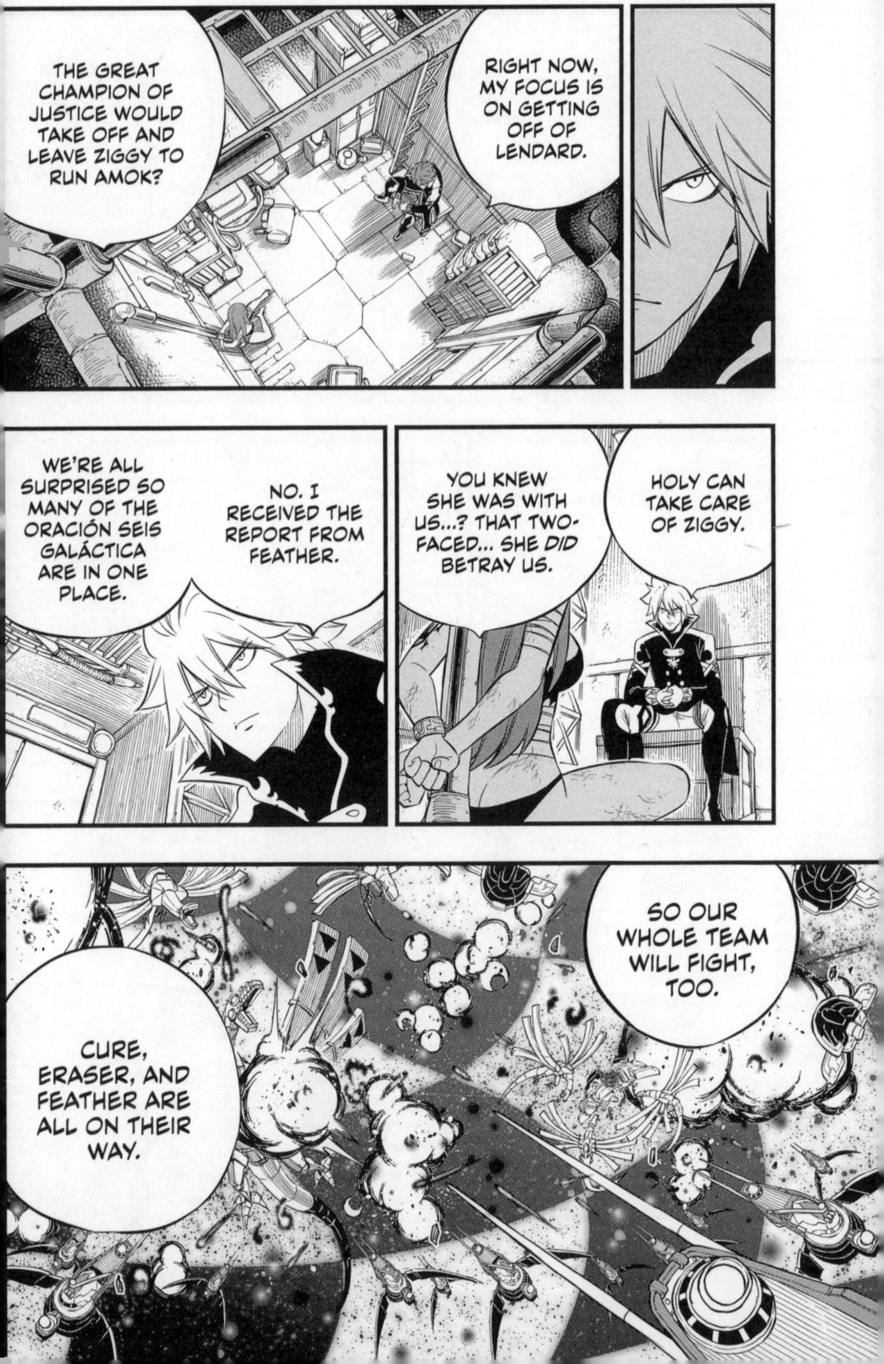
RIGHT NOW, MY FOCUS IS ON GETTING OFF OF LENDARD.
THE GREAT CHAMPION OF JUSTICE WOULD TAKE OFF AND LEAVE ZIGGY TO RUN AMOK?
HOLY CAN TAKE CARE OF ZIGGY.
YOU KNEW SHE WAS WITH US...? THAT TWO-FACED... SHE *DID* BETRAY US.
NO. I RECEIVED THE REPORT FROM FEATHER.
WE'RE ALL SURPRISED SO MANY OF THE ORACIÓN SEIS GALÁCTICA ARE IN ONE PLACE.
SO OUR WHOLE TEAM WILL FIGHT, TOO.
CURE, ERASER, AND FEATHER ARE ALL ON THEIR WAY.

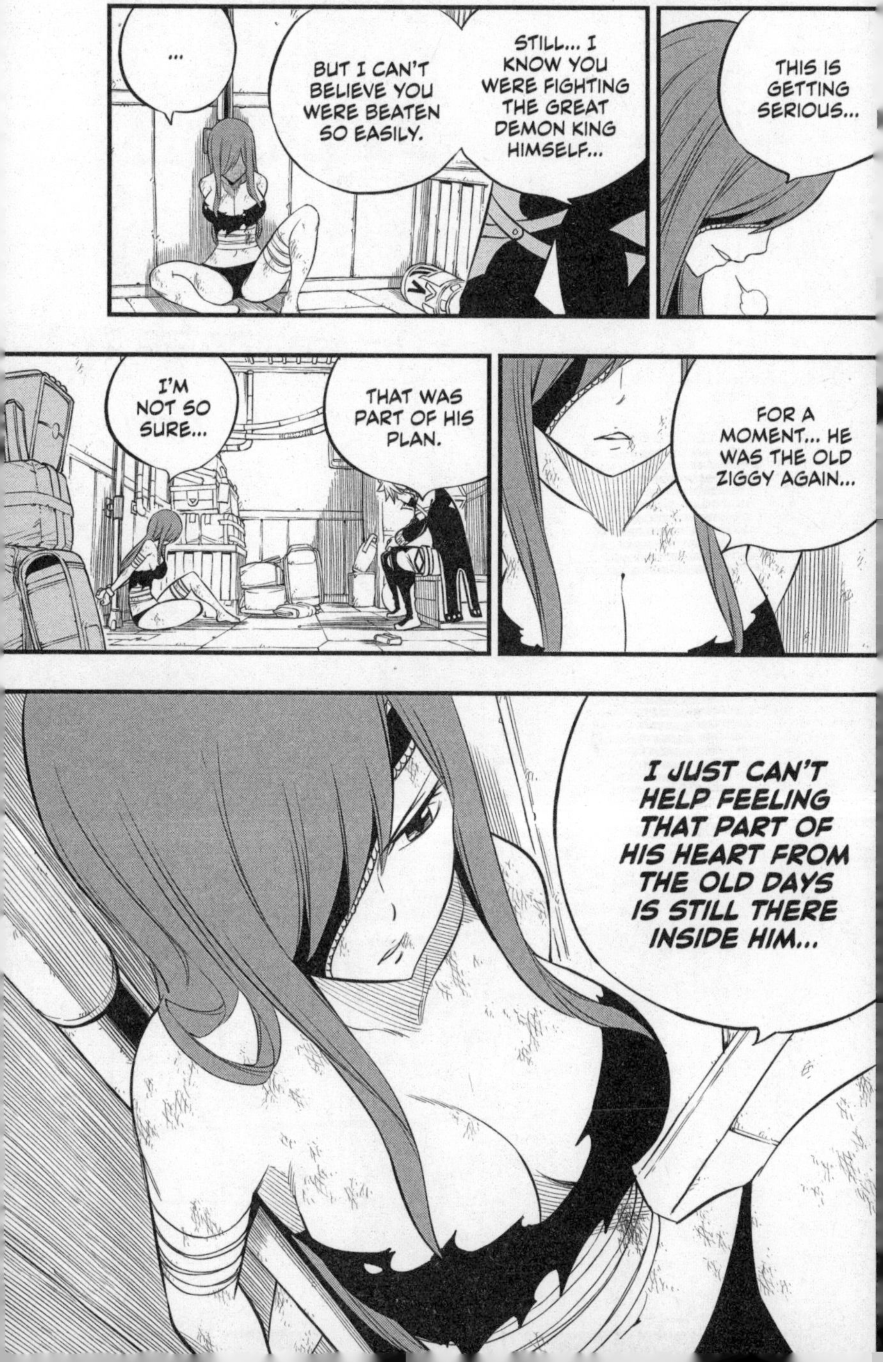
THIS IS GETTING SERIOUS...
STILL... I KNOW YOU WERE FIGHTING THE GREAT DEMON KING HIMSELF...
BUT I CAN'T BELIEVE YOU WERE BEATEN SO EASILY.
...
FOR A MOMENT... HE WAS THE OLD ZIGGY AGAIN...
THAT WAS PART OF HIS PLAN.
I'M NOT SO SURE...
I JUST CAN'T HELP FEELING THAT PART OF HIS HEART FROM THE OLD DAYS IS STILL THERE INSIDE HIM...

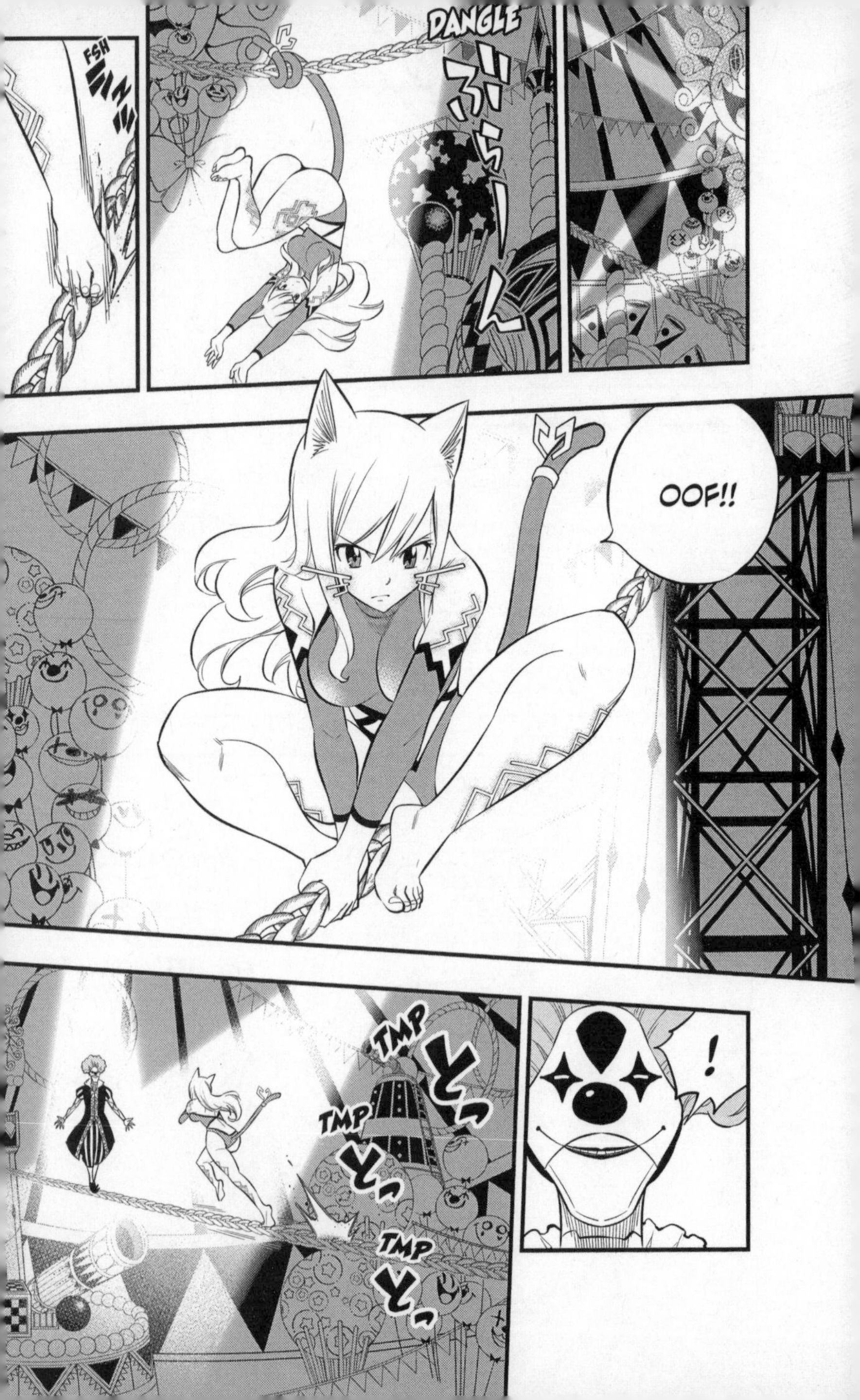
DANGLE
ぶらーん
FSH
OOF!!
!
TMP
ど
TMP
ど
TMP
ど

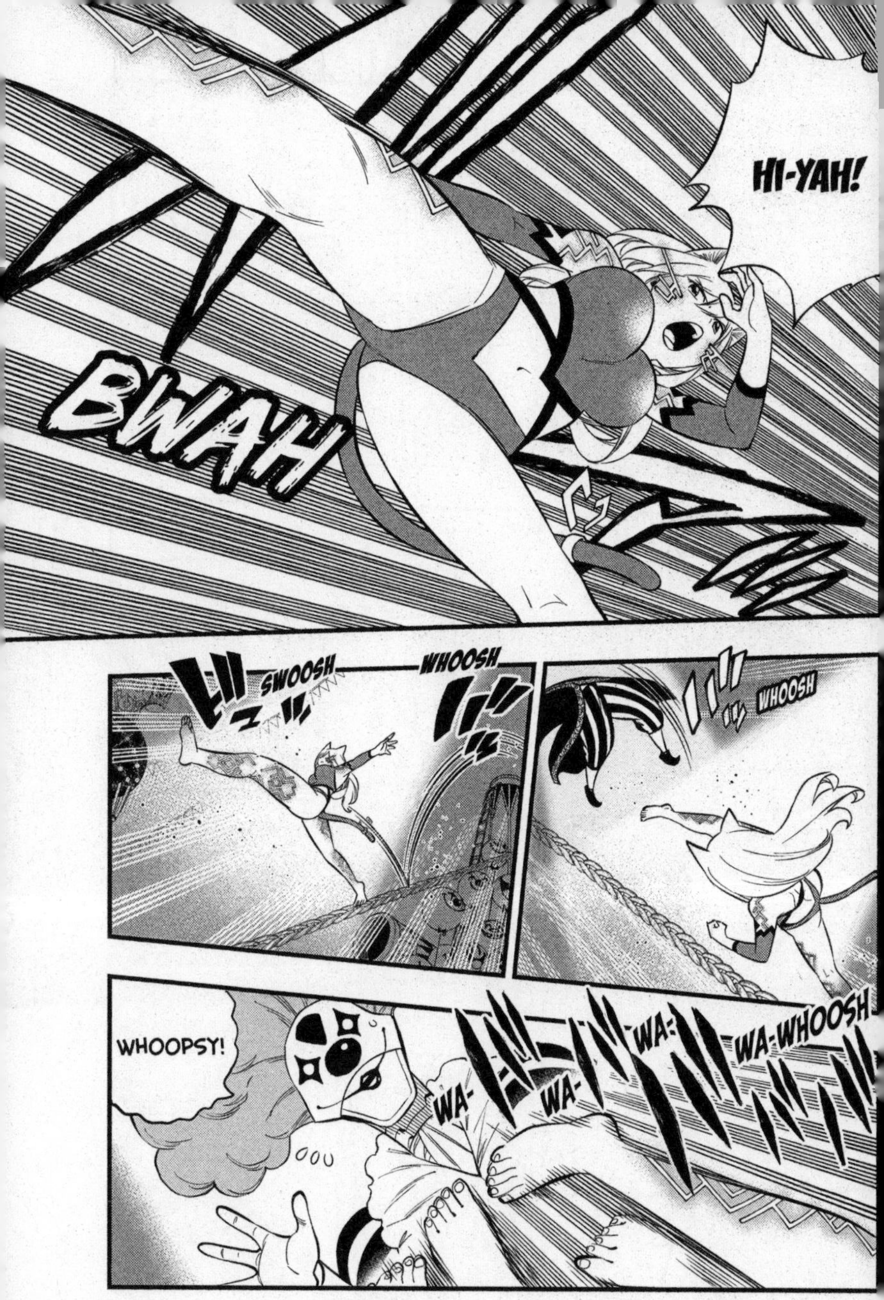
HI-YAH!
BWAH
WHOOSH
WHOOSH
SWOOSH
WA-WHOOSH
WA-
WA-
WA-
WHOOPSY!

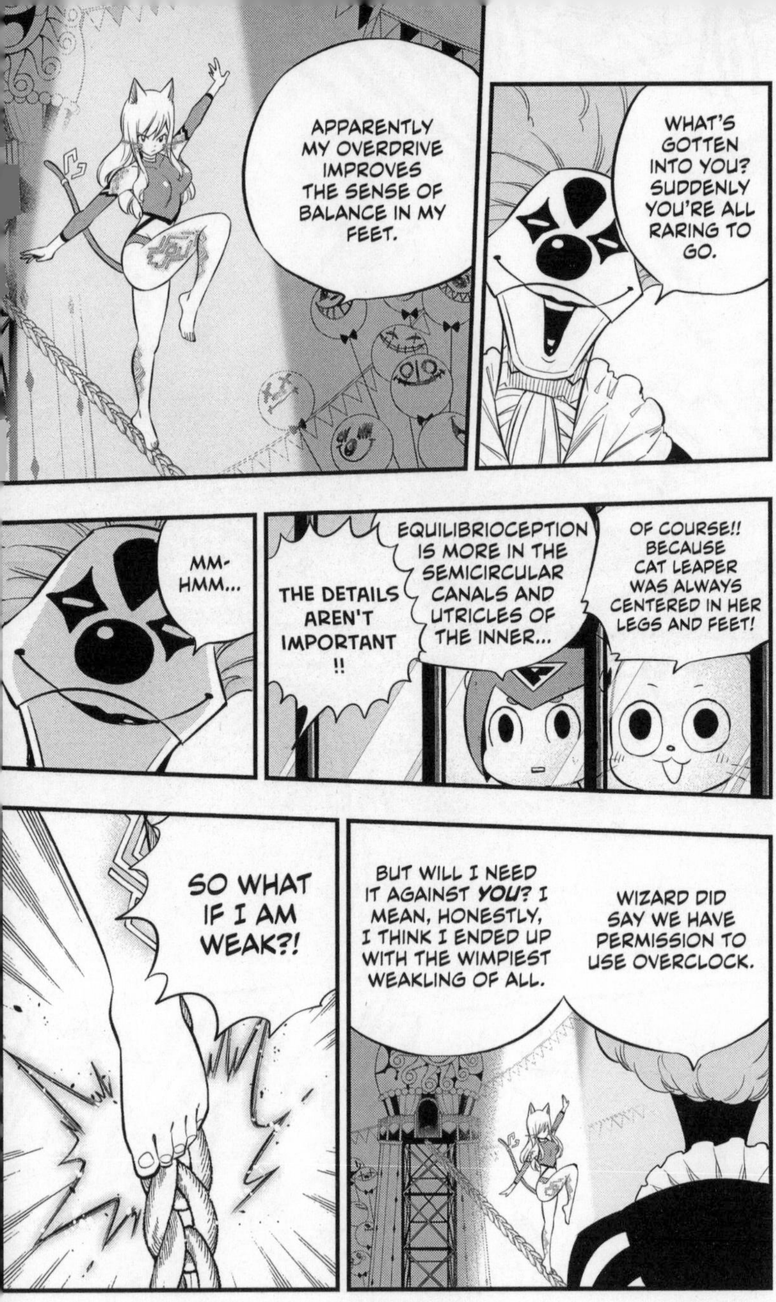
WHAT'S GOTTEN INTO YOU? SUDDENLY YOU'RE ALL RARING TO GO.
APPARENTLY MY OVERDRIVE IMPROVES THE SENSE OF BALANCE IN MY FEET.
OF COURSE!! BECAUSE CAT LEAPER WAS ALWAYS CENTERED IN HER LEGS AND FEET!
EQUILIBRIOCEPTION IS MORE IN THE SEMICIRCULAR CANALS AND UTRICLES OF THE INNER...
THE DETAILS AREN'T IMPORTANT !!
MM-HMM...
WIZARD DID SAY WE HAVE PERMISSION TO USE OVERCLOCK.
BUT WILL I NEED IT AGAINST *YOU*? I MEAN, HONESTLY, I THINK I ENDED UP WITH THE WIMPIEST WEAKLING OF ALL.
SO WHAT IF I AM WEAK?!

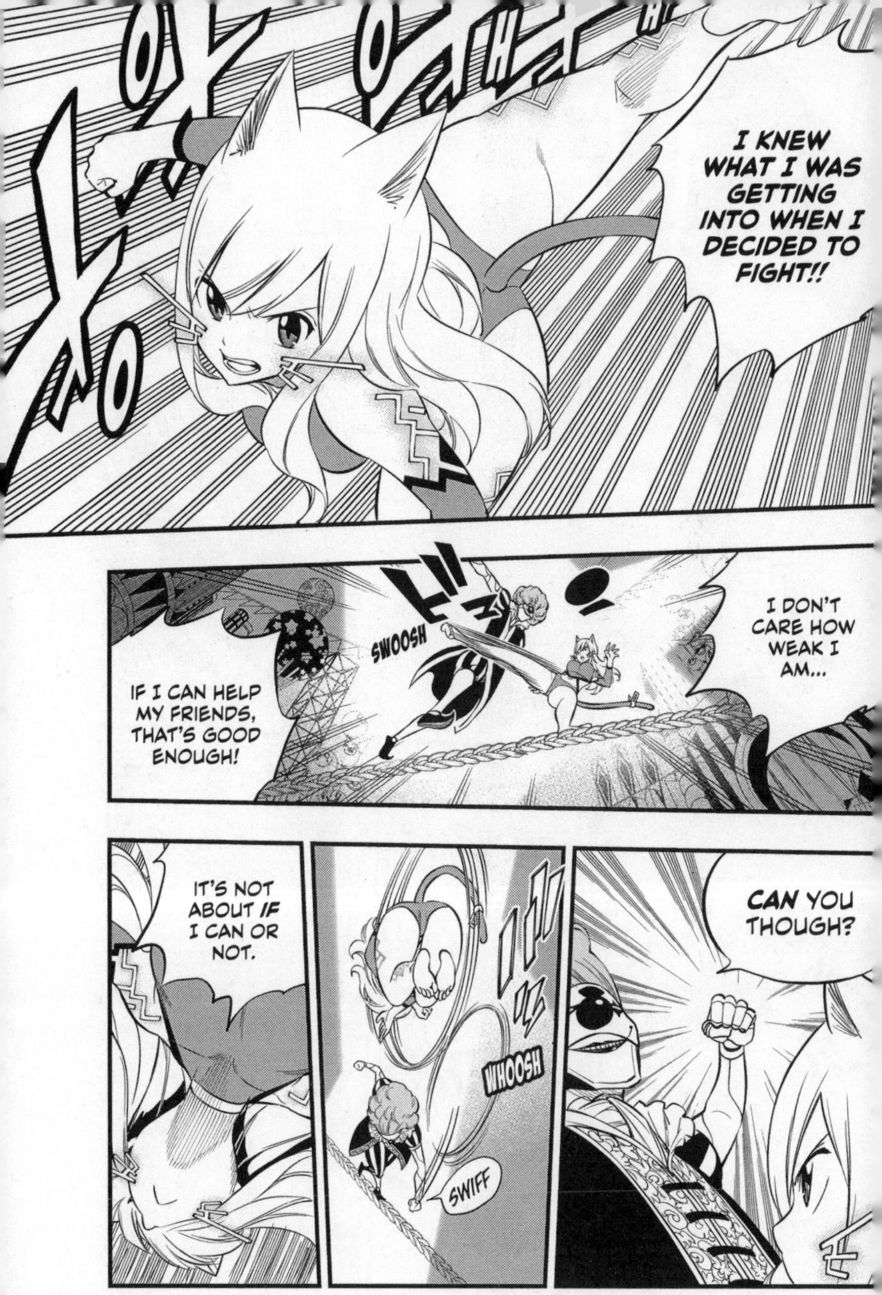
I KNEW WHAT I WAS GETTING INTO WHEN I DECIDED TO FIGHT!!
I DON'T CARE HOW WEAK I AM...
SWOOSH
IF I CAN HELP MY FRIENDS, THAT'S GOOD ENOUGH!
CAN YOU THOUGH?
WHOOSH
SWIFF
IT'S NOT ABOUT IF I CAN OR NOT.

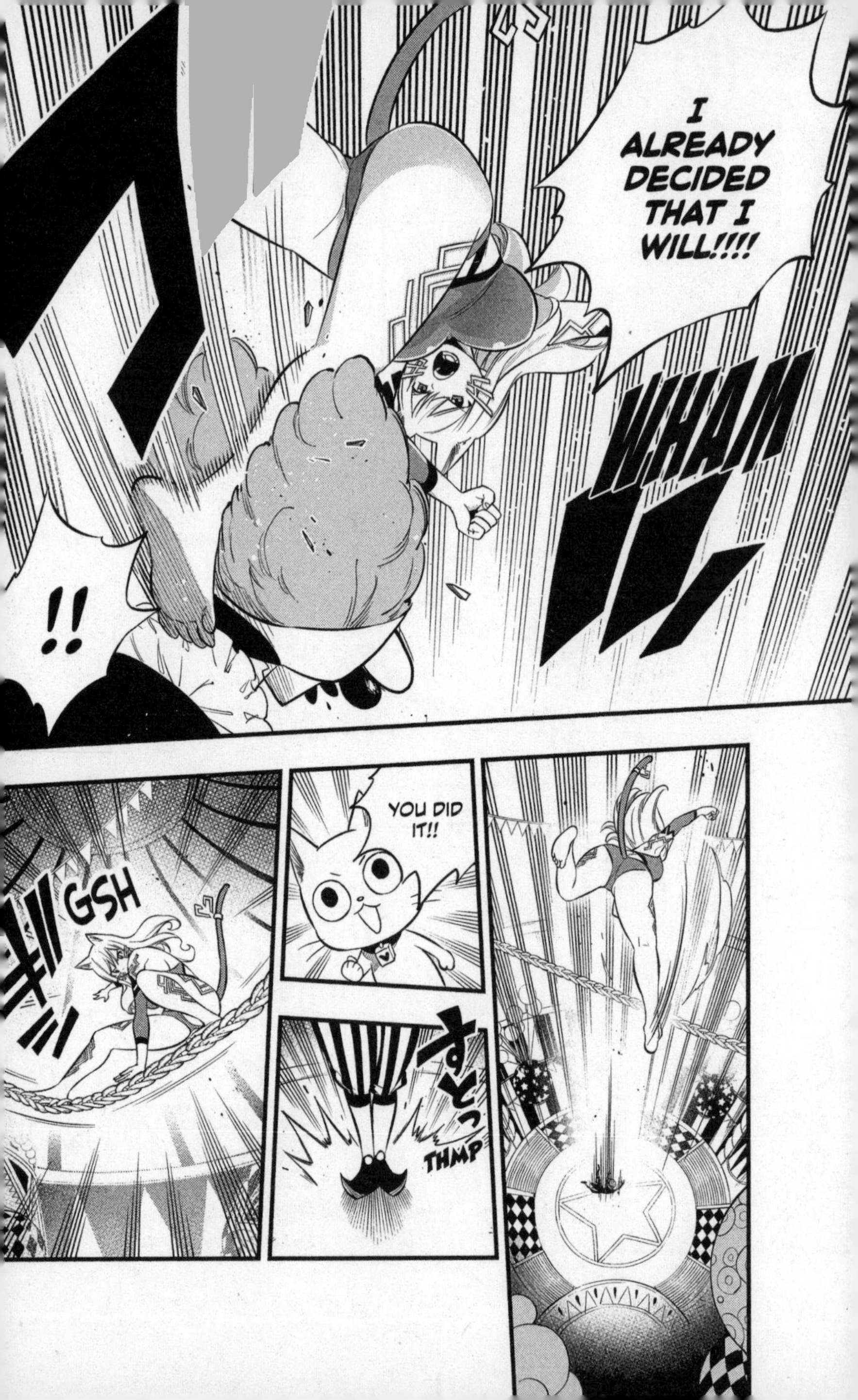
I ALREADY DECIDED THAT I WILL!!!!
WHAM
!!
YOU DID IT!!
すとっ
THMP
GSH

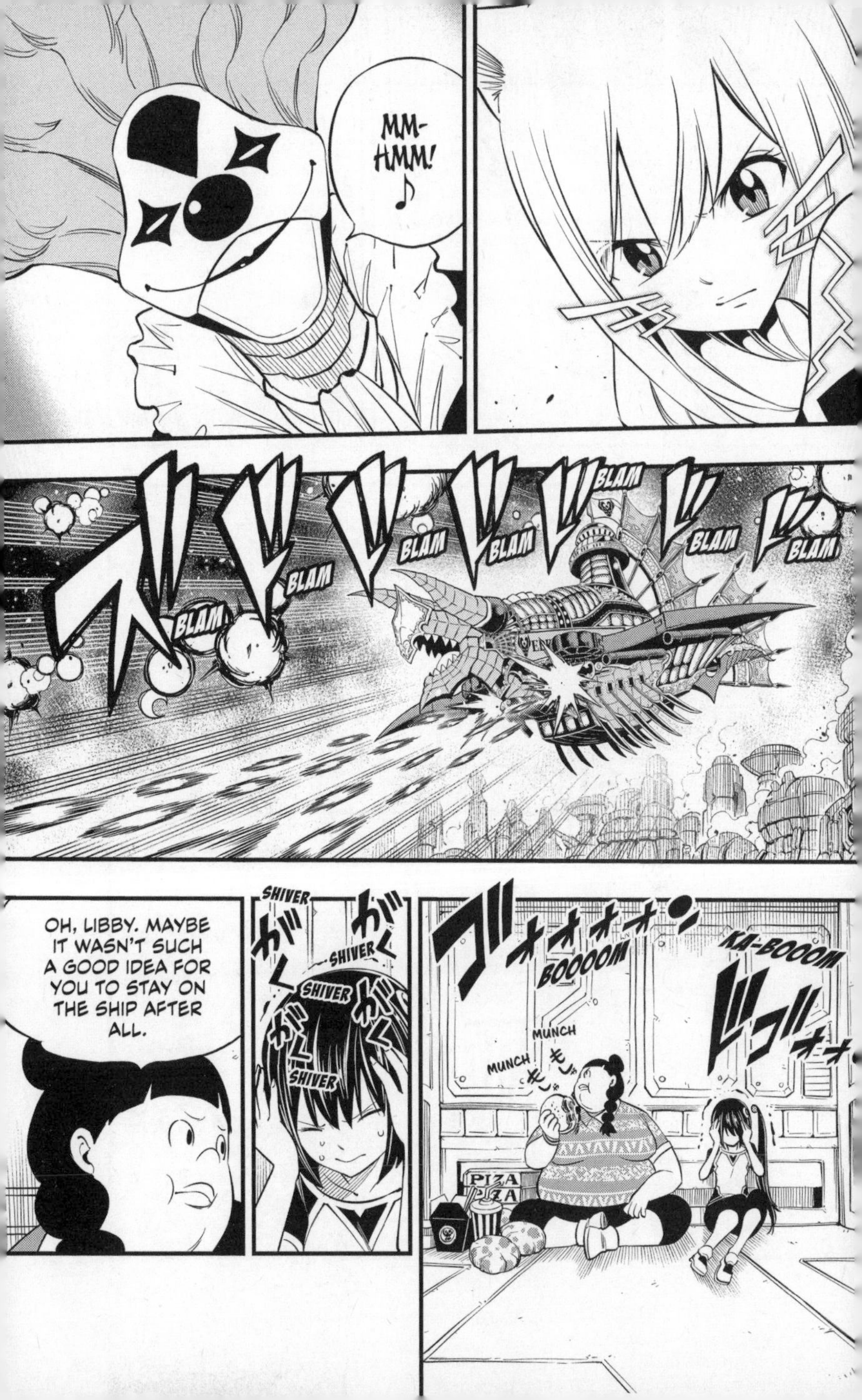
MM-HMM! ♪
BLAM
BLAM
BLAM
BLAM
BLAM
BLAM
BLAM
KA-BOOOM
BOOOOM
MUNCH
MUNCH
SHIVER
SHIVER
SHIVER
SHIVER
OH, LIBBY. MAYBE IT WASN'T SUCH A GOOD IDEA FOR YOU TO STAY ON THE SHIP AFTER ALL.

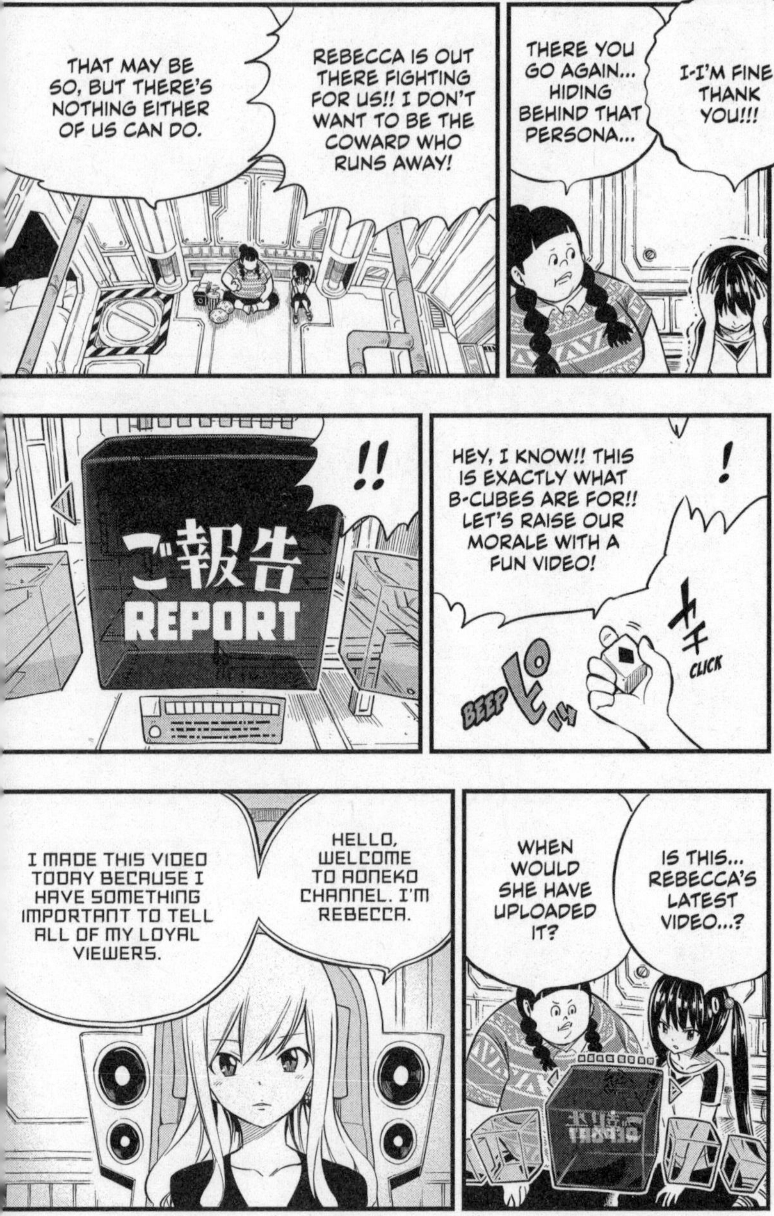
I-I'M FINE, THANK YOU!!!
THERE YOU GO AGAIN... HIDING BEHIND THAT PERSONA...
REBECCA IS OUT THERE FIGHTING FOR US!! I DON'T WANT TO BE THE COWARD WHO RUNS AWAY!
THAT MAY BE SO, BUT THERE'S NOTHING EITHER OF US CAN DO.
!
HEY, I KNOW!! THIS IS EXACTLY WHAT B-CUBES ARE FOR!! LET'S RAISE OUR MORALE WITH A FUN VIDEO!
カチ
CLICK
ピッ
BEEP
!!
ご報告
REPORT
IS THIS... REBECCA'S LATEST VIDEO...?
WHEN WOULD SHE HAVE UPLOADED IT?
HELLO, WELCOME TO AONEKO CHANNEL. I'M REBECCA.
I MADE THIS VIDEO TODAY BECAUSE I HAVE SOMETHING IMPORTANT TO TELL ALL OF MY LOYAL VIEWERS.

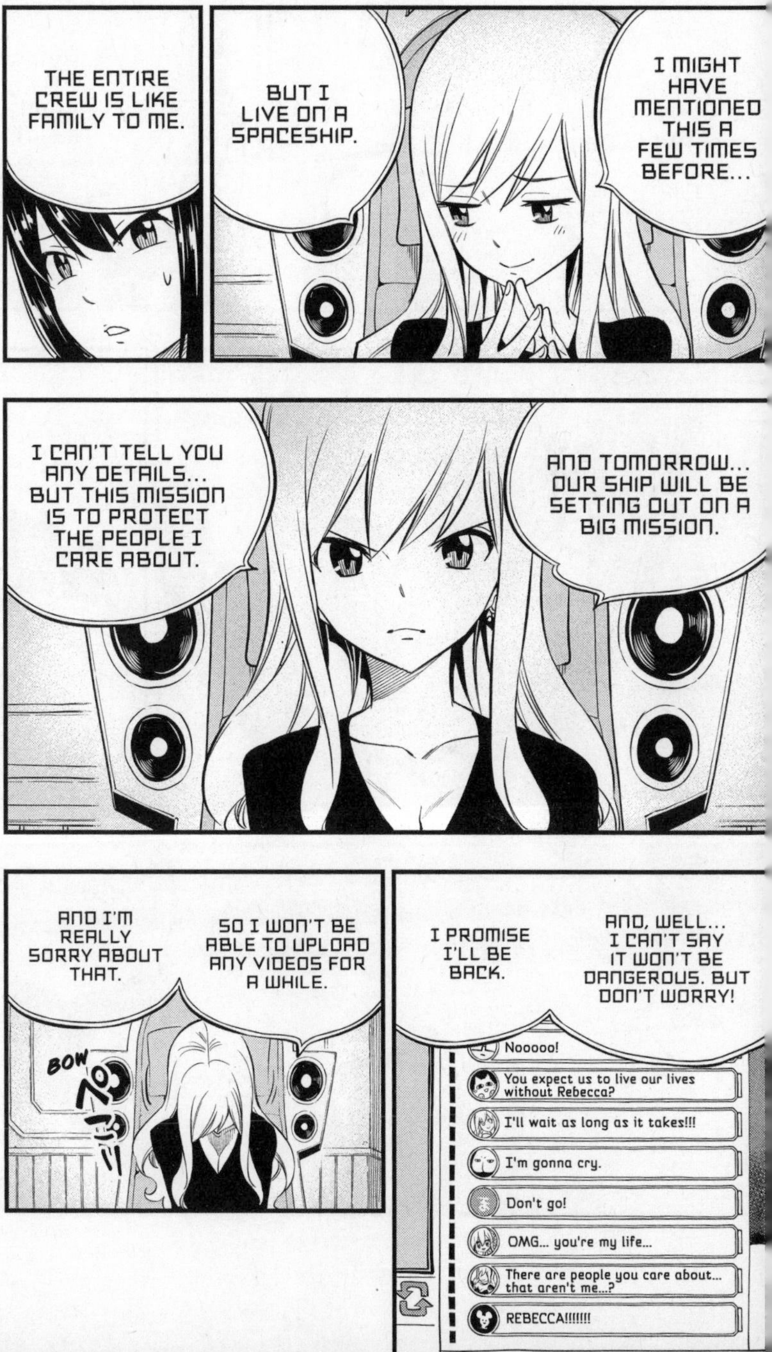
I MIGHT HAVE MENTIONED THIS A FEW TIMES BEFORE...
BUT I LIVE ON A SPACESHIP.
THE ENTIRE CREW IS LIKE FAMILY TO ME.
AND TOMORROW... OUR SHIP WILL BE SETTING OUT ON A BIG MISSION.
I CAN'T TELL YOU ANY DETAILS... BUT THIS MISSION IS TO PROTECT THE PEOPLE I CARE ABOUT.
AND, WELL... I CAN'T SAY IT WON'T BE DANGEROUS. BUT DON'T WORRY!
I PROMISE I'LL BE BACK.
Nooooo!
You expect us to live our lives without Rebecca?
I'll wait as long as it takes!!!
I'm gonna cry.
Don't go!
OMG... you're my life...
There are people you care about... that aren't me...?
REBECCA!!!!!!
SO I WON'T BE ABLE TO UPLOAD ANY VIDEOS FOR A WHILE.
AND I'M REALLY SORRY ABOUT THAT.
BOW

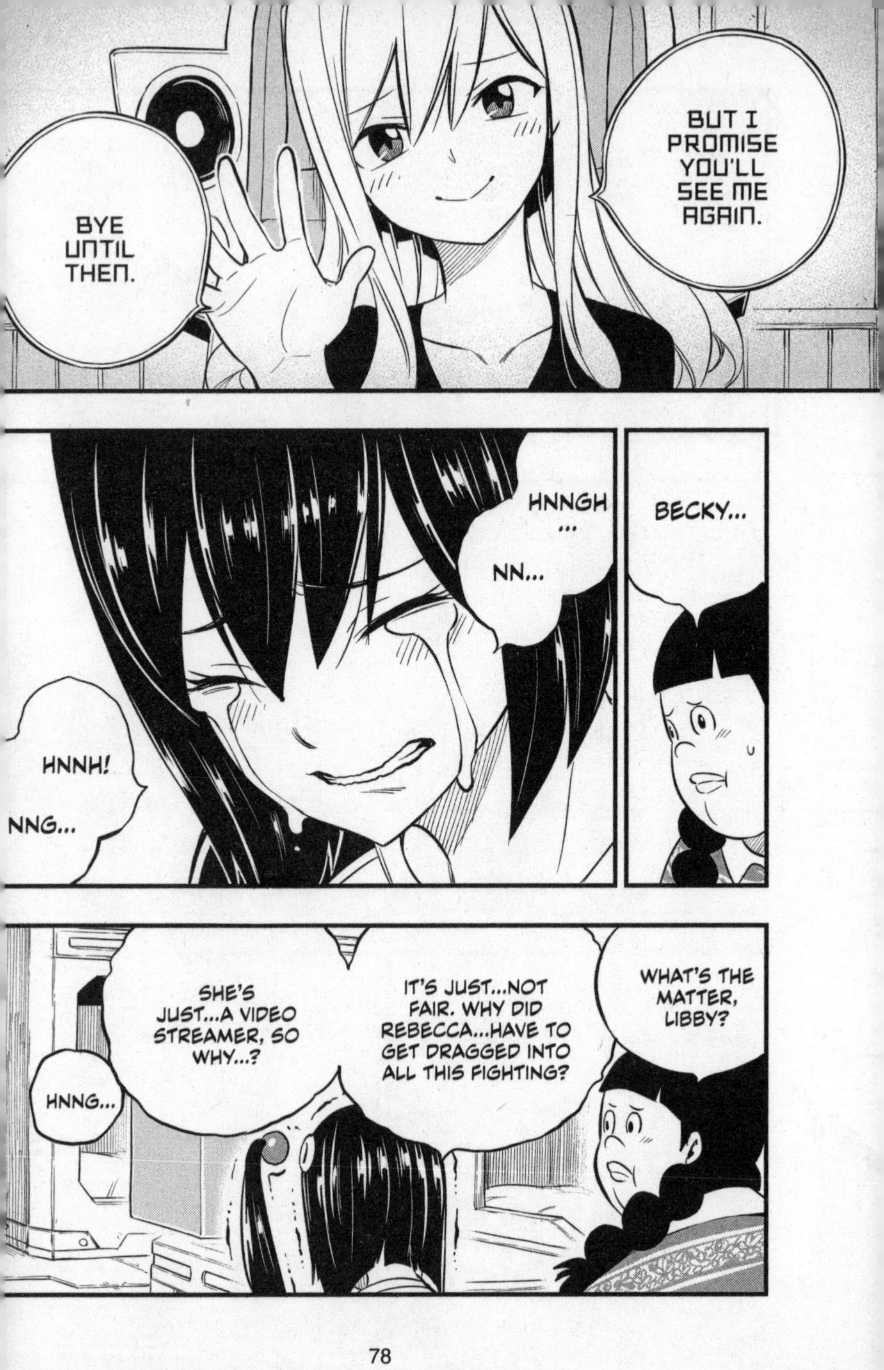
BUT I PROMISE YOU'LL SEE ME AGAIN.
BYE UNTIL THEN.
BECKY...
HNNGH... NN...
HNNH! NNG...
WHAT'S THE MATTER, LIBBY?
IT'S JUST...NOT FAIR. WHY DID REBECCA...HAVE TO GET DRAGGED INTO ALL THIS FIGHTING?
SHE'S JUST...A VIDEO STREAMER, SO WHY...?
HNNG...

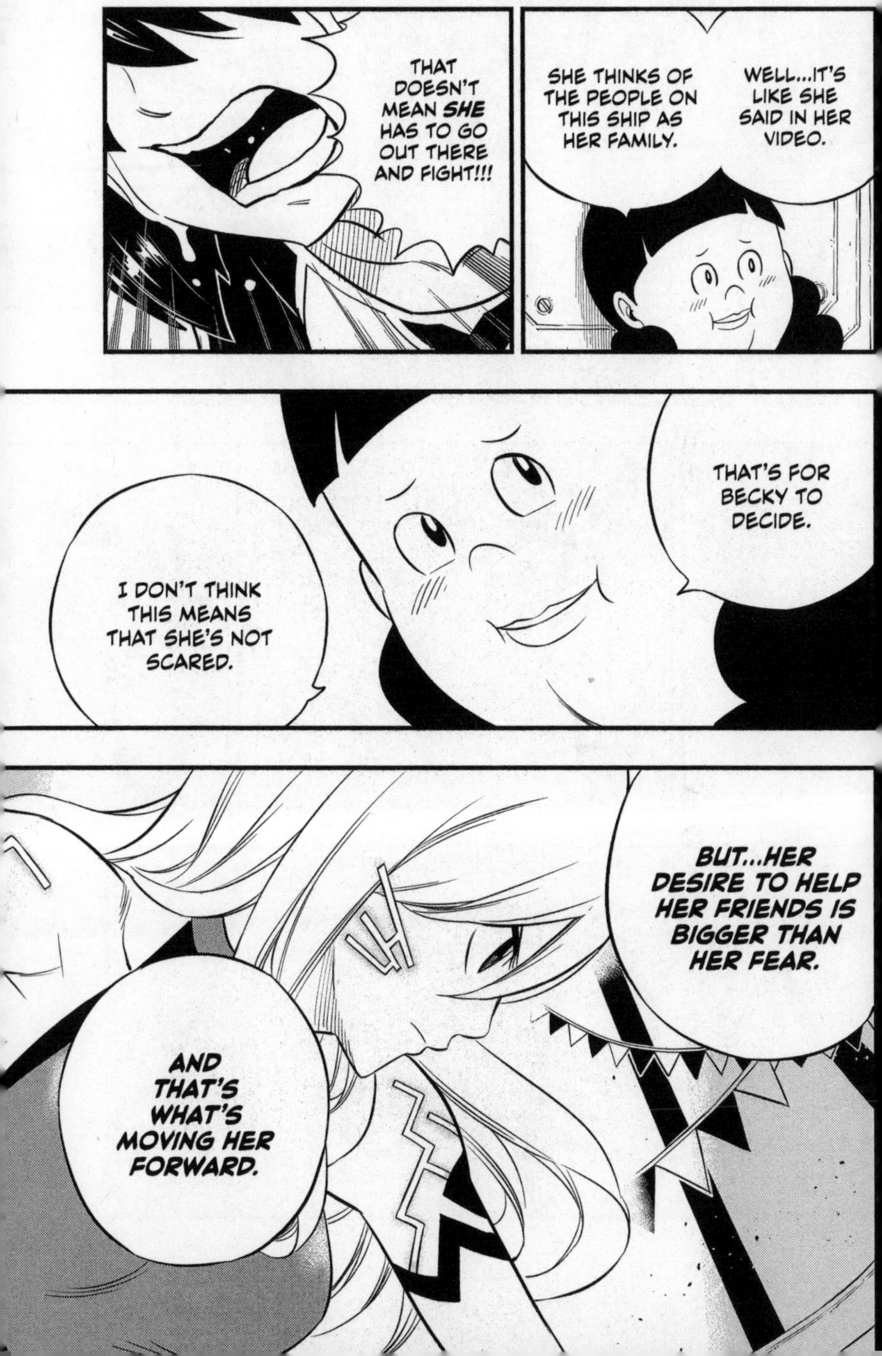
WELL...IT'S LIKE SHE SAID IN HER VIDEO.
SHE THINKS OF THE PEOPLE ON THIS SHIP AS HER FAMILY.
THAT DOESN'T MEAN *SHE* HAS TO GO OUT THERE AND FIGHT!!!
THAT'S FOR BECKY TO DECIDE.
I DON'T THINK THIS MEANS THAT SHE'S NOT SCARED.
BUT...HER DESIRE TO HELP HER FRIENDS IS BIGGER THAN HER FEAR.
AND THAT'S WHAT'S MOVING HER FORWARD.

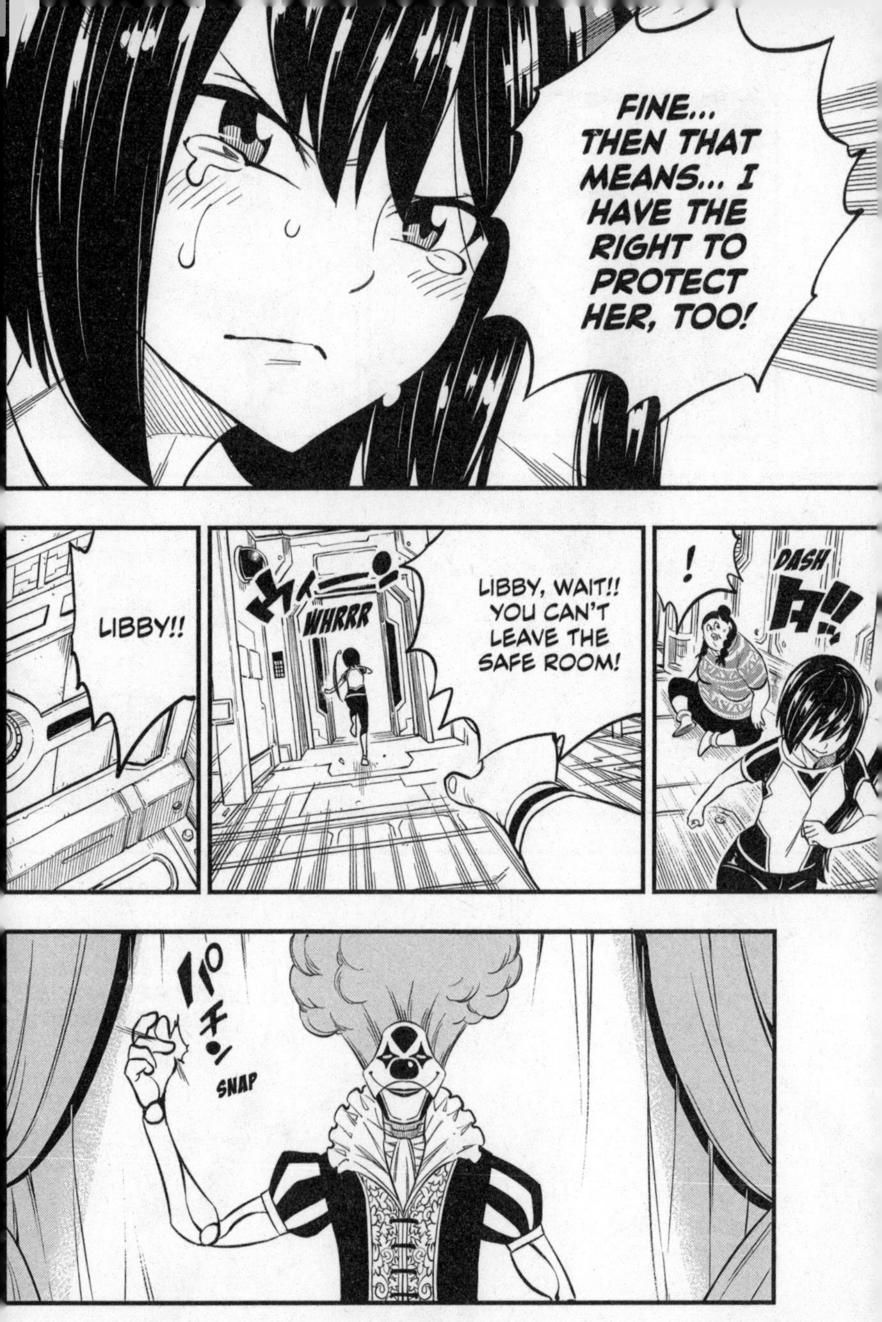
FINE... THEN THAT MEANS... I HAVE THE RIGHT TO PROTECT HER, TOO!
!
DASH
ドッ!!
WHRRR
LIBBY, WAIT!! YOU CAN'T LEAVE THE SAFE ROOM!
LIBBY!!
パチン
SNAP

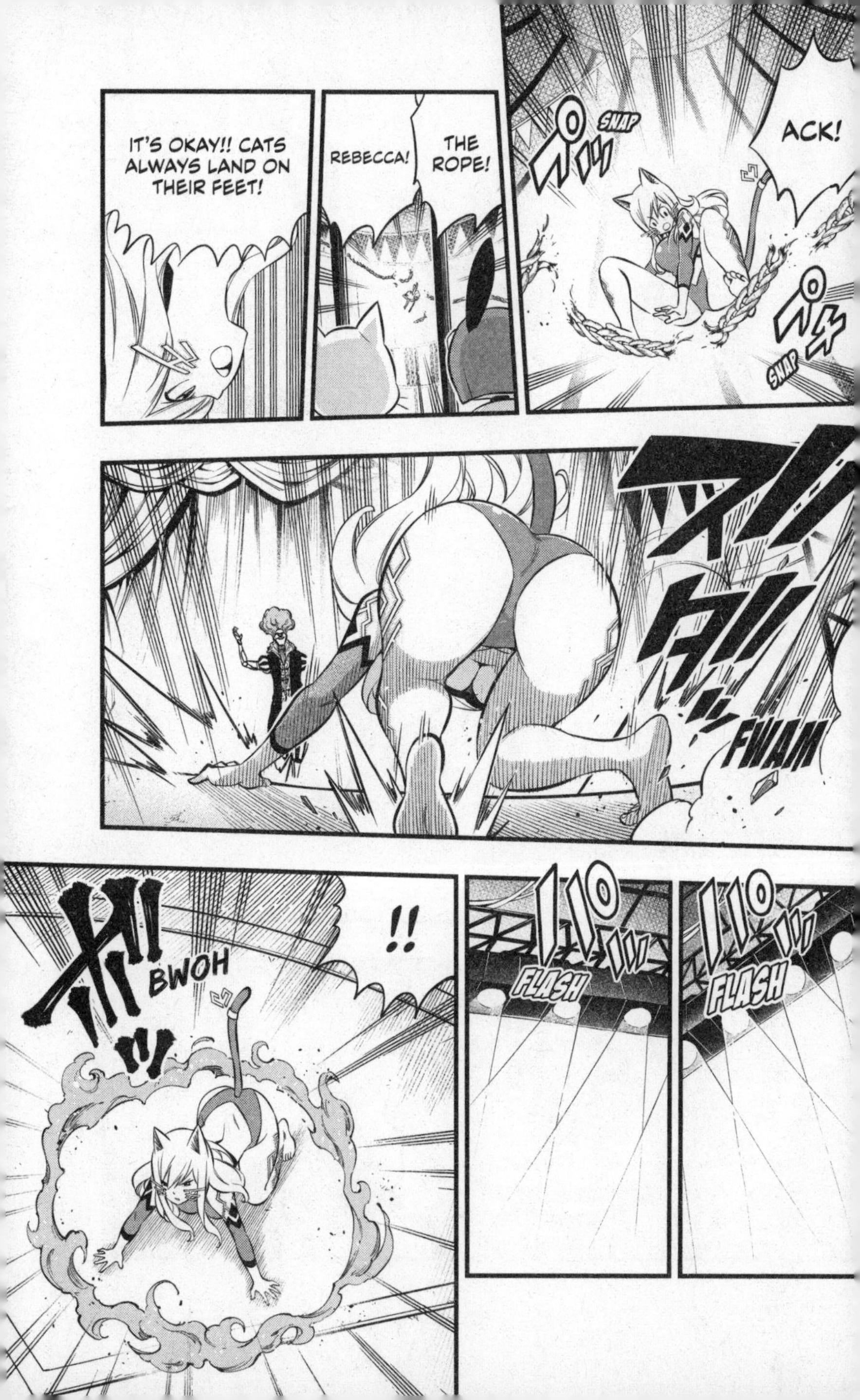
ACK!
SNAP
SNAP
THE ROPE!
REBECCA!
IT'S OKAY!! CATS ALWAYS LAND ON THEIR FEET!
FWAM
FLASH
FLASH
!!
BWOH

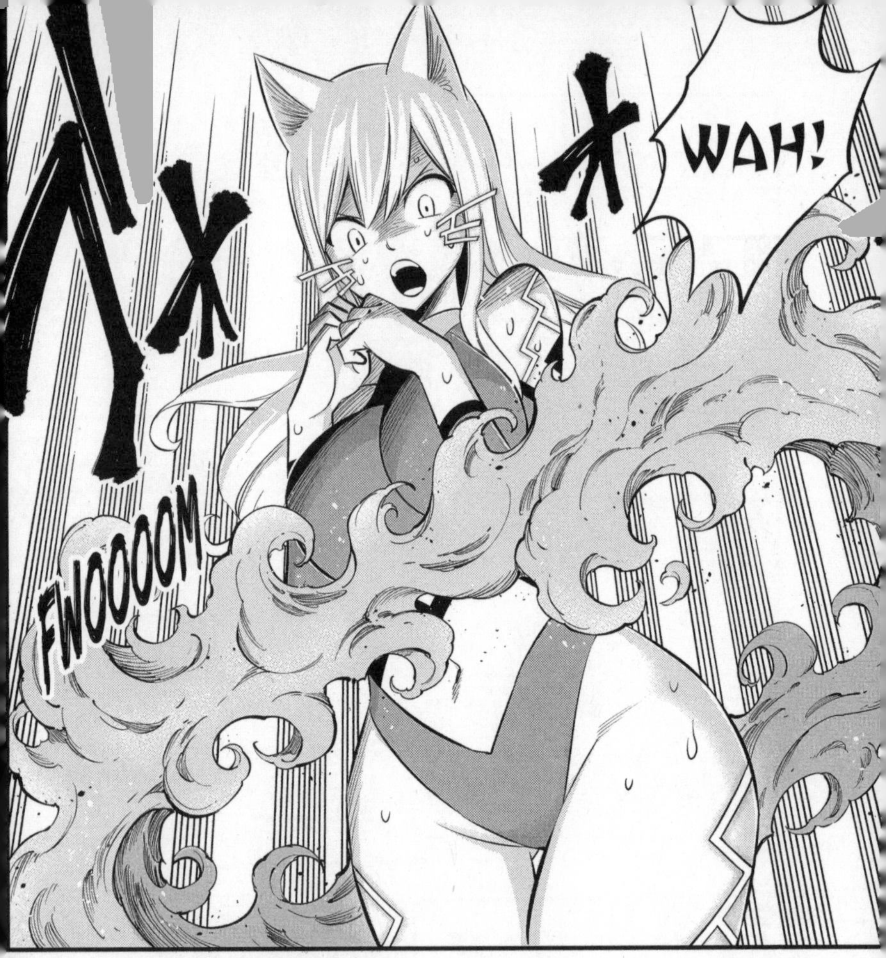
WAH!
FWOOOOM
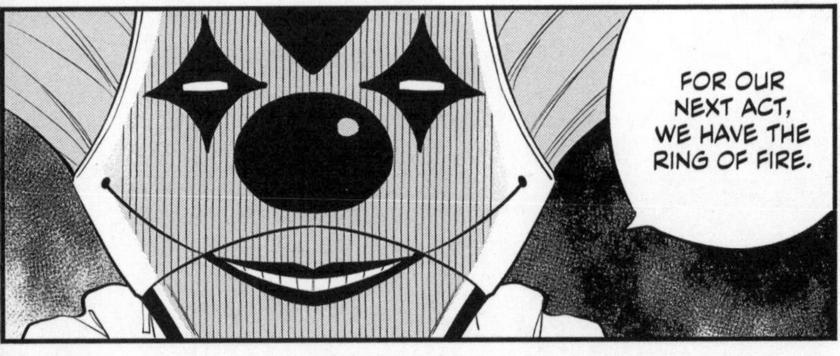
FOR OUR NEXT ACT, WE HAVE THE RING OF FIRE.

EDENS ZERO

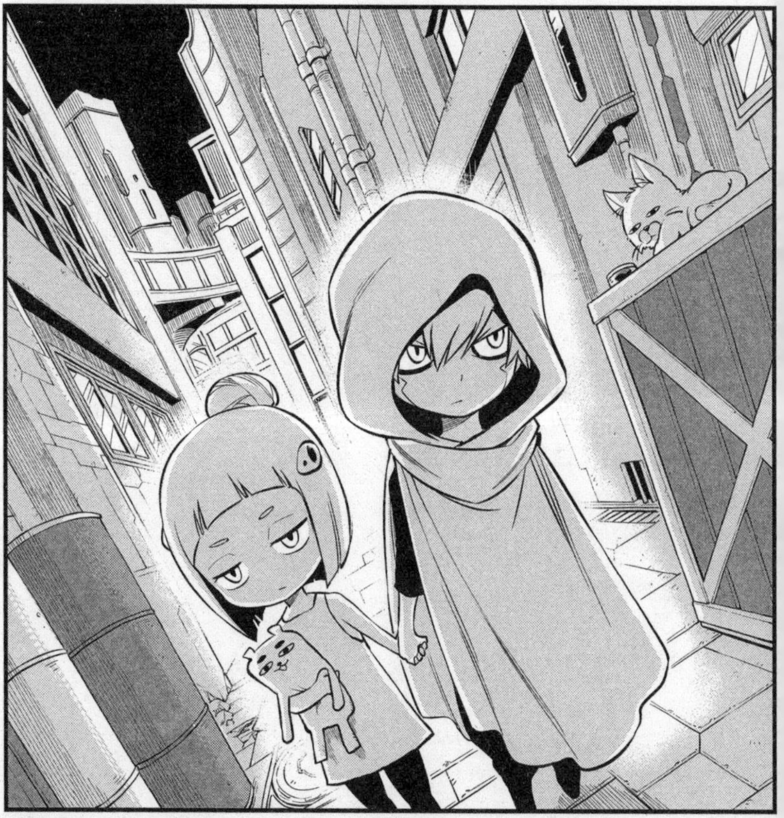

CHAPTER 190: THE GREATEST SHOW FROM HELL

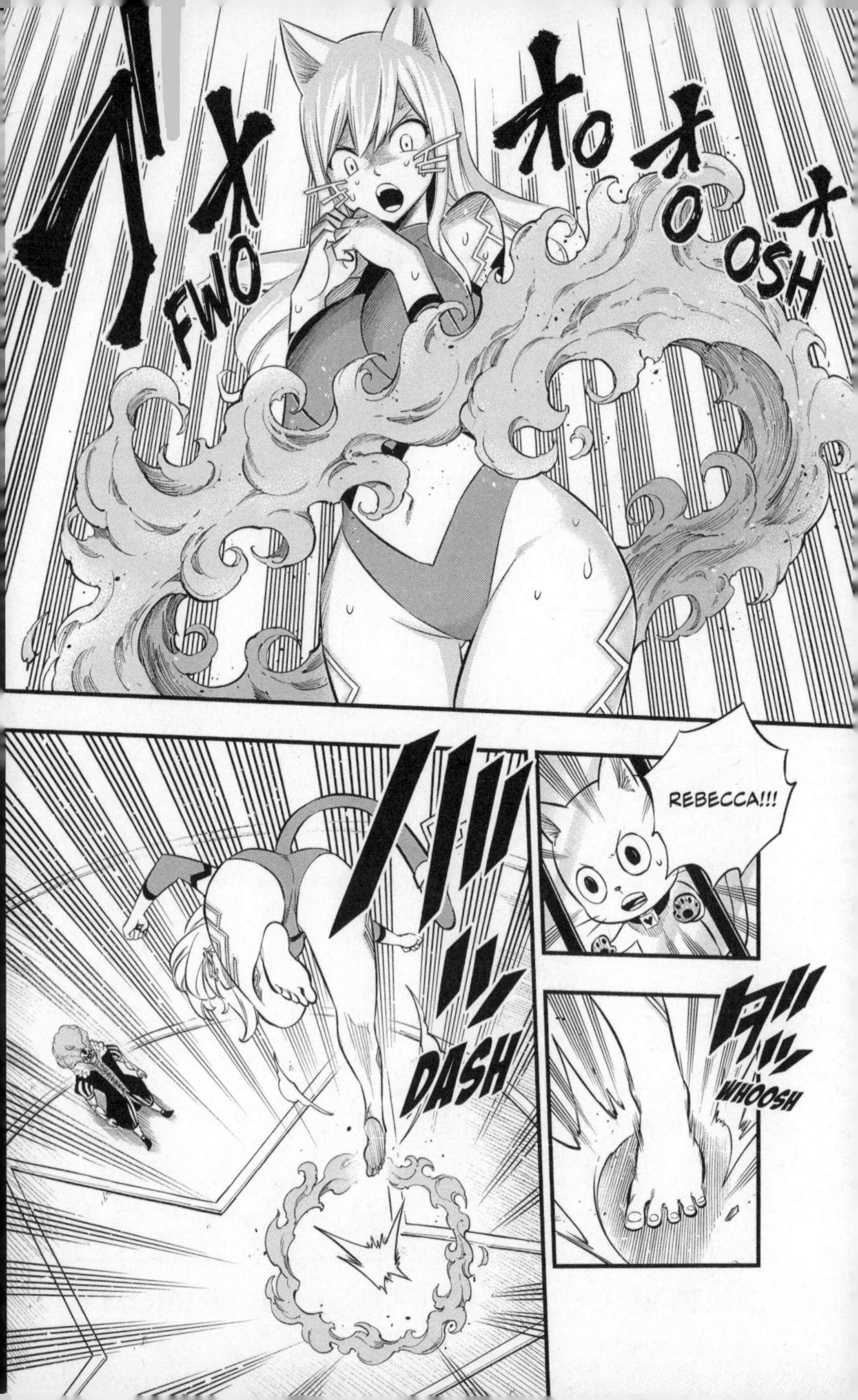
FWOOOOSH
REBECCA!!!
WHOOSH
DASH

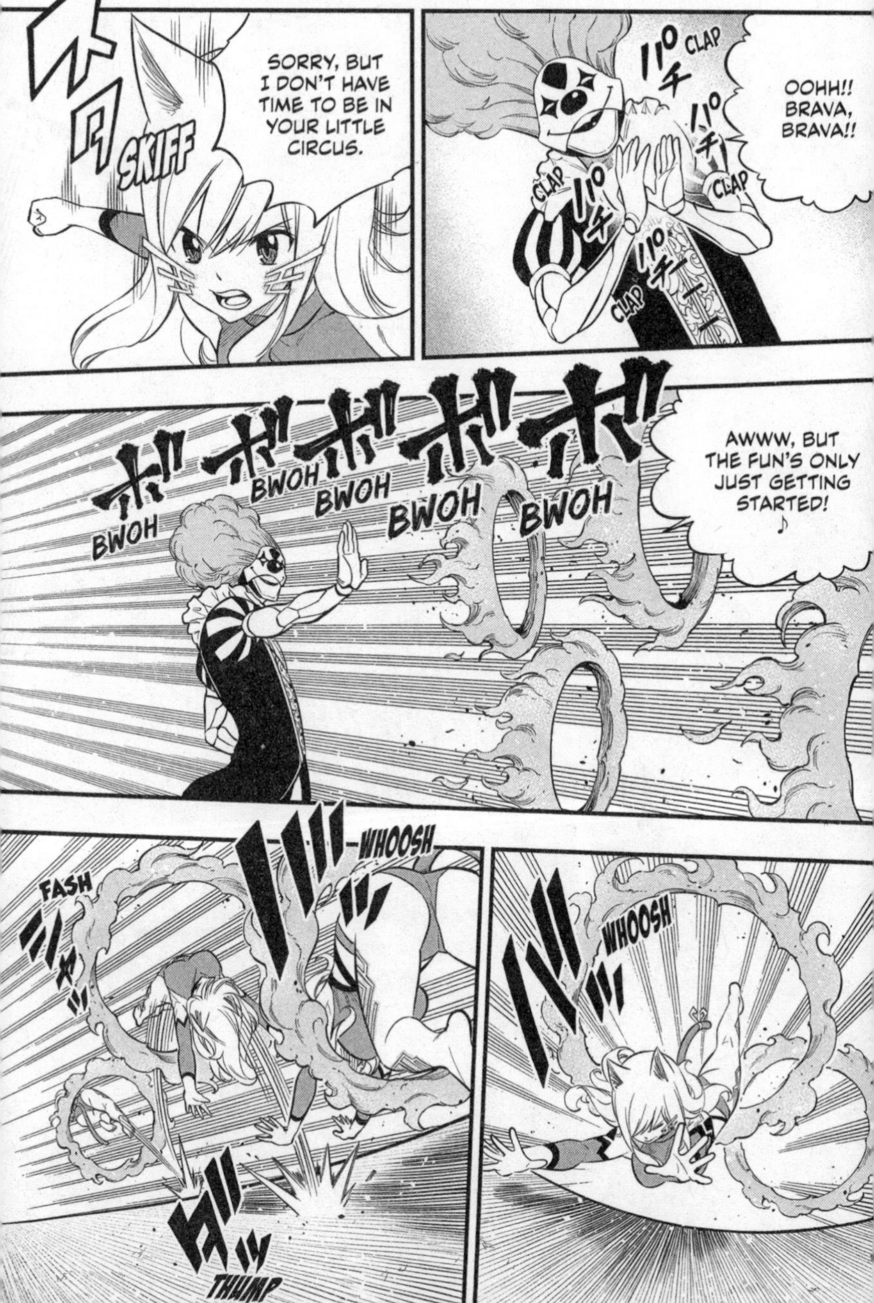

CLAP
CLAP
CLAP
CLAP
OOHH!! BRAVA, BRAVA!!
SKIFF
SORRY, BUT I DON'T HAVE TIME TO BE IN YOUR LITTLE CIRCUS.
AWWW, BUT THE FUN'S ONLY JUST GETTING STARTED! ♪
BWOH
BWOH
BWOH
BWOH
BWOH
WHOOSH
WHOOSH
FASH
THUMP

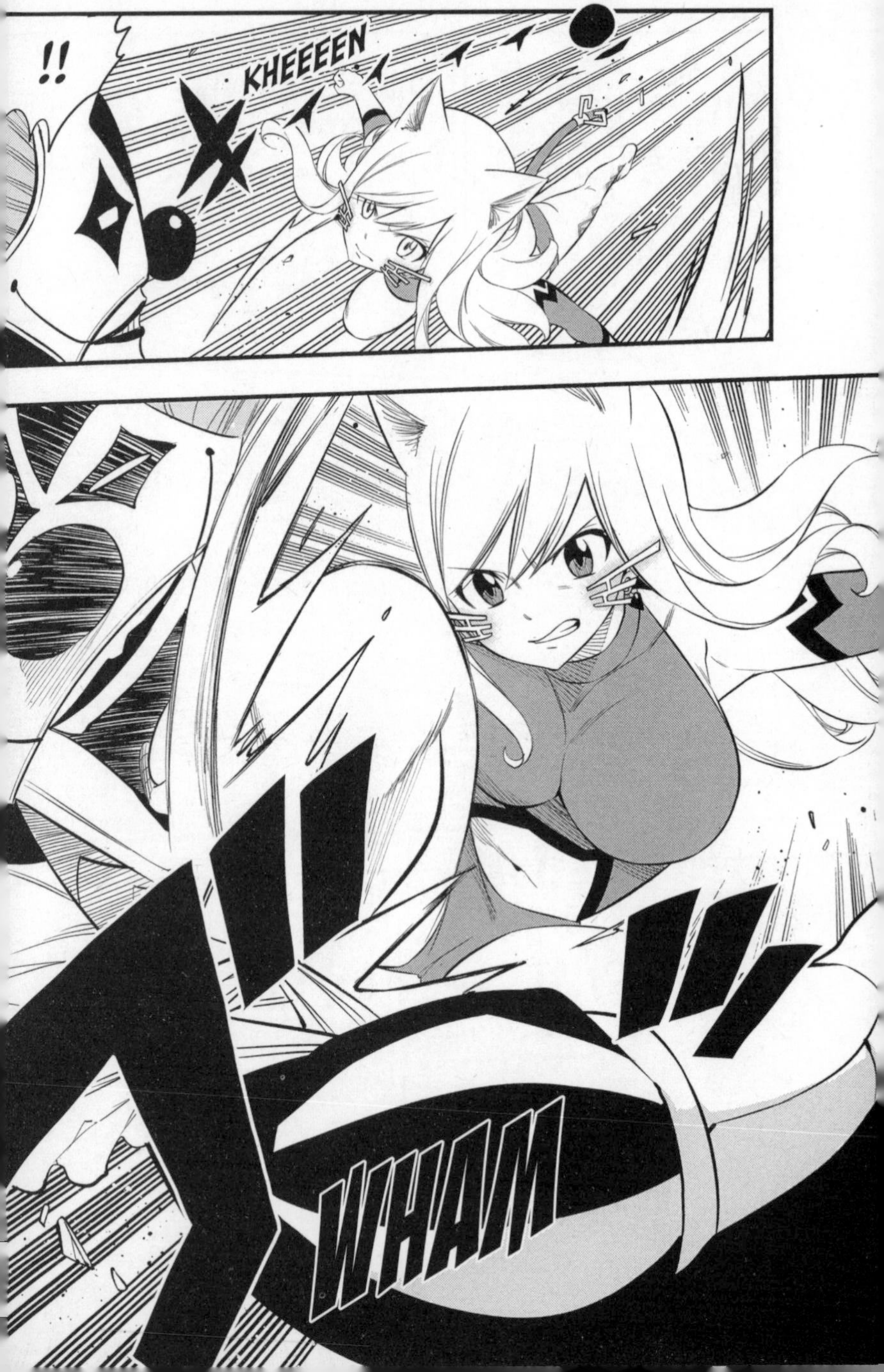
KHEEEEN
!!
WHAM

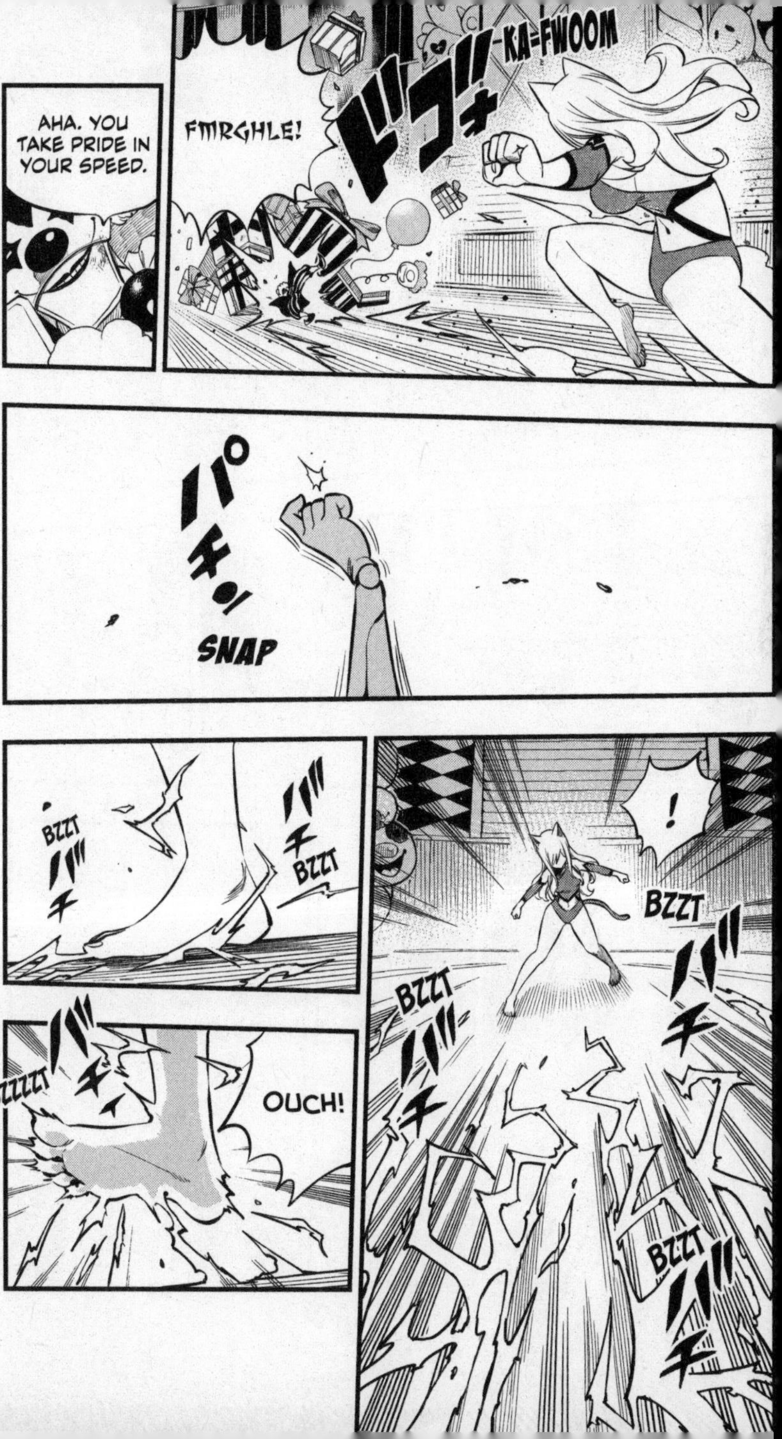
KA-FWOOM
FMRGHLE!
AHA. YOU TAKE PRIDE IN YOUR SPEED.
SNAP
!
BZZT
BZZT
BZZT
BZZT
BZZT
BZZZZT
OUCH!

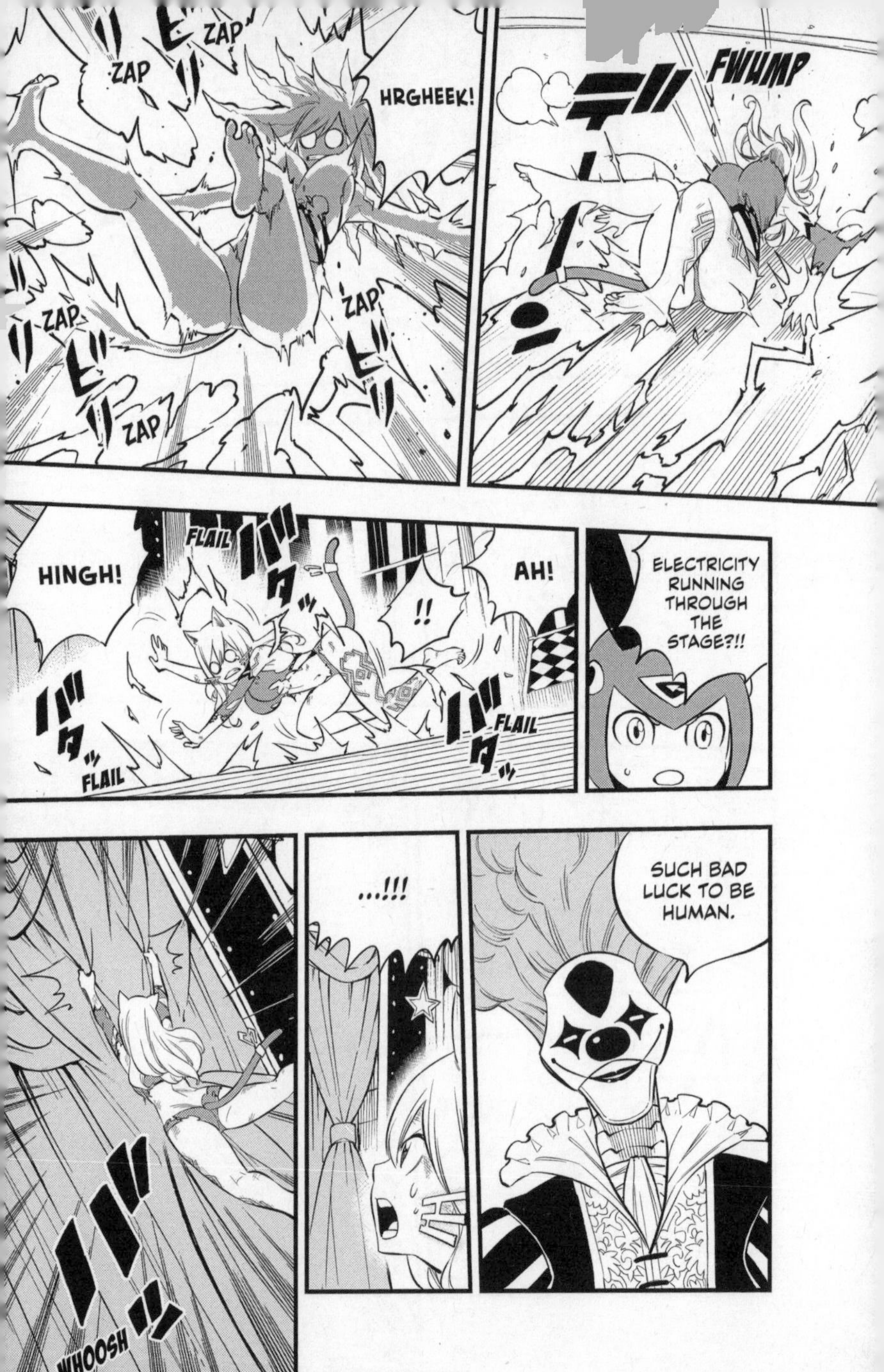
FWUMP
ZAP
ZAP
HRGHEEK!
ZAP
ZAP
ZAP
ZAP
ELECTRICITY RUNNING THROUGH THE STAGE?!!
AH!
!!
FLAIL
FLAIL
HINGH!
FLAIL
SUCH BAD LUCK TO BE HUMAN.
...!!!
WHOOSH

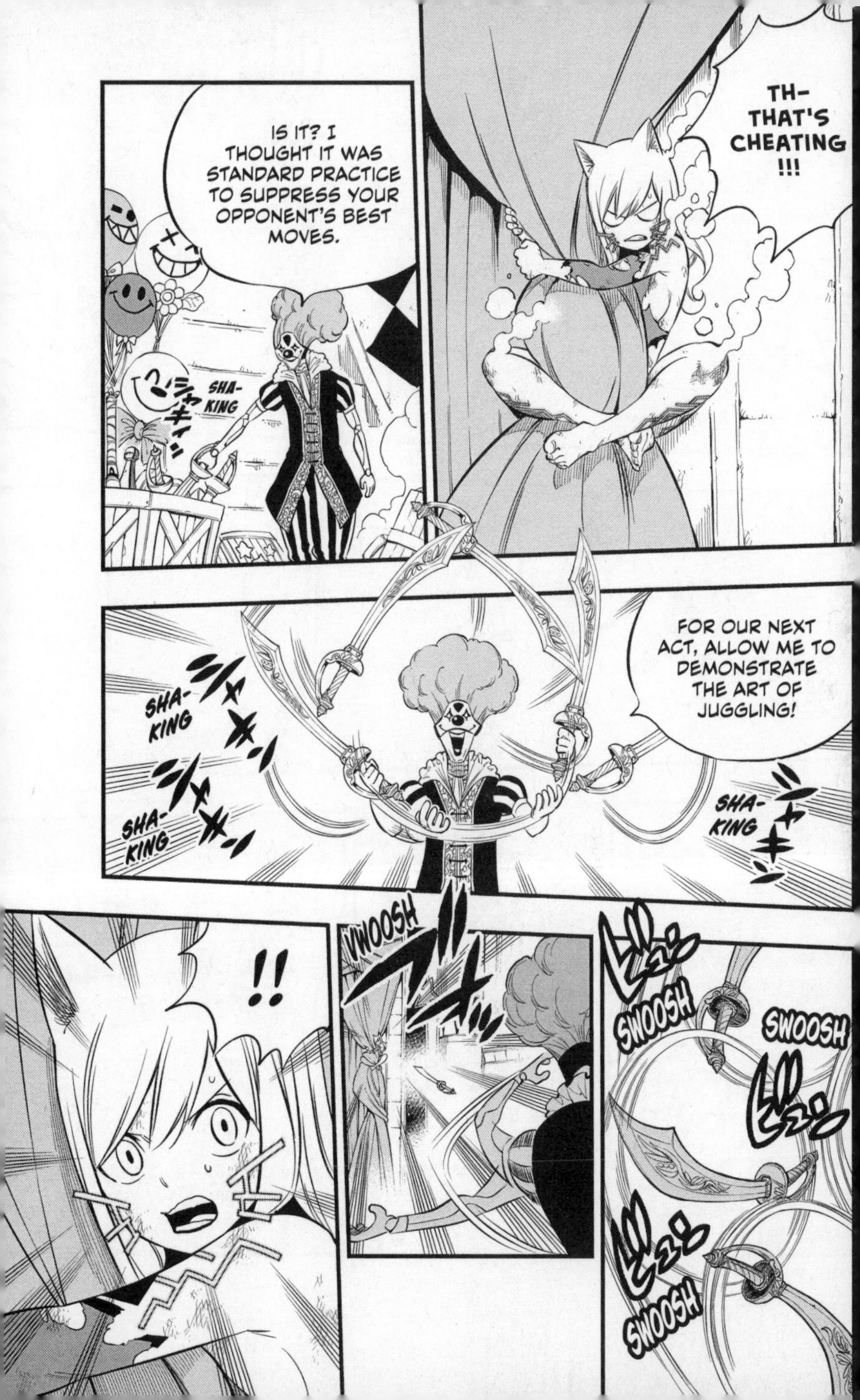
TH- THAT'S CHEATING !!!
IS IT? I THOUGHT IT WAS STANDARD PRACTICE TO SUPPRESS YOUR OPPONENT'S BEST MOVES.
SHA-KING
FOR OUR NEXT ACT, ALLOW ME TO DEMONSTRATE THE ART OF JUGGLING!
SHA-KING
SHA-KING
SHA-KING
SWOOSH
SWOOSH
SWOOSH
VWOOSH
!!

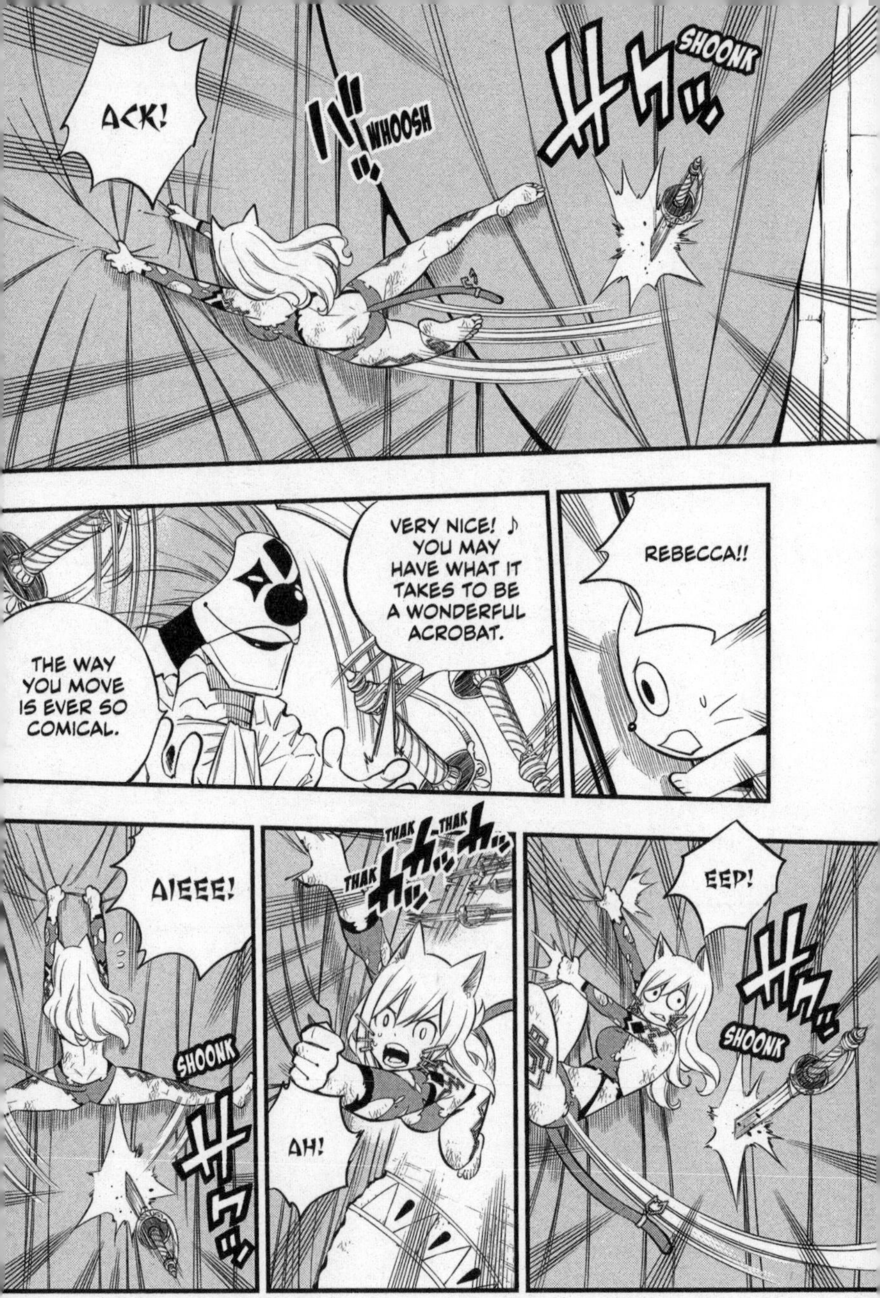
SHOONK
WHOOSH
ACK!
REBECCA!!
VERY NICE! ♪ YOU MAY HAVE WHAT IT TAKES TO BE A WONDERFUL ACROBAT.
THE WAY YOU MOVE IS EVER SO COMICAL.
EEP!
SHOONK
THAK THAK THAK
AH!
AIEEE!
SHOONK

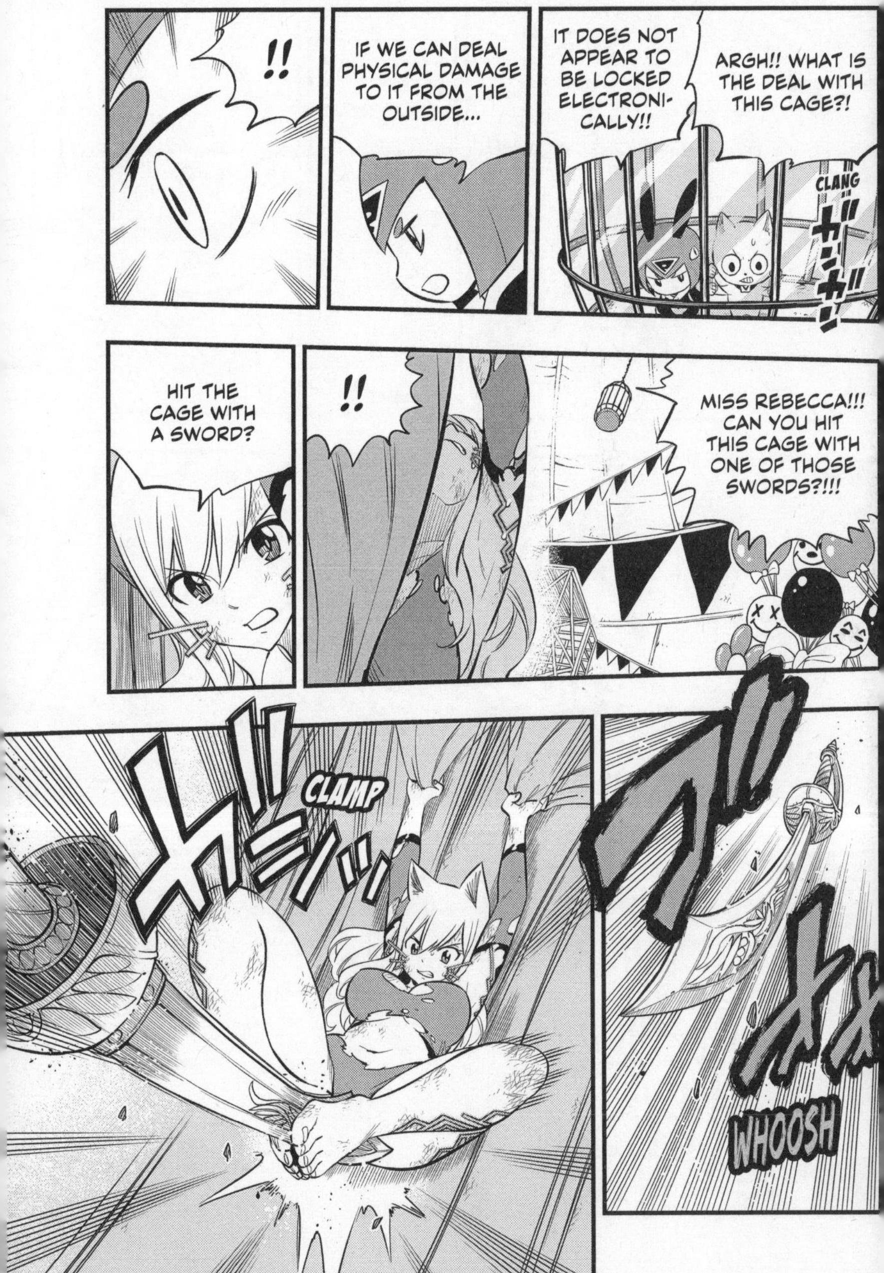
ARGH!! WHAT IS THE DEAL WITH THIS CAGE?!
IT DOES NOT APPEAR TO BE LOCKED ELECTRONI-CALLY!!
CLANG
IF WE CAN DEAL PHYSICAL DAMAGE TO IT FROM THE OUTSIDE...
!!
MISS REBECCA!!! CAN YOU HIT THIS CAGE WITH ONE OF THOSE SWORDS?!!!
!!
HIT THE CAGE WITH A SWORD?
WHOOSH
CLAMP

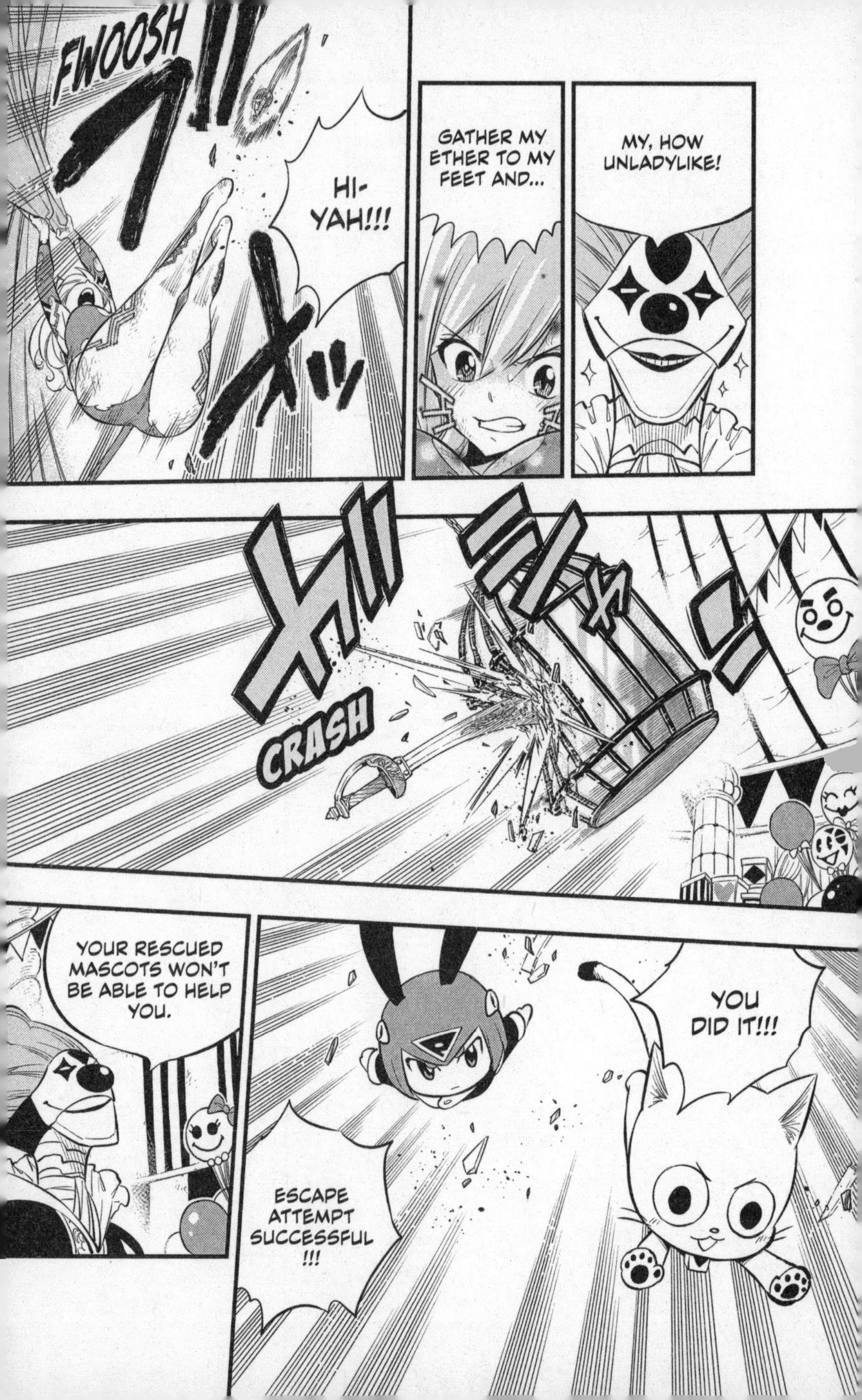
MY, HOW UNLADYLIKE!
GATHER MY ETHER TO MY FEET AND...
FWOOSH
HI-YAH!!!
CRASH
YOU DID IT!!!
ESCAPE ATTEMPT SUCCESSFUL !!!
YOUR RESCUED MASCOTS WON'T BE ABLE TO HELP YOU.

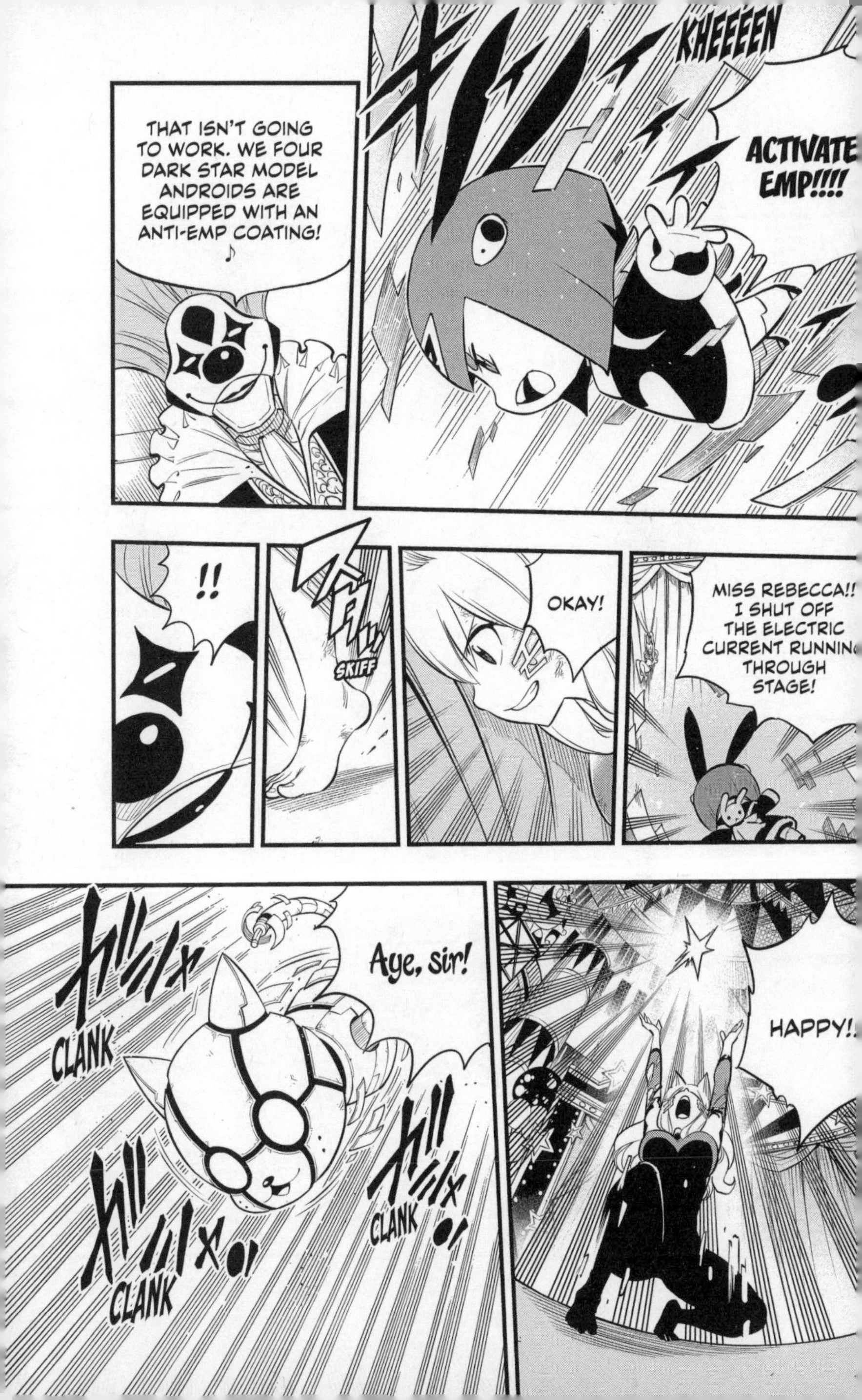
KHEEEEN
ACTIVATE EMP!!!!
THAT ISN'T GOING TO WORK. WE FOUR DARK STAR MODEL ANDROIDS ARE EQUIPPED WITH AN ANTI-EMP COATING! ♪
MISS REBECCA!! I SHUT OFF THE ELECTRIC CURRENT RUNNIN THROUGH STAGE!
OKAY!
SKIFF
!!
HAPPY!
Aye, sir!
CLANK
CLANK
CLANK

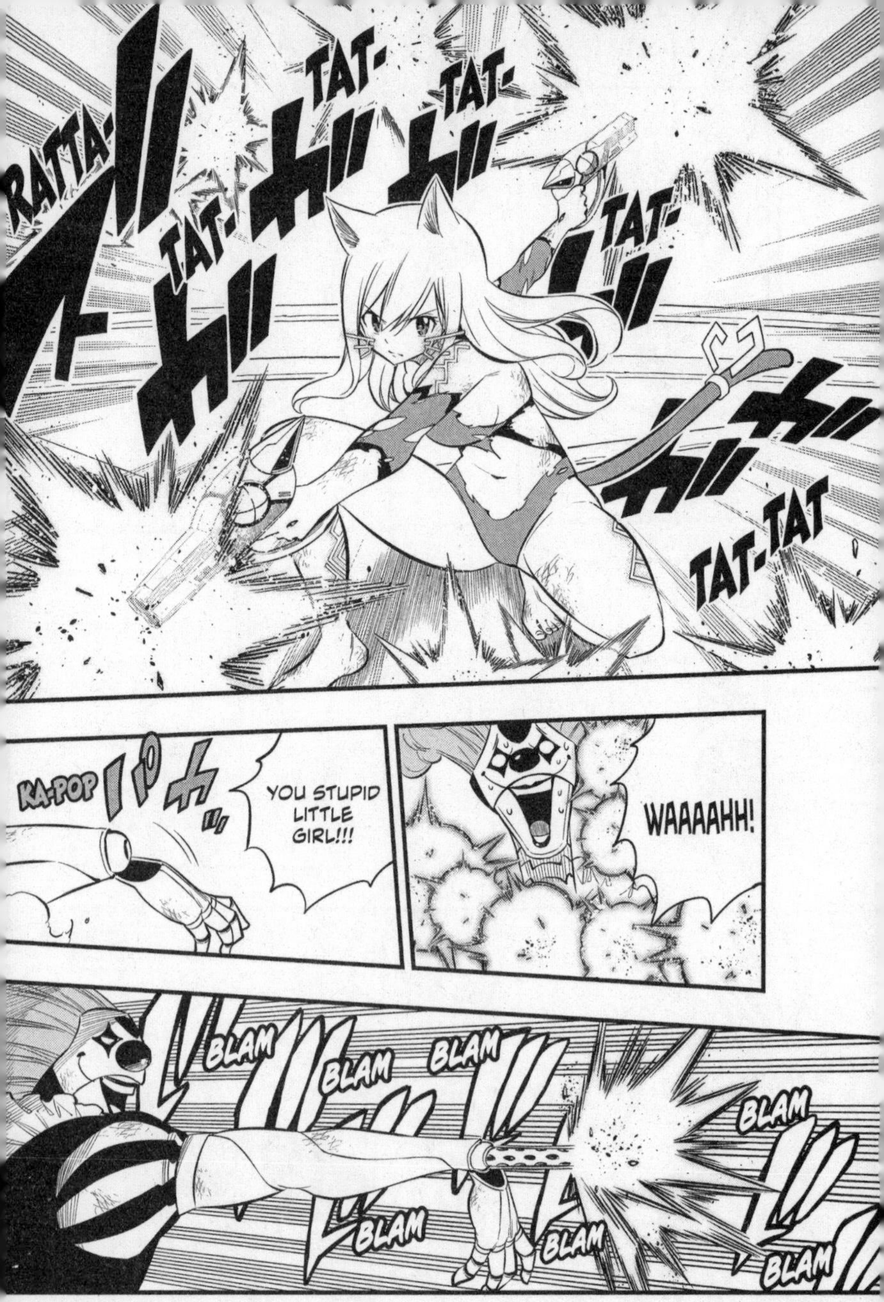
RATTA-
TAT-
TAT-
TAT-
TAT-
TAT-TAT
WAAAAHH!
YOU STUPID LITTLE GIRL!!!
KA-POP
BLAM
BLAM
BLAM
BLAM
BLAM
BLAM
BLAM

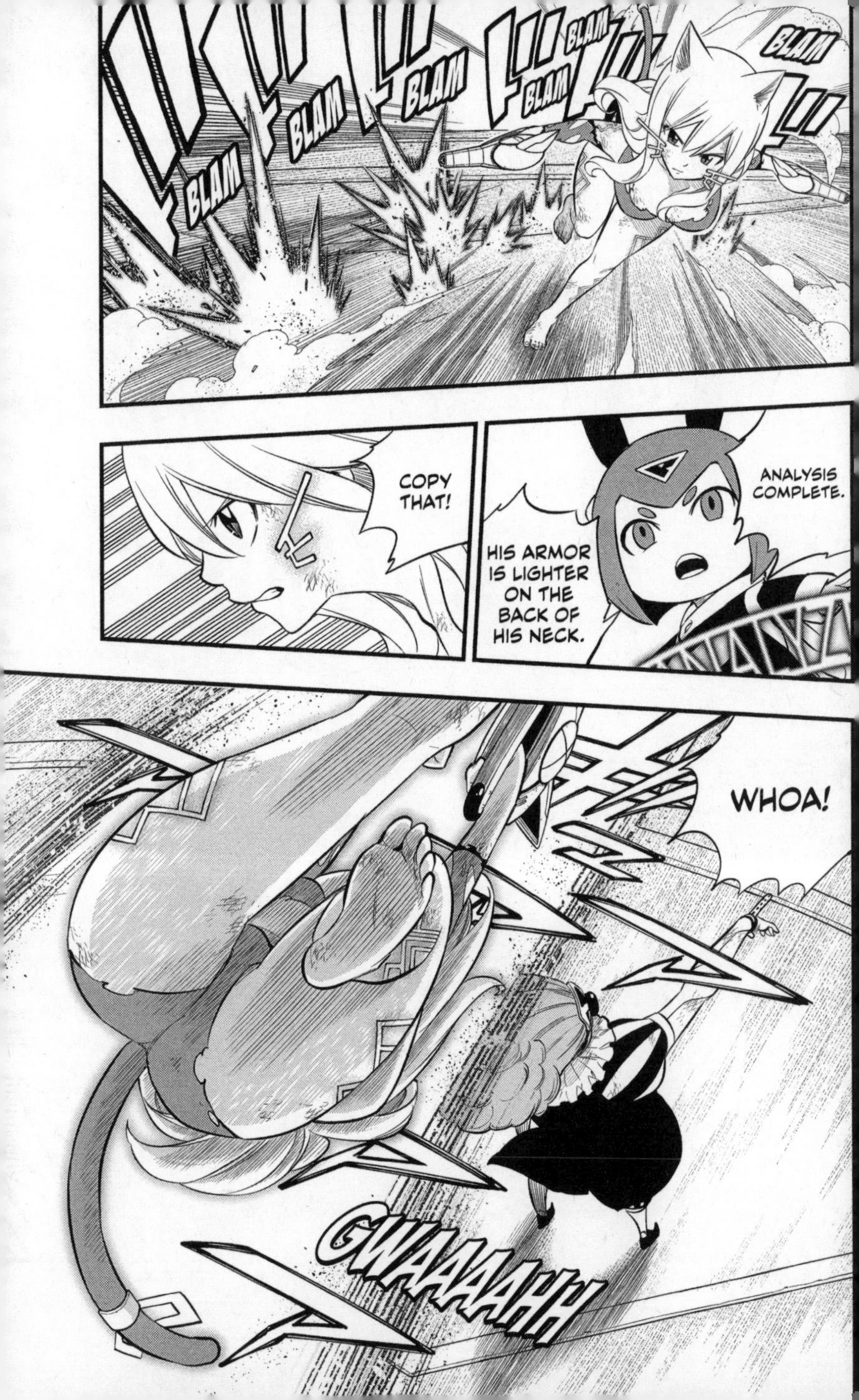
BLAM
BLAM
BLAM
BLAM
BLAM
BLAM
BLAM
ANALYSIS COMPLETE.
HIS ARMOR IS LIGHTER ON THE BACK OF HIS NECK.
COPY THAT!
WHOA!
GWAAAAHH

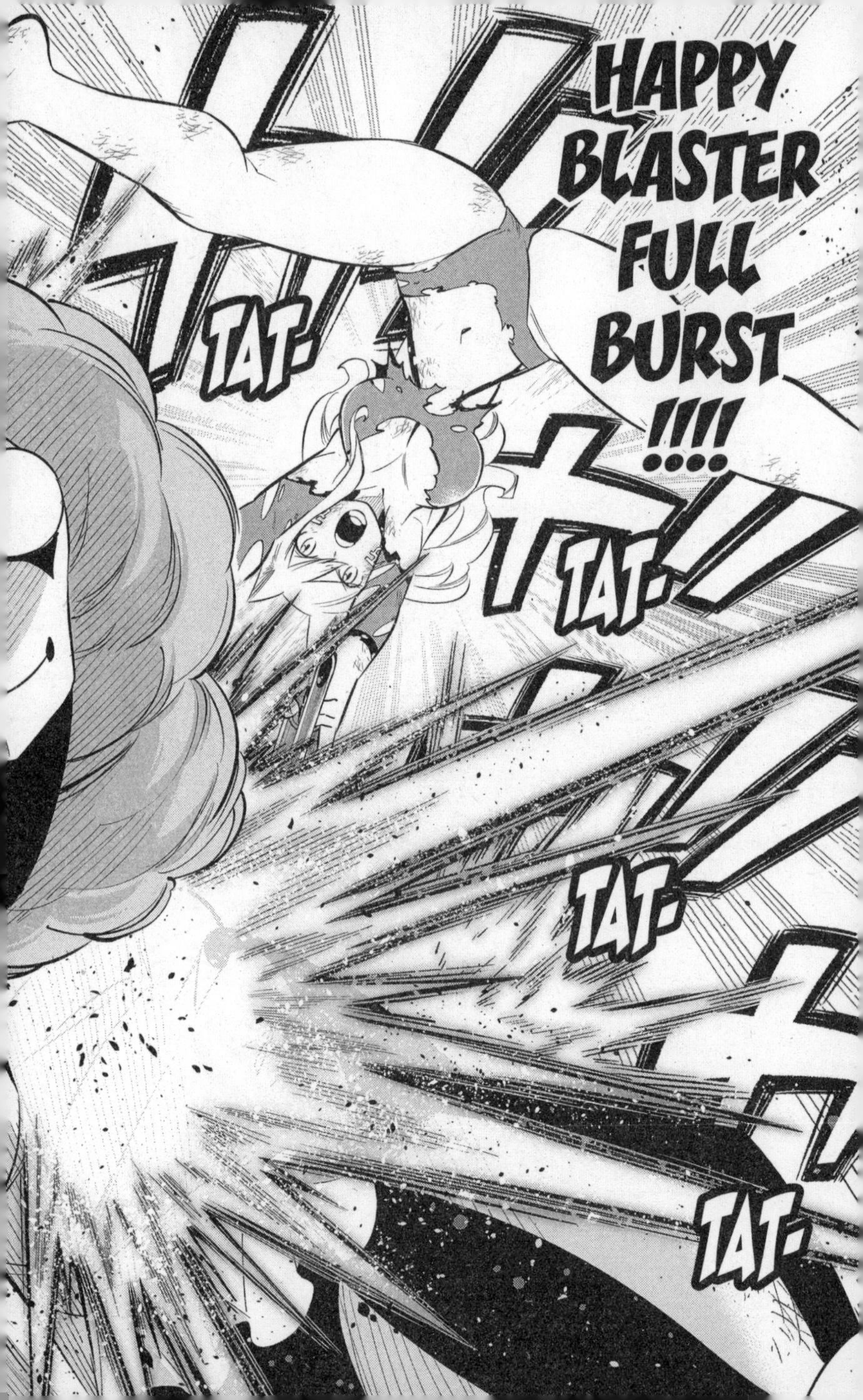
HAPPY BLASTER FULL BURST !!!!
TAT-
TAT-
TAT-
TAT-

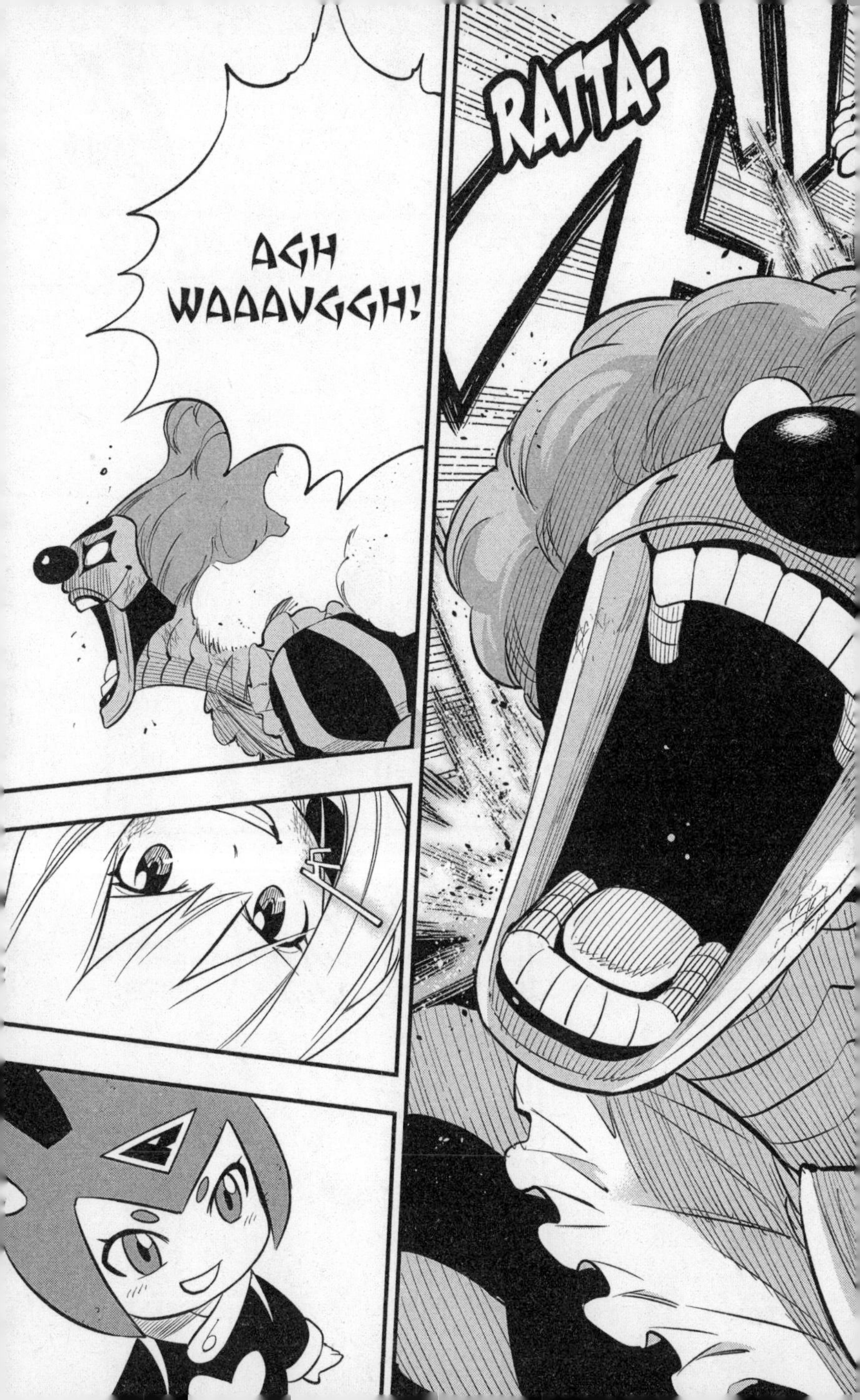
RATTA-
AGH
WAAAUGGH!

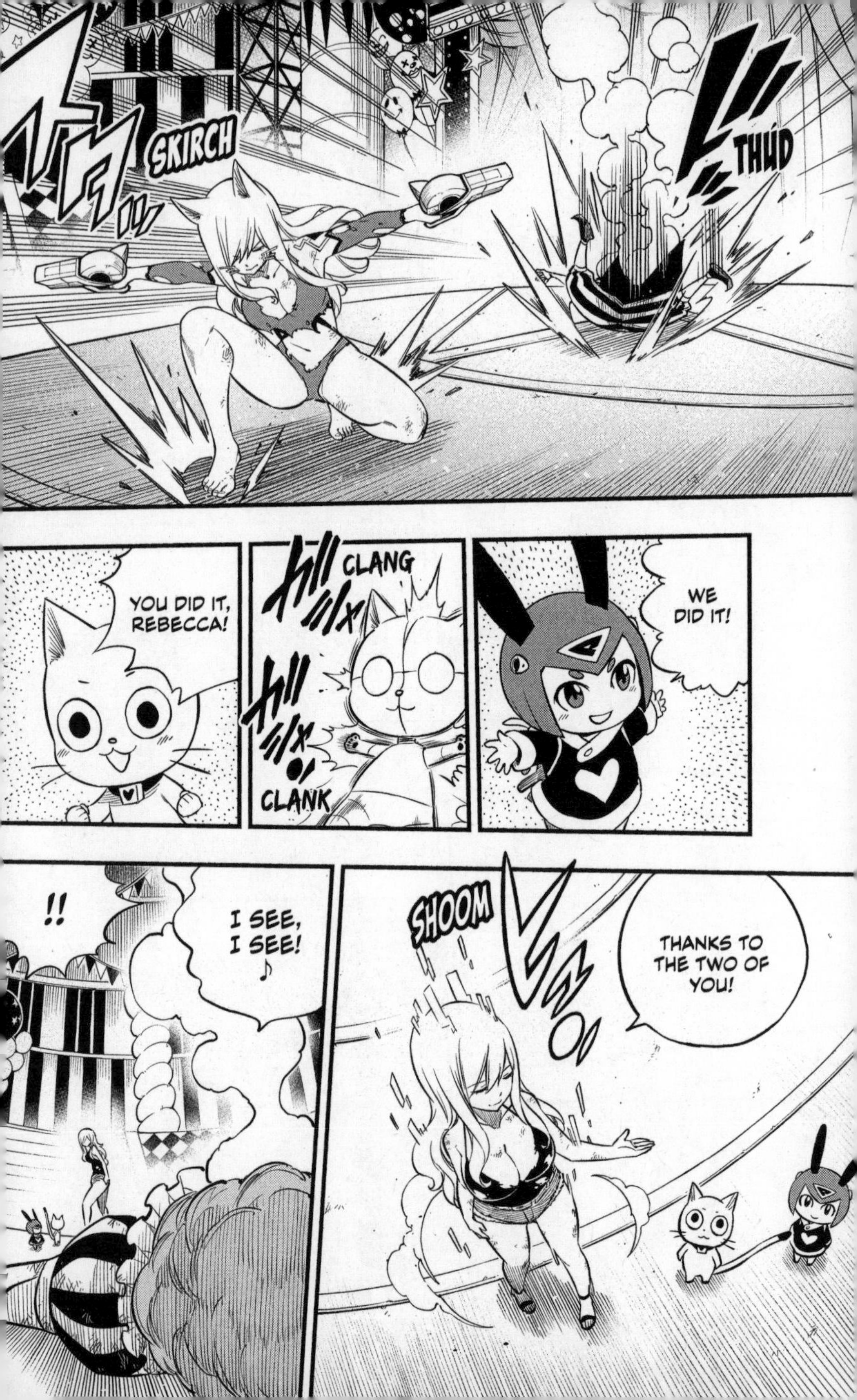
THUD
SKIRCH
WE DID IT!
CLANG
CLANK
YOU DID IT, REBECCA!
SHOOM
THANKS TO THE TWO OF YOU!
!!
I SEE, I SEE! ♪

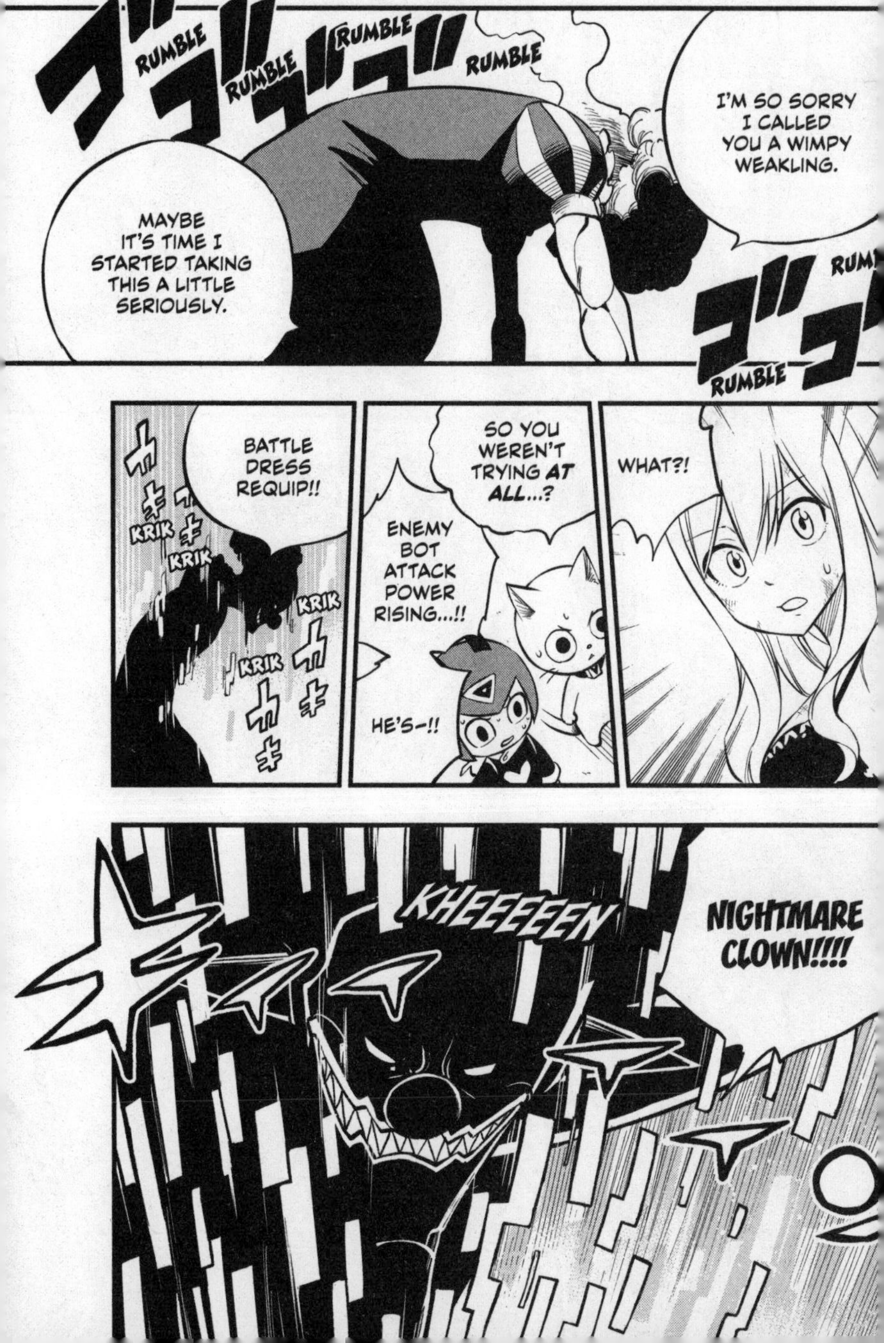
I'M SO SORRY I CALLED YOU A WIMPY WEAKLING.
RUMBLE RUMBLE RUMBLE RUMBLE
MAYBE IT'S TIME I STARTED TAKING THIS A LITTLE SERIOUSLY.
RUMBLE
WHAT?!
SO YOU WEREN'T TRYING **AT ALL**...?
ENEMY BOT ATTACK POWER RISING...!!
HE'S—!!
BATTLE DRESS REQUIP!!
KRIK KRIK KRIK KRIK
NIGHTMARE CLOWN!!!!
KHEEEEEN

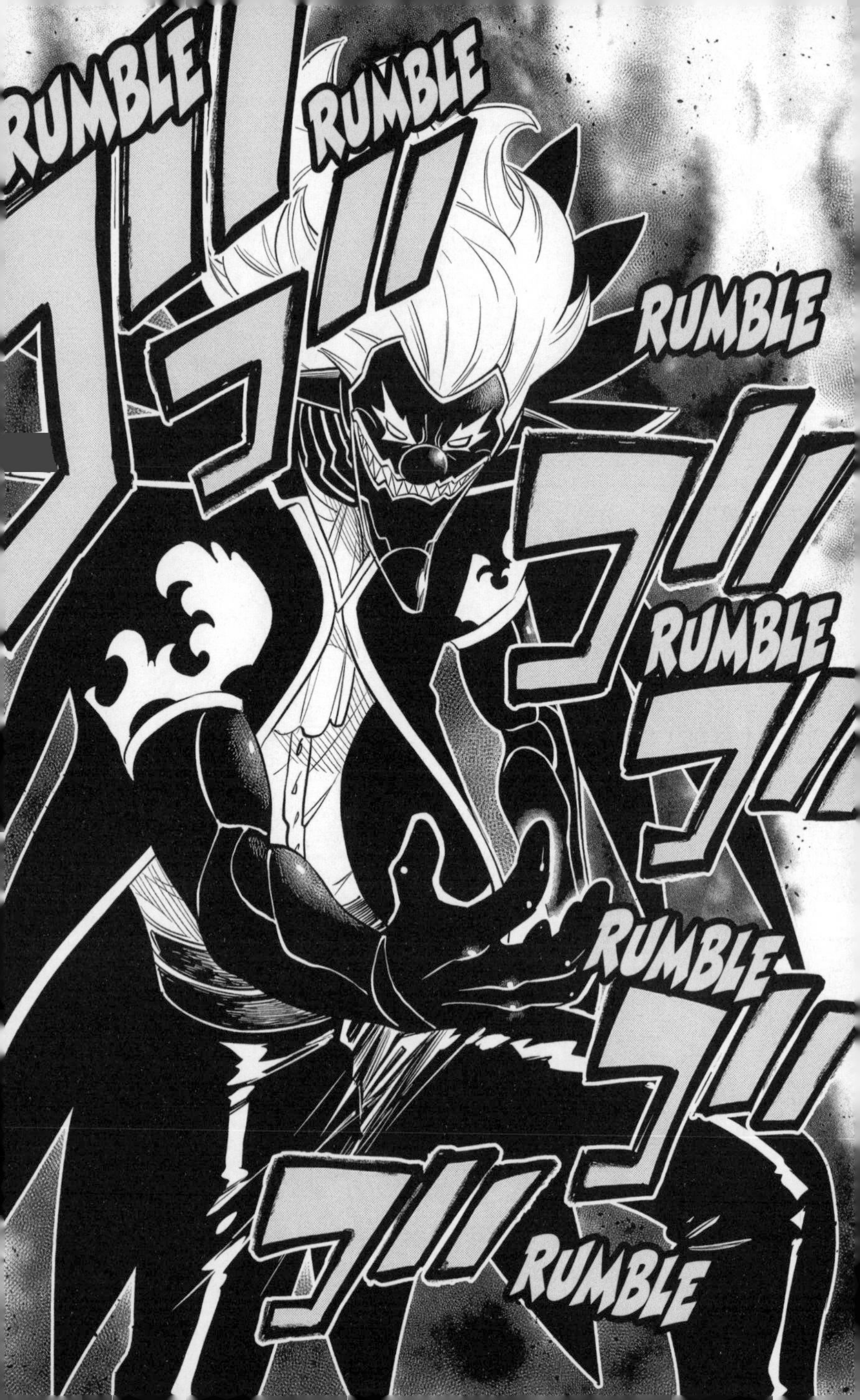
RUMBLE
RUMBLE
RUMBLE
RUMBLE
RUMBLE
RUMBLE

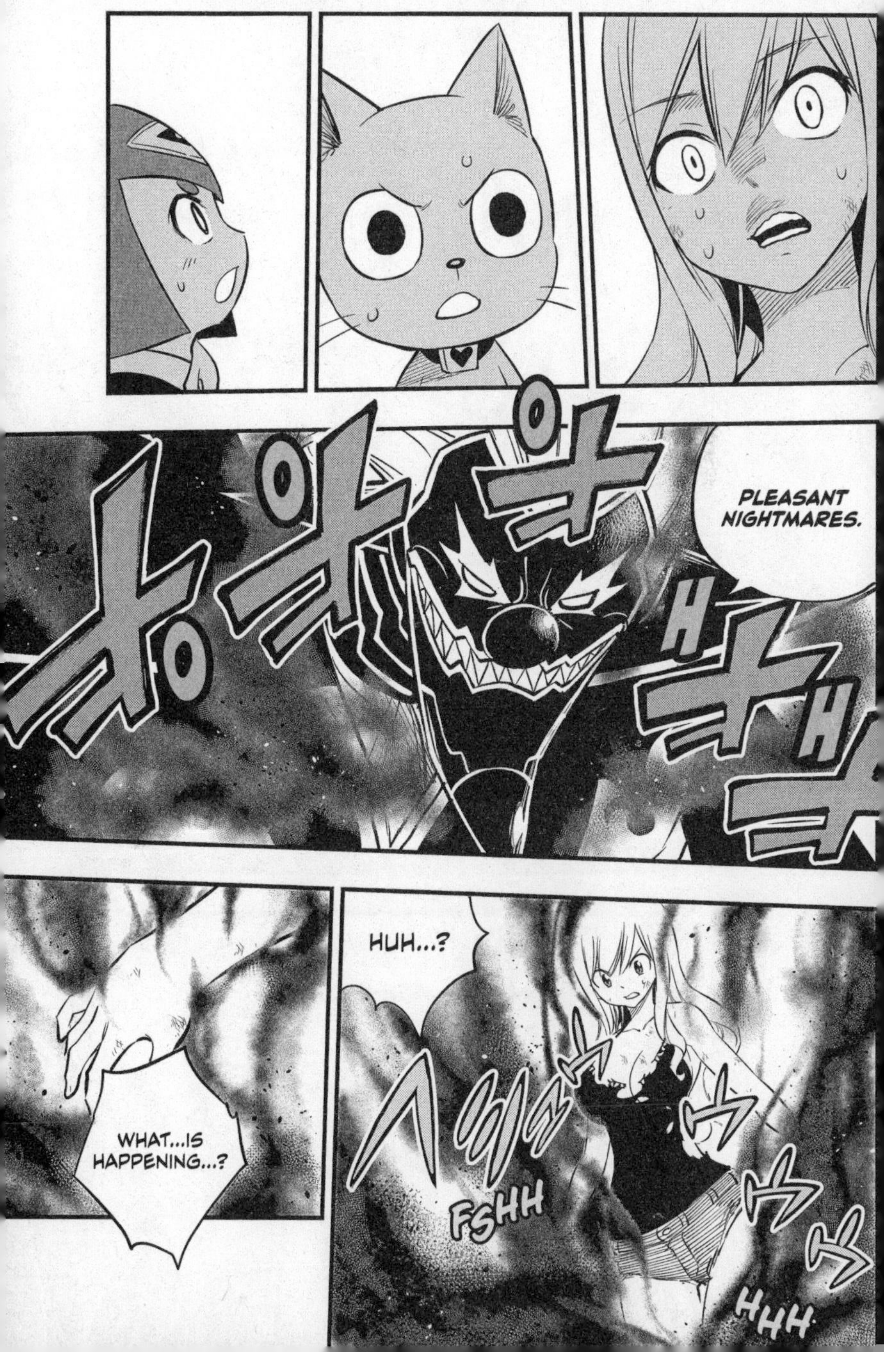
PLEASANT NIGHTMARES.
HH
HUH...?
FSHH
HHH
WHAT...IS HAPPENING...?

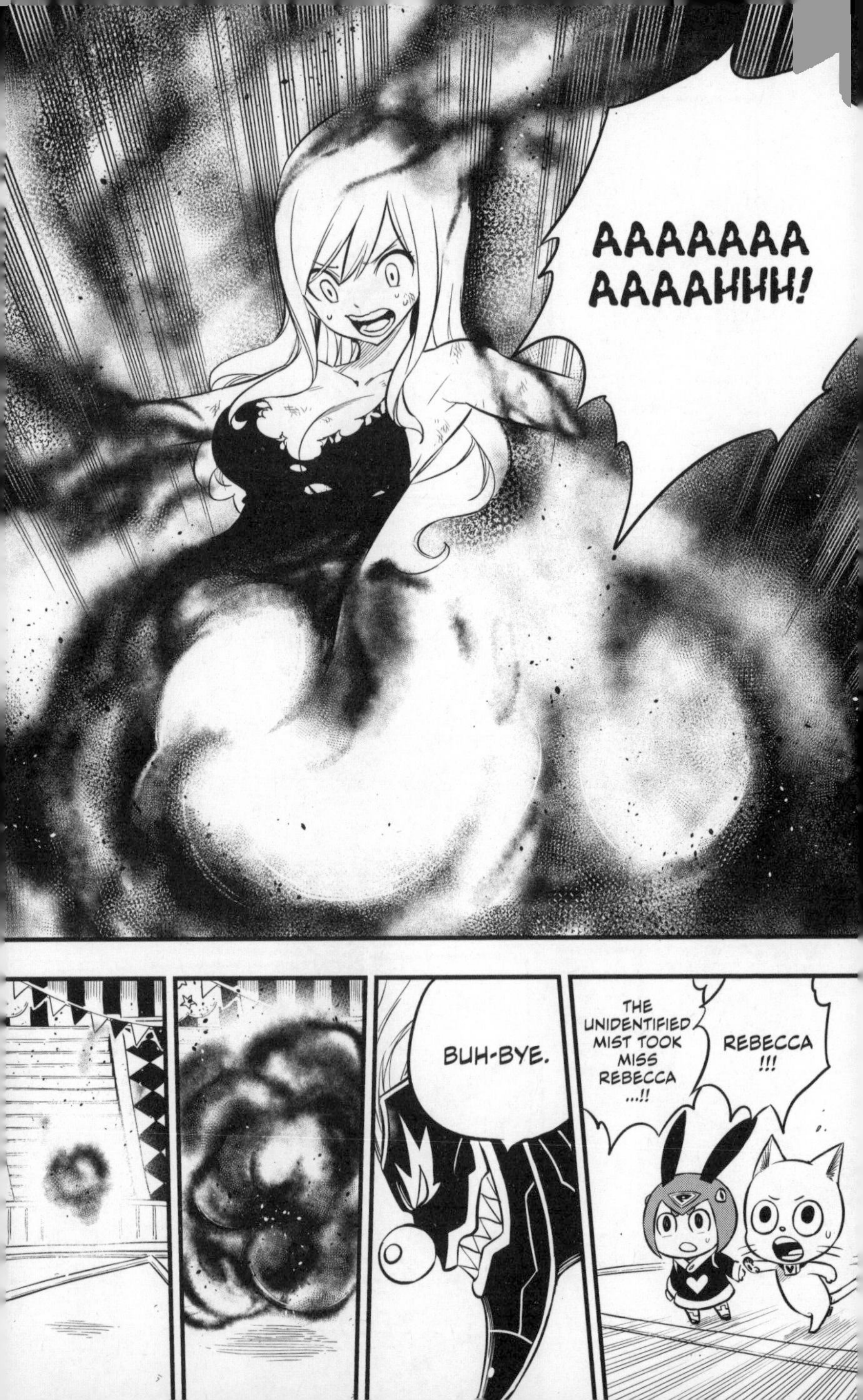
AAAAAAA AAAAHHH!
REBECCA !!!
THE UNIDENTIFIED MIST TOOK MISS REBECCA ...!!
BUH-BYE.

EDENS ZERO

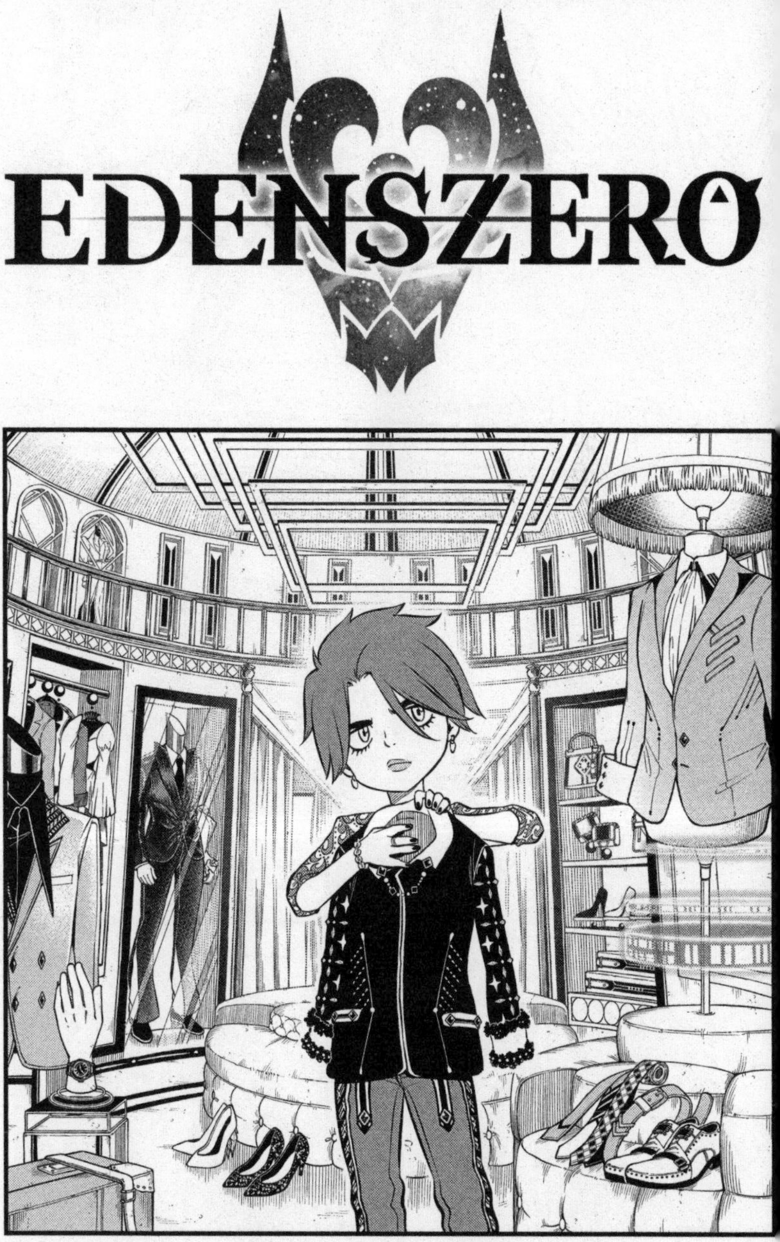

CHAPTER 191: ZOMBIE NURSES

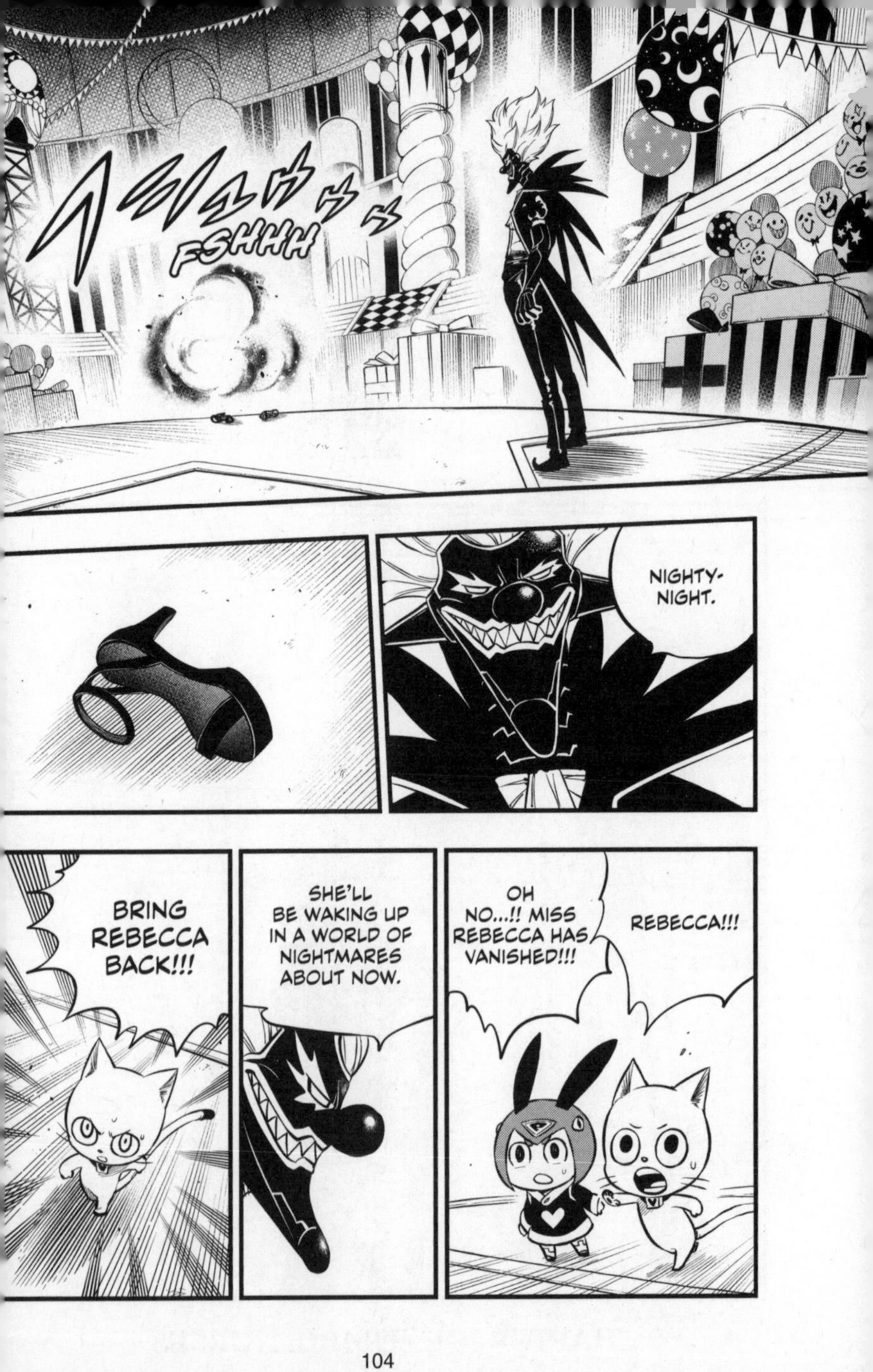
FSHHH
NIGHTY-NIGHT.
REBECCA!!!
OH NO...!! MISS REBECCA HAS VANISHED!!!
SHE'LL BE WAKING UP IN A WORLD OF NIGHTMARES ABOUT NOW.
BRING REBECCA BACK!!!

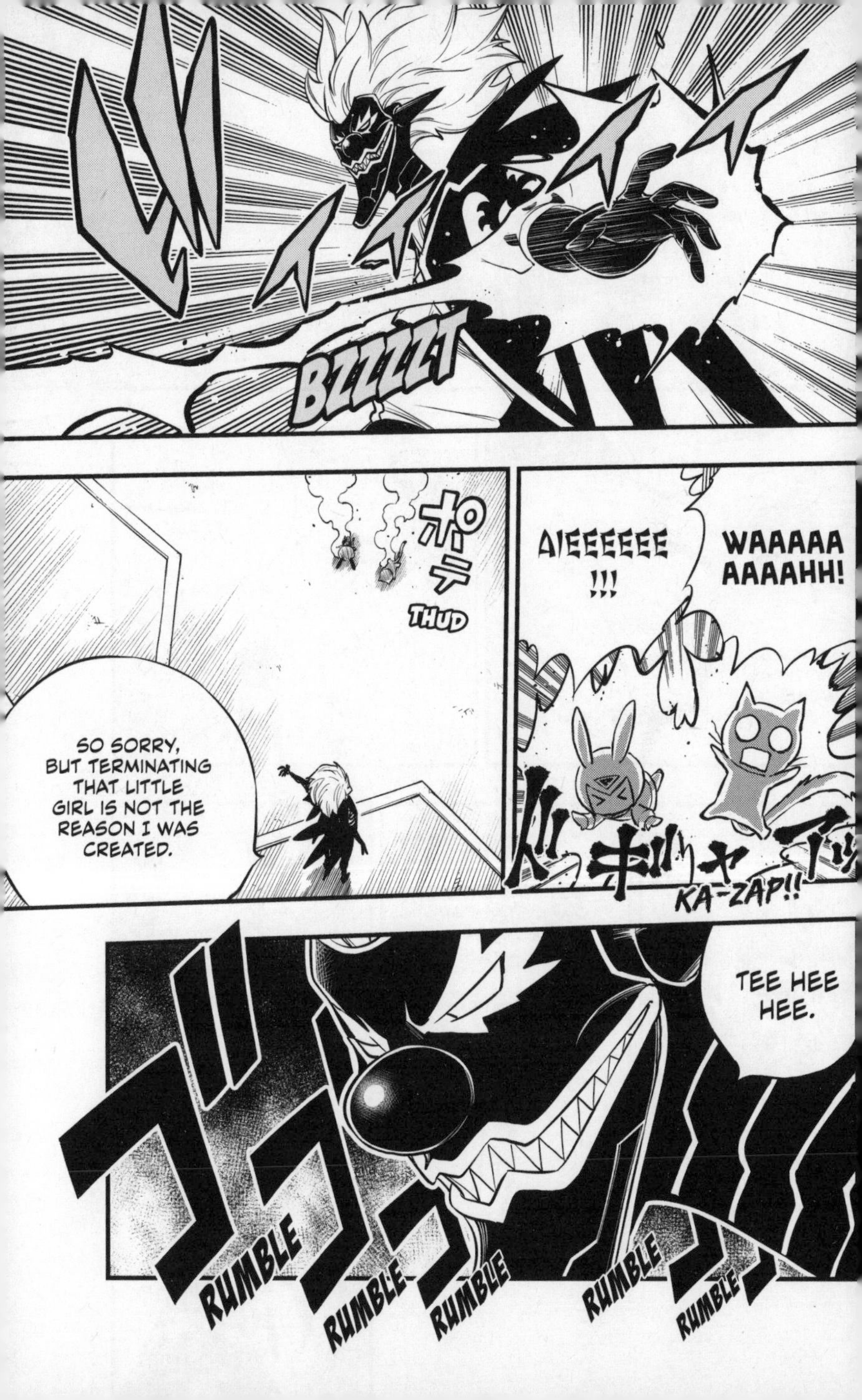
BZZZZZT
WAAAAA AAAAHH!
AIEEEEEE!!!
KA-ZAP!!
ポテ
THUD
SO SORRY, BUT TERMINATING THAT LITTLE GIRL IS NOT THE REASON I WAS CREATED.
TEE HEE HEE.
RUMBLE
RUMBLE
RUMBLE
RUMBLE
RUMBLE

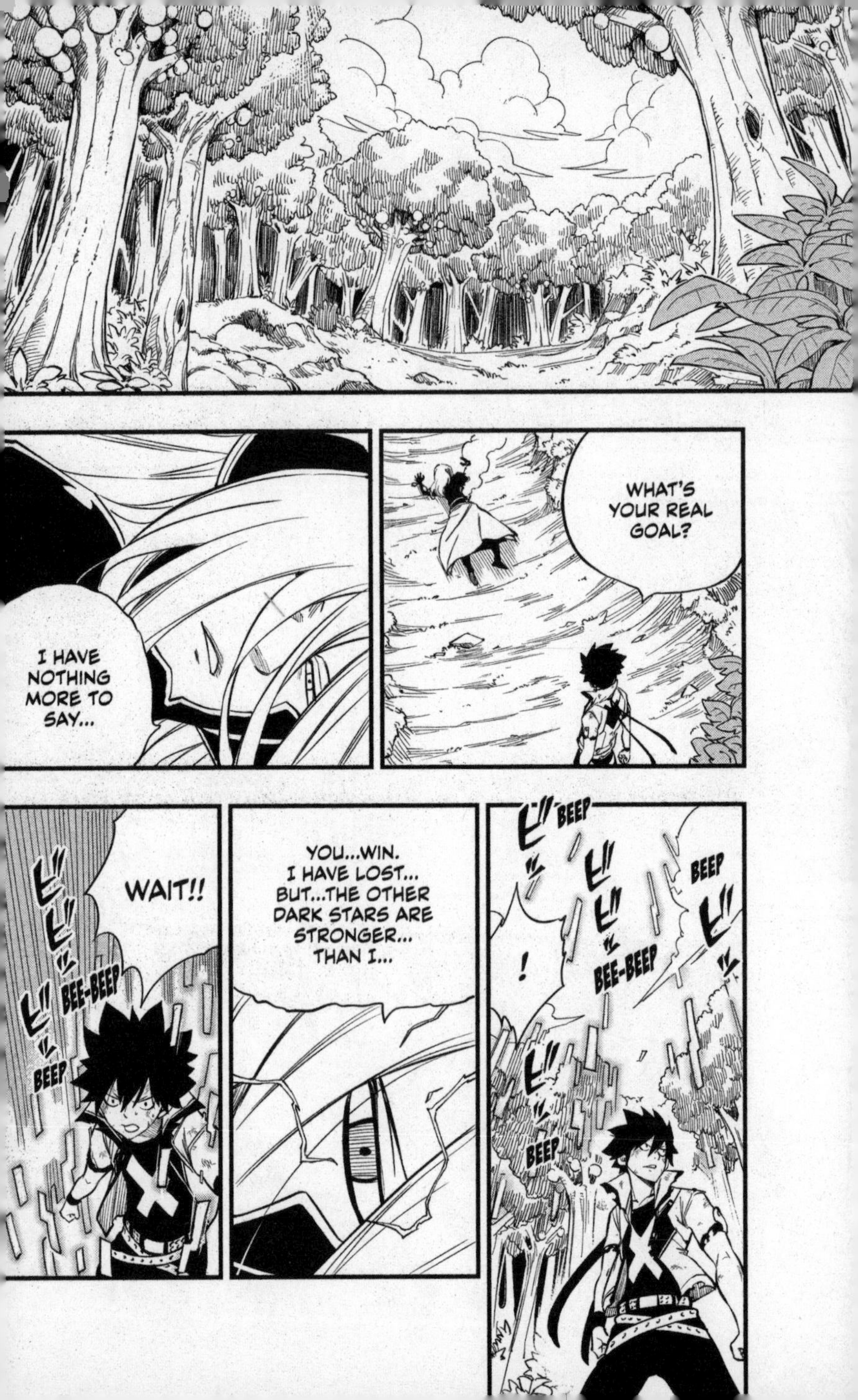

WHAT'S YOUR REAL GOAL?
I HAVE NOTHING MORE TO SAY...
BEEP
!
BEEP
BEE-BEEP
BEEP
YOU...WIN. I HAVE LOST... BUT...THE OTHER DARK STARS ARE STRONGER... THAN I...
WAIT!!
BEE-BEEP
BEEP

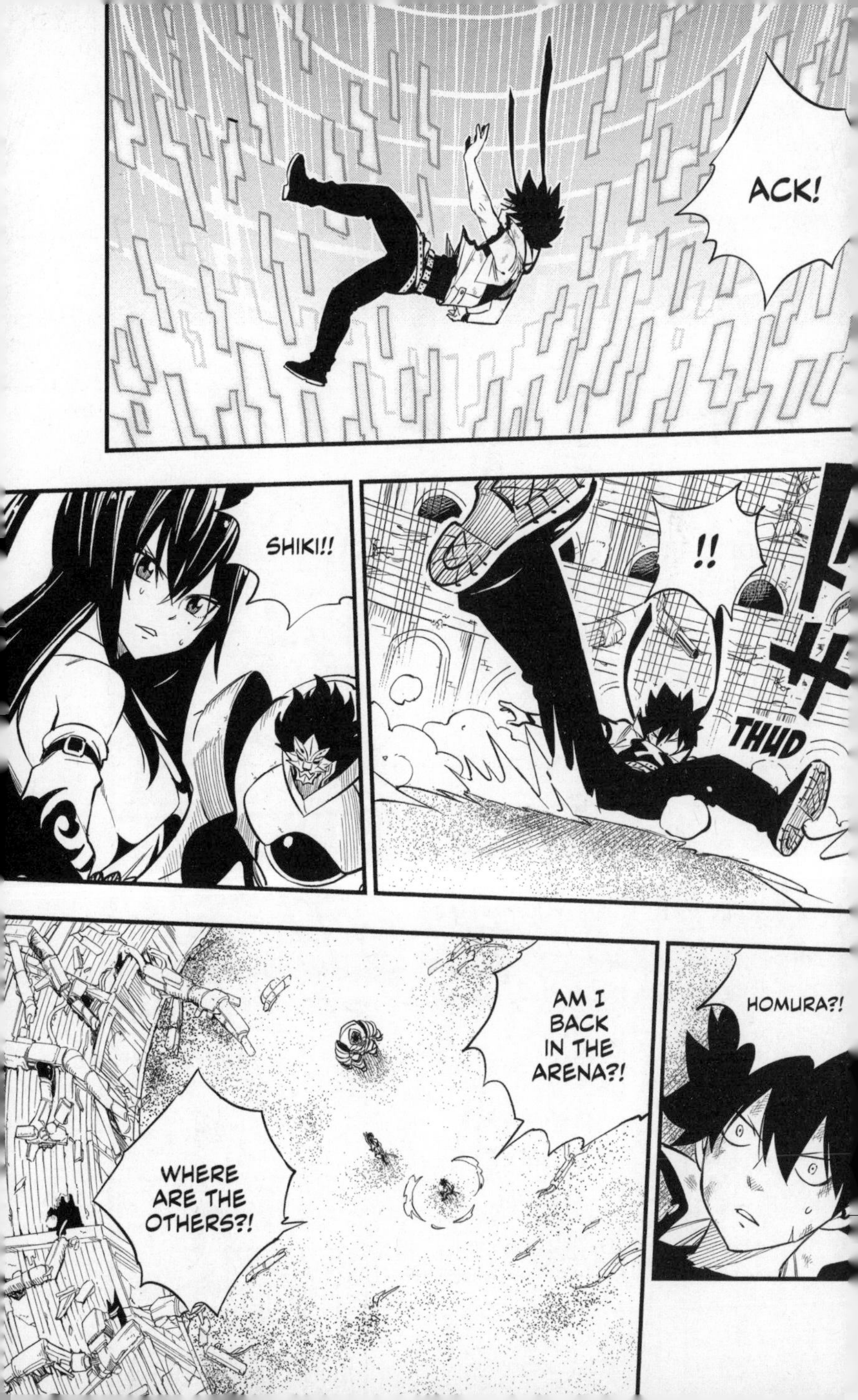
ACK!
!!
THUD
SHIKI!!
HOMURA?!
AM I BACK IN THE ARENA?!
WHERE ARE THE OTHERS?!

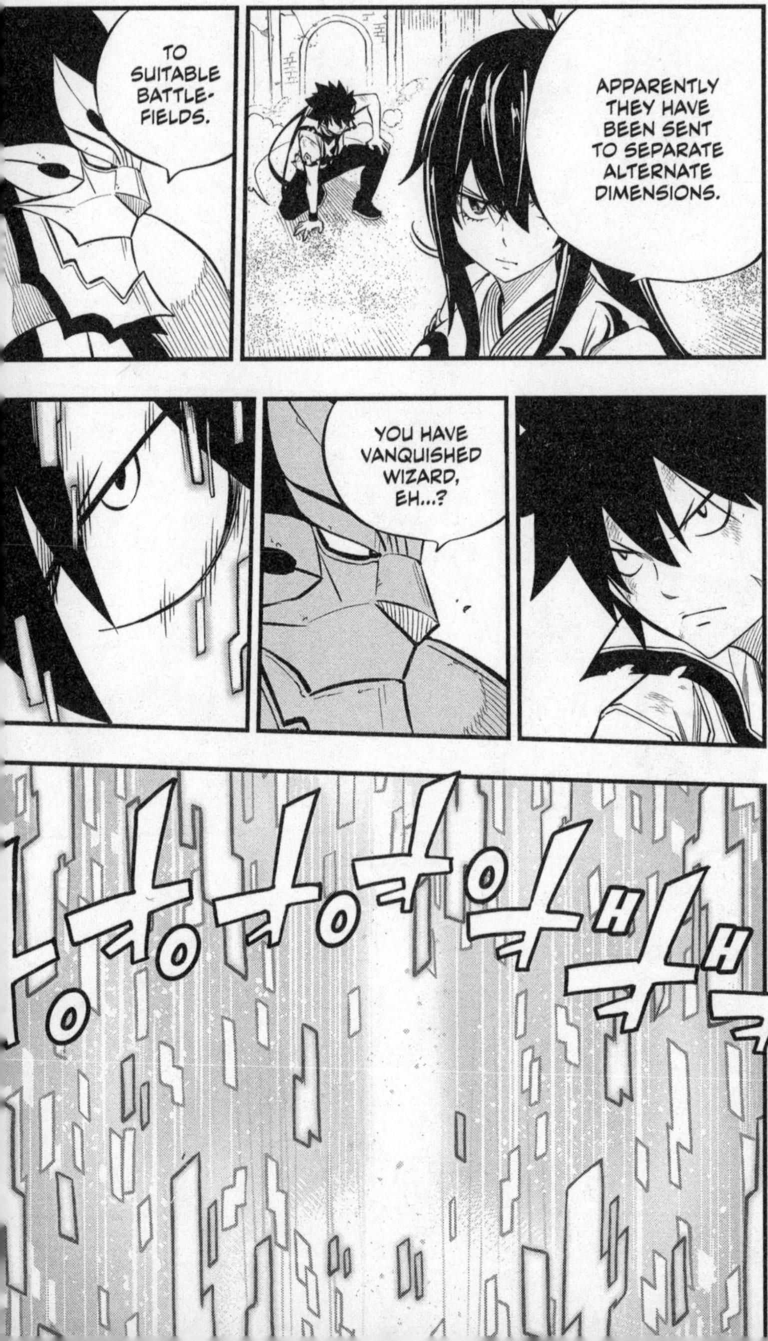
APPARENTLY THEY HAVE BEEN SENT TO SEPARATE ALTERNATE DIMENSIONS.
TO SUITABLE BATTLE-FIELDS.
YOU HAVE VANQUISHED WIZARD, EH...?
HOHOHOHOHHHHHH

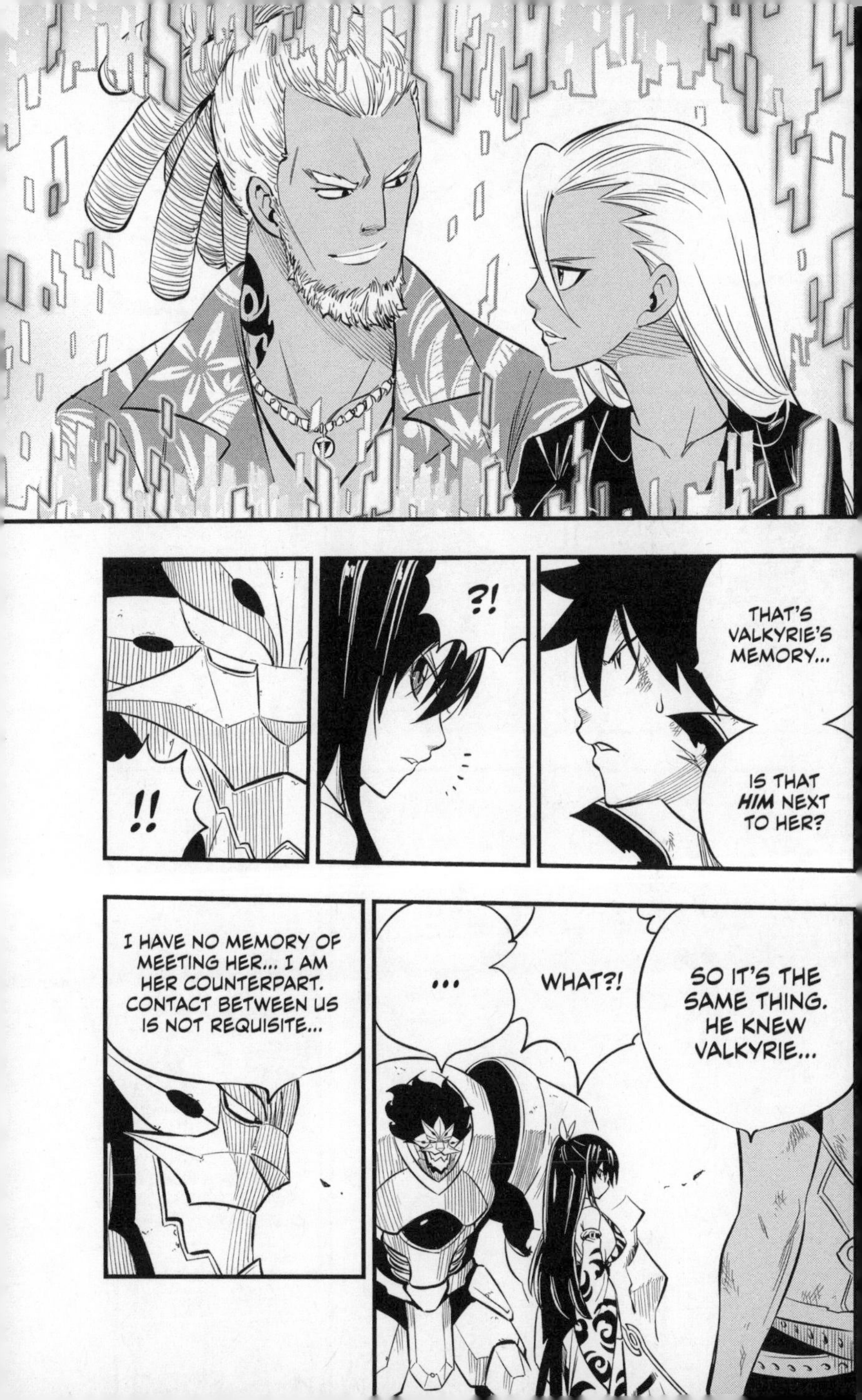
THAT'S VALKYRIE'S MEMORY...
IS THAT *HIM* NEXT TO HER?
?!
!!
SO IT'S THE SAME THING. HE KNEW VALKYRIE...
WHAT?!
...
I HAVE NO MEMORY OF MEETING HER... I AM HER COUNTERPART. CONTACT BETWEEN US IS NOT REQUISITE...

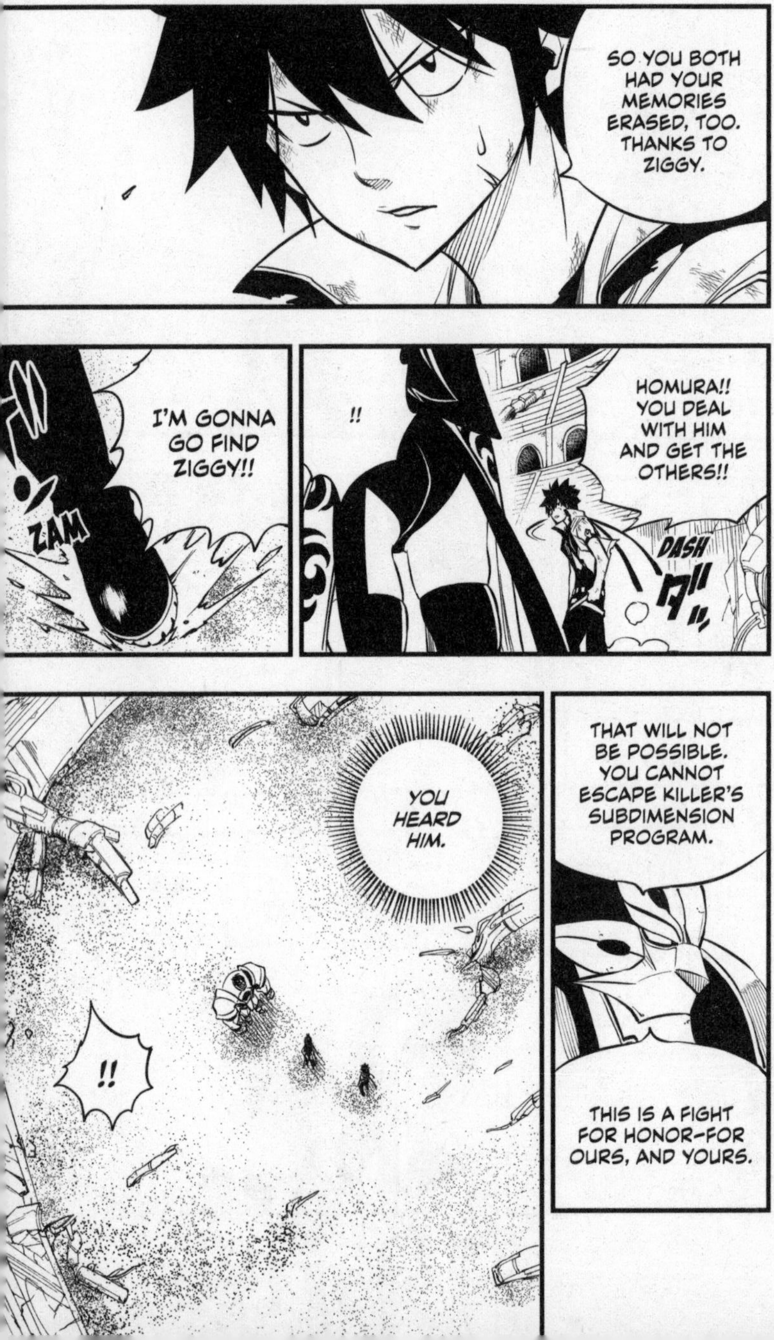
SO YOU BOTH HAD YOUR MEMORIES ERASED, TOO. THANKS TO ZIGGY.
HOMURA!! YOU DEAL WITH HIM AND GET THE OTHERS!!
!!
DASH
I'M GONNA GO FIND ZIGGY!!
ZAM
THAT WILL NOT BE POSSIBLE. YOU CANNOT ESCAPE KILLER'S SUBDIMENSION PROGRAM.
THIS IS A FIGHT FOR HONOR—FOR OURS, AND YOURS.
YOU HEARD HIM.
!!

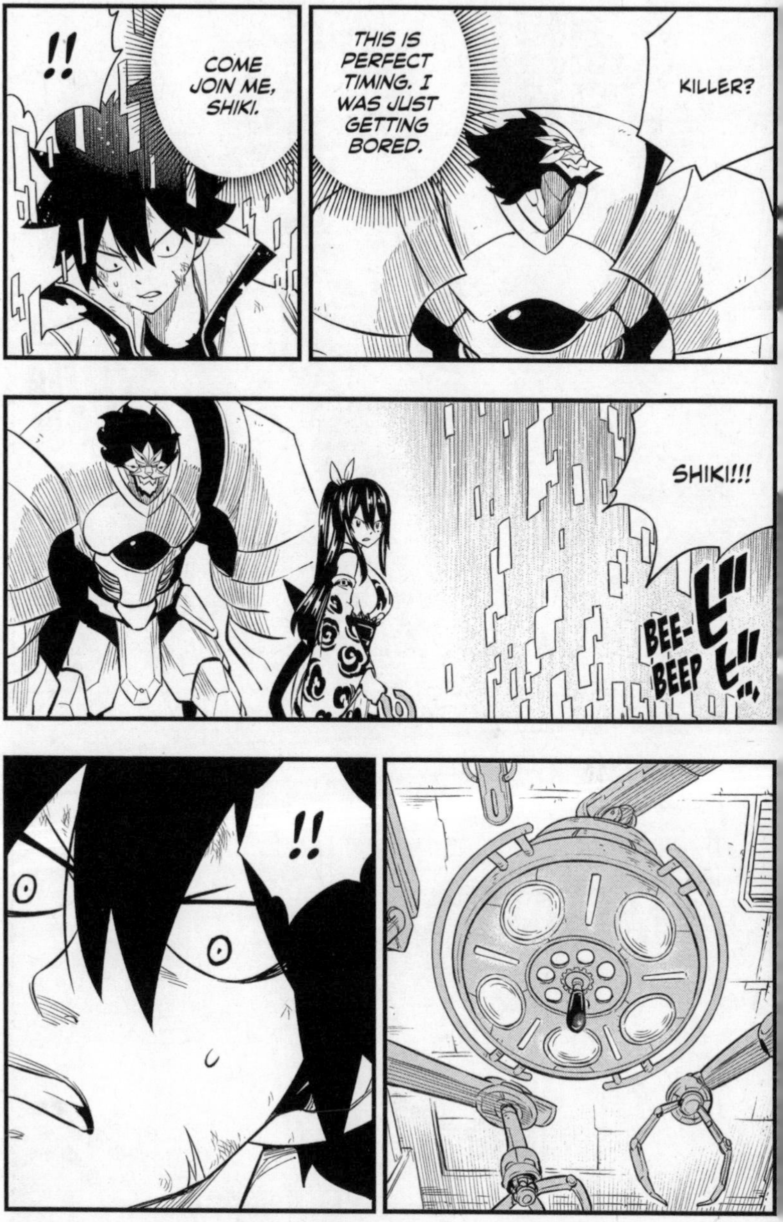
KILLER?
THIS IS PERFECT TIMING. I WAS JUST GETTING BORED.
COME JOIN ME, SHIKI.
!!
SHIKI!!!
BEE-BEEP
!!

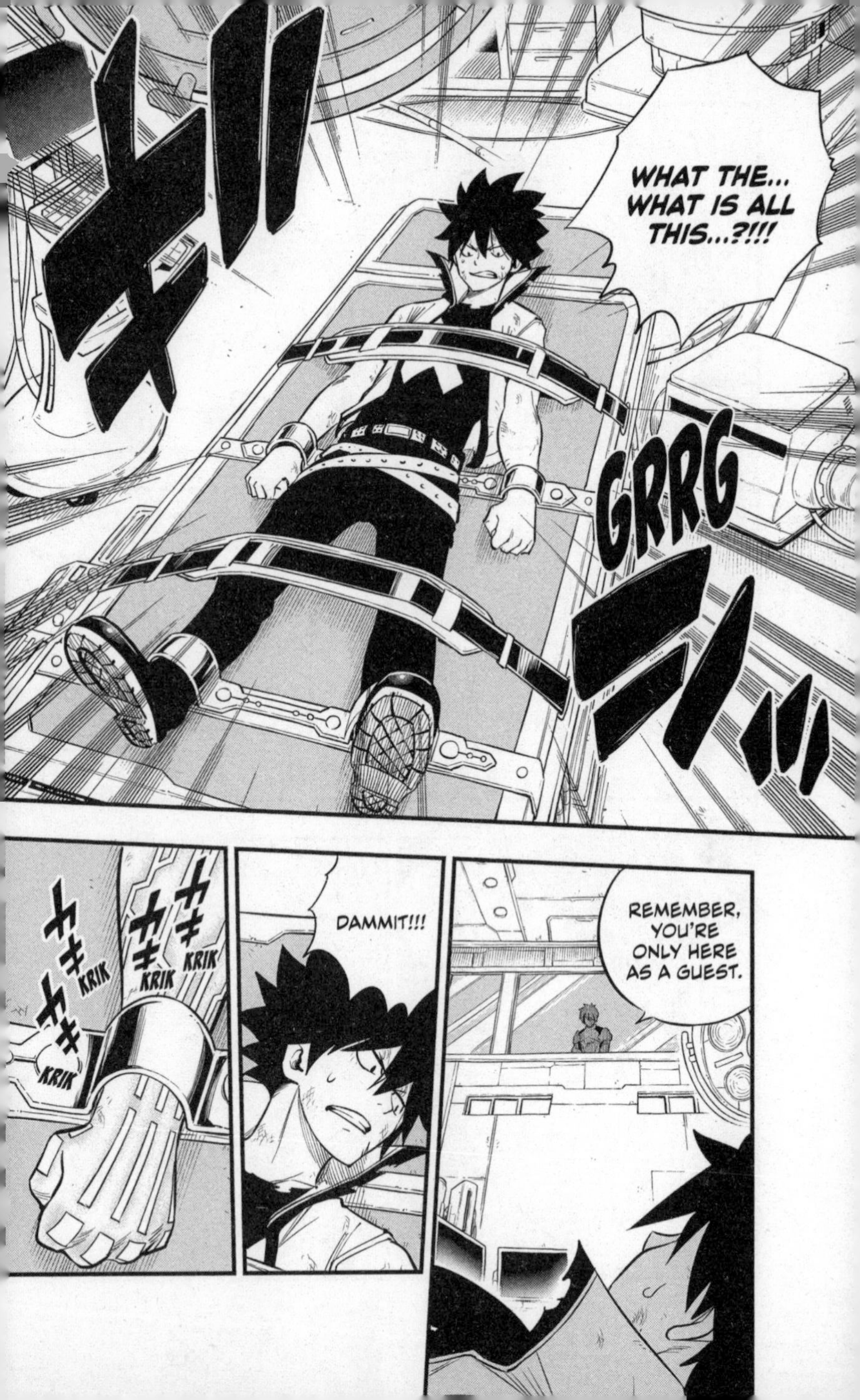
WHAT THE...
WHAT IS ALL
THIS...?!!!
GRRG
REMEMBER,
YOU'RE
ONLY HERE
AS A GUEST.
DAMMIT!!!
KRIK
KRIK
KRIK
KRIK

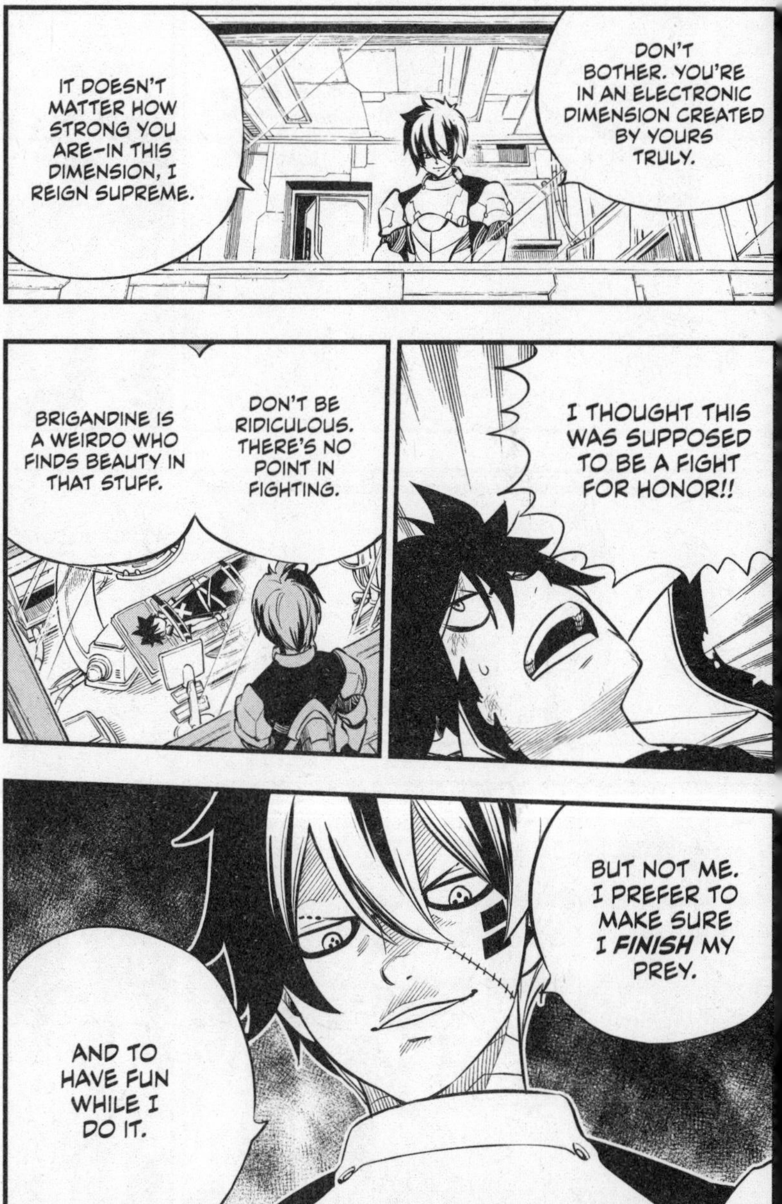
DON'T BOTHER. YOU'RE IN AN ELECTRONIC DIMENSION CREATED BY YOURS TRULY.
IT DOESN'T MATTER HOW STRONG YOU ARE—IN THIS DIMENSION, I REIGN SUPREME.
I THOUGHT THIS WAS SUPPOSED TO BE A FIGHT FOR HONOR!!
DON'T BE RIDICULOUS. THERE'S NO POINT IN FIGHTING.
BRIGANDINE IS A WEIRDO WHO FINDS BEAUTY IN THAT STUFF.
BUT NOT ME. I PREFER TO MAKE SURE I *FINISH* MY PREY.
AND TO HAVE FUN WHILE I DO IT.

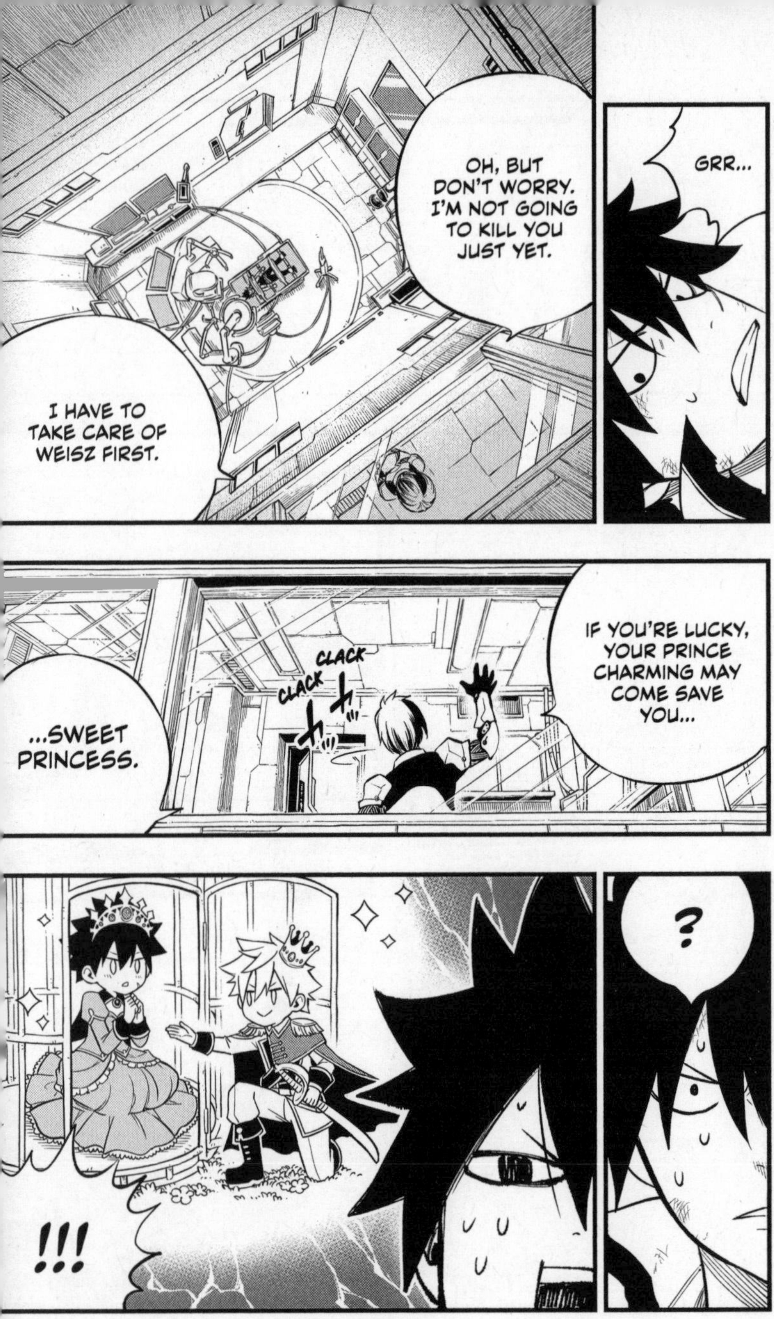
GRR...
OH, BUT DON'T WORRY. I'M NOT GOING TO KILL YOU JUST YET.
I HAVE TO TAKE CARE OF WEISZ FIRST.
IF YOU'RE LUCKY, YOUR PRINCE CHARMING MAY COME SAVE YOU...
CLACK
CLACK
...SWEET PRINCESS.
?
!!!

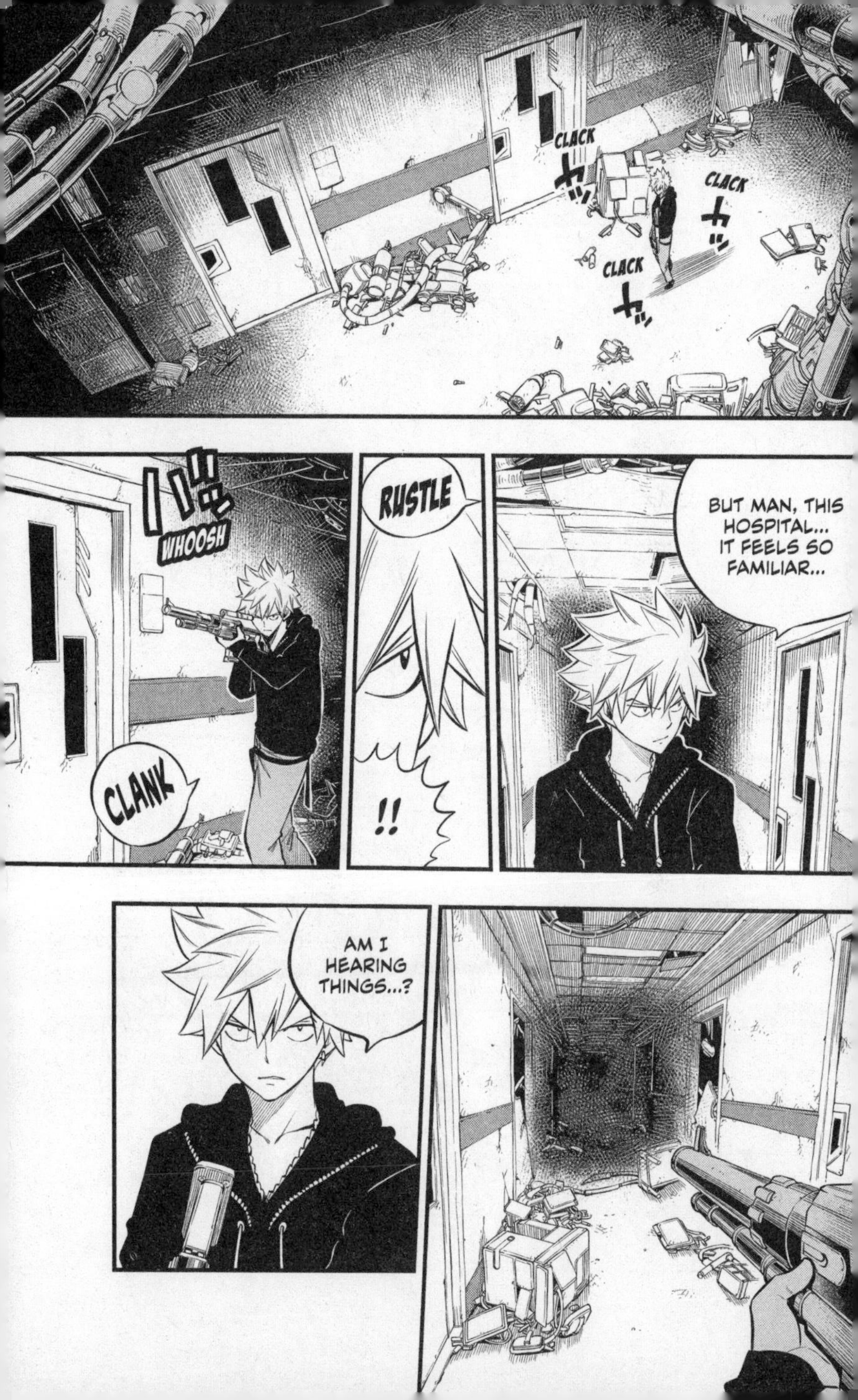
CLACK
CLACK
CLACK
BUT MAN, THIS HOSPITAL... IT FEELS SO FAMILIAR...
RUSTLE
!!
WHOOSH
CLANK
AM I HEARING THINGS...?

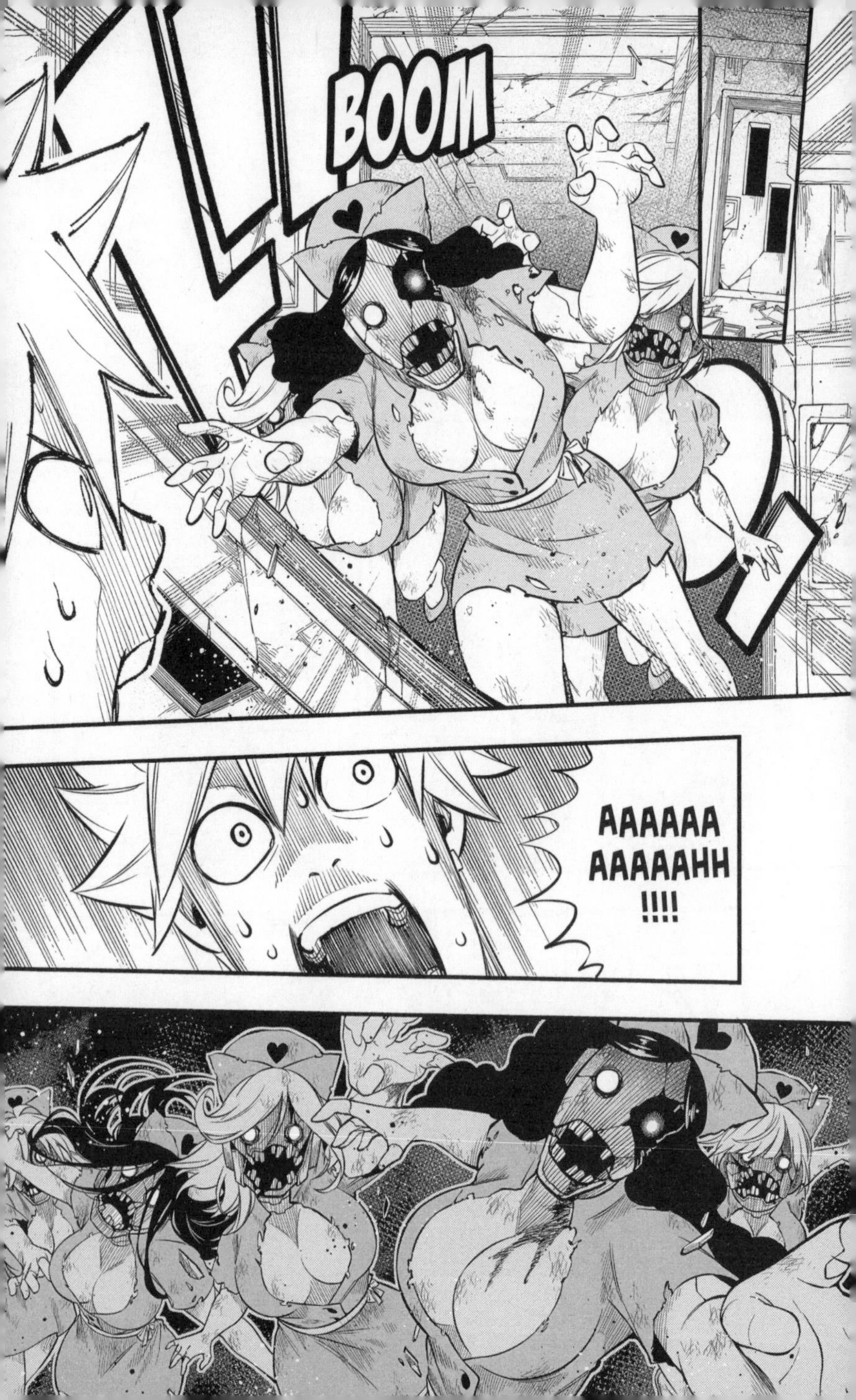
BOOM
AAAAAA AAAAAHH !!!!

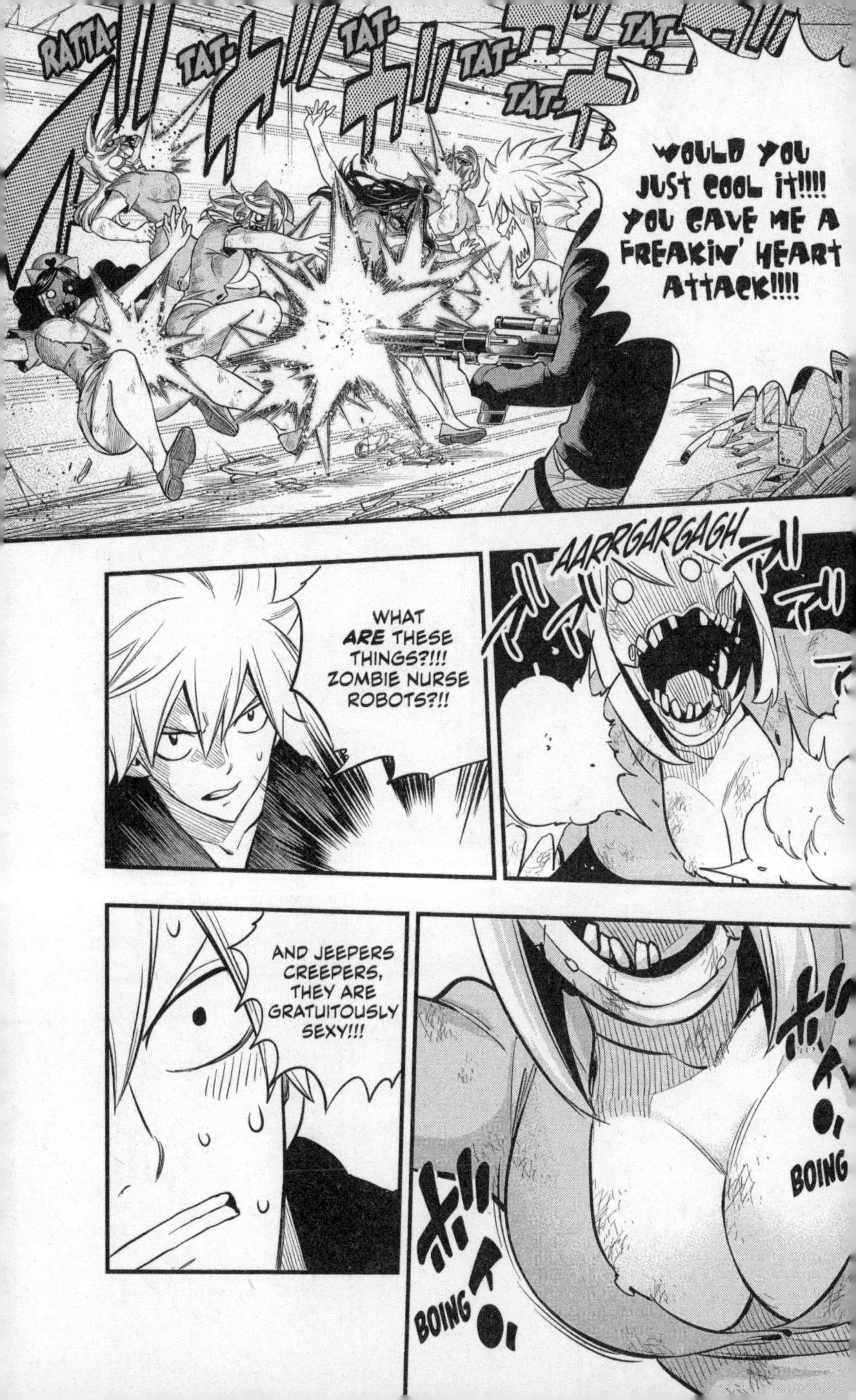
RATTA-
TAT-
TAT-
TAT-
TAT-
TAT
WOULD YOU JUST COOL IT!!!!! YOU GAVE ME A FREAKIN' HEART ATTACK!!!!
AARRGARGAGH
WHAT ARE THESE THINGS?!!! ZOMBIE NURSE ROBOTS?!!
BOING
BOING
AND JEEPERS CREEPERS, THEY ARE GRATUITOUSLY SEXY!!!

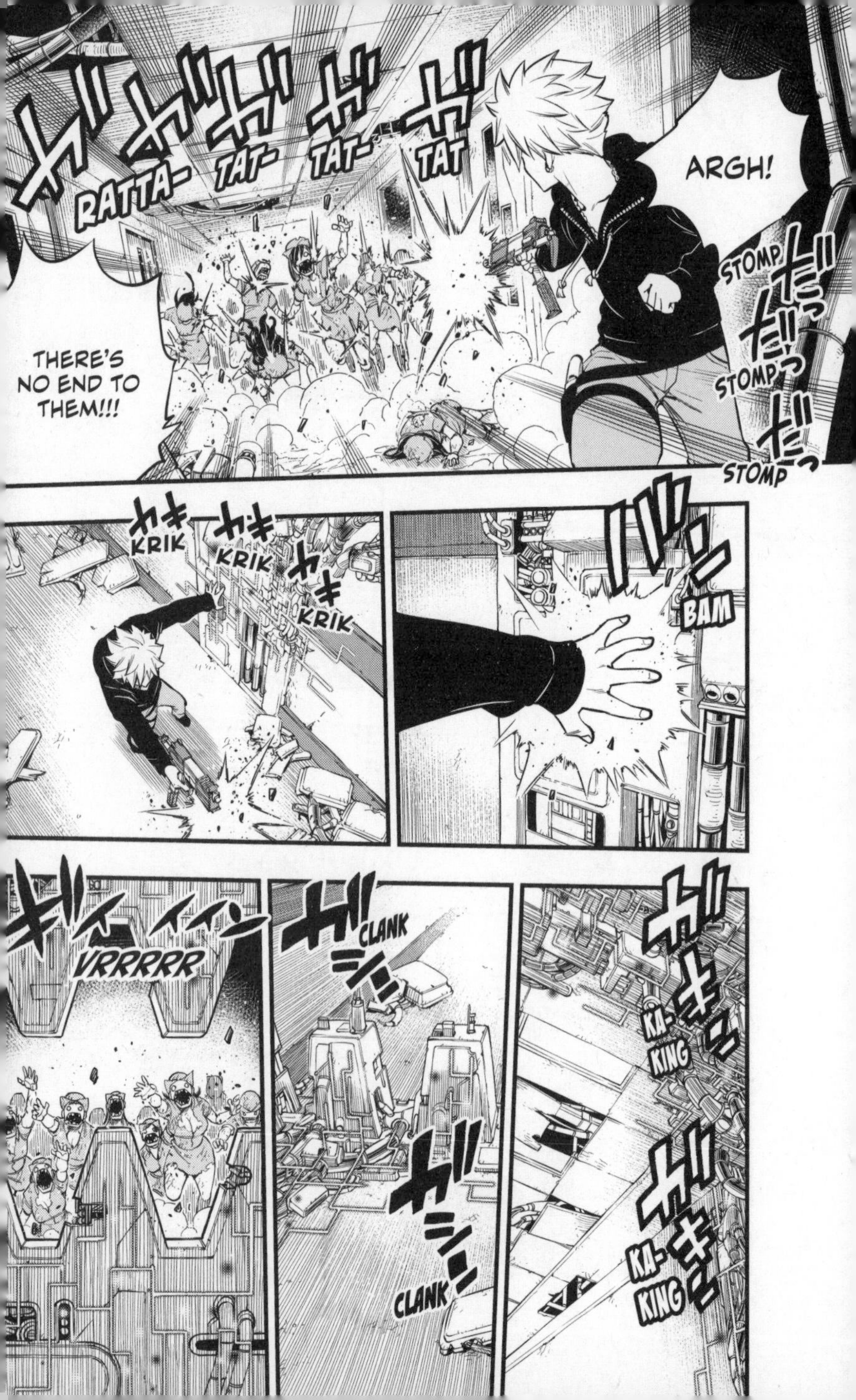
ARGH!
RATTA- TAT- TAT- TAT
THERE'S NO END TO THEM!!!
STOMP STOMP STOMP
BAM
KRIK KRIK KRIK
KA-KING KA-KING
CLANK CLANK
VRRRRR

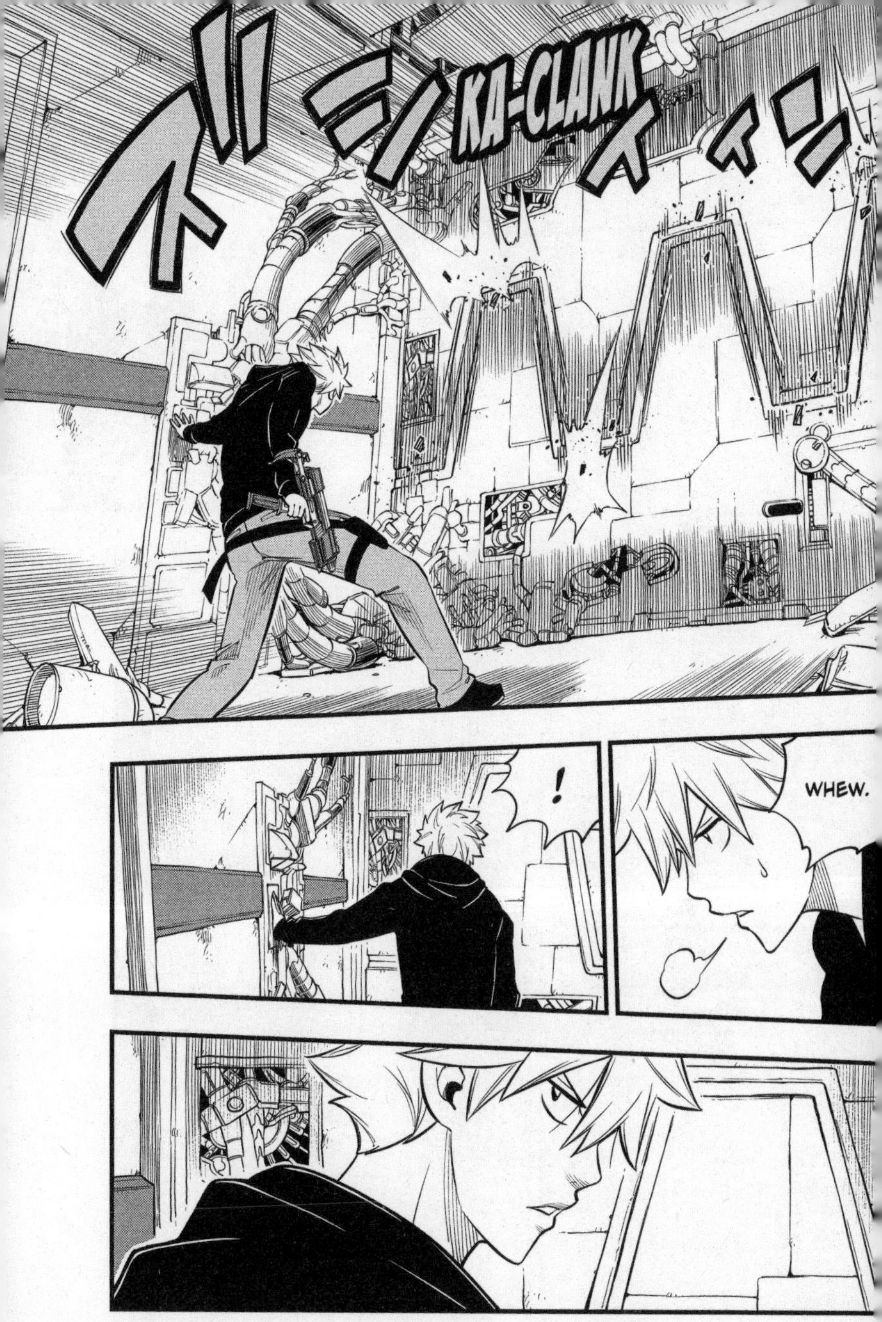
KA-CLANK
WHEW.
!

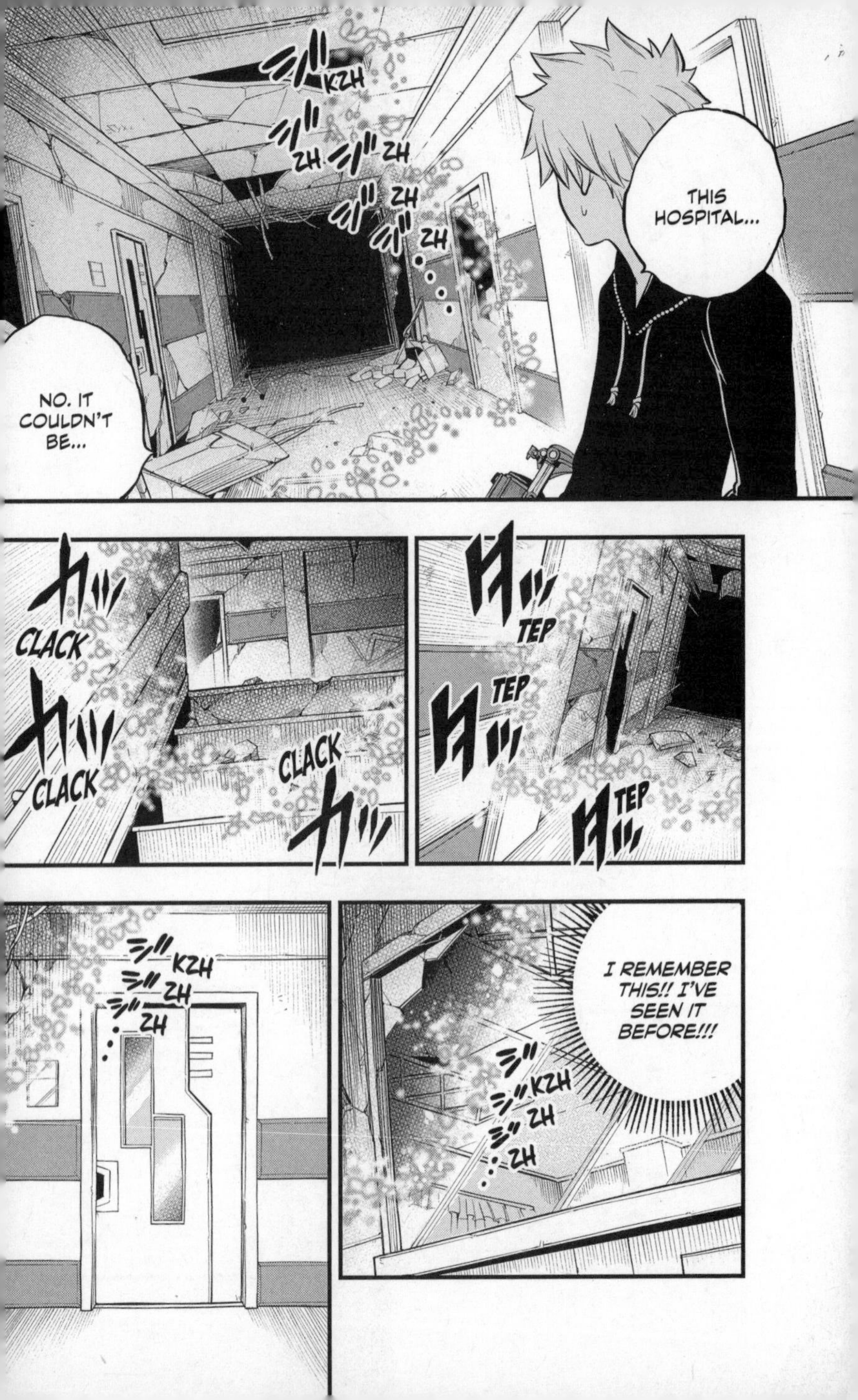
KZH
ZH
ZH
ZH
ZH
THIS HOSPITAL...
NO. IT COULDN'T BE...
TEP
TEP
TEP
CLACK
CLACK
CLACK
I REMEMBER THIS!! I'VE SEEN IT BEFORE!!!
KZH
ZH
ZH
KZH
ZH
ZH

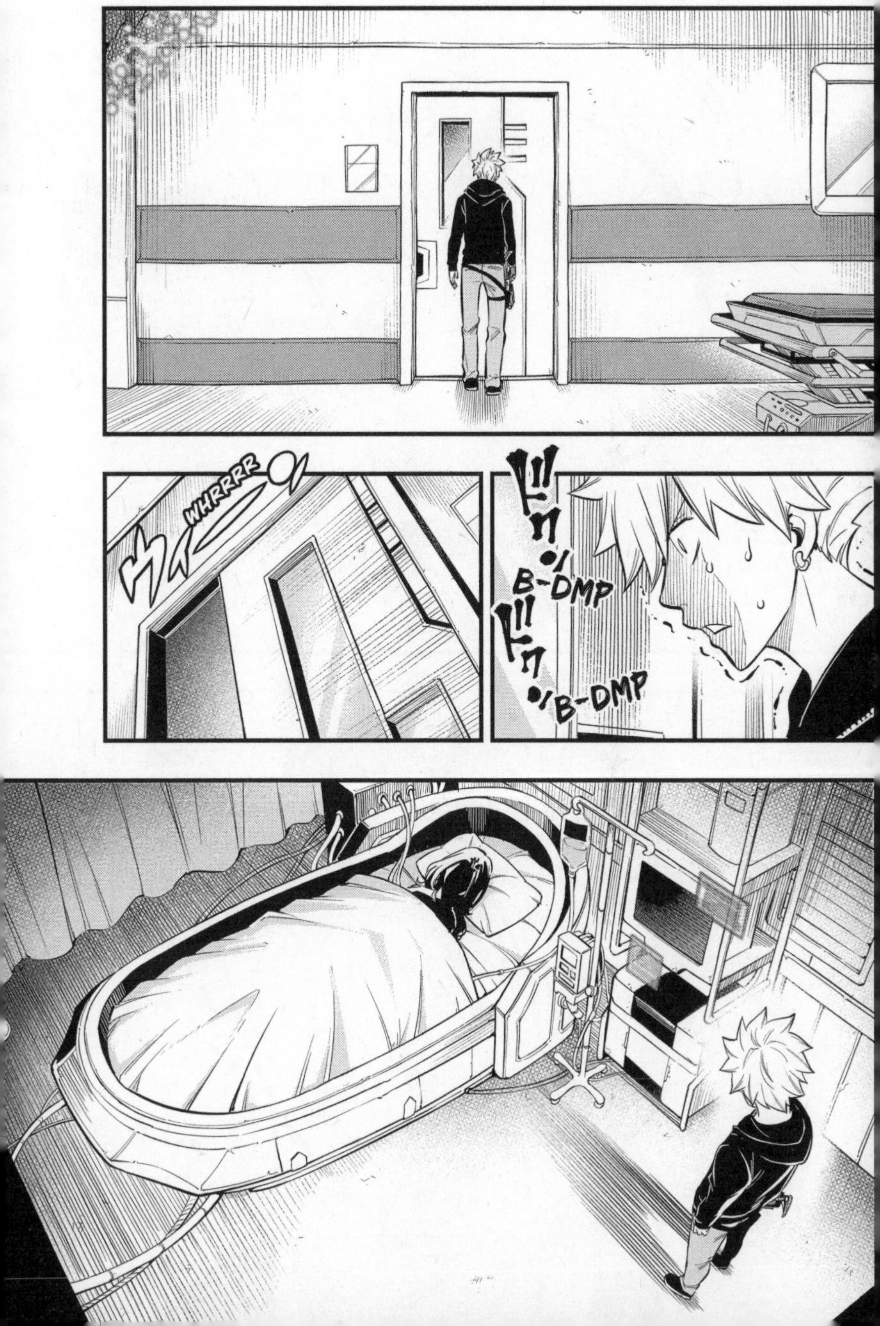
B-DMP
B-DMP
WHRRRR

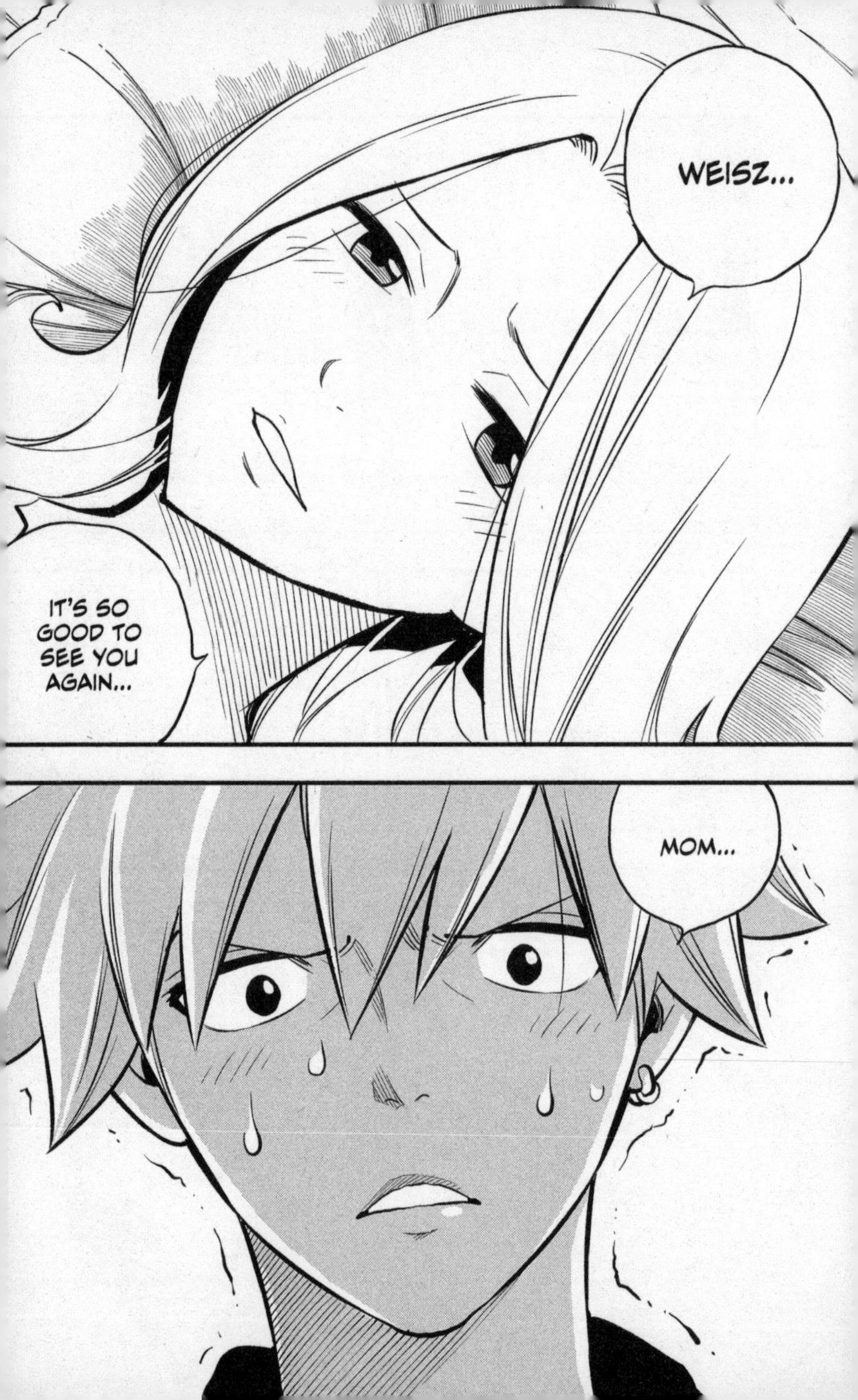
WEISZ...
IT'S SO GOOD TO SEE YOU AGAIN...
MOM...

EDENSZERO

CHAPTER 192: WEISZ VS. KILLER

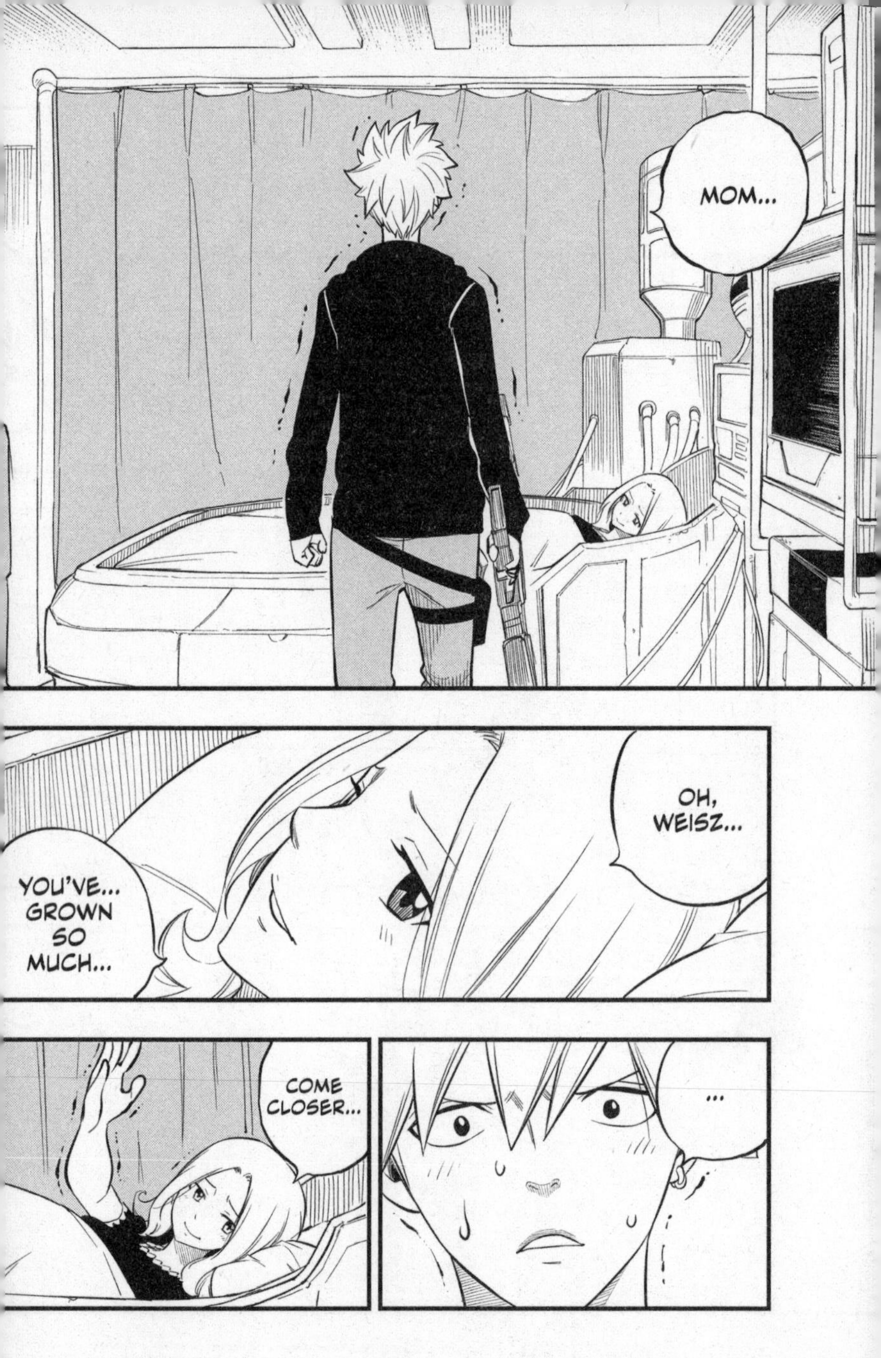
MOM...
OH, WEISZ...
YOU'VE... GROWN SO MUCH...
...
COME CLOSER...

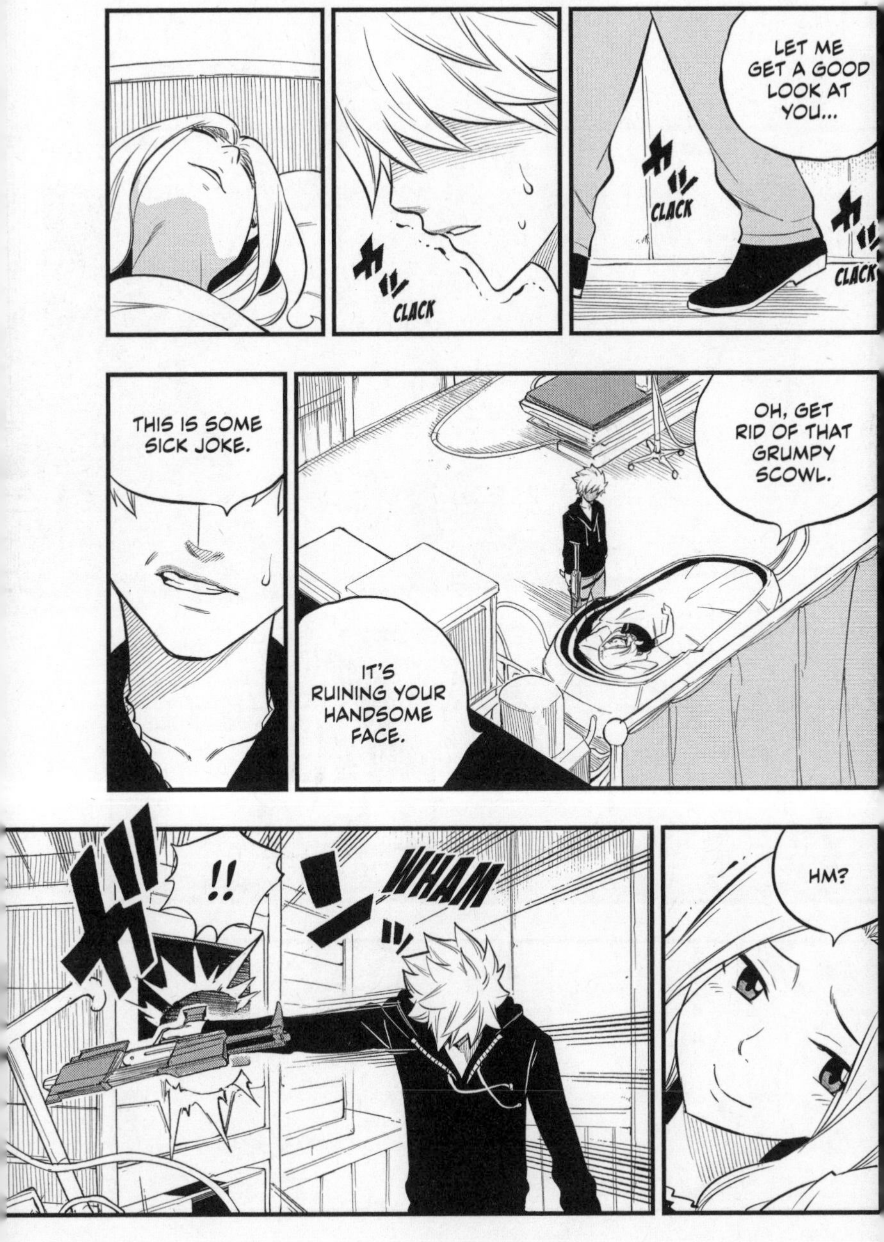
LET ME GET A GOOD LOOK AT YOU...
CLACK
CLACK
CLACK
OH, GET RID OF THAT GRUMPY SCOWL.
IT'S RUINING YOUR HANDSOME FACE.
THIS IS SOME SICK JOKE.
HM?
WHAM
!!

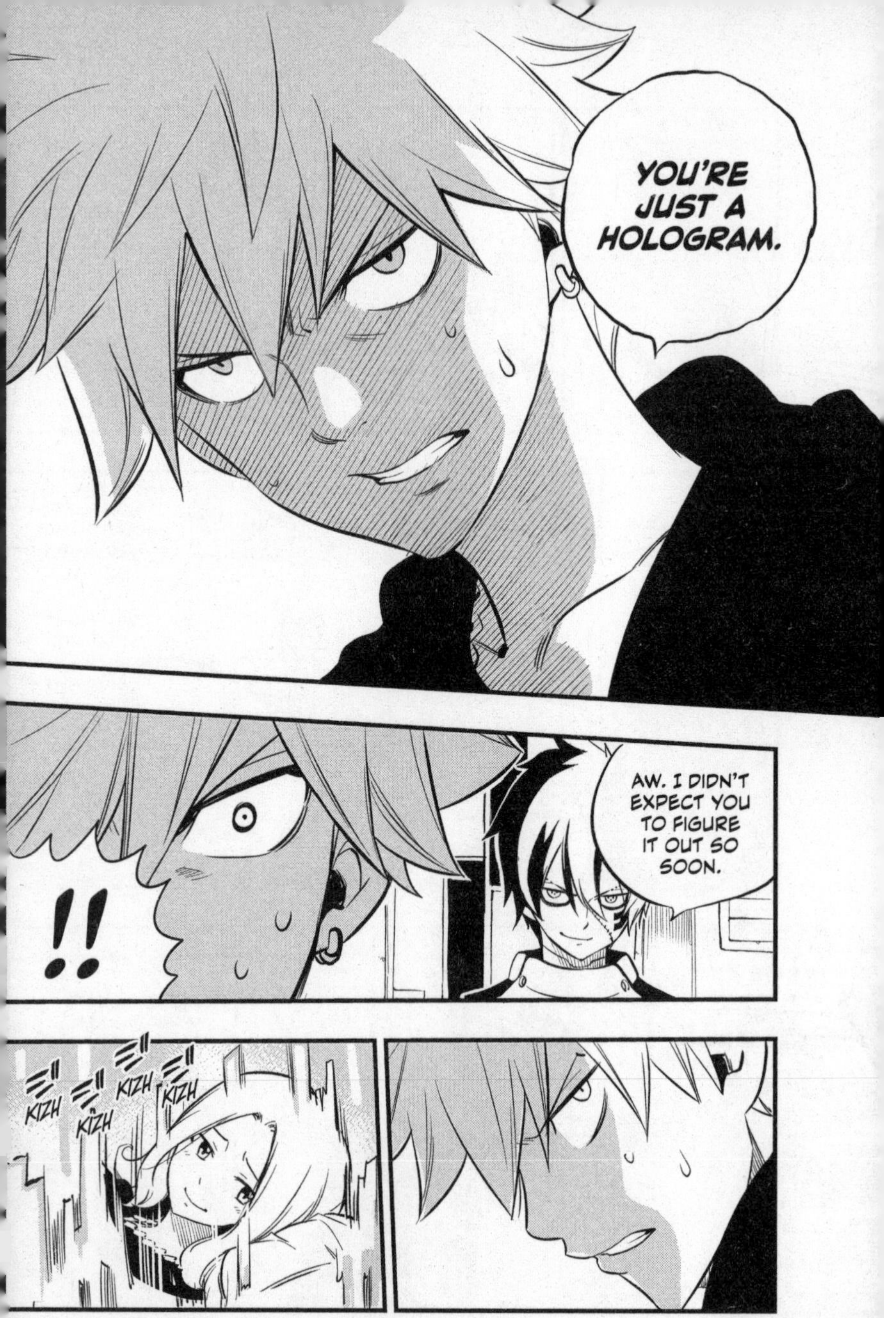
YOU'RE JUST A HOLOGRAM.
AW. I DIDN'T EXPECT YOU TO FIGURE IT OUT SO SOON.
!!
KIZH
KIZH
KIZH
KIZH

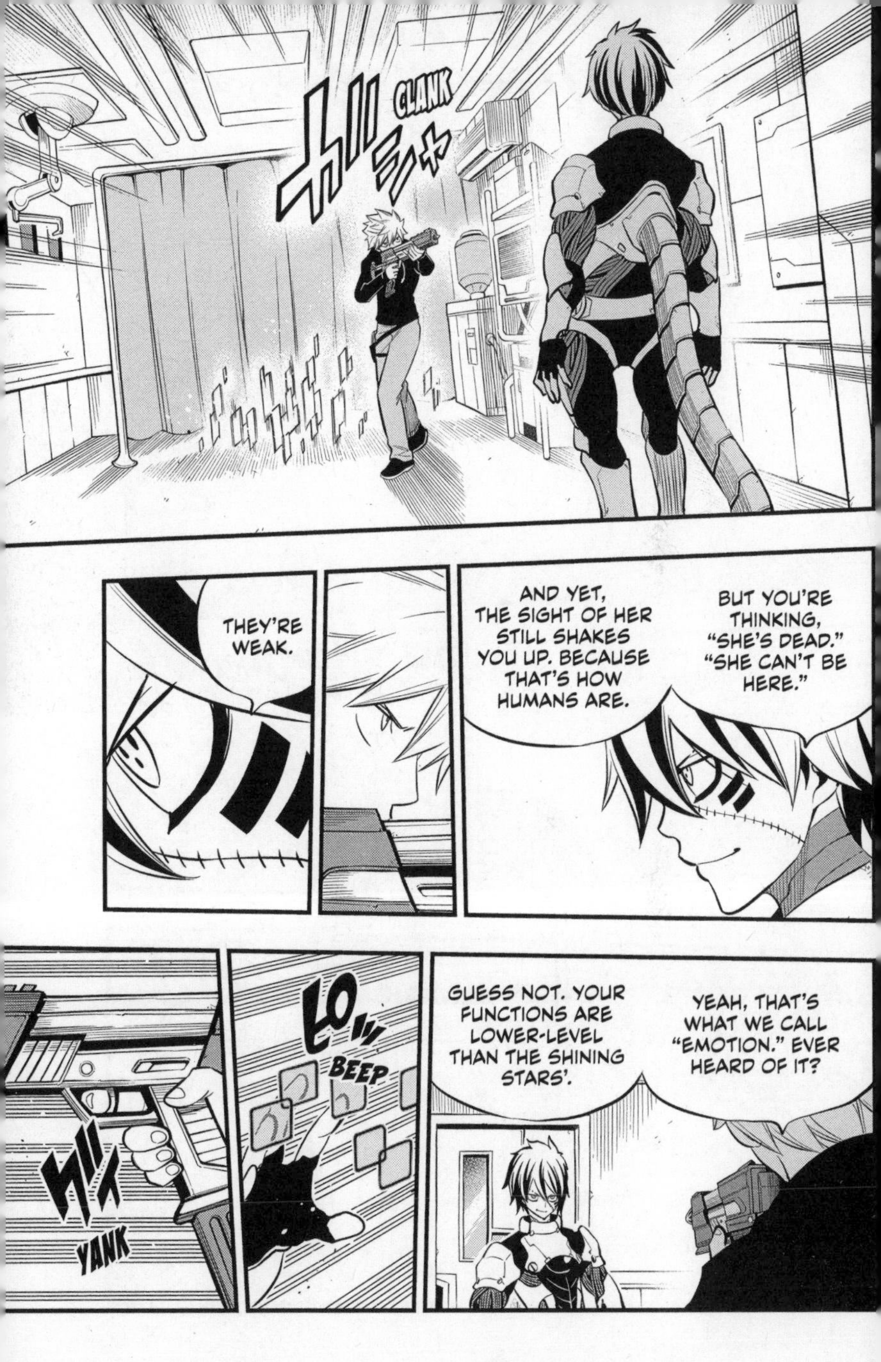
CLANK
BUT YOU'RE THINKING, "SHE'S DEAD." "SHE CAN'T BE HERE."
AND YET, THE SIGHT OF HER STILL SHAKES YOU UP. BECAUSE THAT'S HOW HUMANS ARE.
THEY'RE WEAK.
YEAH, THAT'S WHAT WE CALL "EMOTION." EVER HEARD OF IT?
GUESS NOT. YOUR FUNCTIONS ARE LOWER-LEVEL THAN THE SHINING STARS'.
BEEP
YANK

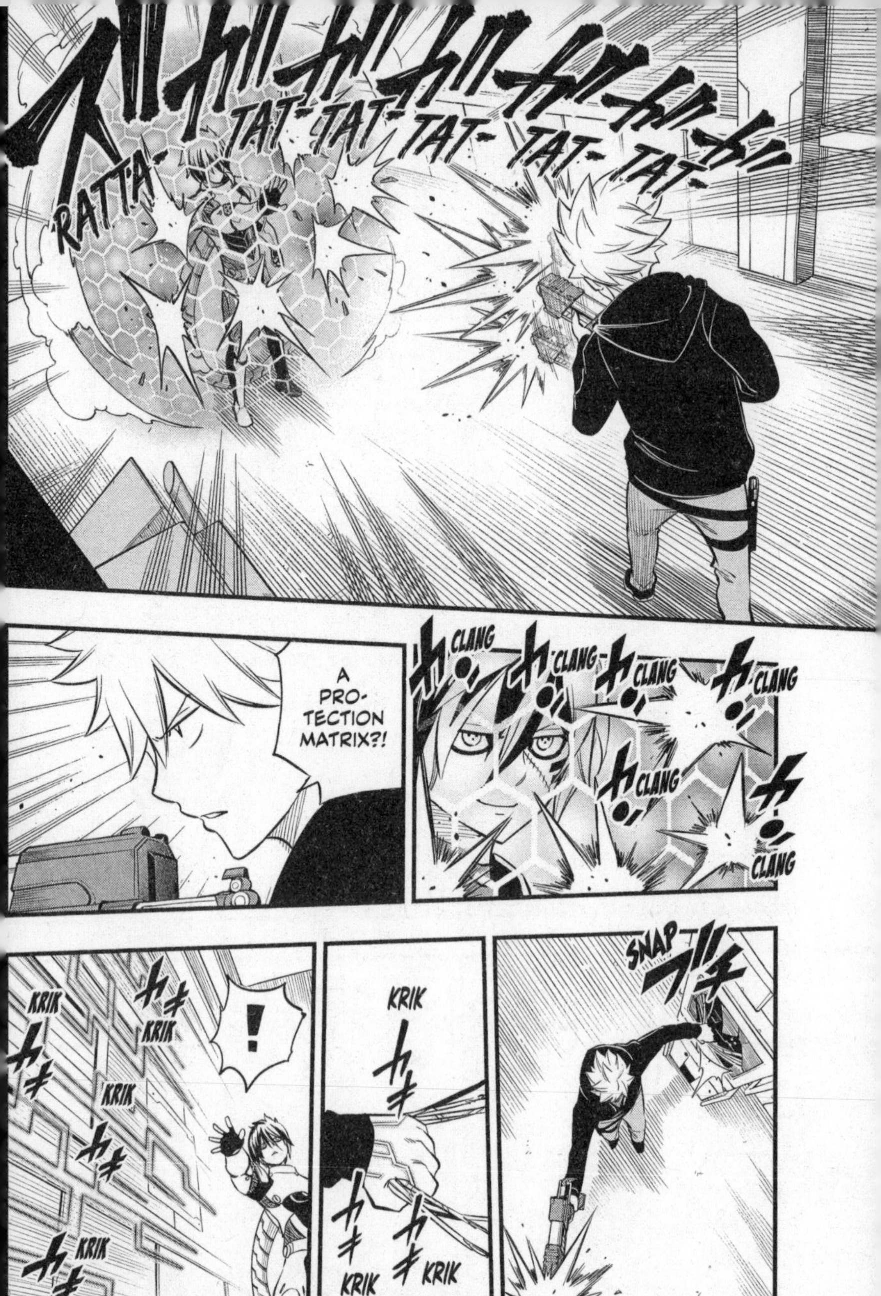
RATTA-TAT-TAT-TAT-TAT-TAT
CLANG
CLANG
CLANG
CLANG
CLANG
CLANG
A PROTECTION MATRIX?!
SNAP
KRIK
KRIK
KRIK
KRIK
!
KRIK
KRIK
KRIK

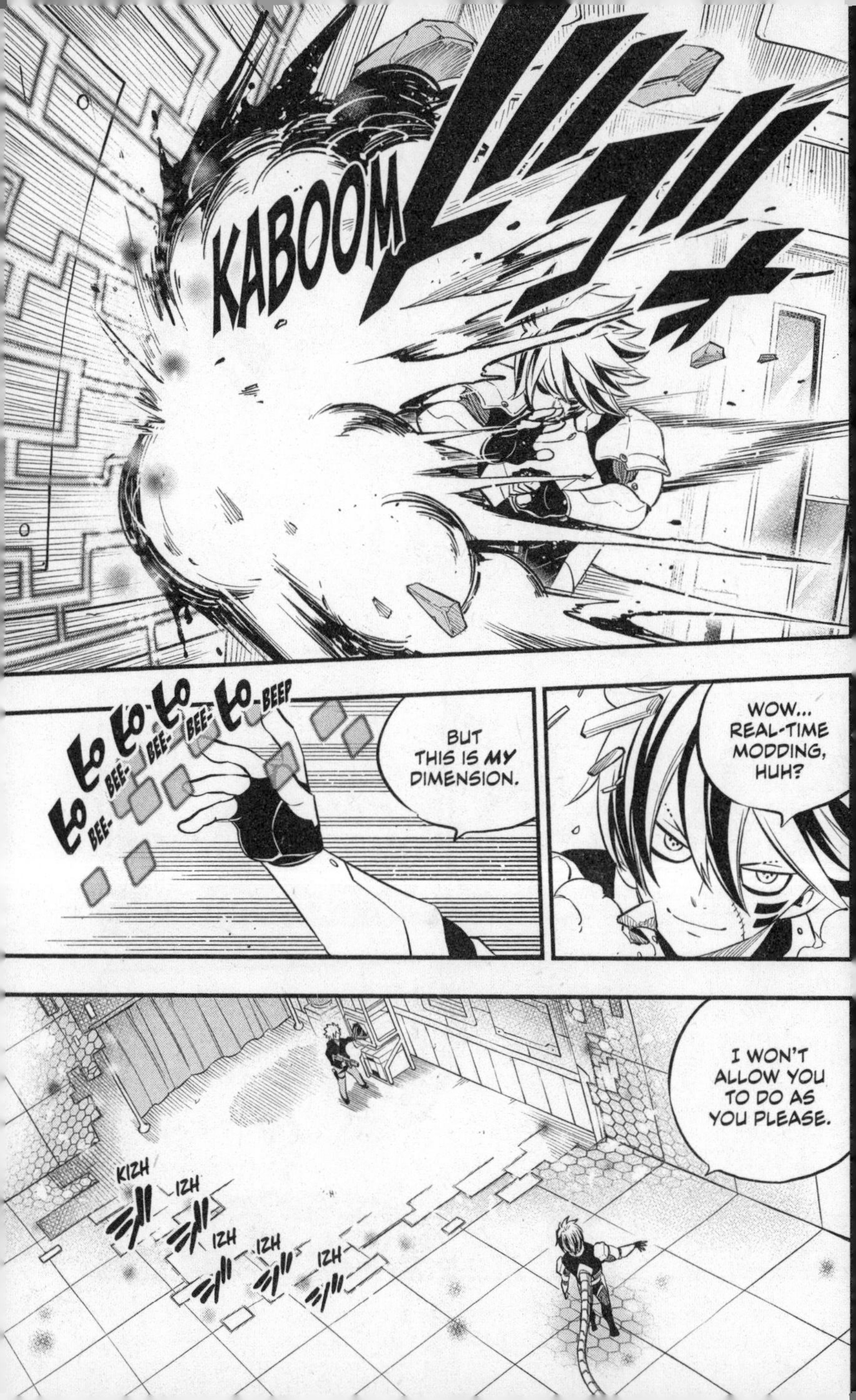
KABOOM
WOW... REAL-TIME MODDING, HUH?
BUT THIS IS MY DIMENSION.
BEE- BEE- BEE- BEE- BEEP
I WON'T ALLOW YOU TO DO AS YOU PLEASE.
KIZH
IZH
IZH
IZH
IZH

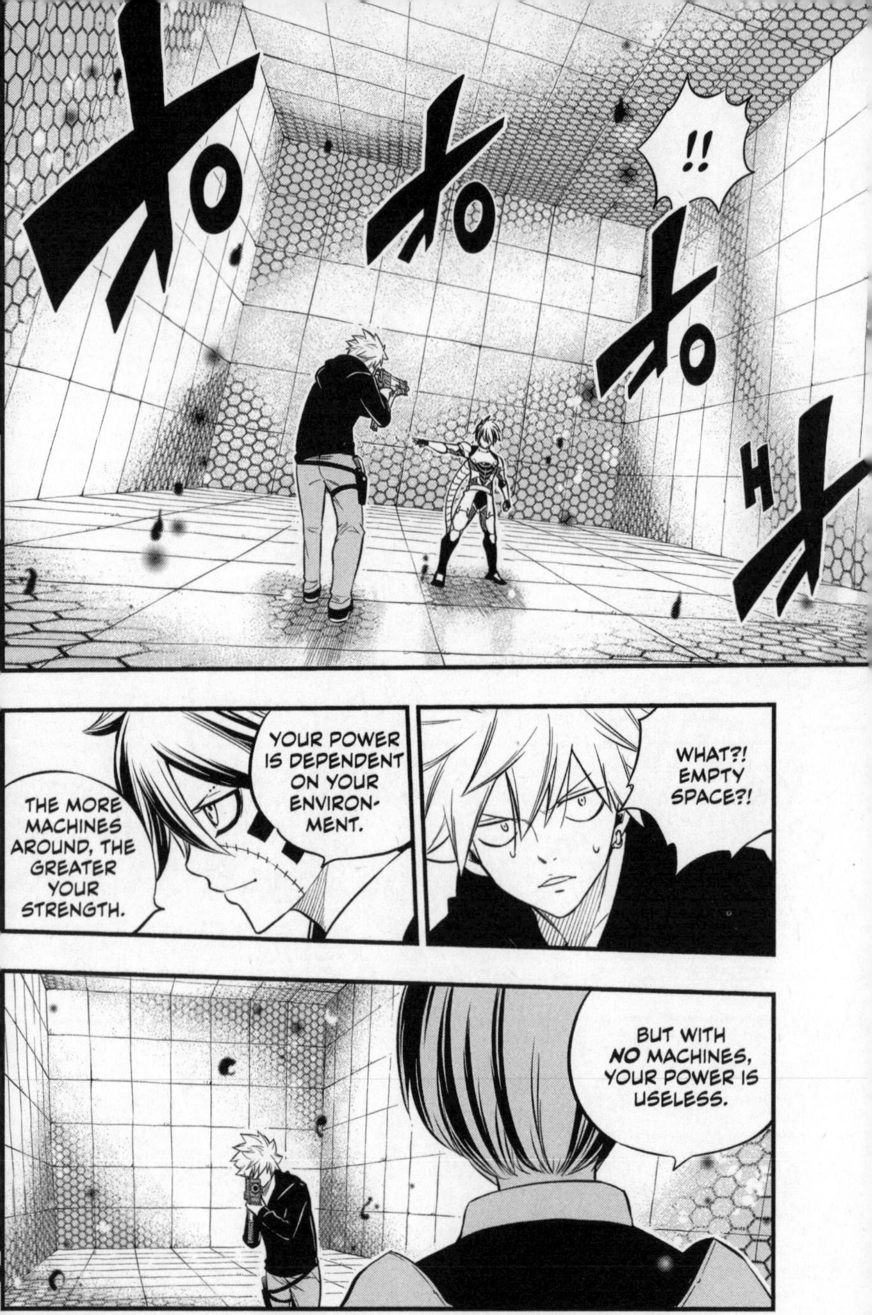
!!
WHAT?! EMPTY SPACE?!
YOUR POWER IS DEPENDENT ON YOUR ENVIRON-MENT.
THE MORE MACHINES AROUND, THE GREATER YOUR STRENGTH.
BUT WITH *NO* MACHINES, YOUR POWER IS USELESS.

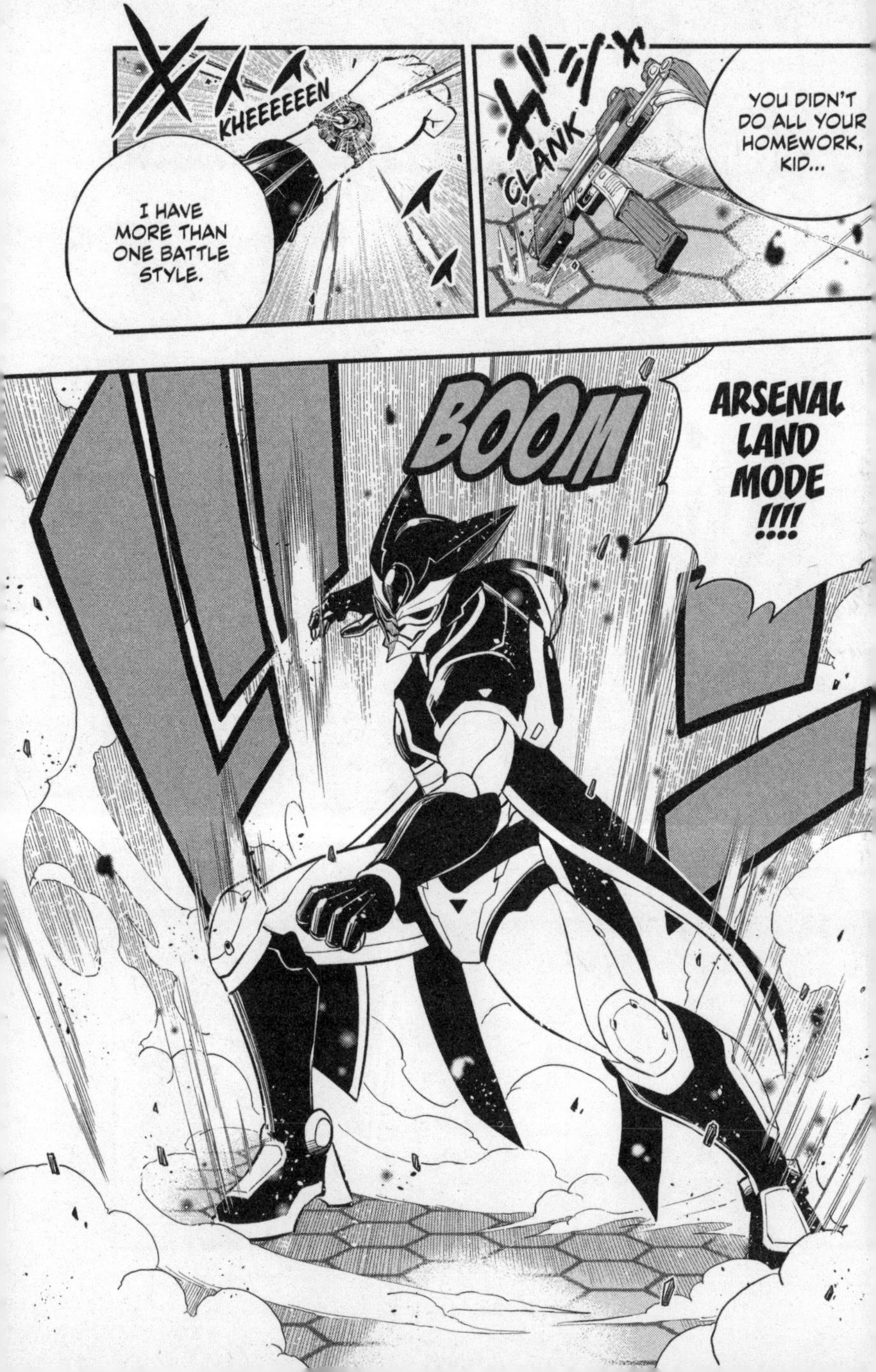
CLANK
YOU DIDN'T DO ALL YOUR HOMEWORK, KID...
KHEEEEEEN
I HAVE MORE THAN ONE BATTLE STYLE.
ARSENAL LAND MODE!!!!
BOOM

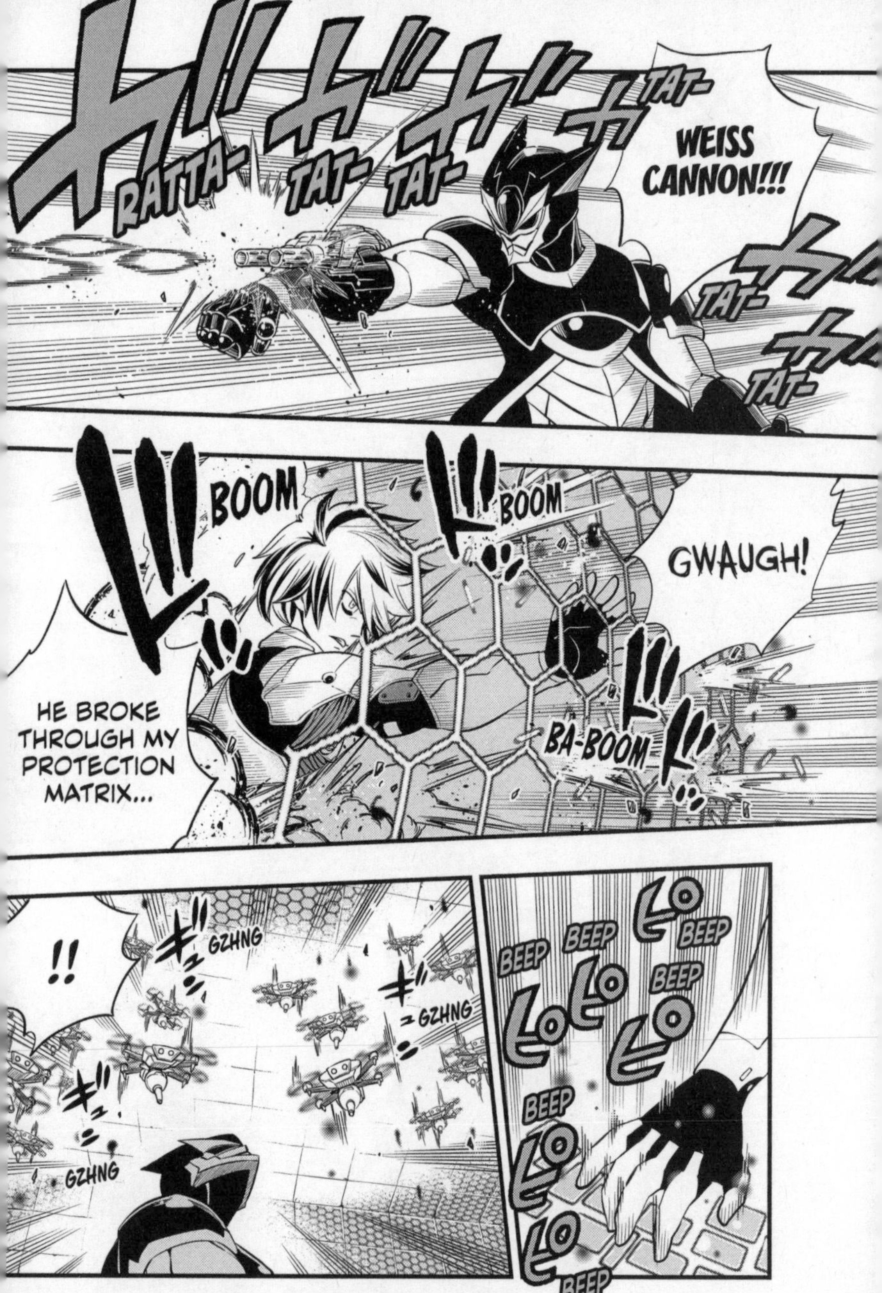

WEISS CANNON!!!
RATTA-TAT-TAT-TAT-
TAT-
TAT-
GWAUGH!
BOOM
BOOM
BA-BOOM
HE BROKE THROUGH MY PROTECTION MATRIX...
BEEP BEEP BEEP BEEP BEEP BEEP
!!
GZHNG
GZHNG
GZHNG

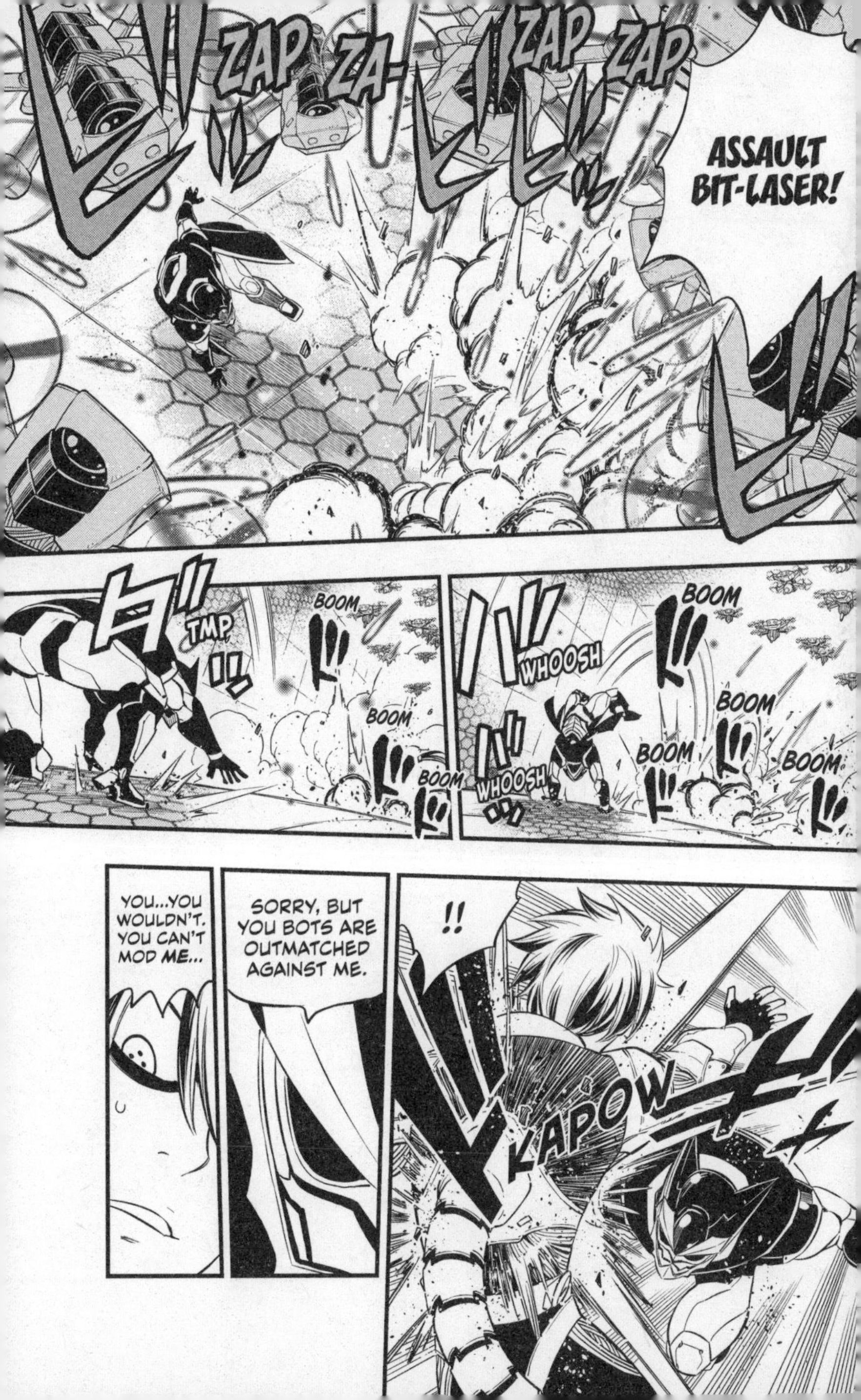
ASSAULT BIT-LASER!
ZAP
ZAP
ZA-
ZAP
BOOM
WHOOSH
BOOM
BOOM
BOOM
WHOOSH
BOOM
TMP
BOOM
BOOM
!!
KAPOW
SORRY, BUT YOU BOTS ARE OUTMATCHED AGAINST ME.
YOU...YOU WOULDN'T. YOU CAN'T MOD ME...

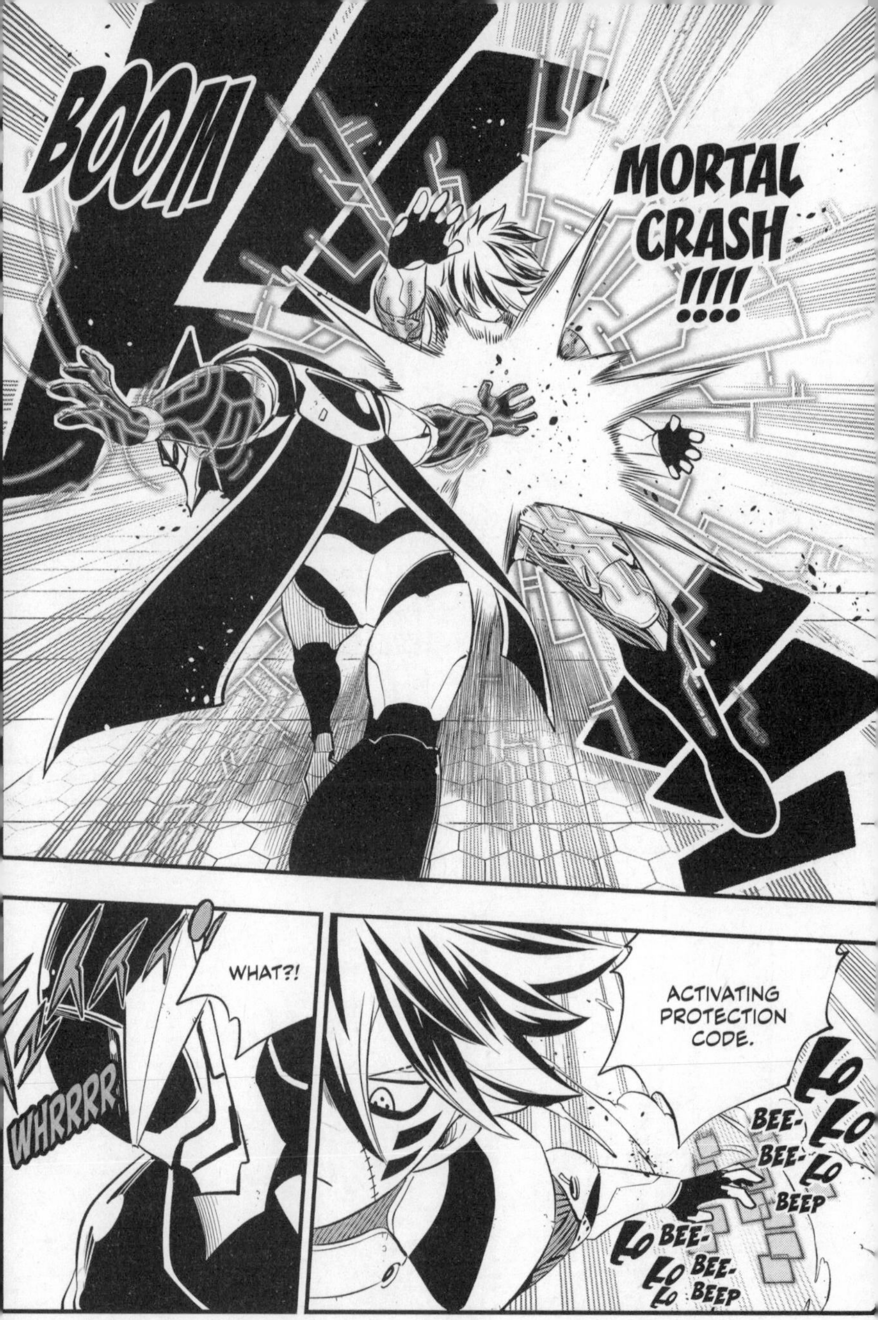
MORTAL CRASH!!!!
BOOM
ACTIVATING PROTECTION CODE.
BEE- BEE- BEEP
BEE- BEE- BEEP
WHAT?!
WHRRRR

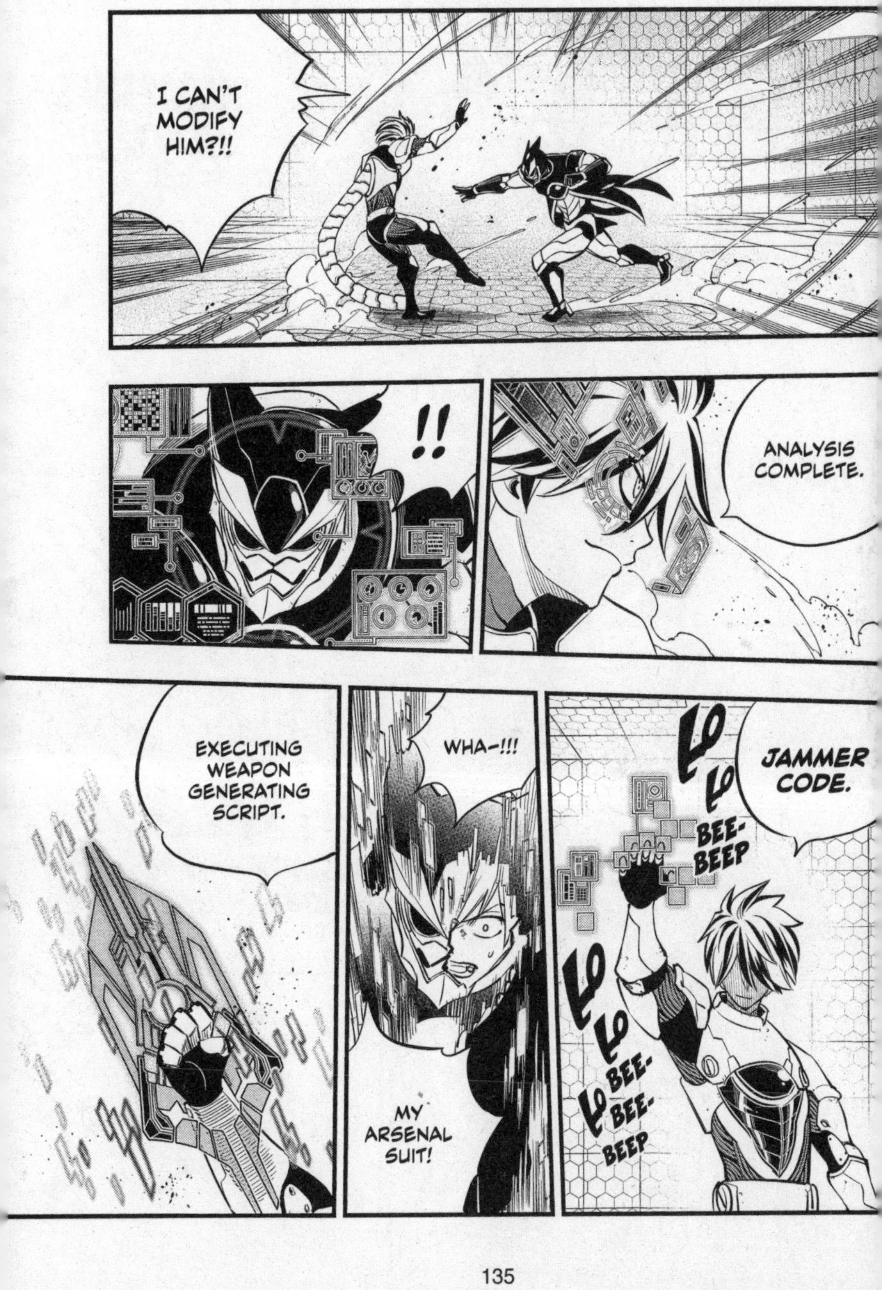
I CAN'T MODIFY HIM?!!
ANALYSIS COMPLETE.
!!
JAMMER CODE.
BEE-BEEP
BEE-BEE-BEEP
WHA-!!!
MY ARSENAL SUIT!
EXECUTING WEAPON GENERATING SCRIPT.

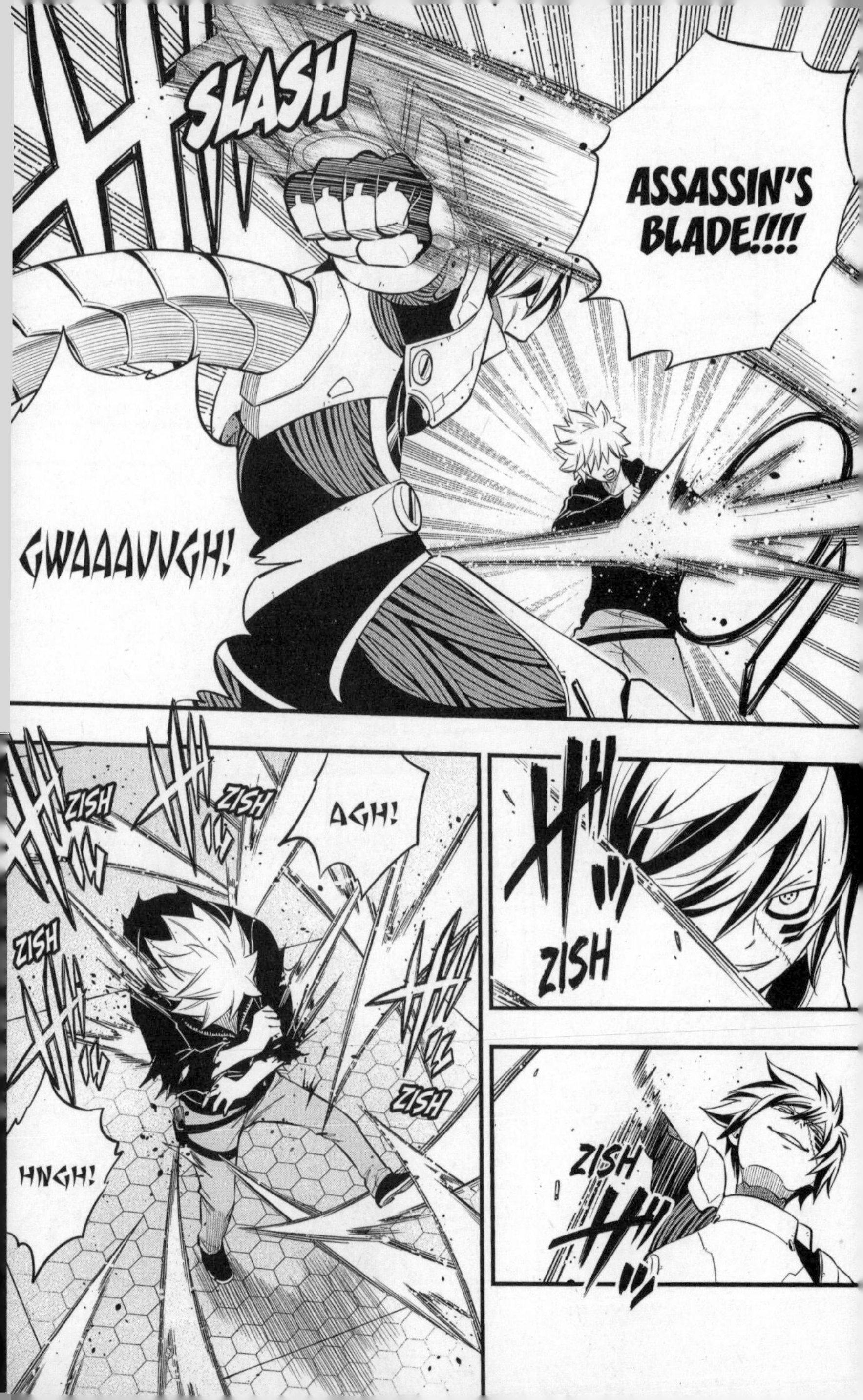
ASSASSIN'S BLADE!!!!
SLASH
GWAAAUUGH!
ZISH
ZISH
AGH!
ZISH
ZISH
ZISH
ZISH
HNGH!

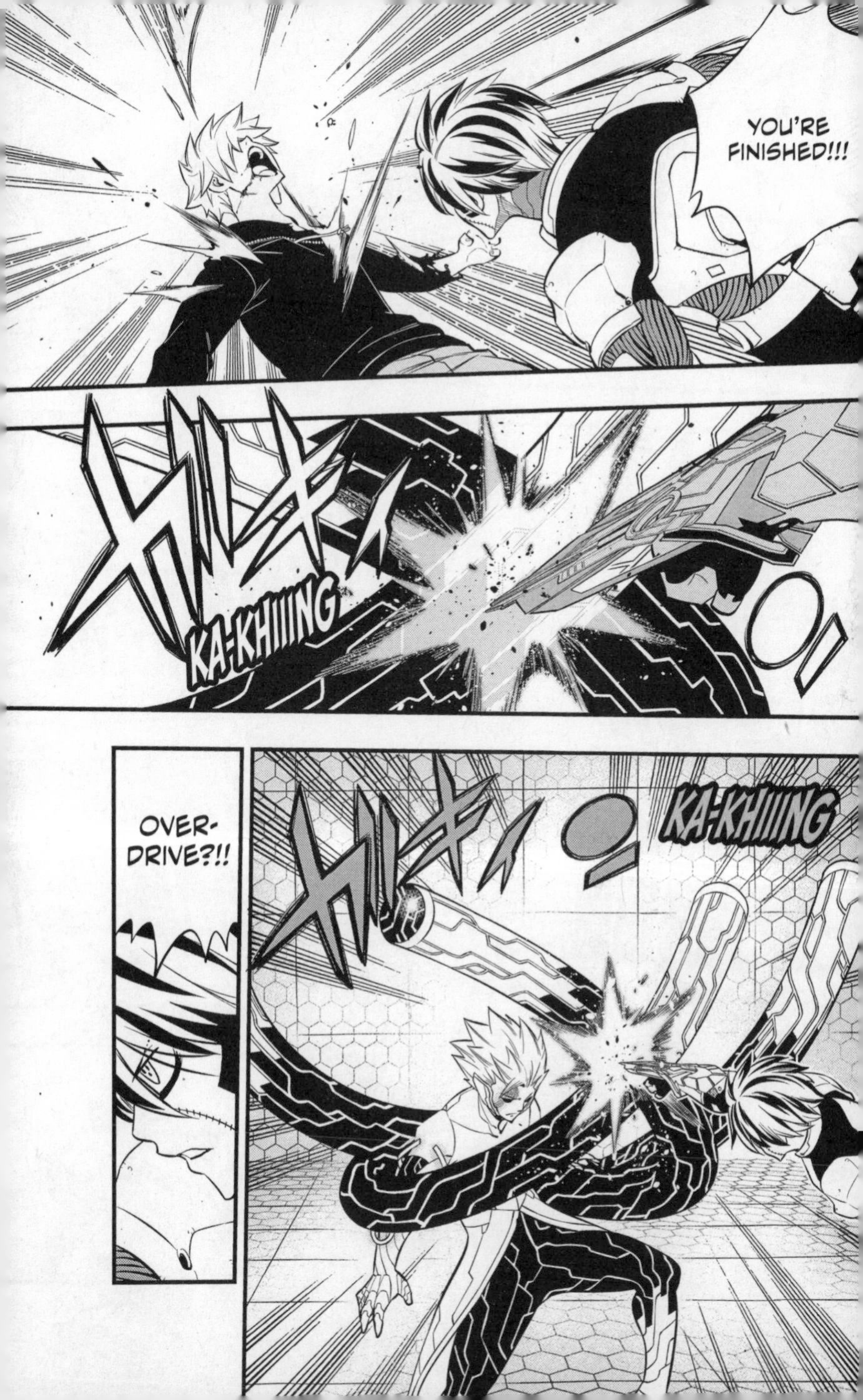
YOU'RE FINISHED!!!
KA-KHIIIING
KA-KHIIIING
OVER-DRIVE?!!

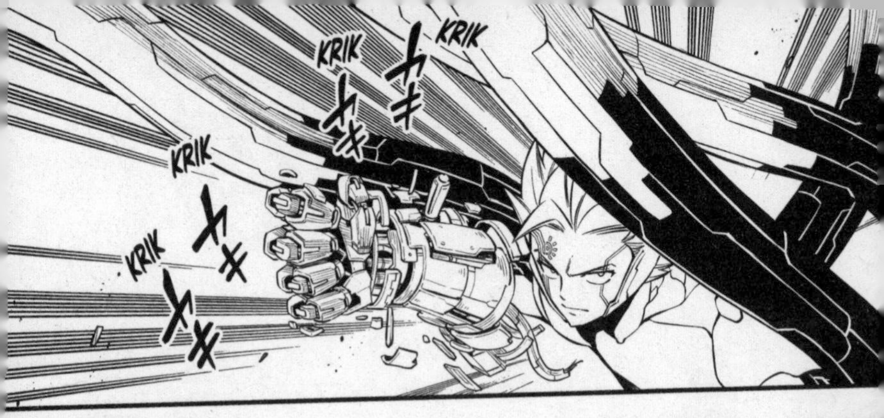
KRIK
KRIK
KRIK
KRIK
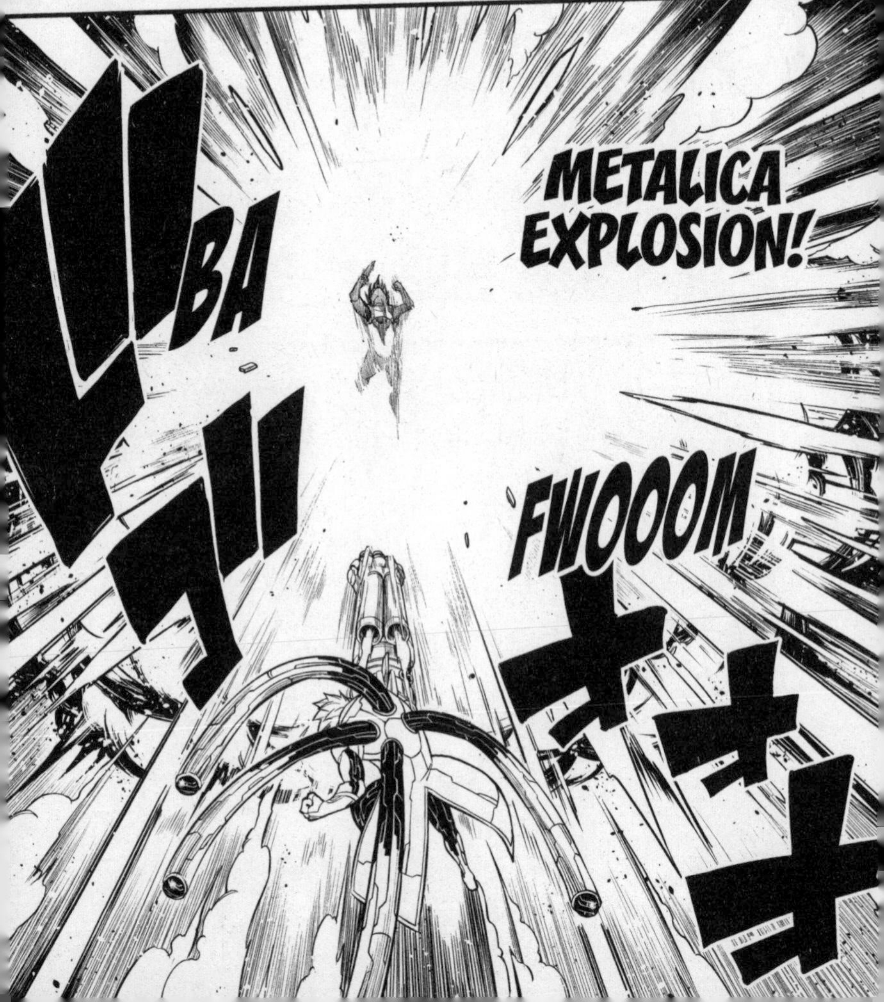
METALICA EXPLOSION!
FWOOOM
BA

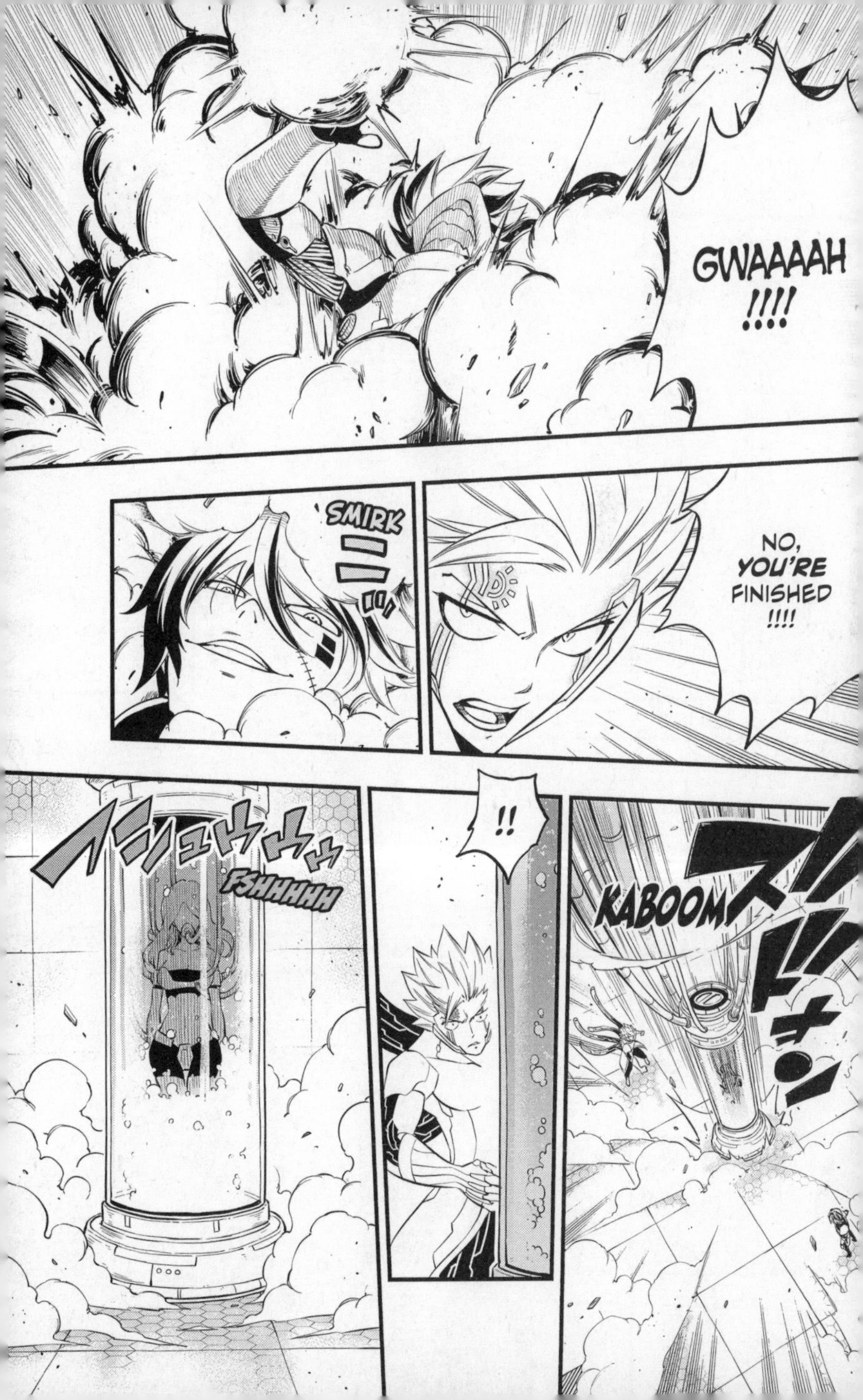
GWAAAAH!!!!
NO, YOU'RE FINISHED!!!!
SMIRK
KABOOM
!!
FSHHHHH

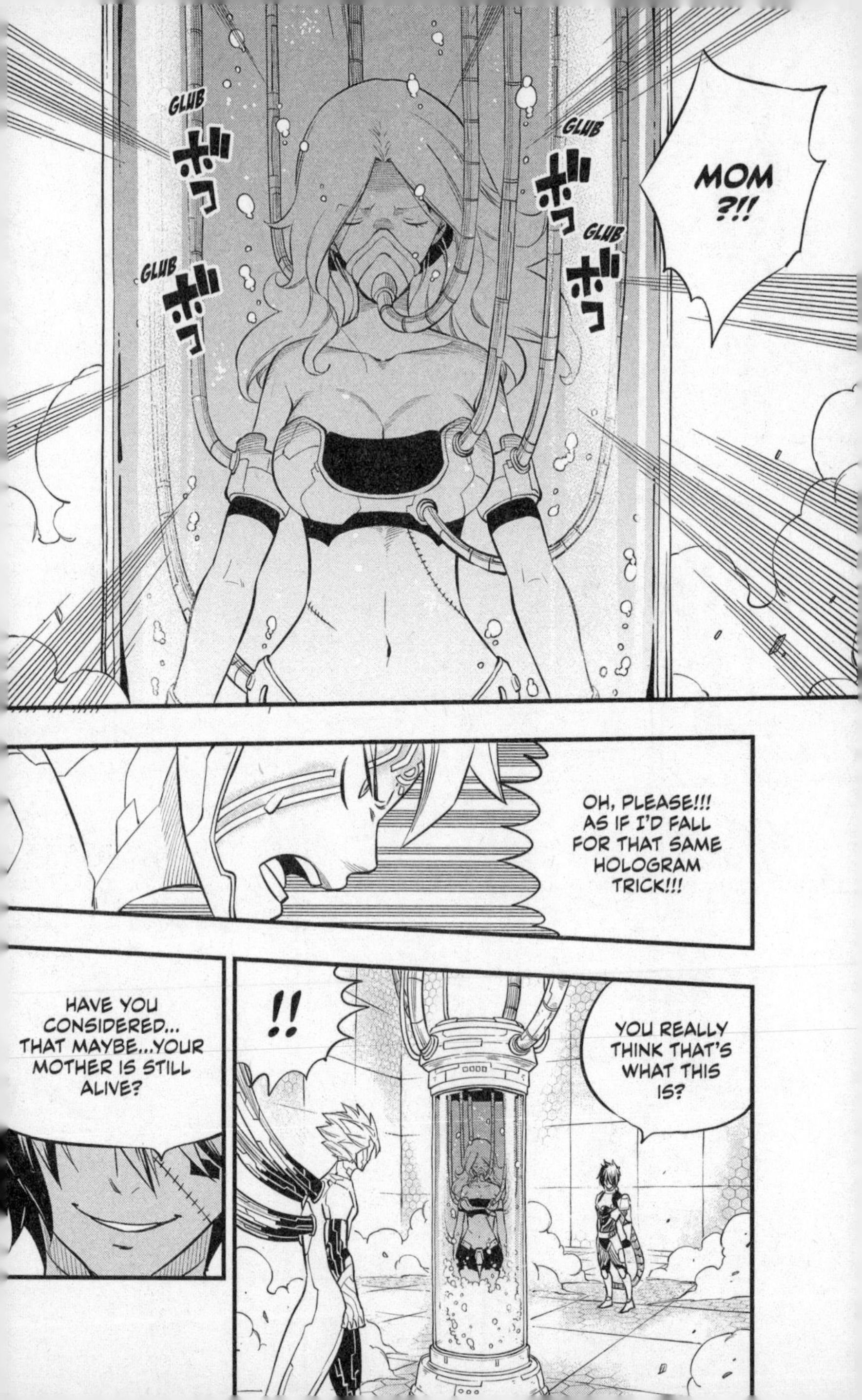
MOM ?!!
GLUB
ボッ
GLUB
ボッ
GLUB
ボッ
GLUB
ボッ
OH, PLEASE!!! AS IF I'D FALL FOR THAT SAME HOLOGRAM TRICK!!!
YOU REALLY THINK THAT'S WHAT THIS IS?
!!
HAVE YOU CONSIDERED... THAT MAYBE...YOUR MOTHER IS STILL ALIVE?

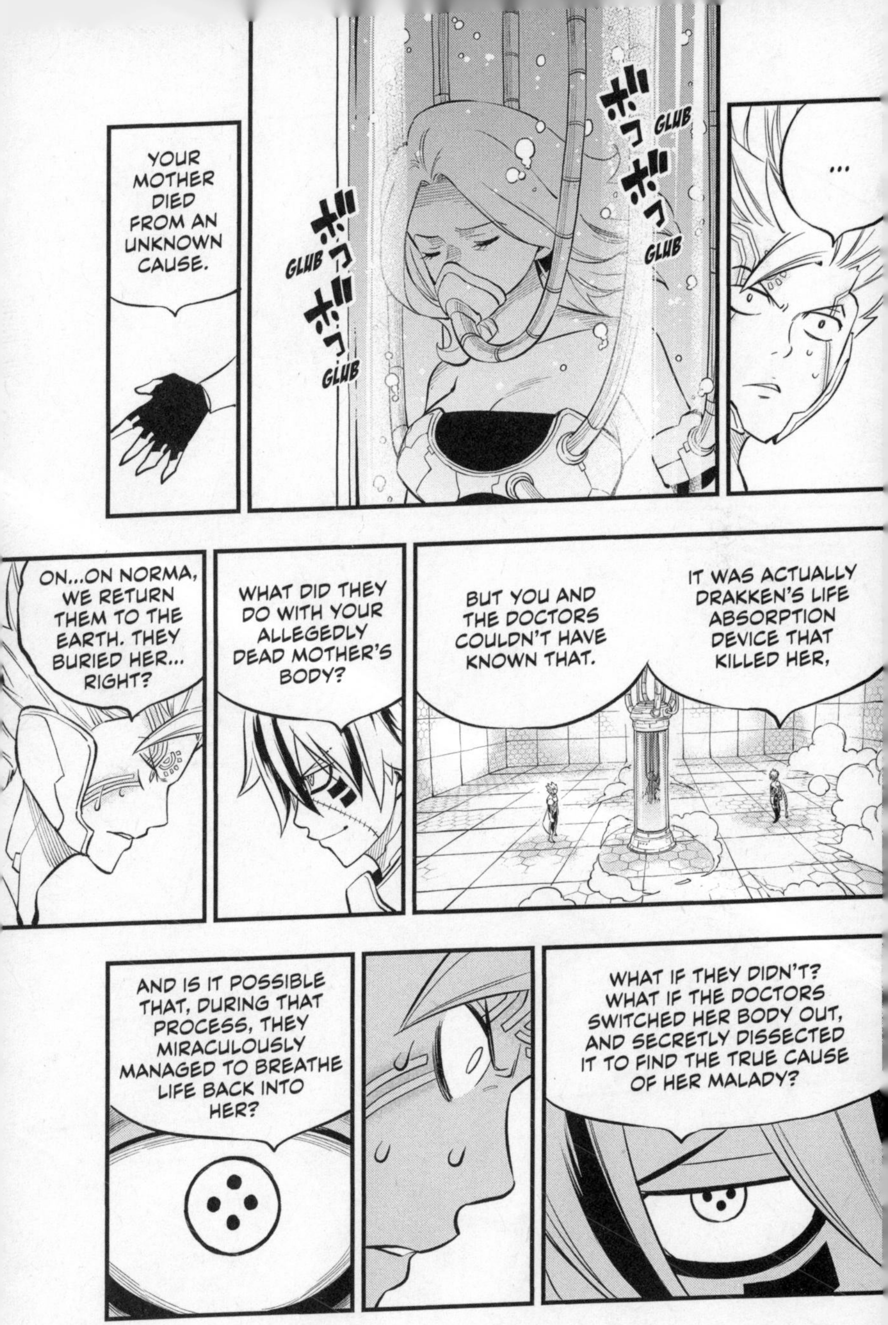
...
ボコ
GLUB
ボコ
GLUB
ボコ
GLUB
ボコ
GLUB
YOUR MOTHER DIED FROM AN UNKNOWN CAUSE.
IT WAS ACTUALLY DRAKKEN'S LIFE ABSORPTION DEVICE THAT KILLED HER,
BUT YOU AND THE DOCTORS COULDN'T HAVE KNOWN THAT.
WHAT DID THEY DO WITH YOUR ALLEGEDLY DEAD MOTHER'S BODY?
ON...ON NORMA, WE RETURN THEM TO THE EARTH. THEY BURIED HER... RIGHT?
WHAT IF THEY DIDN'T? WHAT IF THE DOCTORS SWITCHED HER BODY OUT, AND SECRETLY DISSECTED IT TO FIND THE TRUE CAUSE OF HER MALADY?
AND IS IT POSSIBLE THAT, DURING THAT PROCESS, THEY MIRACULOUSLY MANAGED TO BREATHE LIFE BACK INTO HER?

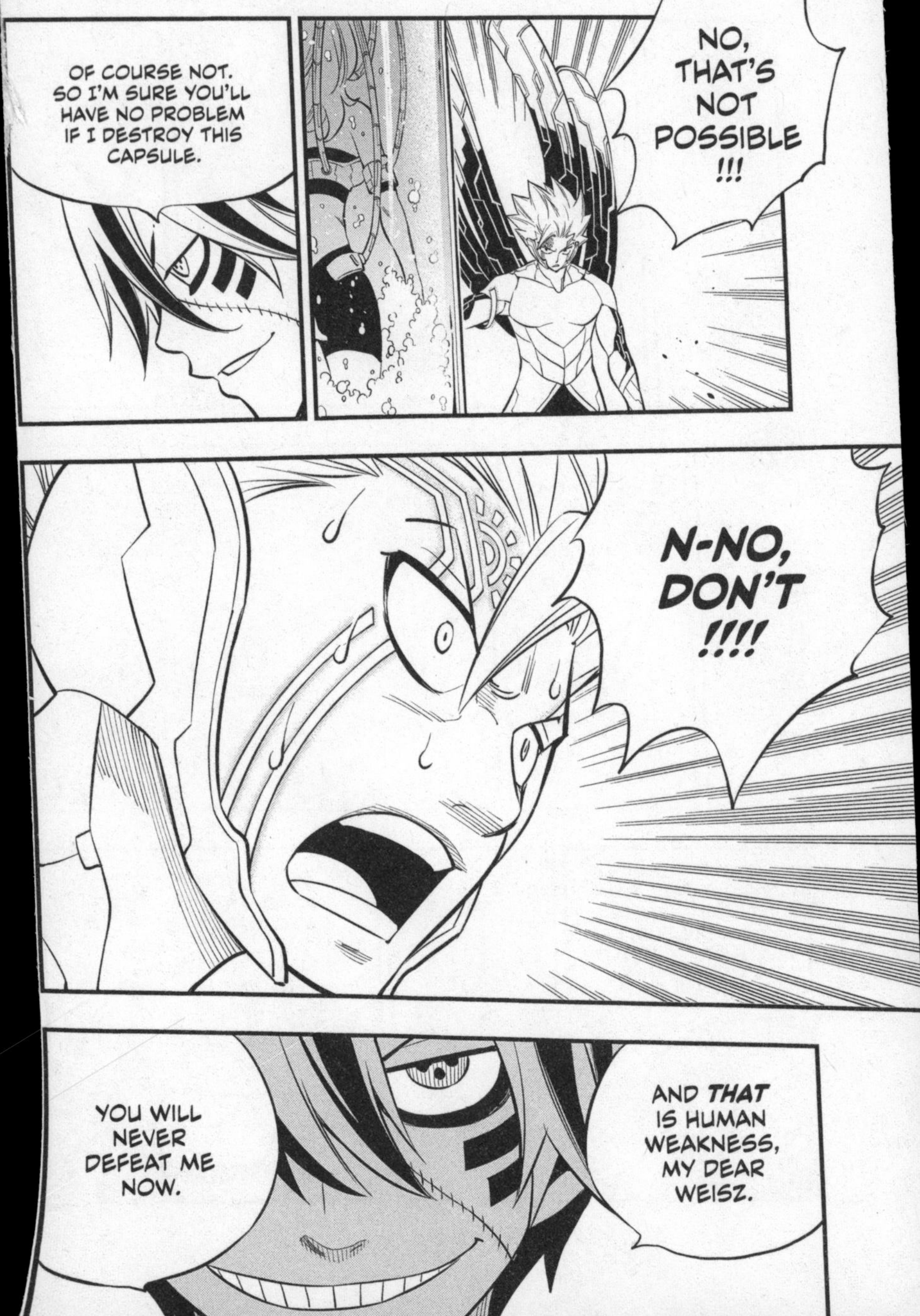
NO, THAT'S NOT POSSIBLE!!!
OF COURSE NOT. SO I'M SURE YOU'LL HAVE NO PROBLEM IF I DESTROY THIS CAPSULE.
N-NO, DON'T!!!!
AND *THAT* IS HUMAN WEAKNESS, MY DEAR WEISZ.
YOU WILL NEVER DEFEAT ME NOW.

EDENSZERO

CHAPTER 193: A GOOD BOY

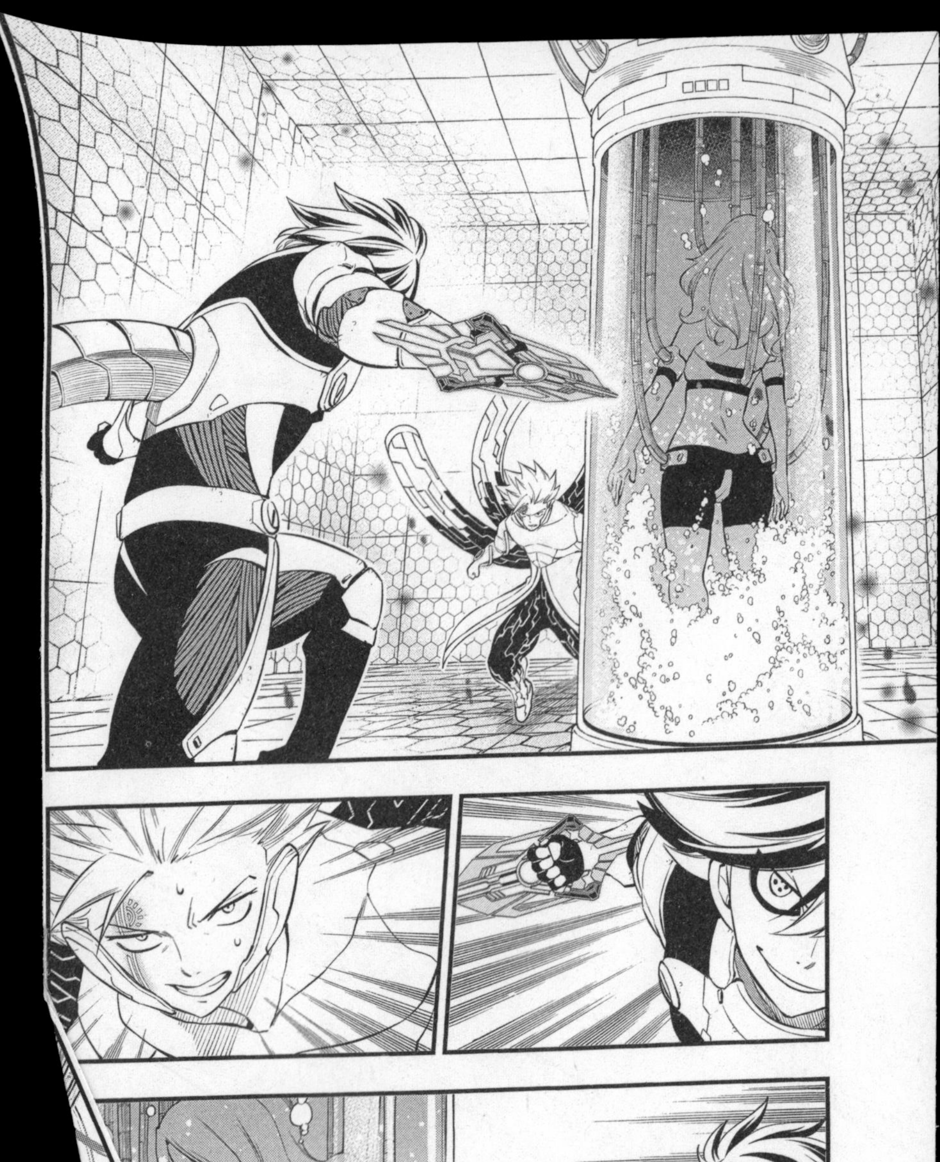

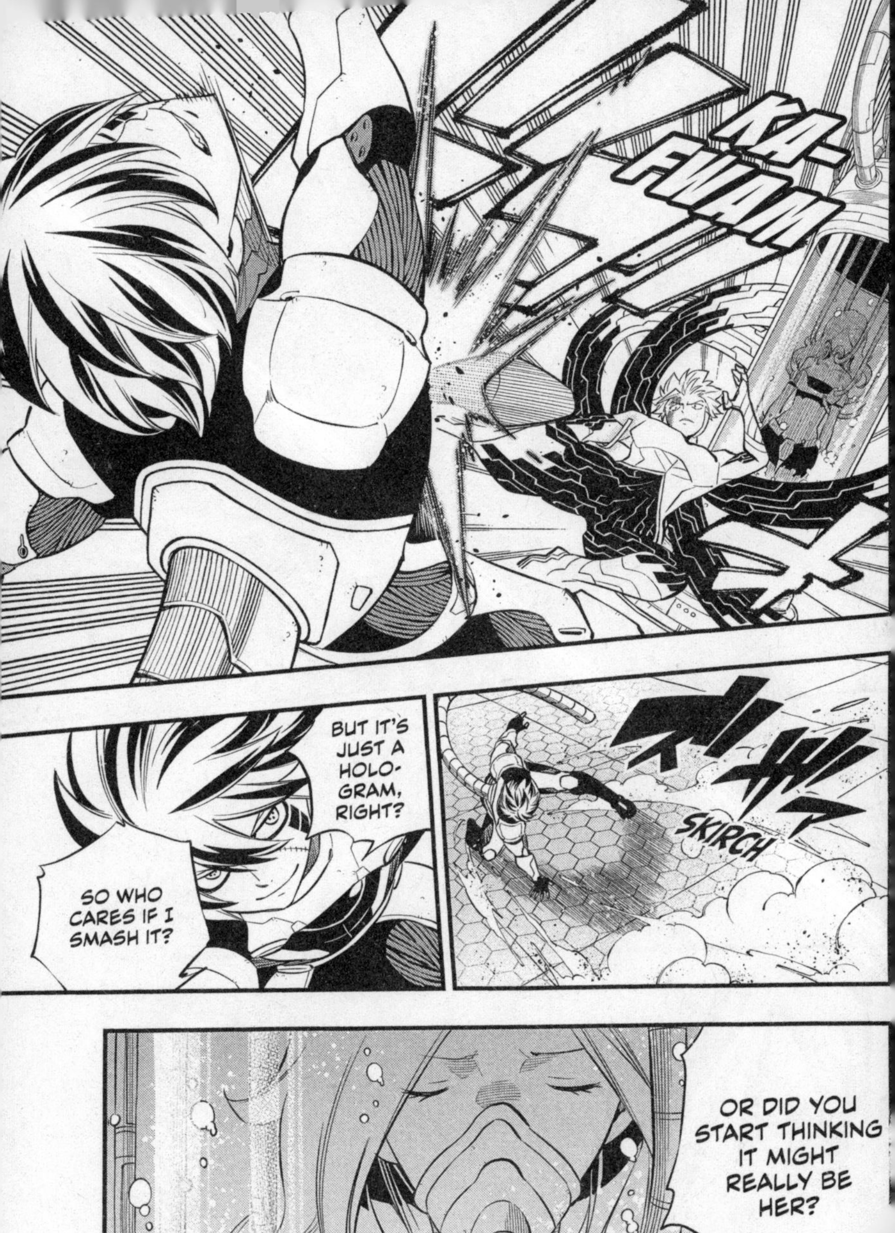
KA-FWAM
SKIRCH
BUT IT'S JUST A HOLOGRAM, RIGHT?
SO WHO CARES IF I SMASH IT?
OR DID YOU START THINKING IT MIGHT REALLY BE HER?

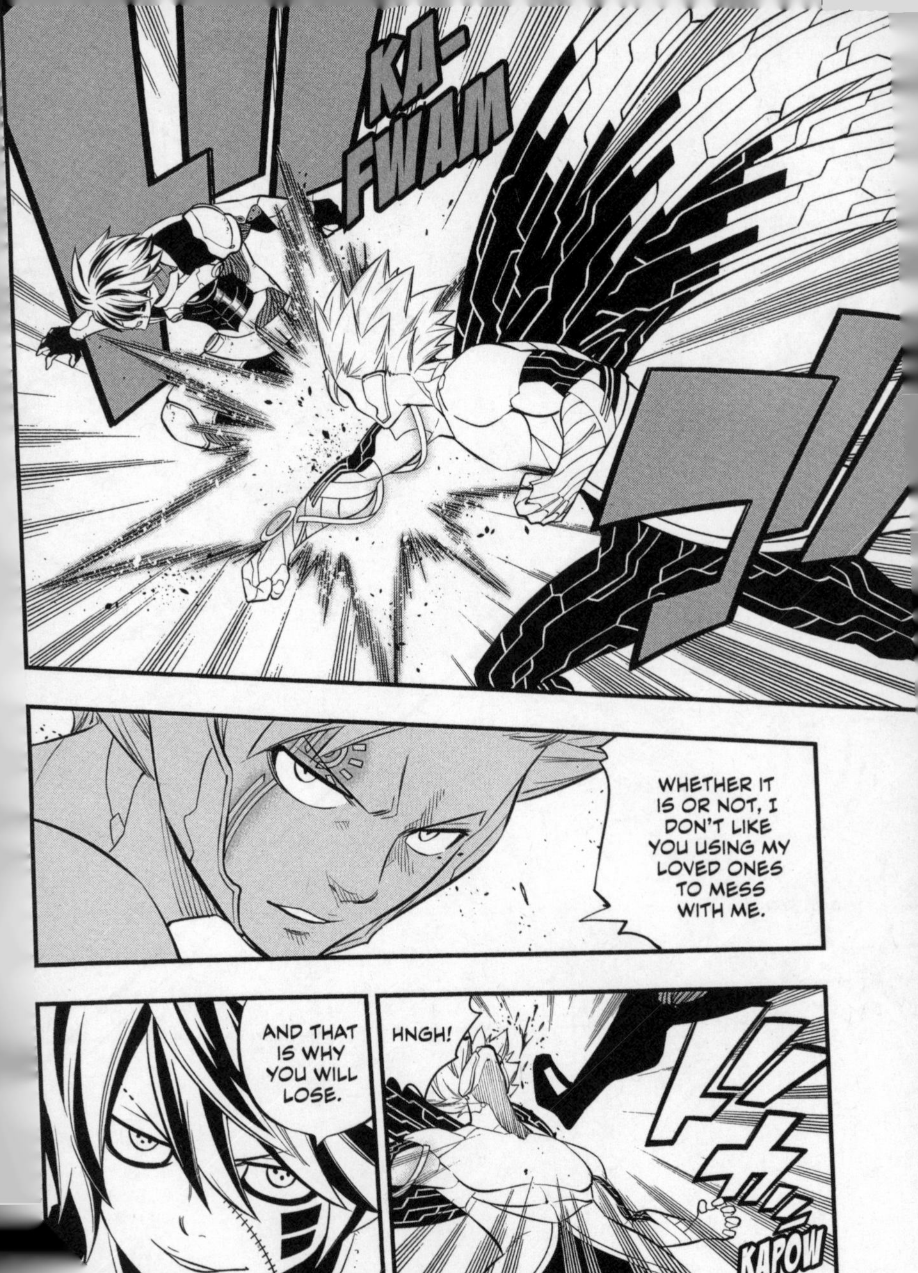
KA-FWAM
WHETHER IT IS OR NOT, I DON'T LIKE YOU USING MY LOVED ONES TO MESS WITH ME.
HNGH!
KAPOW
AND THAT IS WHY YOU WILL LOSE.

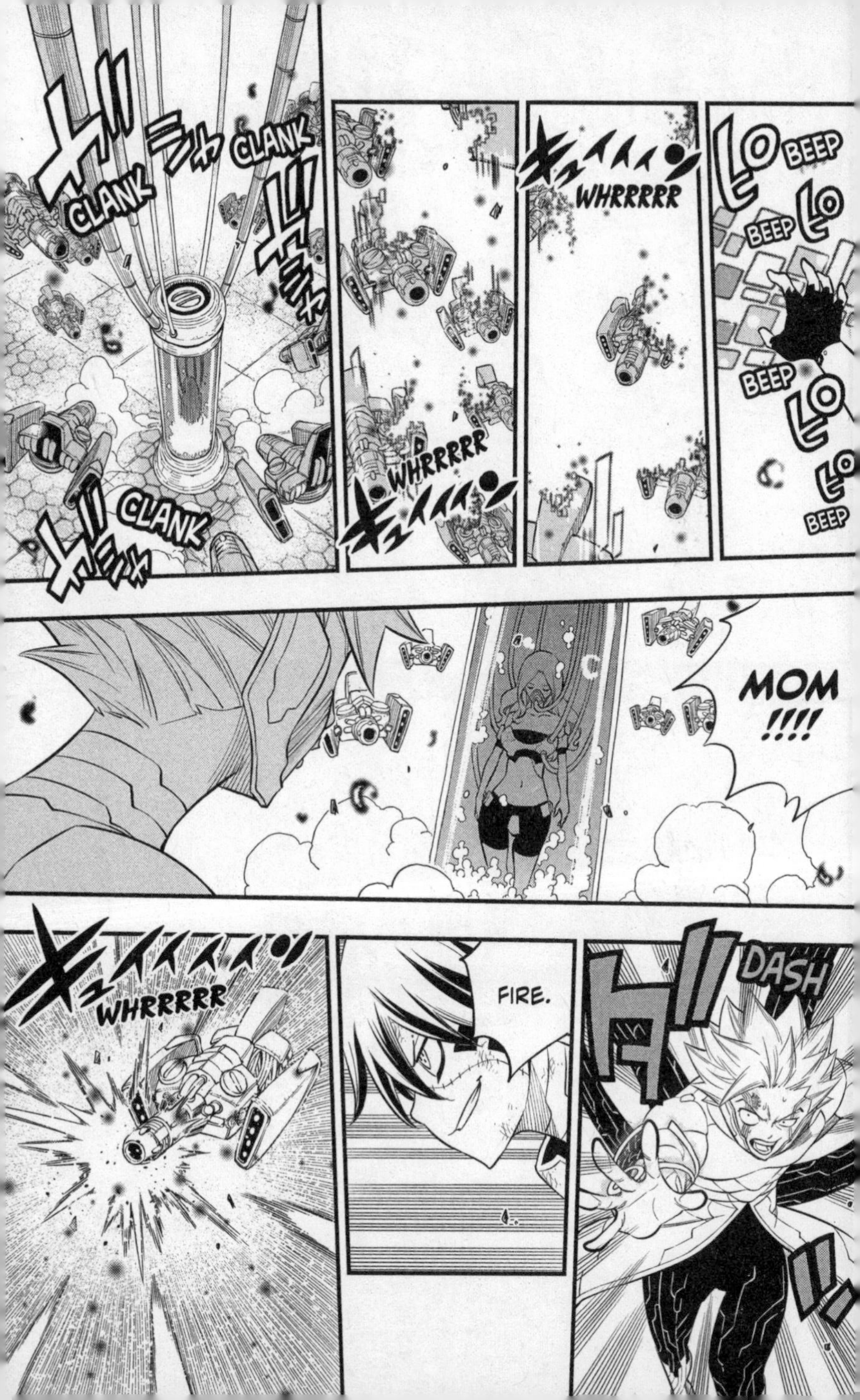
BEEP
BEEP
BEEP
BEEP
WHRRRR
WHRRRR
CLANK
CLANK
CLANK
MOM!!!!
DASH
FIRE.
WHRRRR

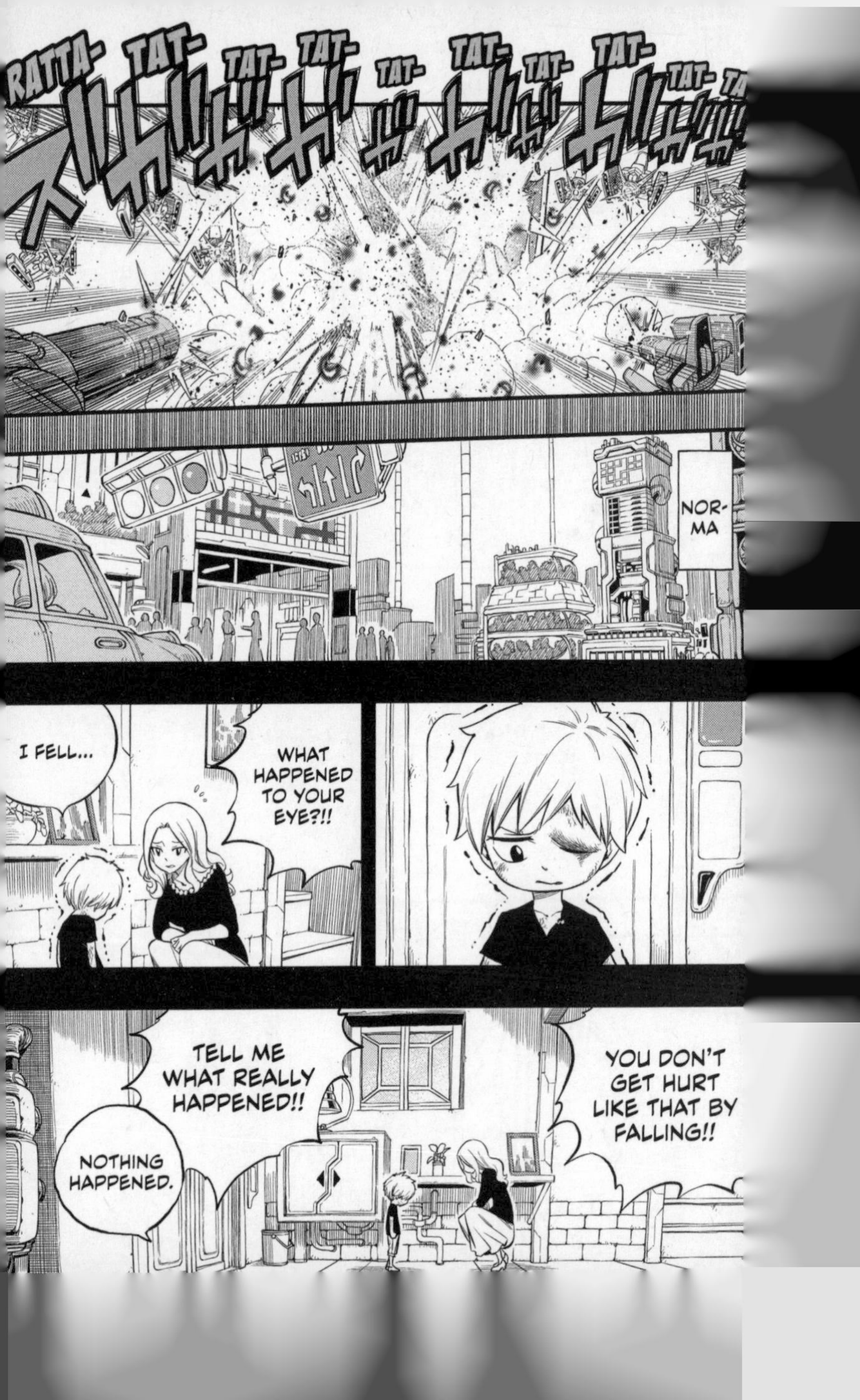
RATTA- TAT- TAT- TAT- TAT- TAT- TAT- TAT- TAT-
NOR-MA
WHAT HAPPENED TO YOUR EYE?!!
I FELL...
YOU DON'T GET HURT LIKE THAT BY FALLING!!
TELL ME WHAT REALLY HAPPENED!!
NOTHING HAPPENED.

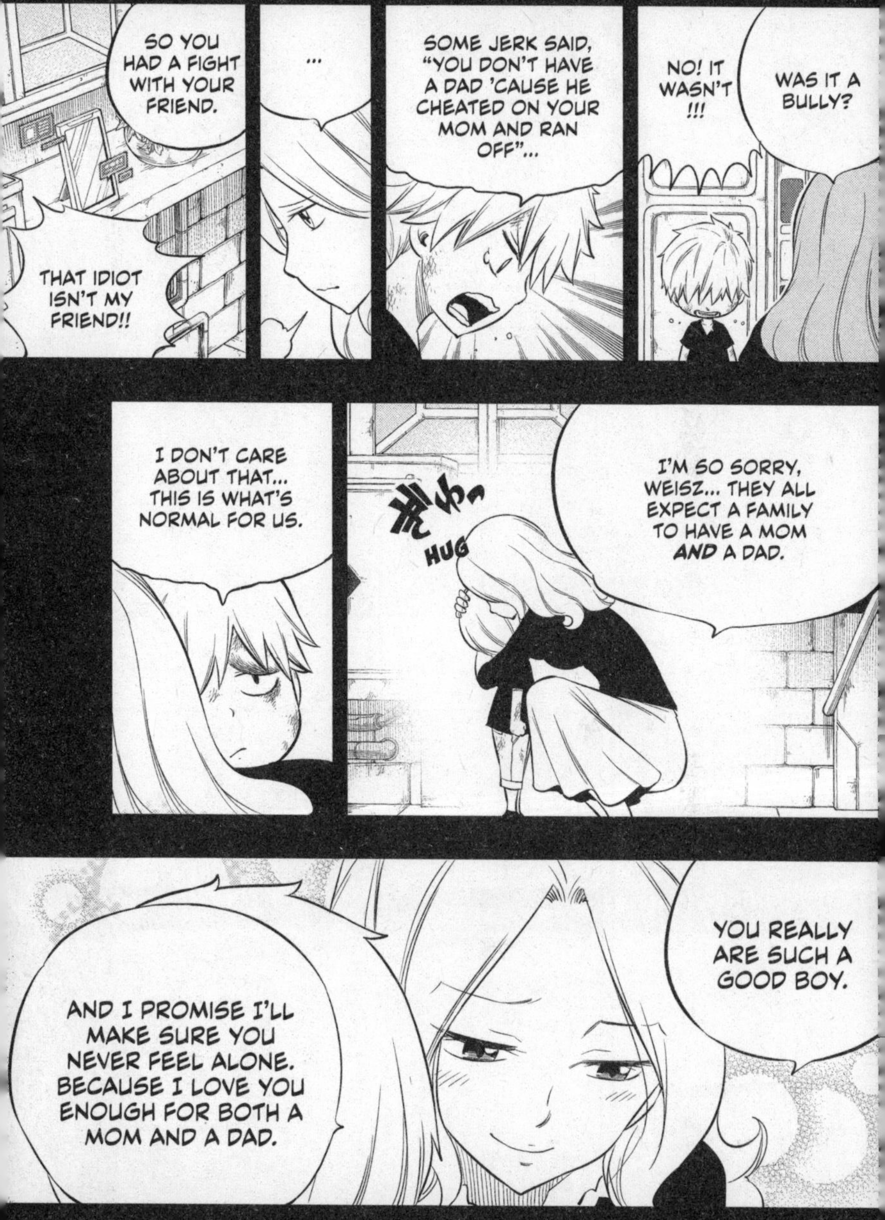
WAS IT A BULLY?
NO! IT WASN'T !!!
SOME JERK SAID, "YOU DON'T HAVE A DAD 'CAUSE HE CHEATED ON YOUR MOM AND RAN OFF"...
...
SO YOU HAD A FIGHT WITH YOUR FRIEND.
THAT IDIOT ISN'T MY FRIEND!!
I'M SO SORRY, WEISZ... THEY ALL EXPECT A FAMILY TO HAVE A MOM *AND* A DAD.
HUG
I DON'T CARE ABOUT THAT... THIS IS WHAT'S NORMAL FOR US.
YOU REALLY ARE SUCH A GOOD BOY.
AND I PROMISE I'LL MAKE SURE YOU NEVER FEEL ALONE. BECAUSE I LOVE YOU ENOUGH FOR BOTH A MOM AND A DAD.

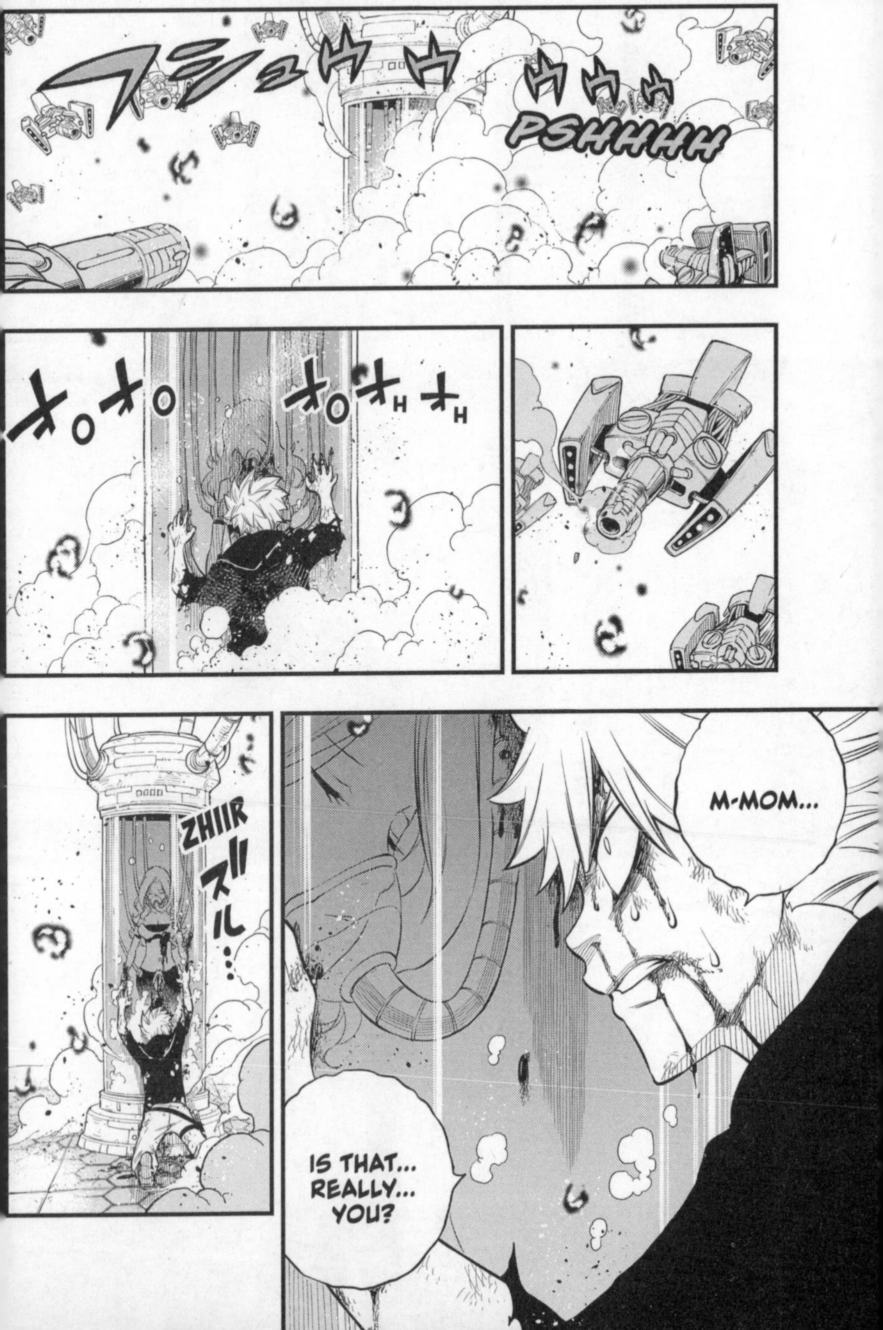

スシュゥゥゥゥゥ
PSHHHHH
ォ○ォ○ ォ○ォHォH
ZHIIR
ズル…
M-MOM...
IS THAT... REALLY... YOU?

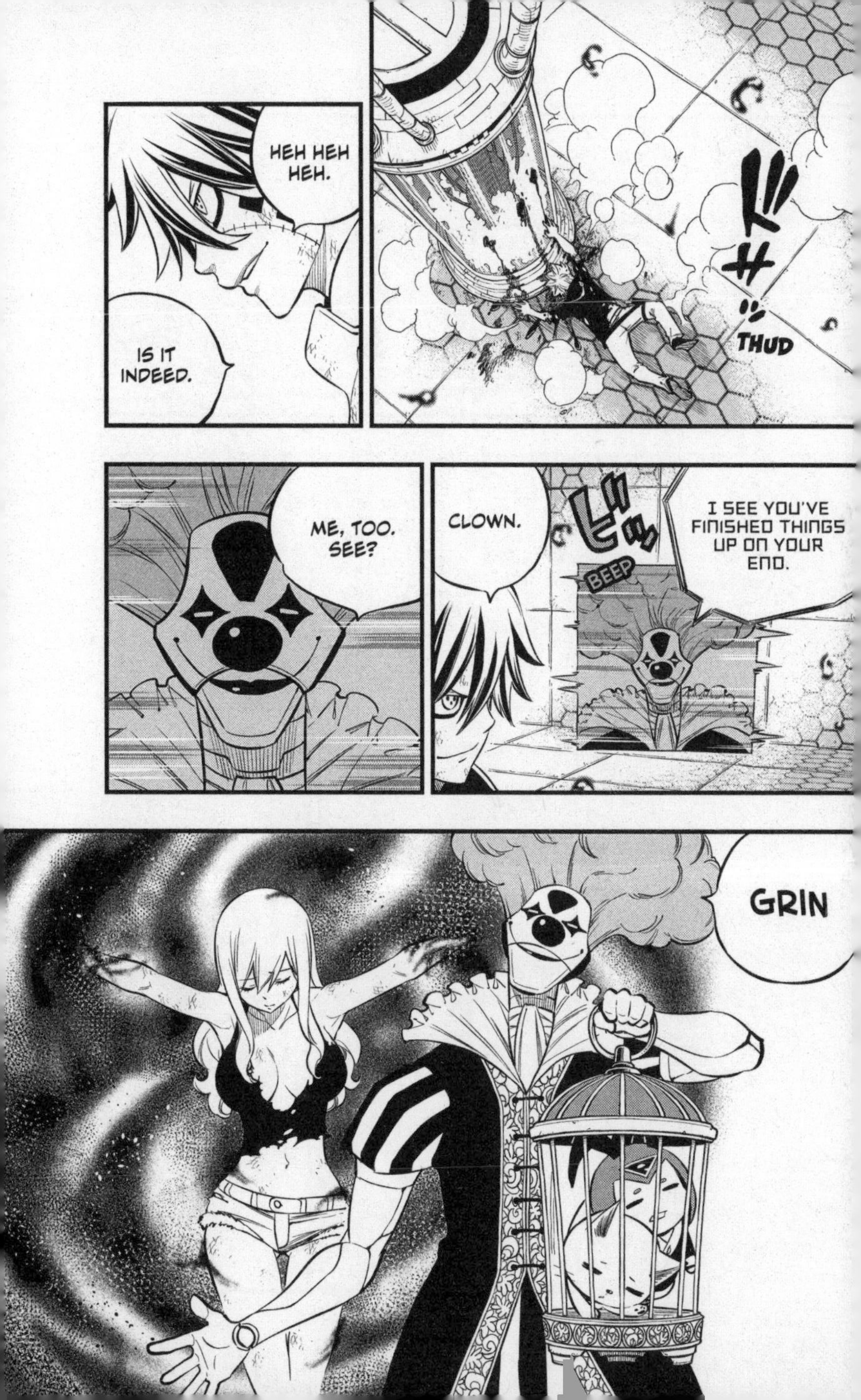
THUD
HEH HEH HEH.
IS IT INDEED.
I SEE YOU'VE FINISHED THINGS UP ON YOUR END.
BEEP
CLOWN.
ME, TOO. SEE?
GRIN

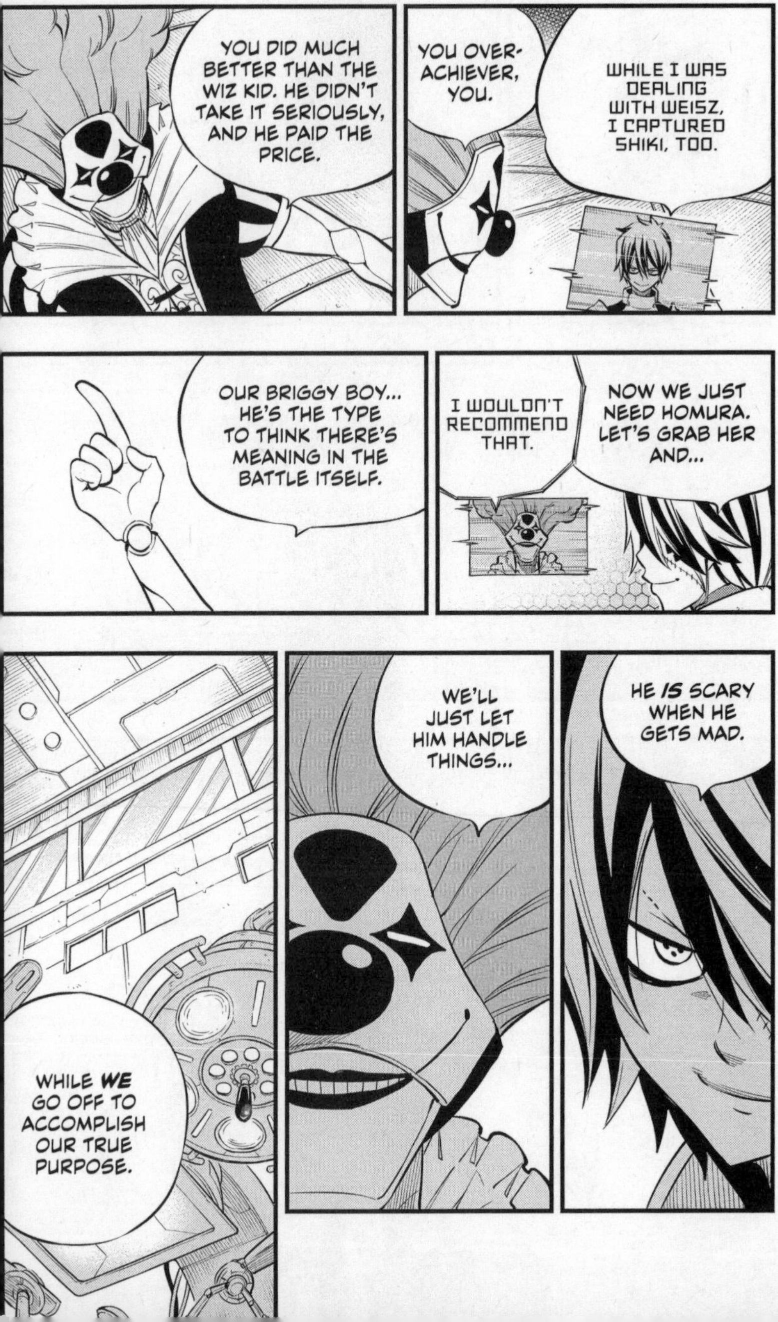
WHILE I WAS DEALING WITH WEISZ, I CAPTURED SHIKI, TOO.
YOU OVER-ACHIEVER, YOU.
YOU DID MUCH BETTER THAN THE WIZ KID. HE DIDN'T TAKE IT SERIOUSLY, AND HE PAID THE PRICE.
NOW WE JUST NEED HOMURA. LET'S GRAB HER AND...
I WOULDN'T RECOMMEND THAT.
OUR BRIGGY BOY... HE'S THE TYPE TO THINK THERE'S MEANING IN THE BATTLE ITSELF.
HE *IS* SCARY WHEN HE GETS MAD.
WE'LL JUST LET HIM HANDLE THINGS...
WHILE *WE* GO OFF TO ACCOMPLISH OUR TRUE PURPOSE.

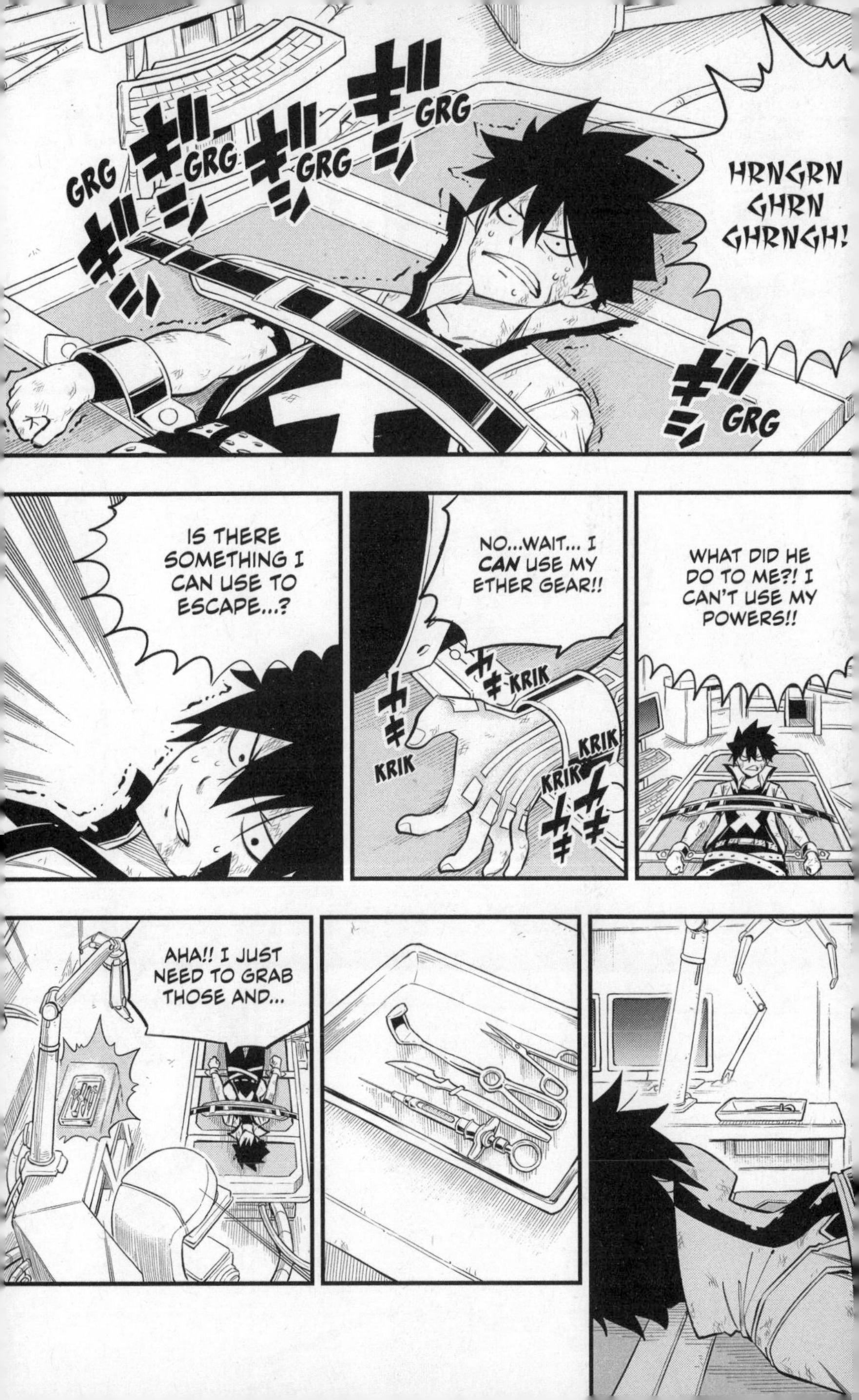
HRNGRN GHRN GHRNGH!
GRG
GRG
GRG
GRG
GRG
WHAT DID HE DO TO ME?! I CAN'T USE MY POWERS!!
NO...WAIT... I CAN USE MY ETHER GEAR!!
KRIK
KRIK
KRIK
KRIK
IS THERE SOMETHING I CAN USE TO ESCAPE...?
AHA!! I JUST NEED TO GRAB THOSE AND...

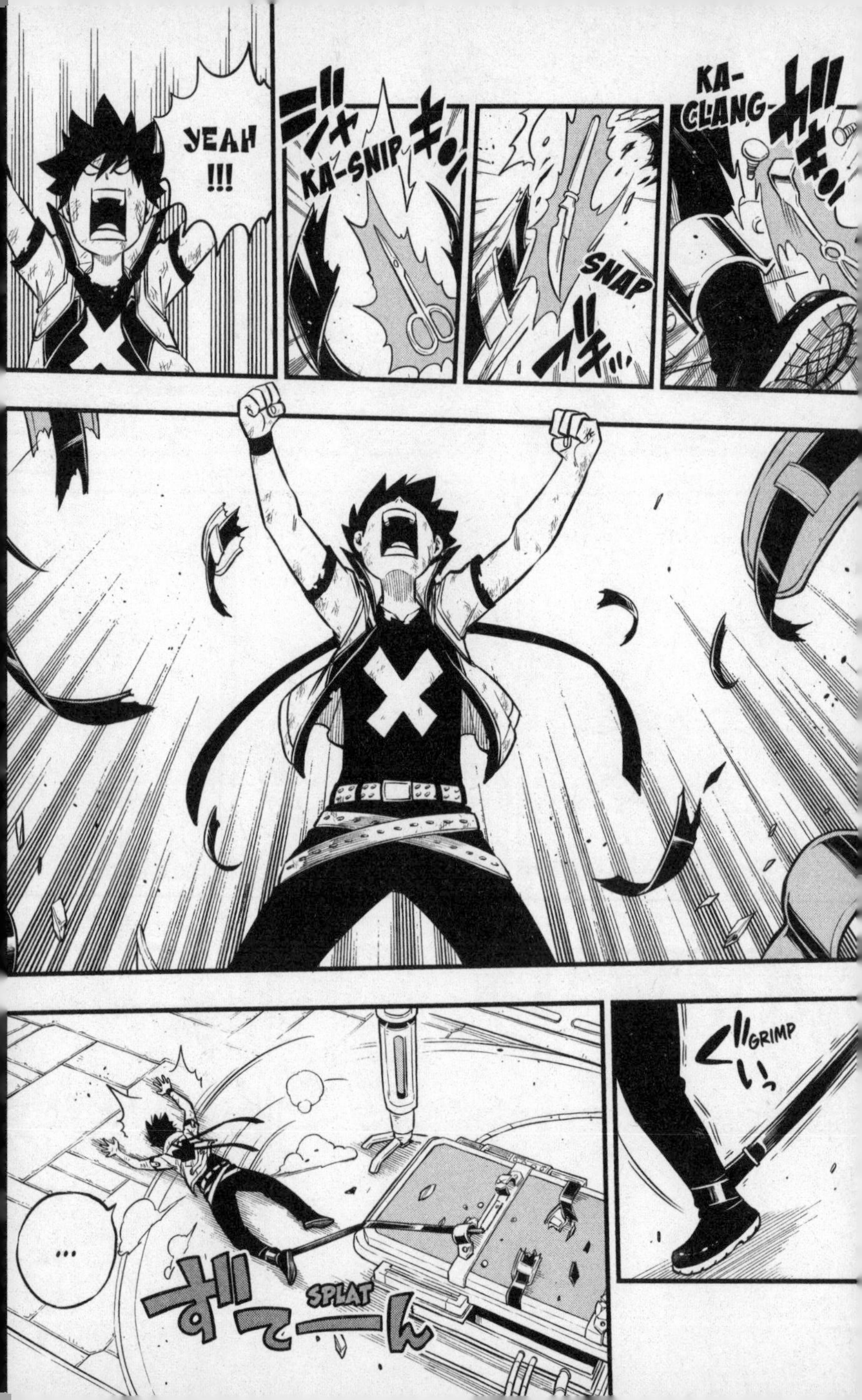

KA-CLANG
SNAP
KA-SNIP
YEAH !!!
GRIMP
...
SPLAT

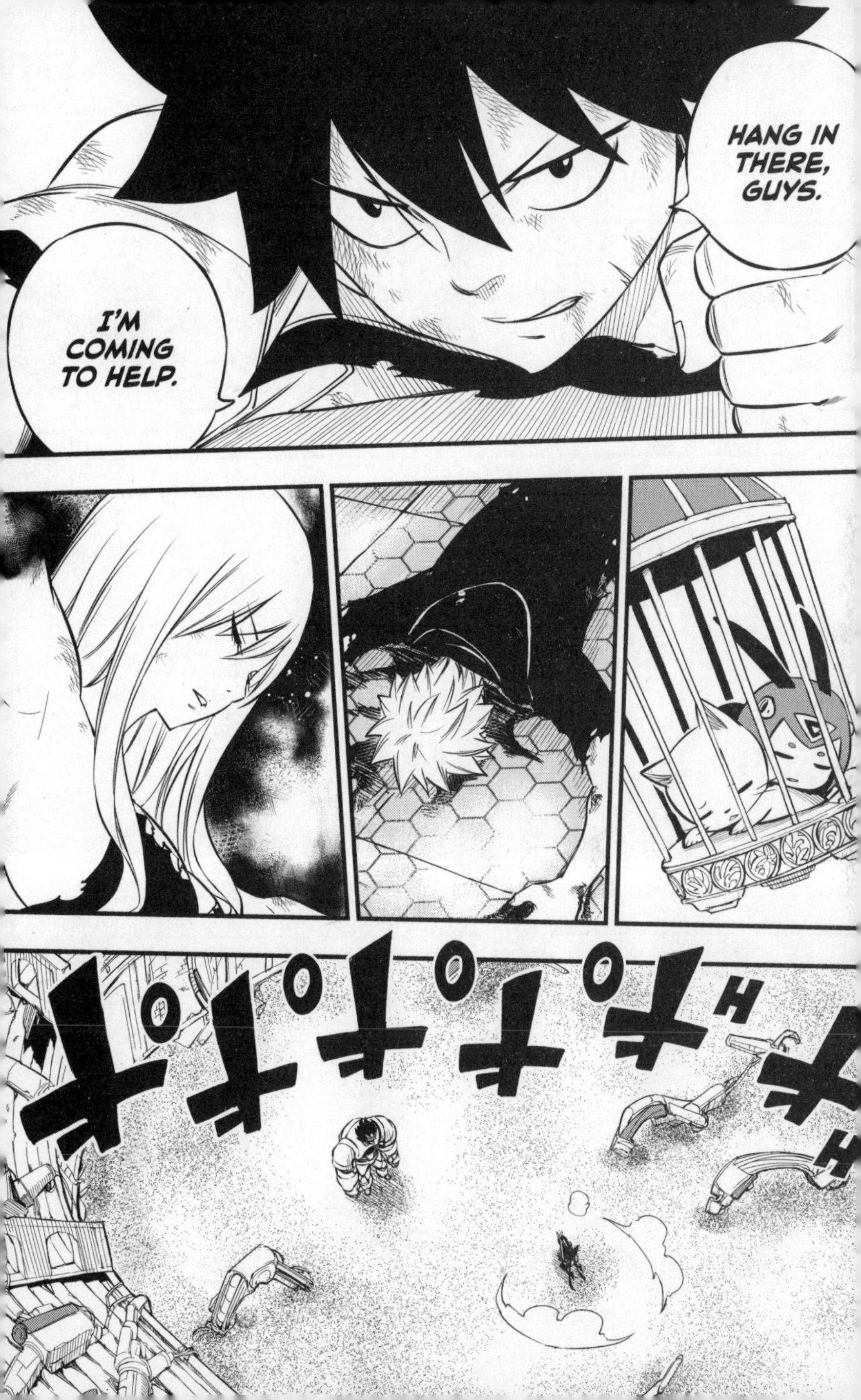
HANG IN THERE, GUYS.
I'M COMING TO HELP.

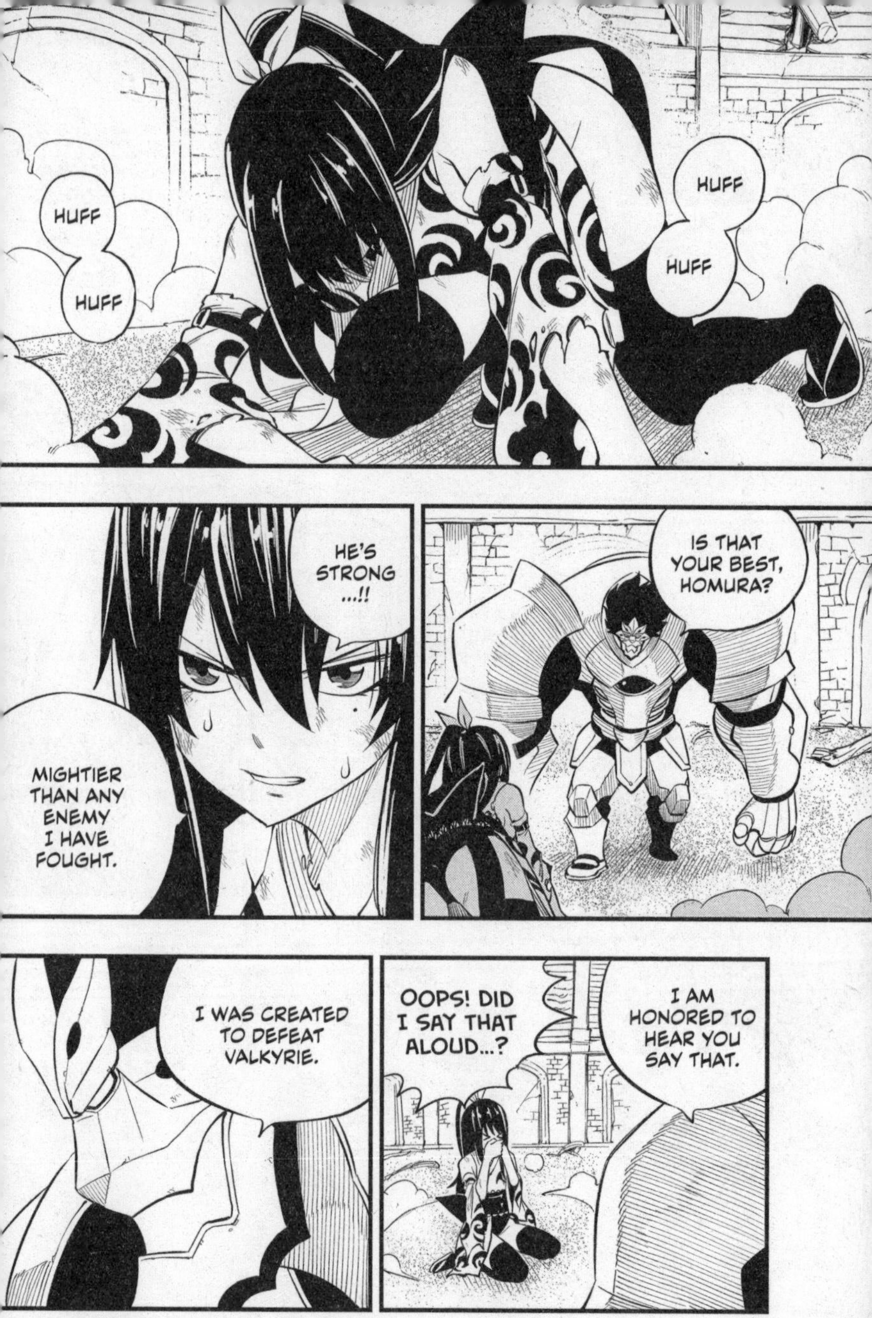
HUFF
HUFF
HUFF
HUFF
IS THAT YOUR BEST, HOMURA?
HE'S STRONG ...!!
MIGHTIER THAN ANY ENEMY I HAVE FOUGHT.
I AM HONORED TO HEAR YOU SAY THAT.
OOPS! DID I SAY THAT ALOUD...?
I WAS CREATED TO DEFEAT VALKYRIE.

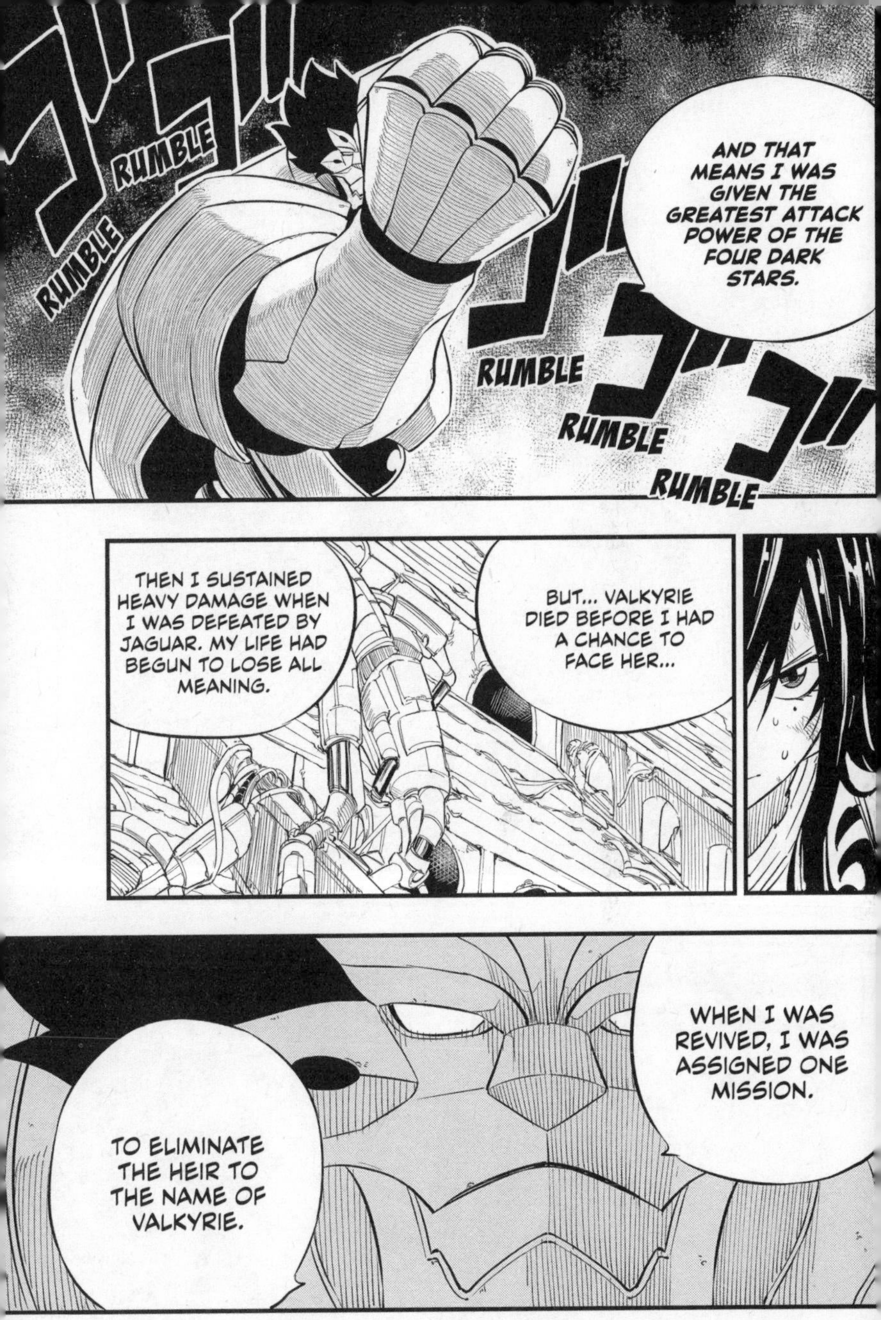
AND THAT MEANS I WAS GIVEN THE GREATEST ATTACK POWER OF THE FOUR DARK STARS.
RUMBLE
RUMBLE
RUMBLE
RUMBLE
RUMBLE
RUMBLE
BUT... VALKYRIE DIED BEFORE I HAD A CHANCE TO FACE HER...
THEN I SUSTAINED HEAVY DAMAGE WHEN I WAS DEFEATED BY JAGUAR. MY LIFE HAD BEGUN TO LOSE ALL MEANING.
WHEN I WAS REVIVED, I WAS ASSIGNED ONE MISSION.
TO ELIMINATE THE HEIR TO THE NAME OF VALKYRIE.

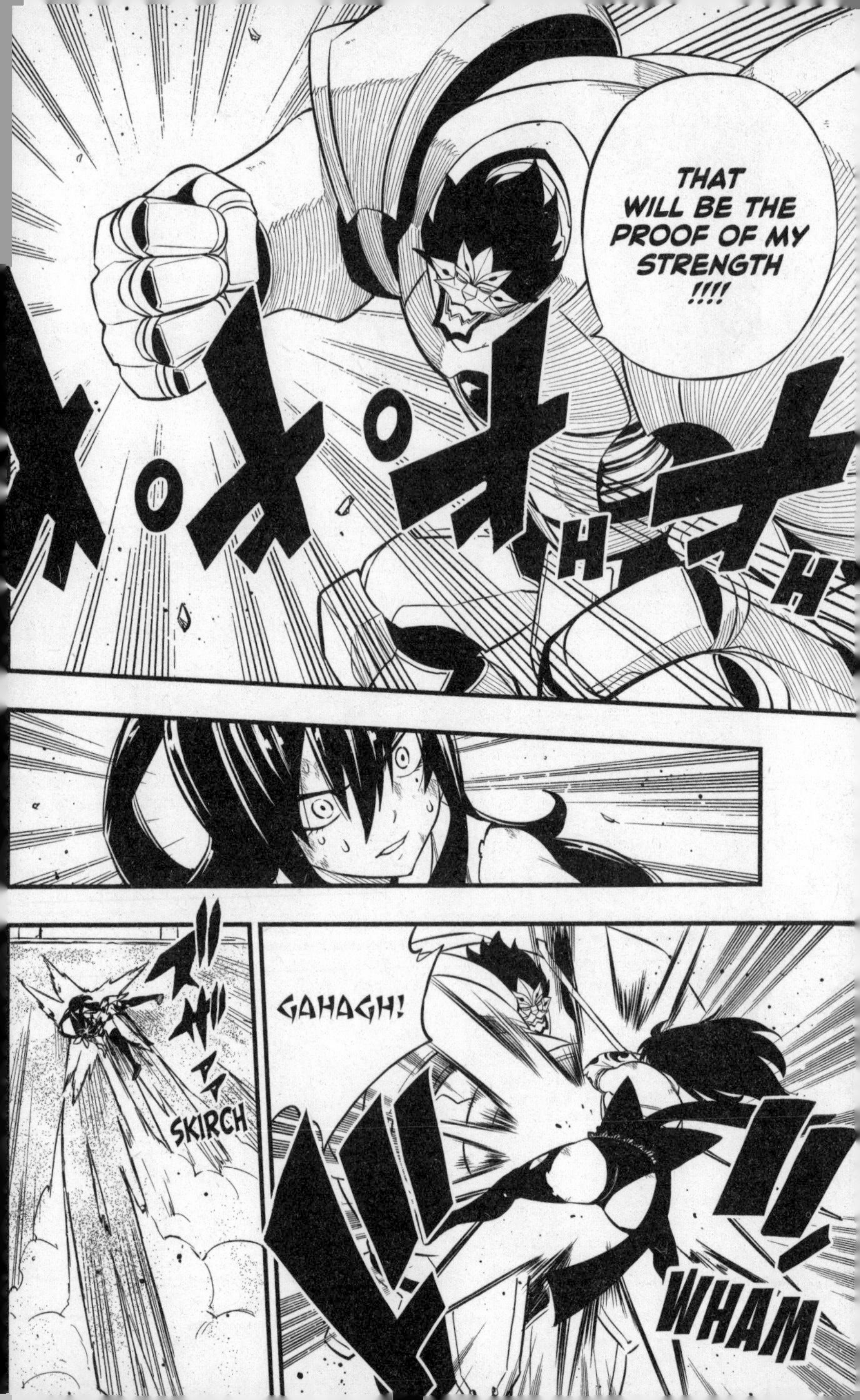
THAT WILL BE THE PROOF OF MY STRENGTH !!!!
H
H
GAHAGH!
WHAM
SKIRCH

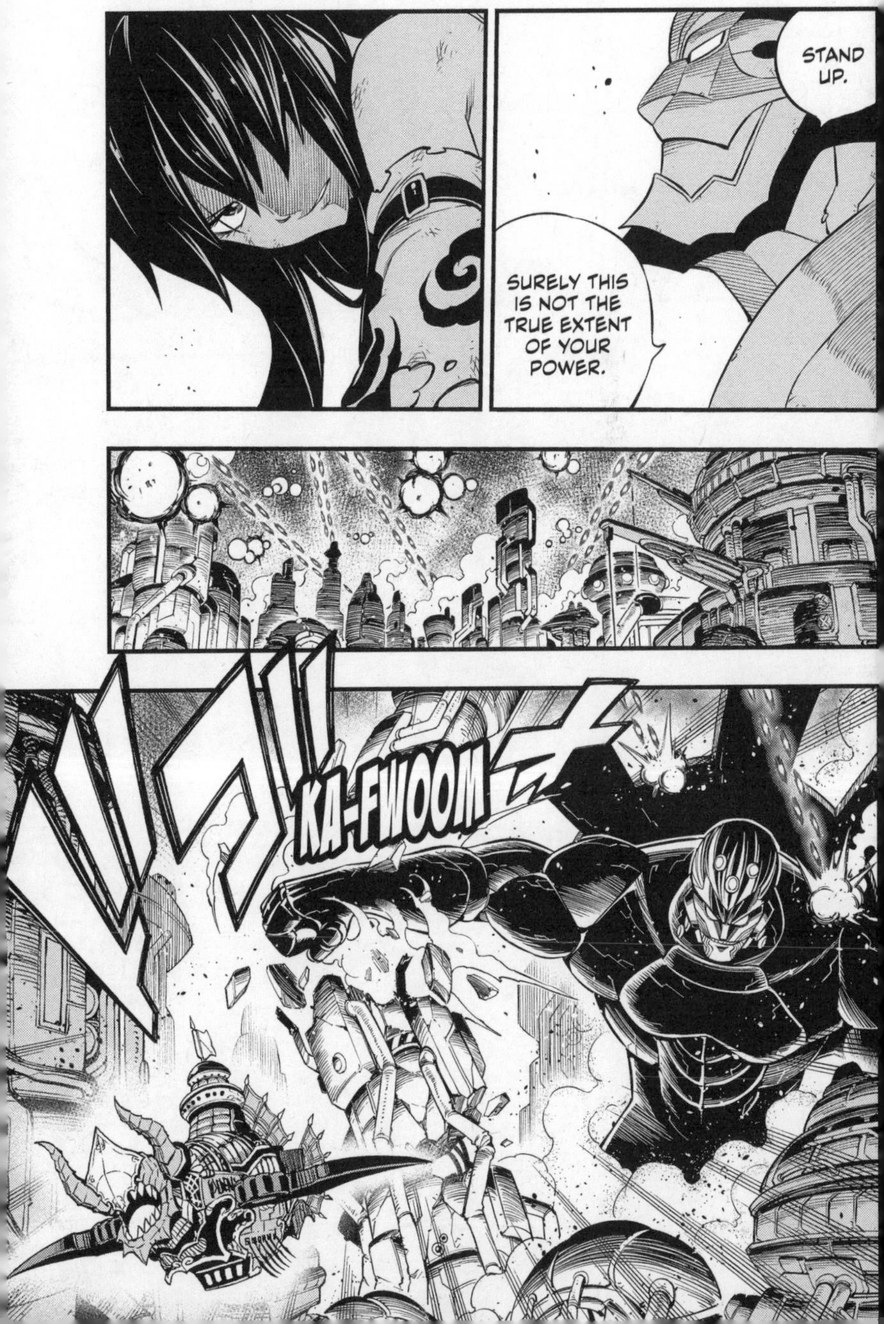
STAND UP.
SURELY THIS IS NOT THE TRUE EXTENT OF YOUR POWER.
KA-FWOOM

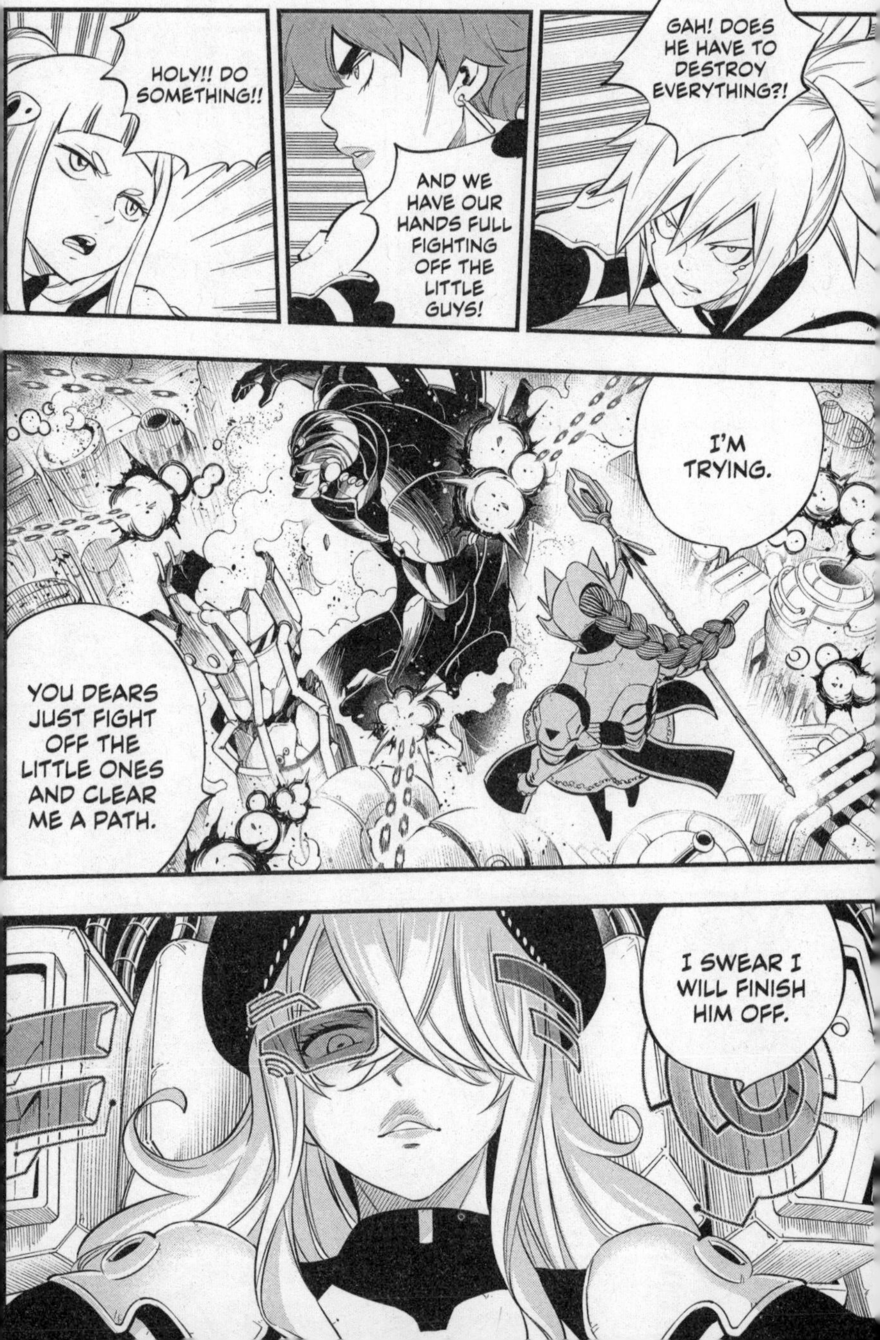
GAH! DOES HE HAVE TO DESTROY EVERYTHING?!
AND WE HAVE OUR HANDS FULL FIGHTING OFF THE LITTLE GUYS!
HOLY!! DO SOMETHING!!
I'M TRYING.
YOU DEARS JUST FIGHT OFF THE LITTLE ONES AND CLEAR ME A PATH.
I SWEAR I WILL FINISH HIM OFF.

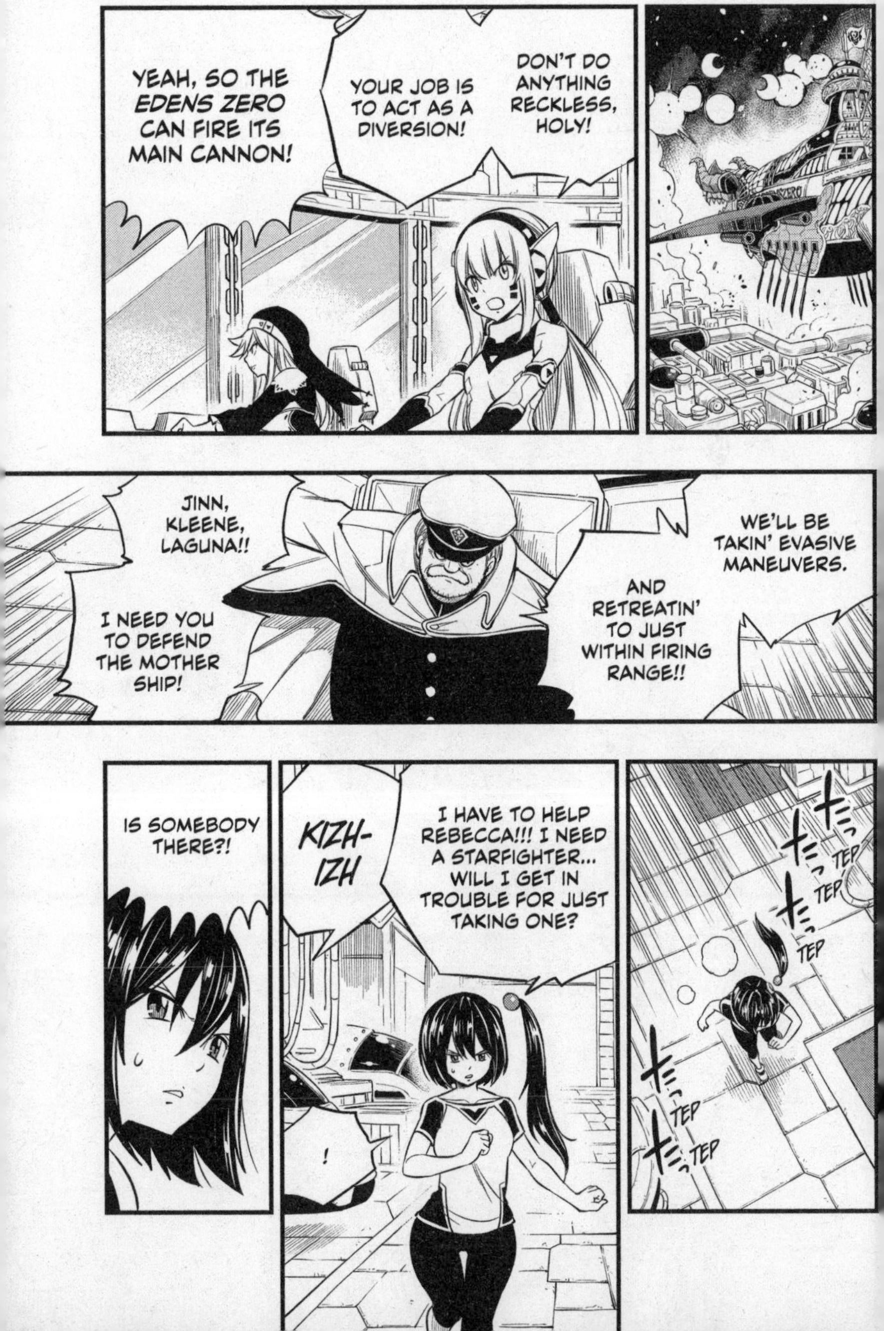

DON'T DO ANYTHING RECKLESS, HOLY!
YOUR JOB IS TO ACT AS A DIVERSION!
YEAH, SO THE *EDENS ZERO* CAN FIRE ITS MAIN CANNON!
WE'LL BE TAKIN' EVASIVE MANEUVERS.
AND RETREATIN' TO JUST WITHIN FIRING RANGE!!
JINN, KLEENE, LAGUNA!!
I NEED YOU TO DEFEND THE MOTHER SHIP!
TEP
TEP
TEP
TEP
TEP
I HAVE TO HELP REBECCA!!! I NEED A STARFIGHTER... WILL I GET IN TROUBLE FOR JUST TAKING ONE?
KIZH-IZH
!
IS SOMEBODY THERE?!

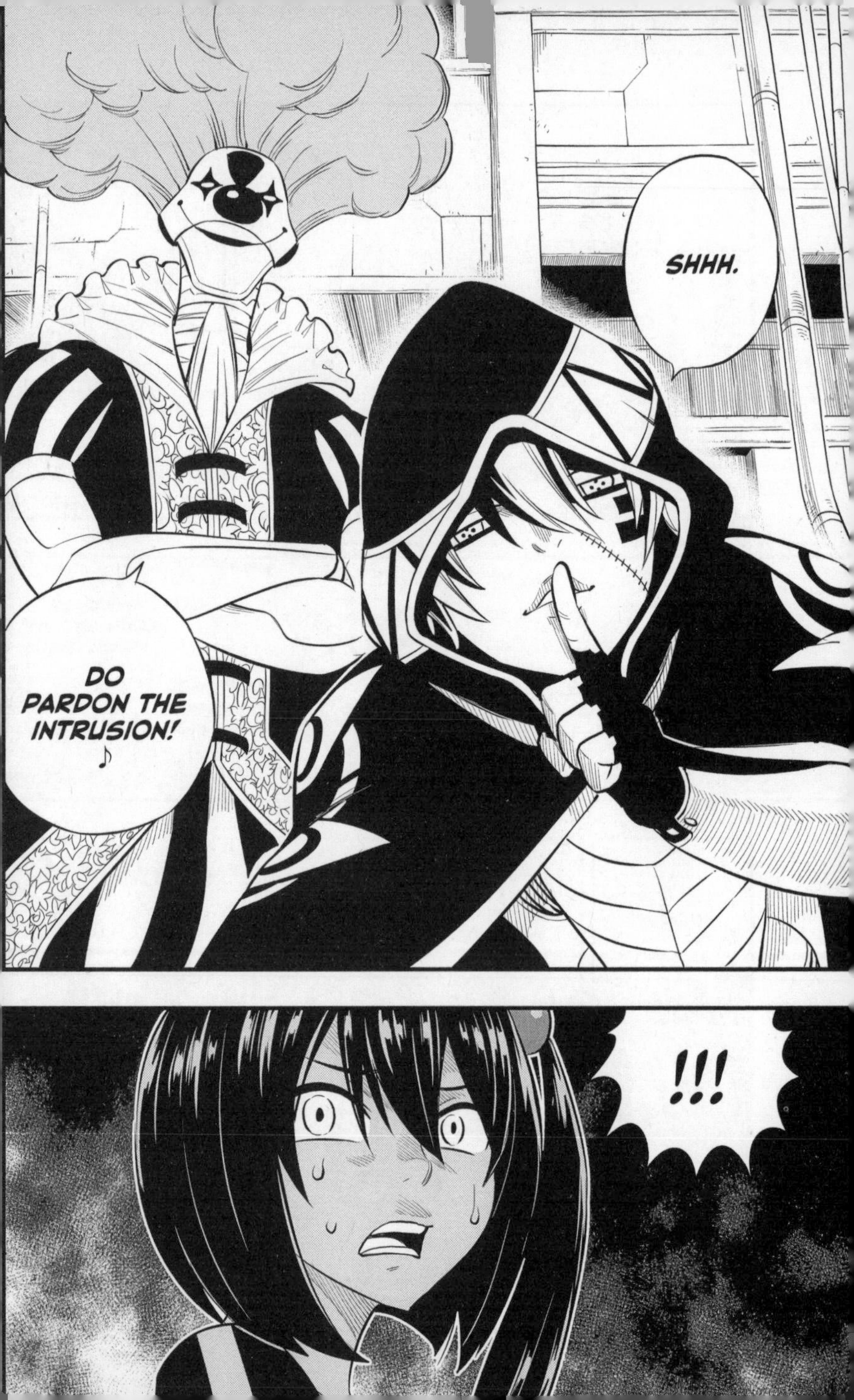
SHHH.
DO PARDON THE INTRUSION! ♪
!!!

EDENS ZERO

Sister Ivory
DON'T

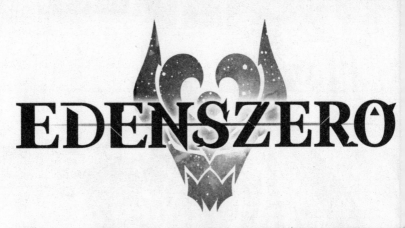

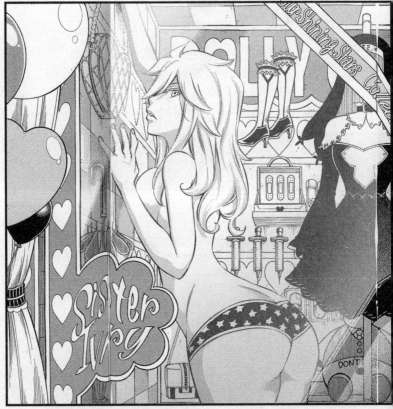

CHAPTER 194: THE ETHER OF ALL THINGS

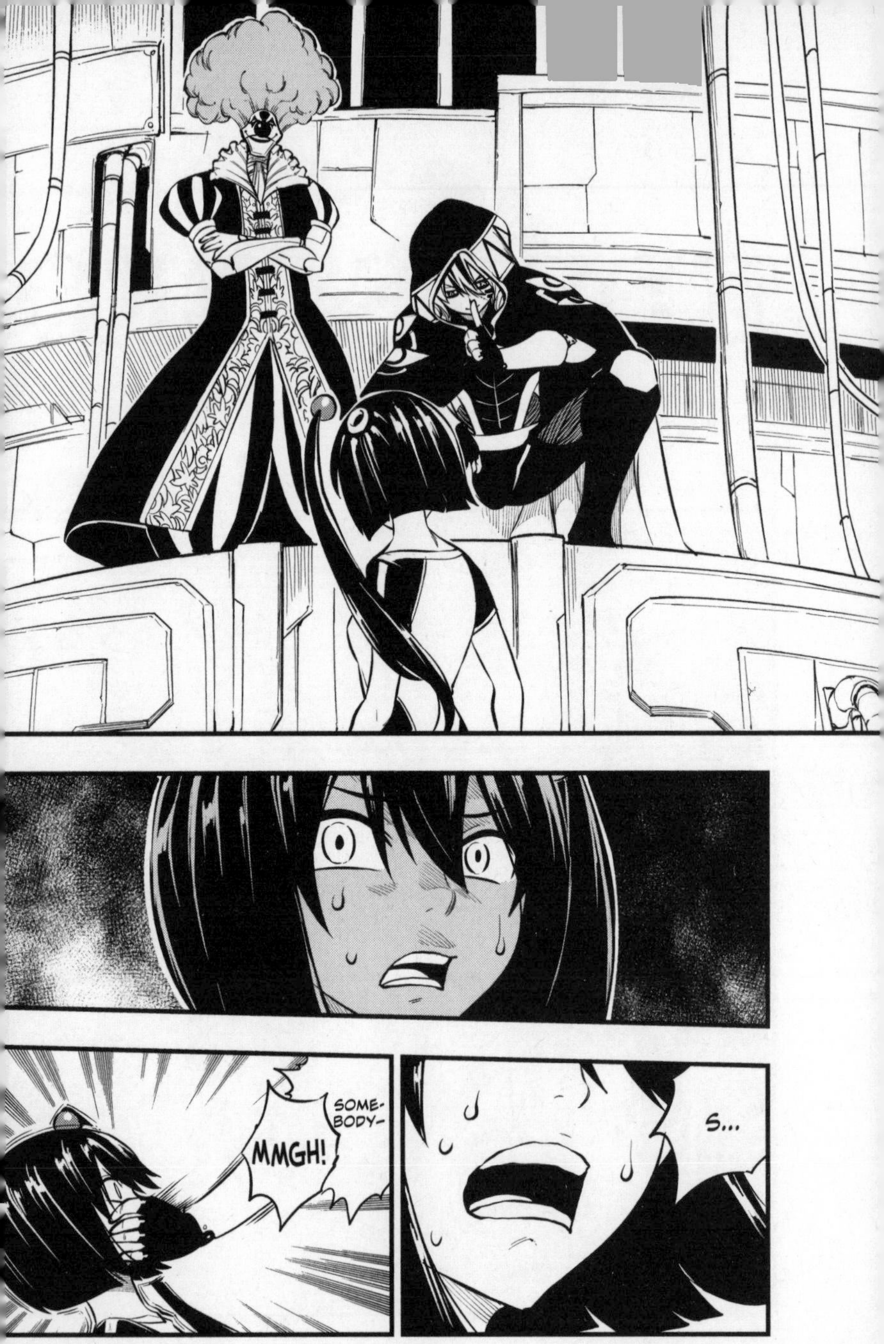
S...
SOME-BODY-
MMGH!

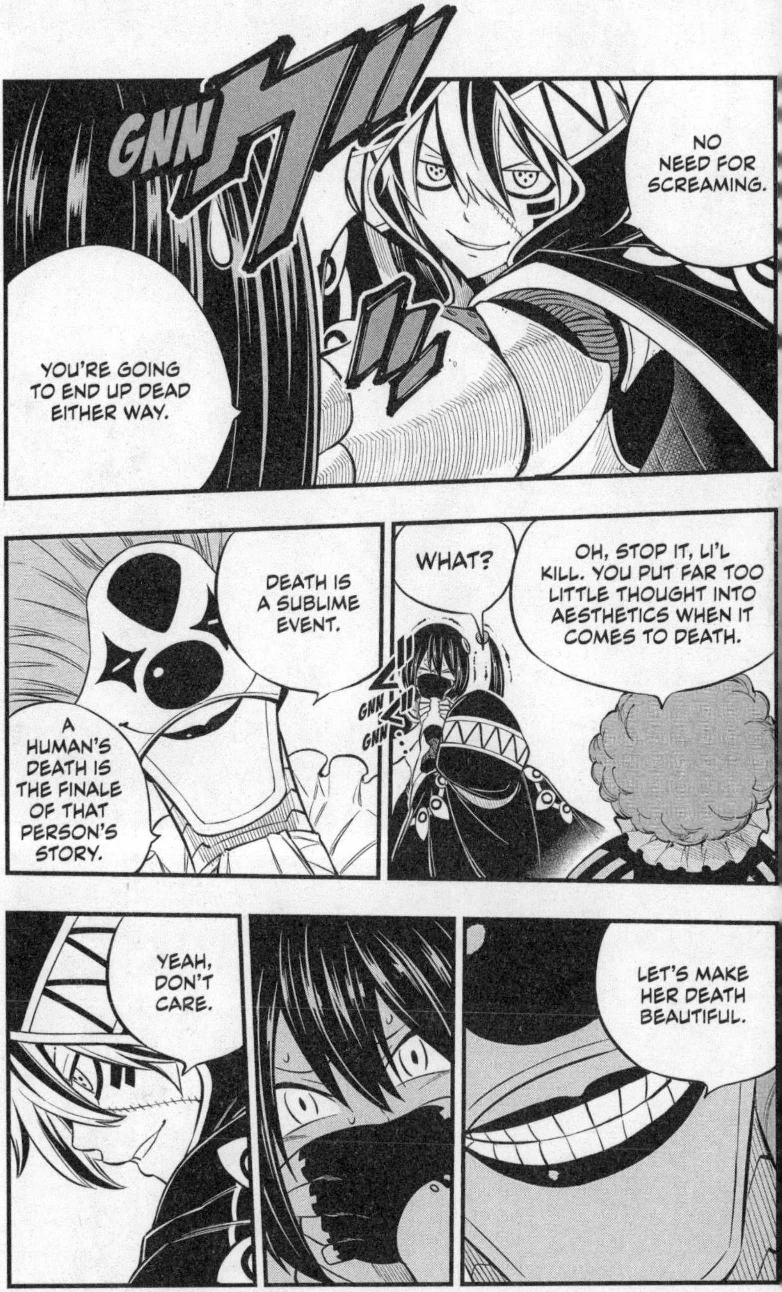
NO NEED FOR SCREAMING.
GNN
YOU'RE GOING TO END UP DEAD EITHER WAY.
OH, STOP IT, LI'L KILL. YOU PUT FAR TOO LITTLE THOUGHT INTO AESTHETICS WHEN IT COMES TO DEATH.
WHAT?
GNN GNN
DEATH IS A SUBLIME EVENT.
A HUMAN'S DEATH IS THE FINALE OF THAT PERSON'S STORY.
LET'S MAKE HER DEATH BEAUTIFUL.
YEAH, DON'T CARE.

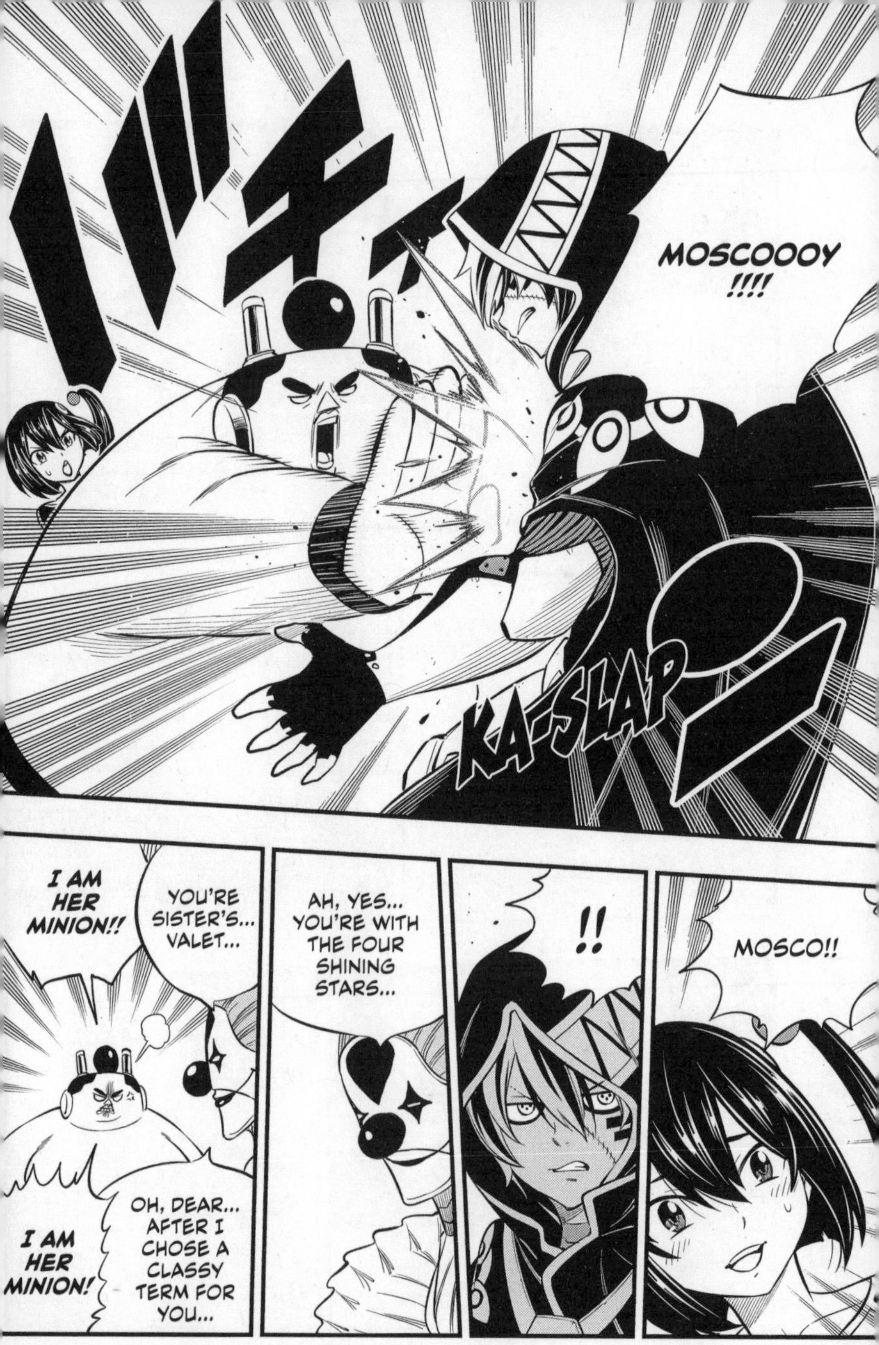
MOSCOOOY !!!!
KA-SLAP
MOSCO!!
!!
AH, YES... YOU'RE WITH THE FOUR SHINING STARS...
YOU'RE SISTER'S... VALET...
I AM HER MINION!!
OH, DEAR... AFTER I CHOSE A CLASSY TERM FOR YOU...
I AM HER MINION!

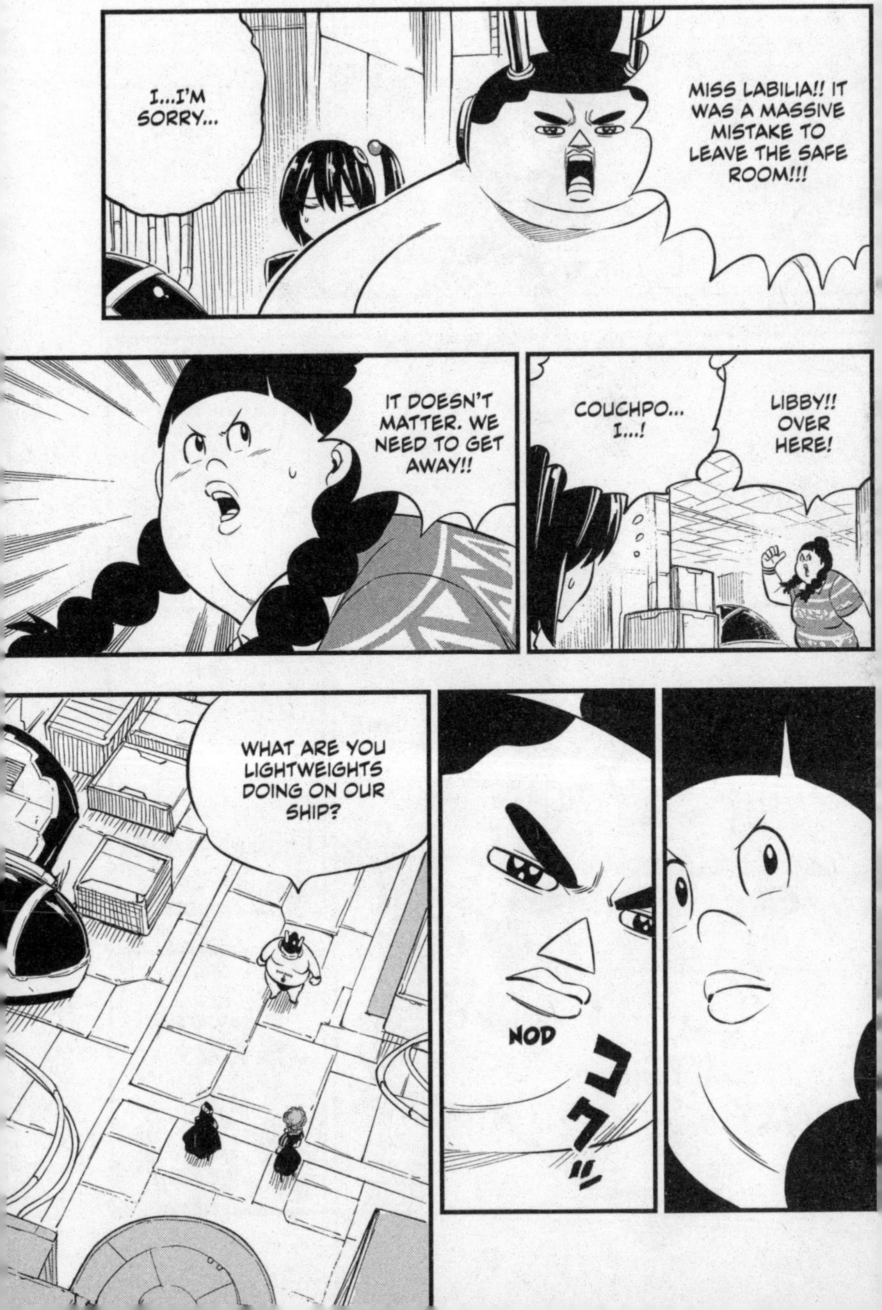
MISS LABILIA!! IT WAS A MASSIVE MISTAKE TO LEAVE THE SAFE ROOM!!!
I...I'M SORRY...
LIBBY!! OVER HERE!
COUCHPO... I...!
IT DOESN'T MATTER. WE NEED TO GET AWAY!!
NOD
コクッ
WHAT ARE YOU LIGHTWEIGHTS DOING ON OUR SHIP?

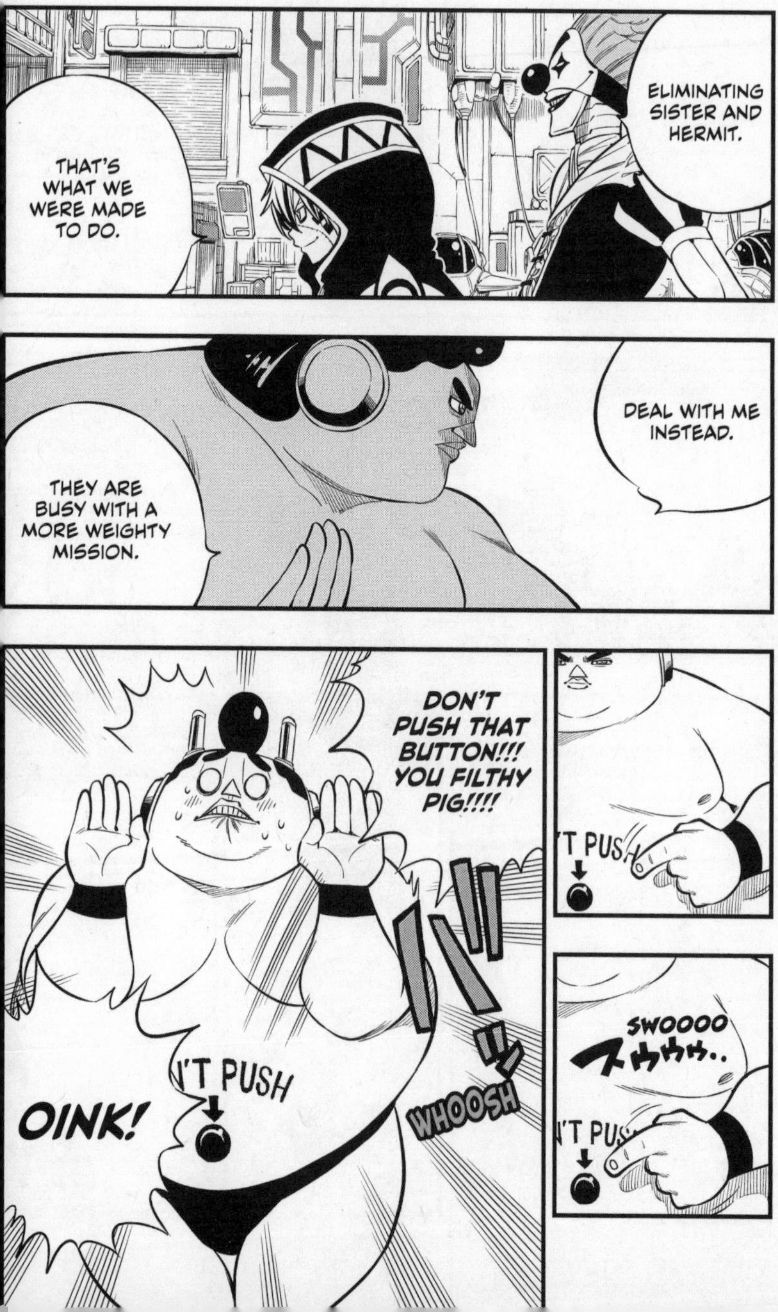
ELIMINATING SISTER AND HERMIT.
THAT'S WHAT WE WERE MADE TO DO.
DEAL WITH ME INSTEAD.
THEY ARE BUSY WITH A MORE WEIGHTY MISSION.
'T PUS
SWOOOO
スゥゥ..
'T PUS
DON'T PUSH THAT BUTTON!!! YOU FILTHY PIG!!!!
WHOOSH
'T PUSH
OINK!

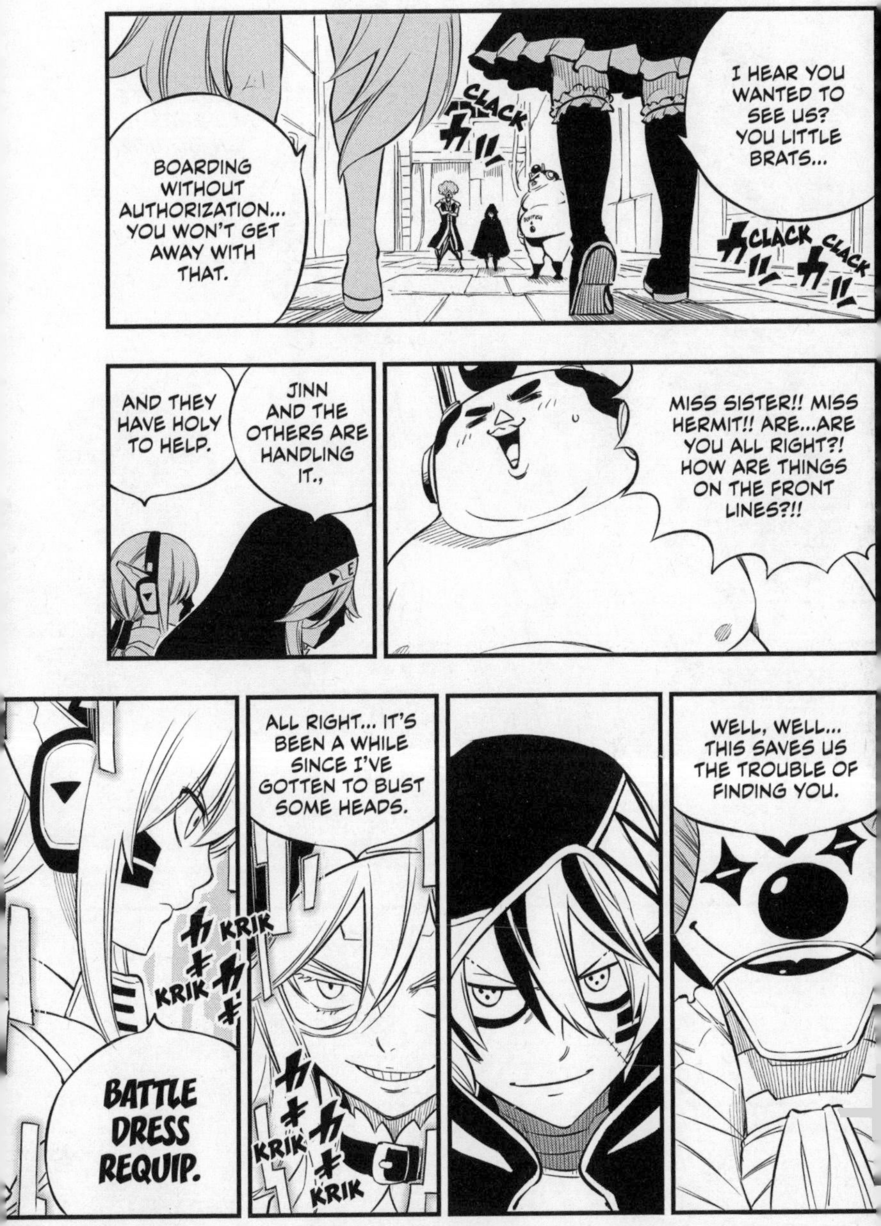
I HEAR YOU WANTED TO SEE US? YOU LITTLE BRATS...
CLACK CLACK
CLACK
BOARDING WITHOUT AUTHORIZATION... YOU WON'T GET AWAY WITH THAT.
MISS SISTER!! MISS HERMIT!! ARE...ARE YOU ALL RIGHT?! HOW ARE THINGS ON THE FRONT LINES?!!
JINN AND THE OTHERS ARE HANDLING IT.,
AND THEY HAVE HOLY TO HELP.
WELL, WELL... THIS SAVES US THE TROUBLE OF FINDING YOU.
ALL RIGHT... IT'S BEEN A WHILE SINCE I'VE GOTTEN TO BUST SOME HEADS.
KRIK KRIK
KRIK KRIK
BATTLE DRESS REQUIP.

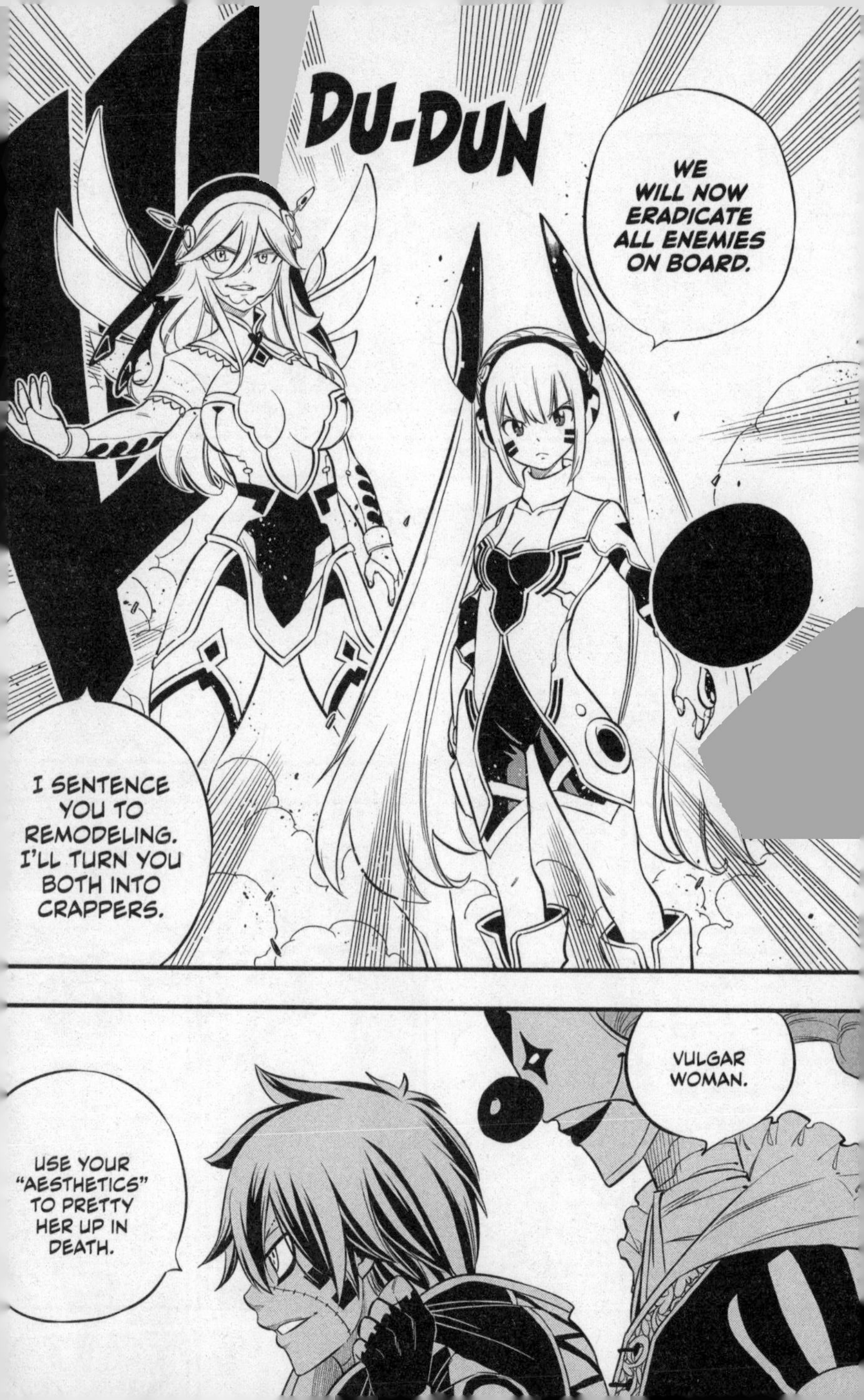
DU-DUN
WE WILL NOW ERADICATE ALL ENEMIES ON BOARD.
I SENTENCE YOU TO REMODELING. I'LL TURN YOU BOTH INTO CRAPPERS.
VULGAR WOMAN.
USE YOUR "AESTHETICS" TO PRETTY HER UP IN DEATH.

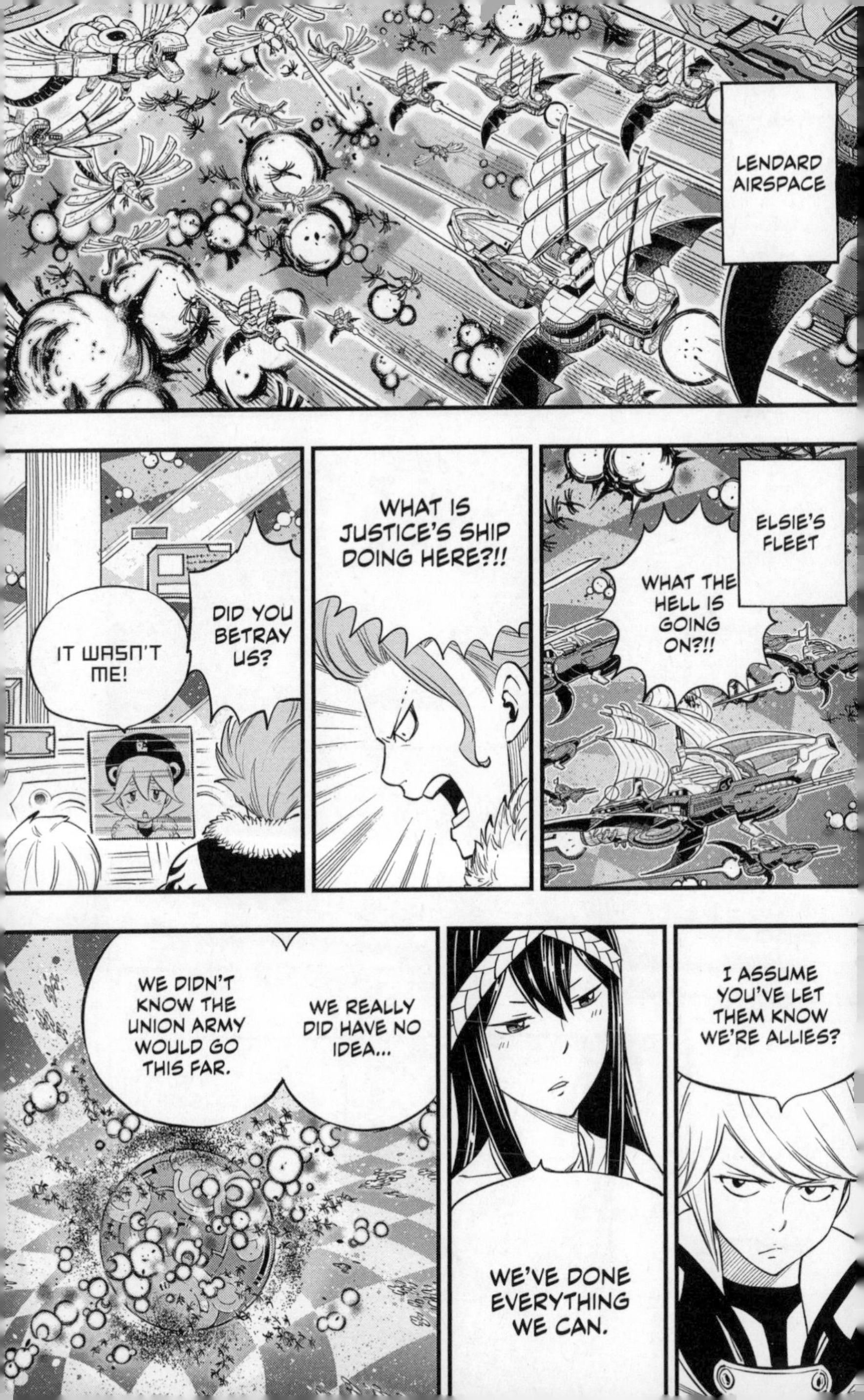
LENDARD AIRSPACE
ELSIE'S FLEET
WHAT THE HELL IS GOING ON?!!
WHAT IS JUSTICE'S SHIP DOING HERE?!!
DID YOU BETRAY US?
IT WASN'T ME!
I ASSUME YOU'VE LET THEM KNOW WE'RE ALLIES?
WE'VE DONE EVERYTHING WE CAN.
WE REALLY DID HAVE NO IDEA...
WE DIDN'T KNOW THE UNION ARMY WOULD GO THIS FAR.

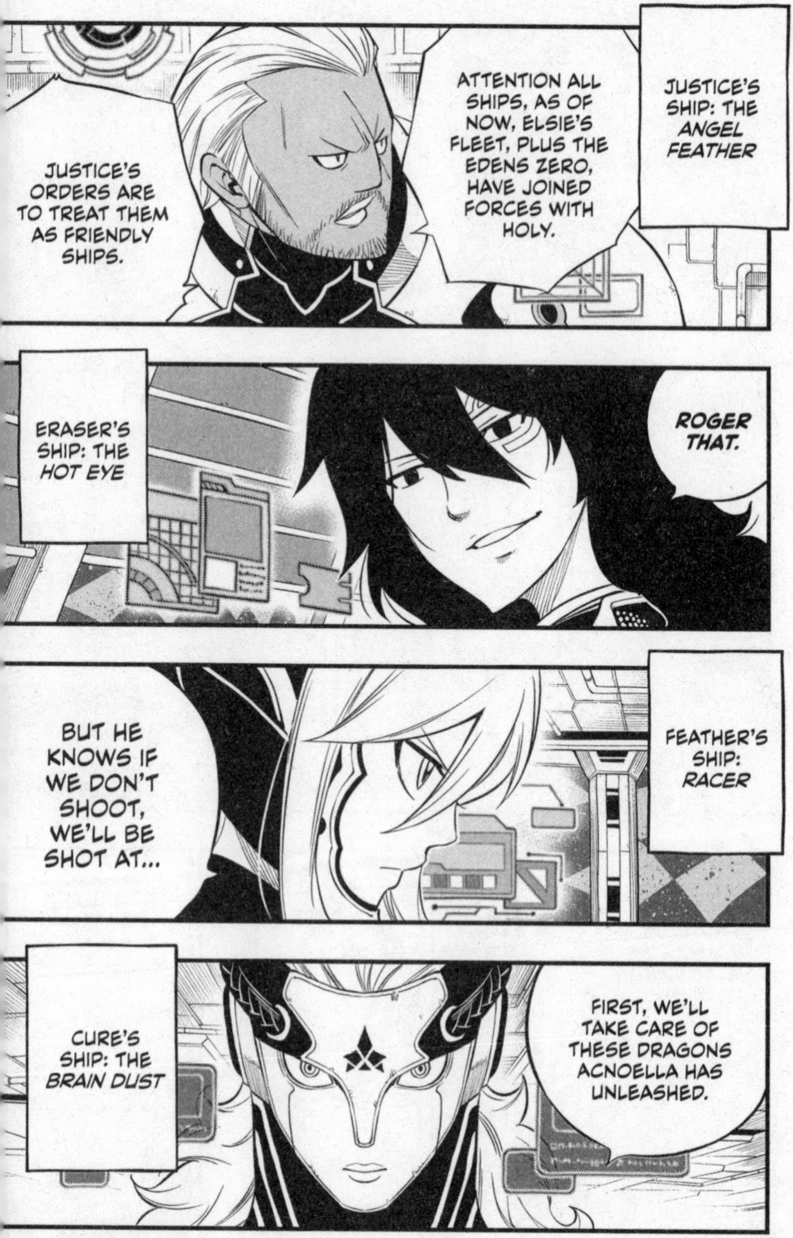
JUSTICE'S SHIP: THE *ANGEL FEATHER*
ATTENTION ALL SHIPS, AS OF NOW, ELSIE'S FLEET, PLUS THE EDENS ZERO, HAVE JOINED FORCES WITH HOLY.
JUSTICE'S ORDERS ARE TO TREAT THEM AS FRIENDLY SHIPS.
ROGER THAT.
ERASER'S SHIP: THE *HOT EYE*
FEATHER'S SHIP: *RACER*
BUT HE KNOWS IF WE DON'T SHOOT, WE'LL BE SHOT AT...
FIRST, WE'LL TAKE CARE OF THESE DRAGONS ACNOELLA HAS UNLEASHED.
CURE'S SHIP: THE *BRAIN DUST*

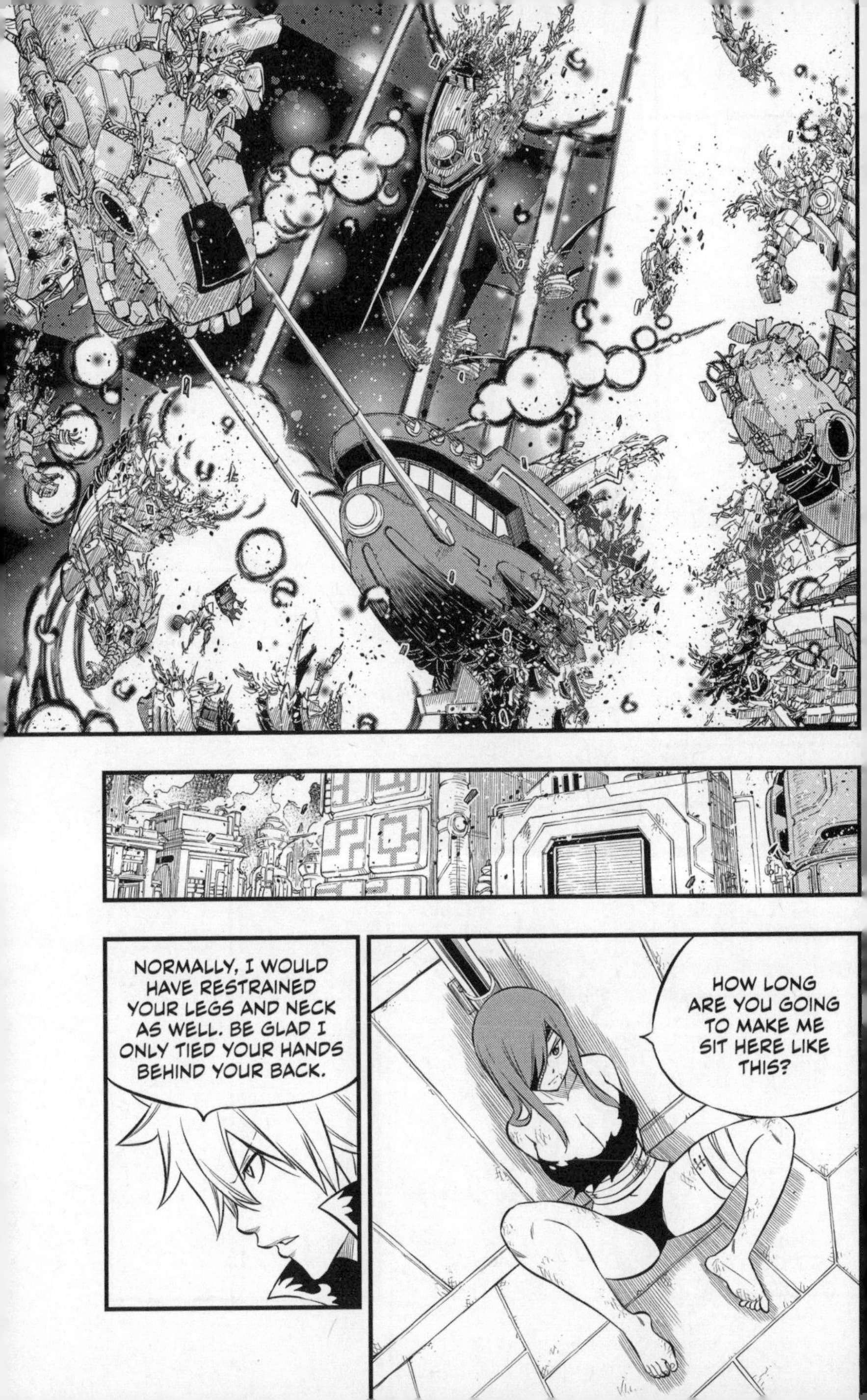
HOW LONG ARE YOU GOING TO MAKE ME SIT HERE LIKE THIS?
NORMALLY, I WOULD HAVE RESTRAINED YOUR LEGS AND NECK AS WELL. BE GLAD I ONLY TIED YOUR HANDS BEHIND YOUR BACK.

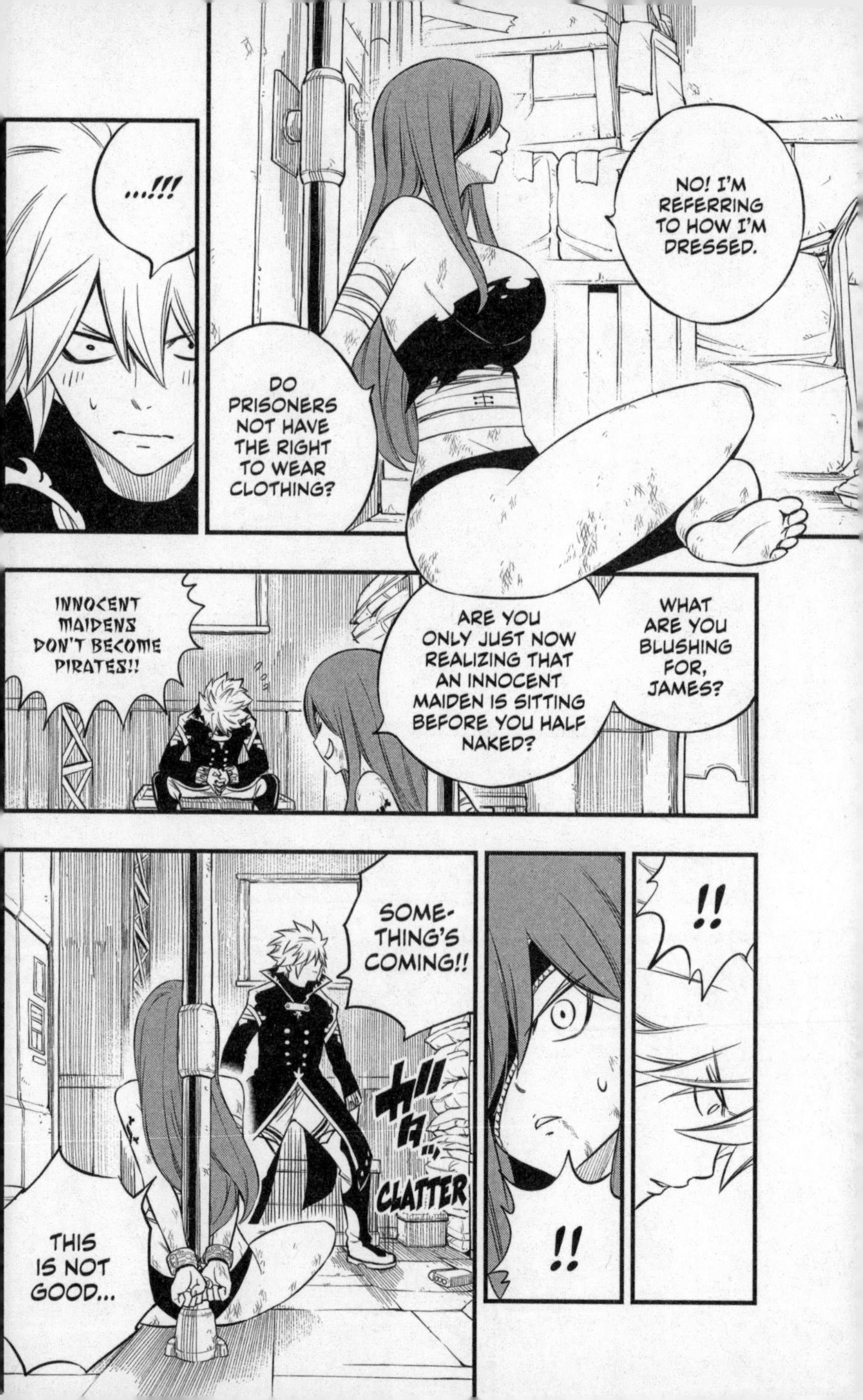
NO! I'M REFERRING TO HOW I'M DRESSED.
DO PRISONERS NOT HAVE THE RIGHT TO WEAR CLOTHING?
...!!!
WHAT ARE YOU BLUSHING FOR, JAMES?
ARE YOU ONLY JUST NOW REALIZING THAT AN INNOCENT MAIDEN IS SITTING BEFORE YOU HALF NAKED?
INNOCENT MAIDENS DON'T BECOME PIRATES!!
!!
!!
SOME-THING'S COMING!!
CLATTER
THIS IS NOT GOOD...

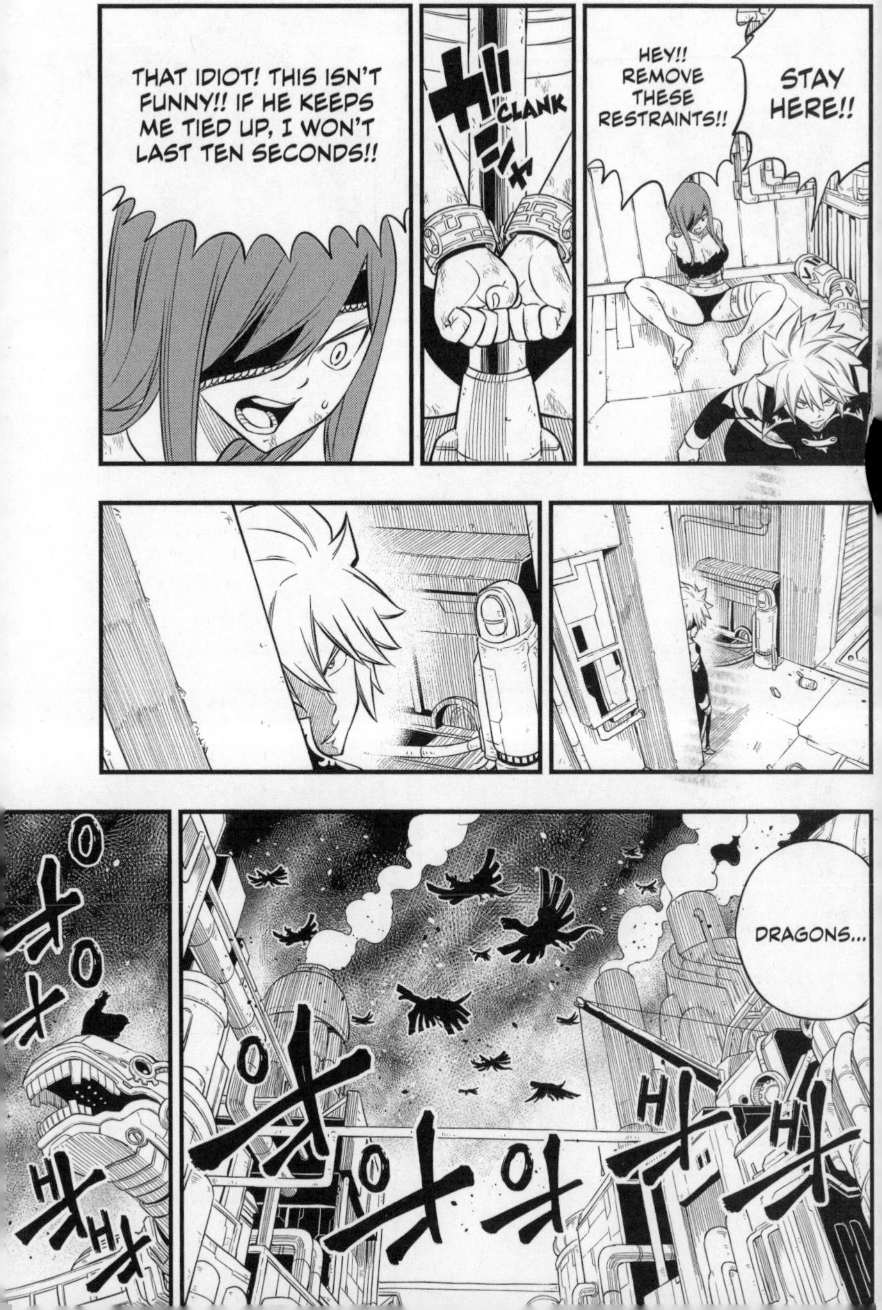
STAY HERE!!
HEY!! REMOVE THESE RESTRAINTS!!
CLANK
THAT IDIOT! THIS ISN'T FUNNY!! IF HE KEEPS ME TIED UP, I WON'T LAST TEN SECONDS!!
DRAGONS...

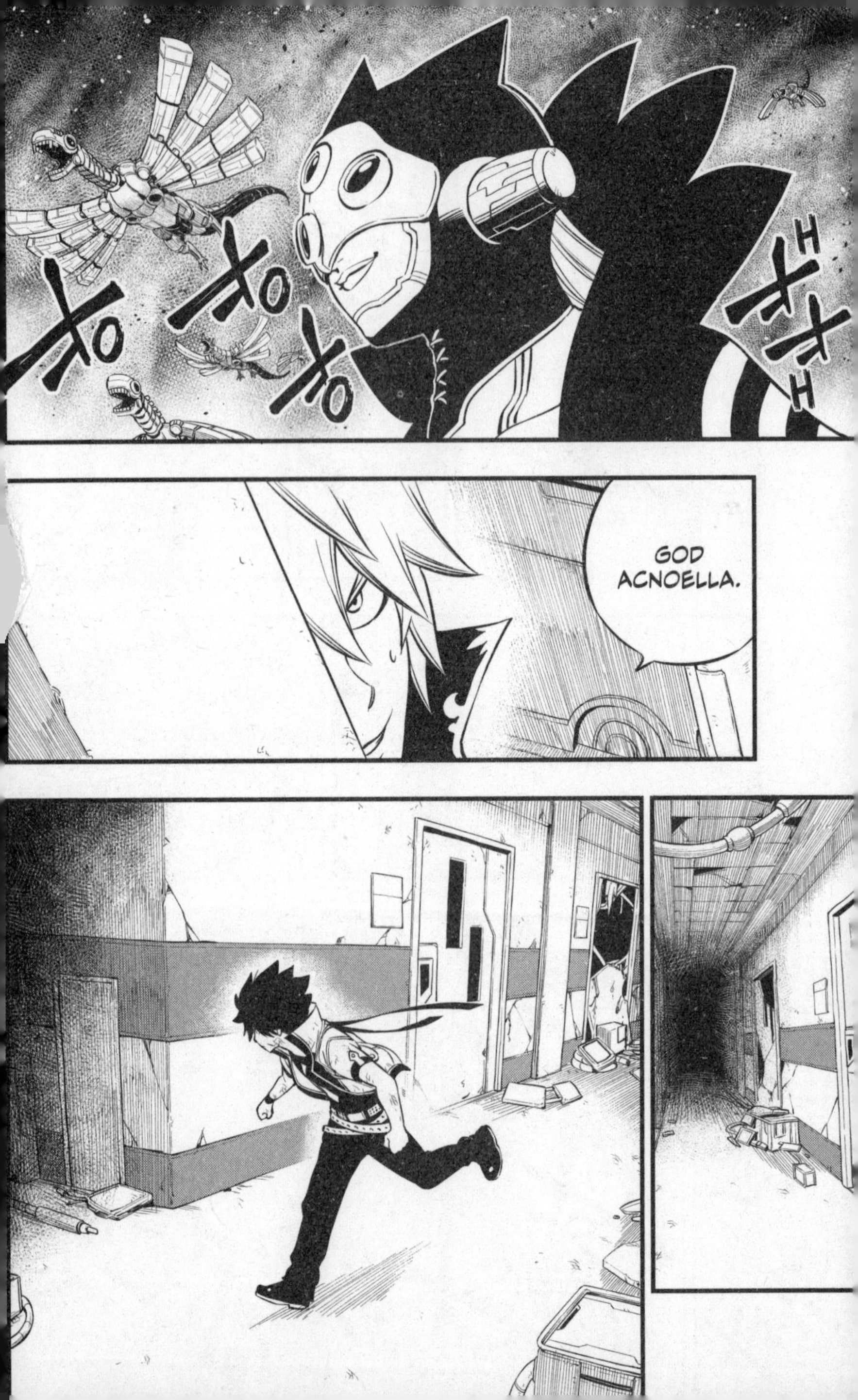
GOD ACNOELLA.

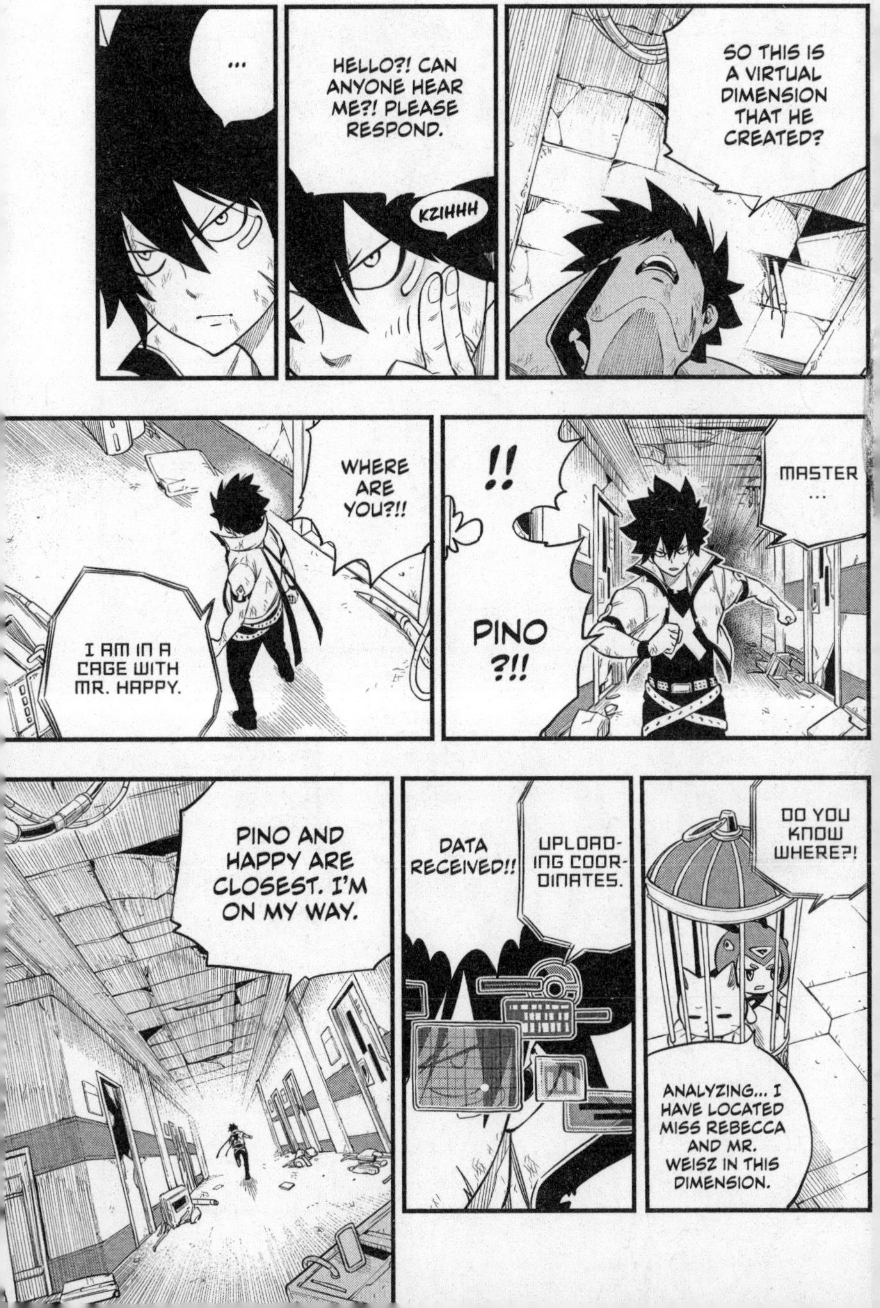
SO THIS IS A VIRTUAL DIMENSION THAT HE CREATED?
HELLO?! CAN ANYONE HEAR ME?! PLEASE RESPOND.
KZIHHH
...
MASTER ...
!!
PINO ?!!
WHERE ARE YOU?!!
I AM IN A CAGE WITH MR. HAPPY.
DO YOU KNOW WHERE?!
ANALYZING... I HAVE LOCATED MISS REBECCA AND MR. WEISZ IN THIS DIMENSION.
UPLOAD-ING COOR-DINATES.
DATA RECEIVED!!
PINO AND HAPPY ARE CLOSEST. I'M ON MY WAY.

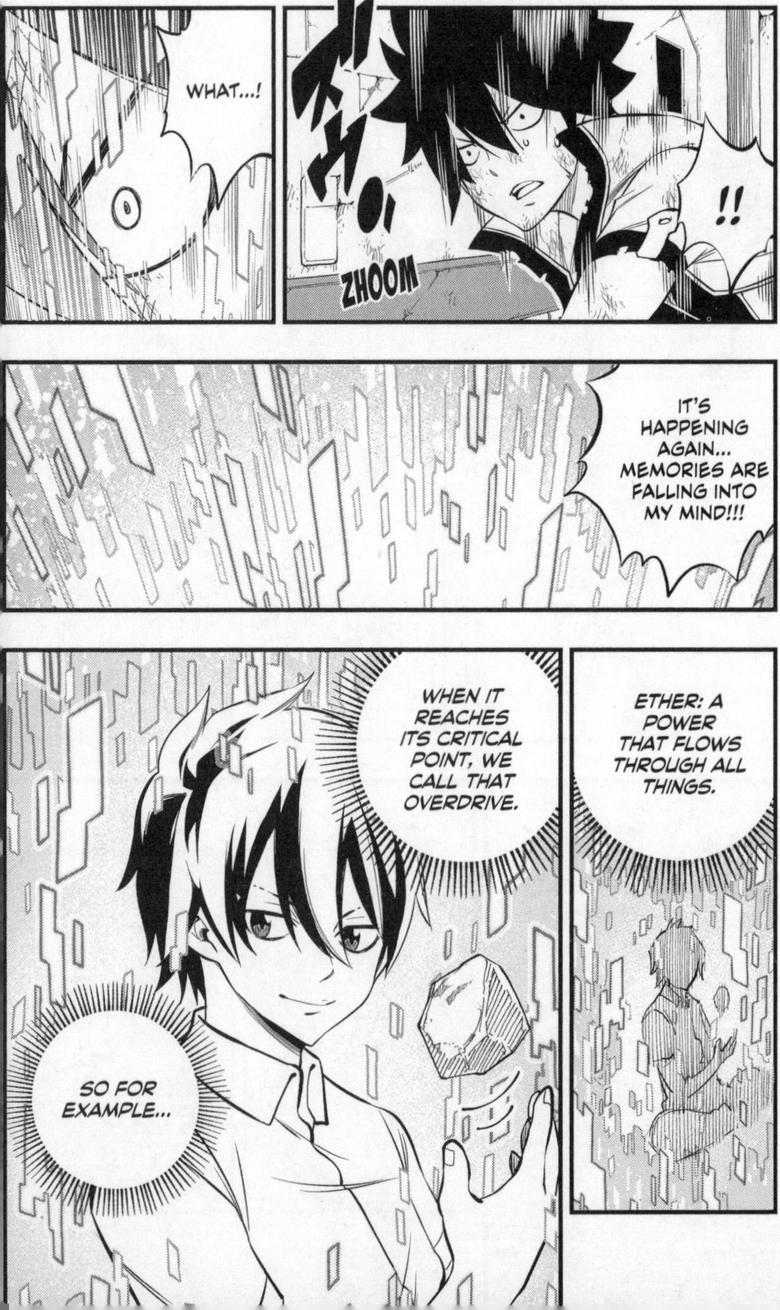
ZHOOM
!!
WHAT...!
IT'S HAPPENING AGAIN... MEMORIES ARE FALLING INTO MY MIND!!!
ETHER: A POWER THAT FLOWS THROUGH ALL THINGS.
WHEN IT REACHES ITS CRITICAL POINT, WE CALL THAT OVERDRIVE.
SO FOR EXAMPLE...

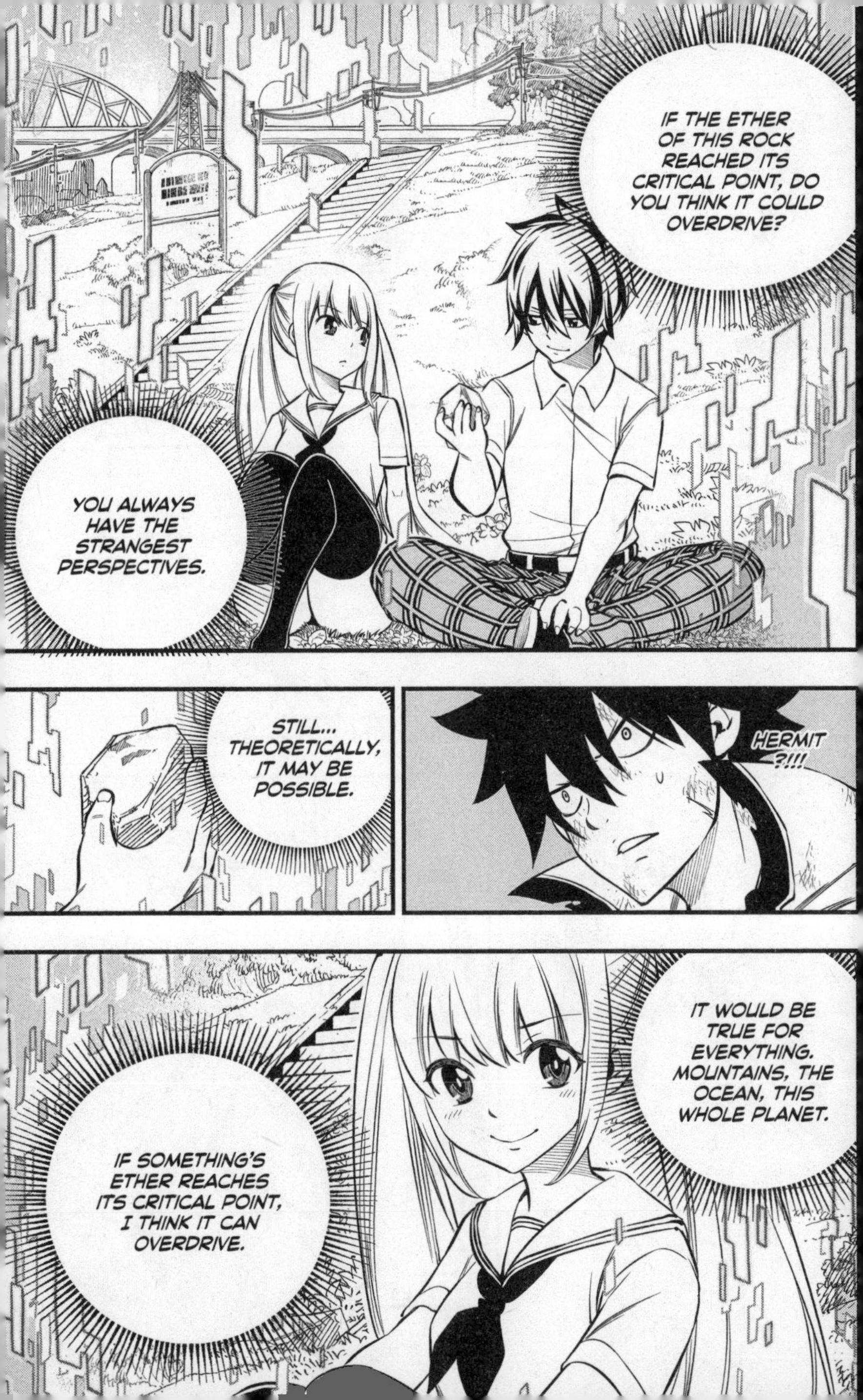
IF THE ETHER OF THIS ROCK REACHED ITS CRITICAL POINT, DO YOU THINK IT COULD OVERDRIVE?
YOU ALWAYS HAVE THE STRANGEST PERSPECTIVES.
HERMIT?!!!
STILL... THEORETICALLY, IT MAY BE POSSIBLE.
IT WOULD BE TRUE FOR EVERYTHING. MOUNTAINS, THE OCEAN, THIS WHOLE PLANET.
IF SOMETHING'S ETHER REACHES ITS CRITICAL POINT, I THINK IT CAN OVERDRIVE.

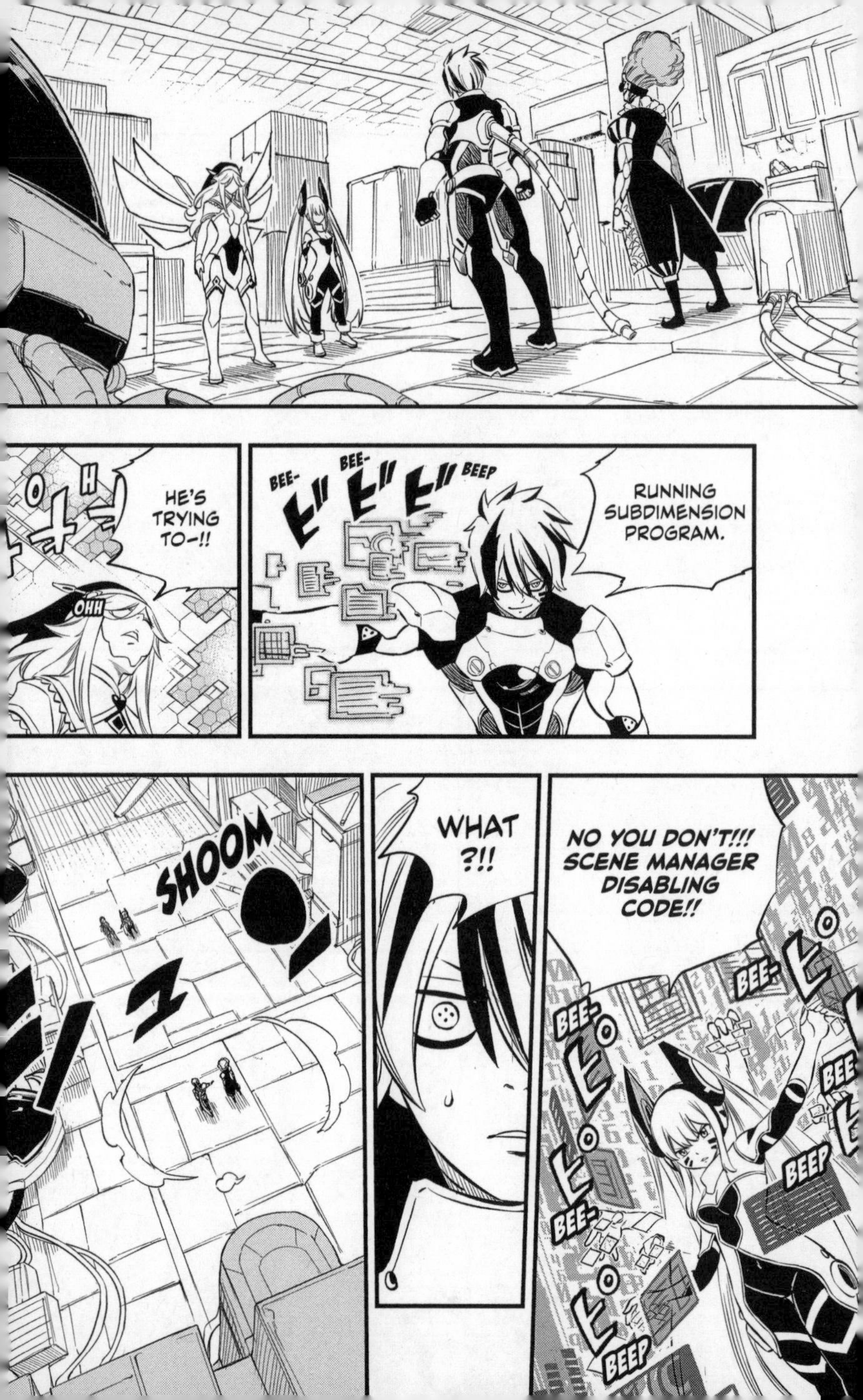
RUNNING SUBDIMENSION PROGRAM.
BEE- BEE- BEEP
HE'S TRYING TO-!!
OHH
NO YOU DON'T!!! SCENE MANAGER DISABLING CODE!!
BEE-
BEE-
BEE
BEEP
BEE-
BEEP
WHAT ?!!
SHOOM

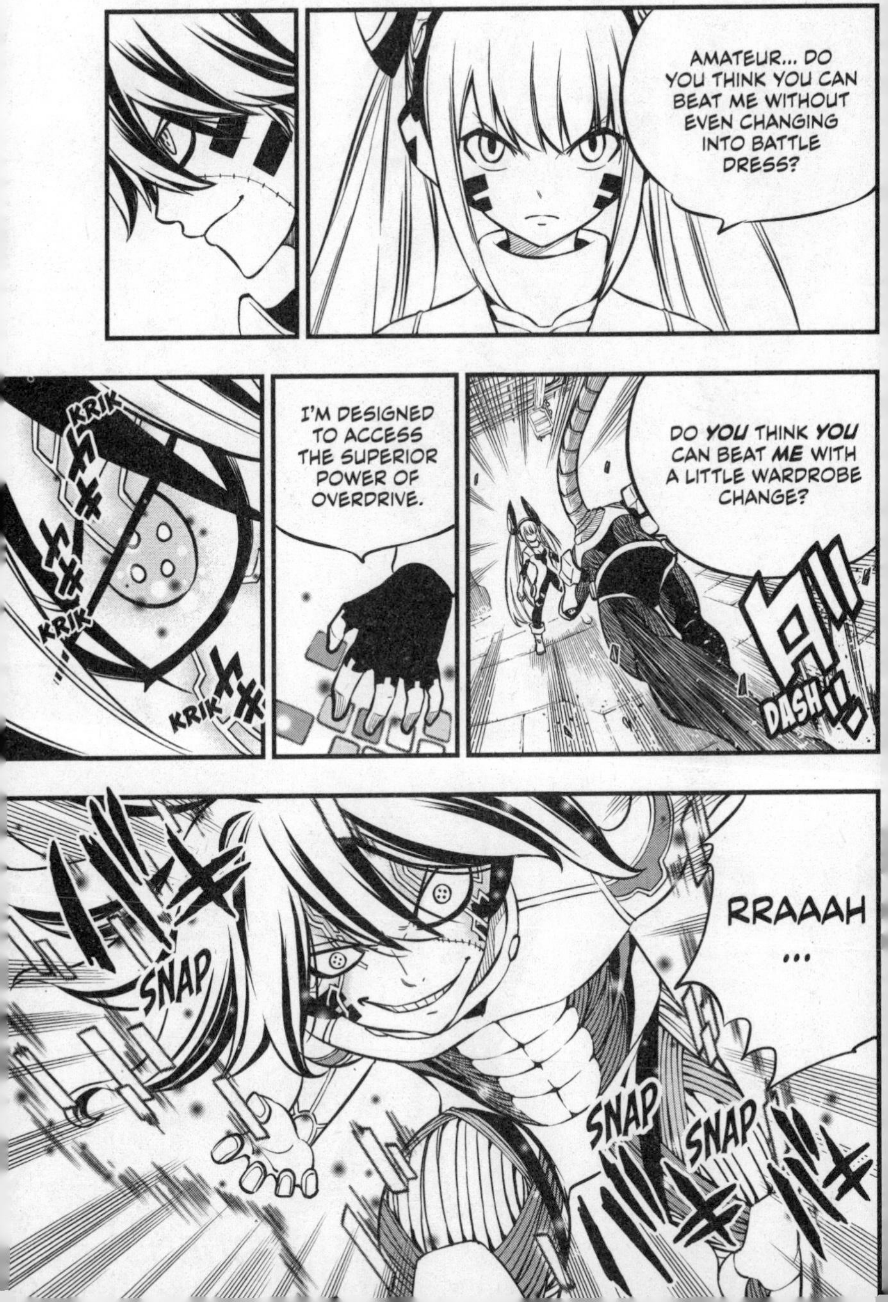
AMATEUR... DO YOU THINK YOU CAN BEAT ME WITHOUT EVEN CHANGING INTO BATTLE DRESS?
DO *YOU* THINK *YOU* CAN BEAT *ME* WITH A LITTLE WARDROBE CHANGE?
DASH
I'M DESIGNED TO ACCESS THE SUPERIOR POWER OF OVERDRIVE.
KRIK
KRIK
KRIK
RRAAAH ...
SNAP
SNAP
SNAP

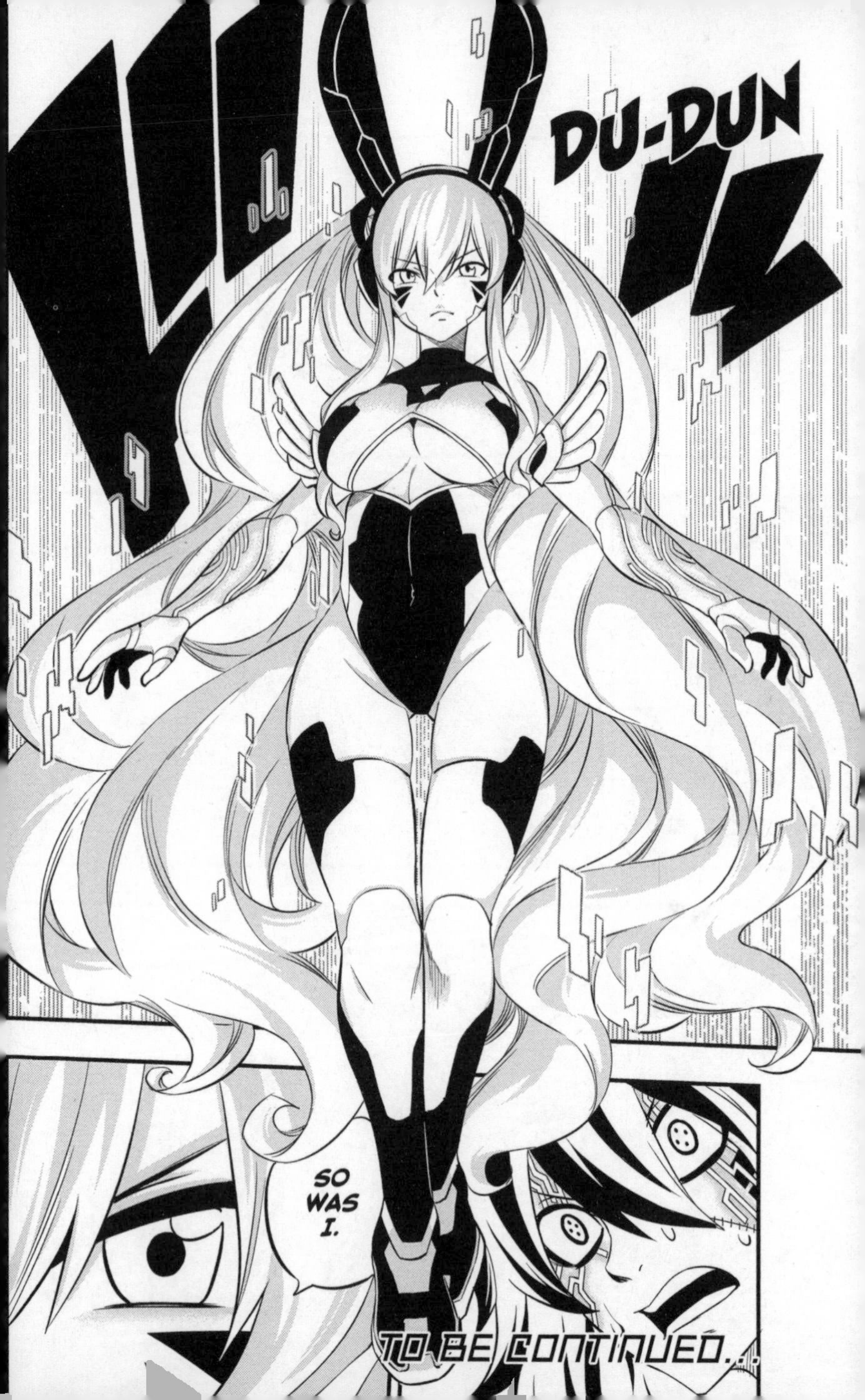
DU-DUN
SO WAS I.
TO BE CONTINUED...

EDENS ZERO

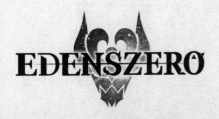

WELCOME TO THE NEXT INSTALLMENT OF...

(Sugasano-san, Gifu)

押せないとゴリゴリ

モスコイ！
自分、前作からのファンス。
エルシーさんにモス恋…
これからもがんばってモス。
応援してるでゴワス！！

DON'T PUSH

◀ Mosco, who may be the number one most popular(?!) character for this corner. We're publishing your drawing, so please don't push it!

(Naru-Naru-san, Hokkaido)

ピーノ
中学生ver

EDENS ZERO 大好きです！
これからも応援してます。

▲ And Pino is every bit as popular. You can really feel the middle-school-ness in this drawing!

(Takoyaki-san, Tokyo)

カウチポ
Chてらつくしゃ
!!!!
ラブ放
たべること
大好き
わたくし好

EDENS ZERO

真島ヒロ先生へ
このイラストはEDENS ZEROの
がんの6ページの1コマ目のイラストです。
これからもがんばってくださいおう
えんしています。

▲ This Couchpo seems to be full of flavor.

(Mio-san, Tokyo)

真島先生のまんがが
大好きです！
EZではハーミット
が一番好きです
これからも
頑張って
(ください)

"Thank you for your hard work!!"

▲ I'm pretty sure Hermit is also "the Soother of Edens."

MASHIMA'S ONE-HIT KO

(White Jack-san, Kagoshima)

ピーノクラゲの大好り。
ごま主人は真島ヒロ先生ですが、どお
これって本当に（EDENS ZERO）の
連載が継続お願いし
ます！！

エデンズゼロ、ウルトラスーパー大好きです！！
フェアリーテイルと同じくらい長期連載に
してほしいです！！

▲ I'll need all of your help to make this wish come true! Please keep reading!

*Fan art submissions are limited to Japan-only.

EZ DRAWING

(Nazuna-san, Niigata)

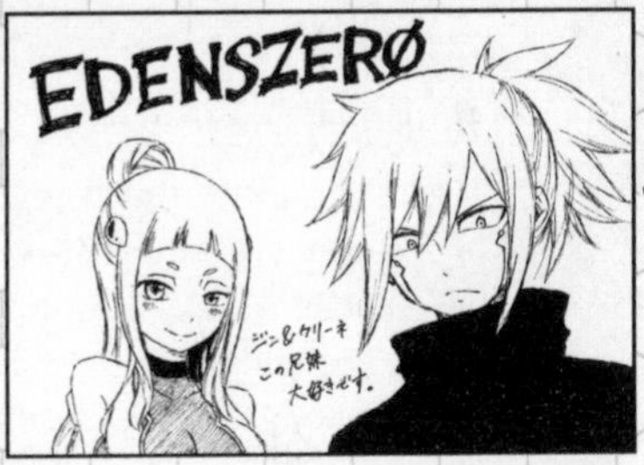
EDENSZERØ
ジン&クリーネ
この兄妹
大好きです。

▶Indispensable members of the Edens Zero's crew, and a really cool duo (as long as they keep their mouths shut).

(Ririshiro-san, Tokyo)

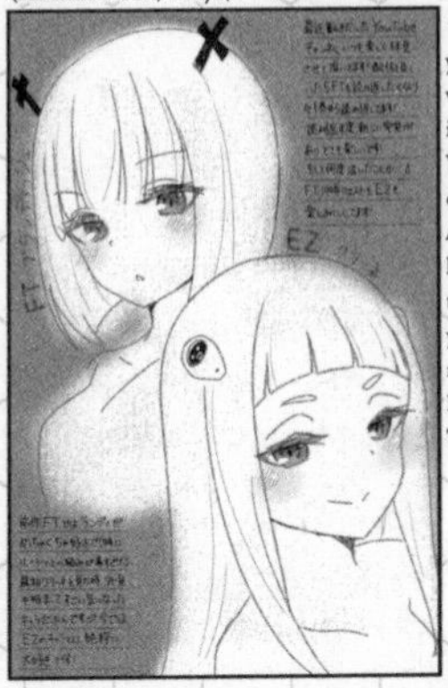

◀Thank you for watching my YouTube channel! And I'm happy to hear you're rereading Fairy Tail!

(LasbellUme-san, Osaka)

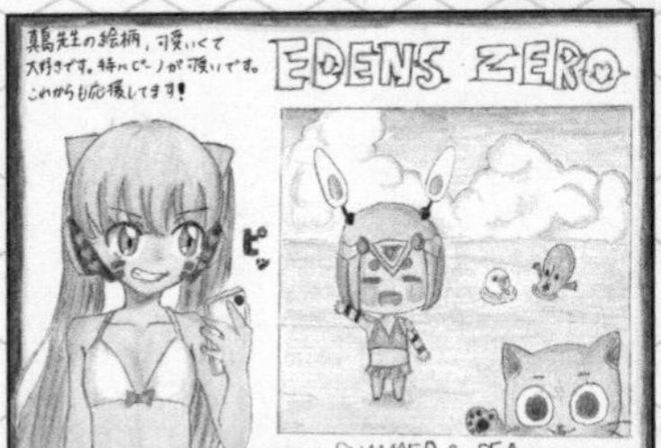
真島先生の絵柄、可愛いくて大好きです。特にピーノが可愛いです。これからも応援してます!
EDENS ZERO
ピッ
SUMMER & SEA

◀So heart-warming. A summer vacation with this gang ♪

(Kyoko Yasuda-san, Tokyo)

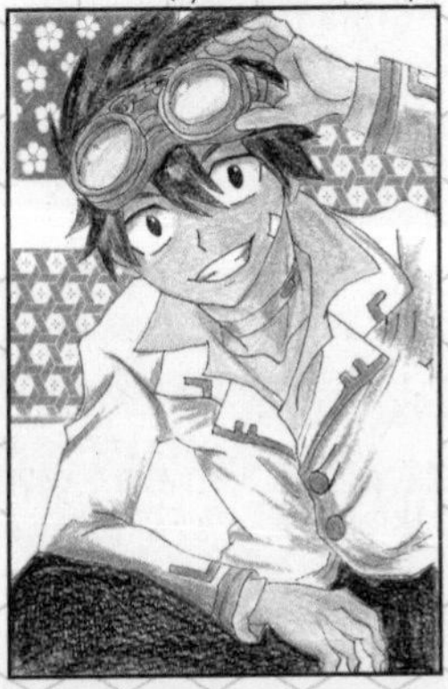

▶A refreshingly suave Shiki with a pose to match! This drawing would be perfect for a summer commercial for bottled water.

(Angelica Campaci-san, Italy)

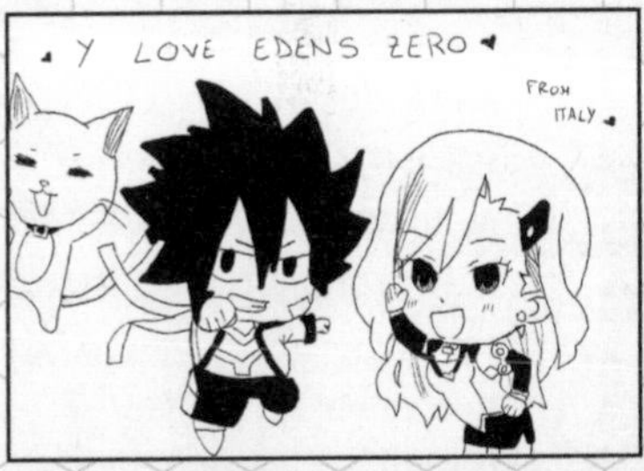
Y LOVE EDENS ZERO
FROM ITALY

▶A submission from Italy! Thank you! Grazie!!

AFTERWORD

I wanted to stream live drawings, so I started a YouTube channel! I was planning to focus on livestreaming, but I figured since I had a channel, I might as well make videos, too, so I tried it, and it was pretty fun! All my videos and streams are archived on the channel, so definitely check it out.

I really am starting from zero with video production—I know nothing about filming or editing or anything, so I'm learning a lot as I go. Editing takes an especially long time, and part of it is that I'm still getting the hang of it. But if I don't figure something out, there's going to be a limit to how much I can do while also doing a weekly manga series. Also, my voice is so hideous it hurts.

It never really bothered me before, but doing these streams and videos, I'm hearing my voice more than I ever have before in my life. I keep thinking, "Has my voice always been this bad? I'm so inarticulate. What's wrong with my intonation?" It's so embarrassing, I just want to curl up in a corner of my room. I figure if I'm going to keep doing streams, I have to improve this somehow, so I started some training to help my articulation and I'm doing vocalization exercises, and it's like, "What are you doing? You're a manga artist!"

That being the case, I'm trying something new, learning more, and working hard. It's the kind of thing that you just do naturally when you're young, and I'm happy to still have experiences like this at my age.

My YouTube channel is something I'm doing 100% as a hobby, so right now my main content is live drawings and how to draw manga, but I'm thinking I'd like to stream games and do game commentating, too. I hope you'll subscribe.

Now about the story. This particular series is one where there are a few big mysteries that need to be revealed. I think it's going to be pretty mind-blowing, so I hope you look forward to it.

The other day, I told my editors, "I can't do dark fantasy," and the reply was, "Depending on how you look at it, **Edens Zero** is pretty dark."

EDENS ZERO

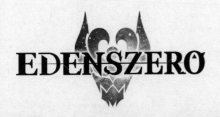

The boys are back, in 400-page hardcovers that are as pretty and badass as they are!

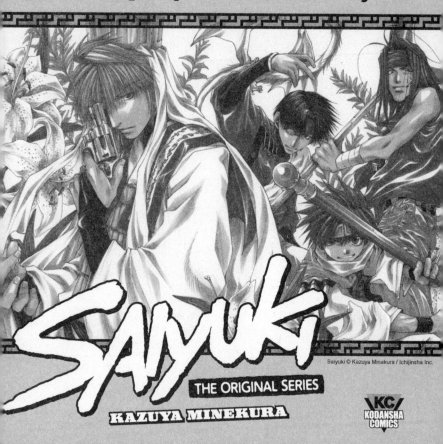

Saiyuki © Kazuya Minekura / Ichijinsha Inc.

SAIYUKI

THE ORIGINAL SERIES

KAZUYA MINEKURA

"AN EDGY COMIC LOOK AT AN ANCIENT CHINESE TALE." —YALSA

Genjo Sanzo is a Buddhist priest in the city of Togenkyo, which is being ravaged by yokai spirits that have fallen out of balance with the natural order. His superiors send him on a journey far to the west to discover why this is happening and how to stop it. His companions are three yokai with human souls. But this is no day trip — the four will encounter many discoveries and horrors on the way.

FEATURES NEW TRANSLATION, COLOR PAGES, AND BEAUTIFUL WRAPAROUND COVER ART!

Young characters and steampunk setting, like *Howl's Moving Castle* and *Battle Angel Alita*

A boy with a talent for machines and a mysterious girl whose wings he's fixed will take you beyond the clouds! In the tradition of the high-flying, resonant adventure stories of Studio Ghibli comes a gorgeous tale about the longing of young hearts for adventure and friendship!

PERFECT WORLD

Rie Aruga

A TOUCHING NEW SERIES ABOUT LOVE AND COPING WITH DISABILITY

An office party reunites Tsugumi with her high school crush Itsuki. He's realized his dream of becoming an architect, but along the way, he experienced a spinal injury that put him in a wheelchair. Now Tsugumi's rekindled feelings will butt up against prejudices she never considered — and Itsuki will have to decide if he's ready to let someone into his heart...

"Depicts with great delicacy and courage the difficulties some with disabilities experience getting involved in romantic relationships... Rie Aruga refuses to romanticize, pushing her heroine to face the reality of disability. She invites her readers to the same tasks of empathy, knowledge and recognition."
—Slate.fr

"An important entry [in manga romance]... The emotional core of both plot and characters indicates thoughtfulness... [Aruga's] research is readily apparent in the text and artwork, making this feel like a real story."
—Anime News Network

The adorable new odd-couple cat comedy manga from the creator of the beloved *Chi's Sweet Home*, in full color!

Sue & Tai-chan

Konami Kanata

Sue is an aging housecat who's looking forward to living out her life in peace... but her plans change when the mischievous black tomcat Tai-chan enters the picture! Hey! Sue never signed up to be a catsitter! *Sue & Tai-chan* is the latest from the reigning meow-narch of cute kitty comics, Konami Kanata.

KC
KODANSHA
COMICS

A Kodansha Comics Trade Paperback Original
EDENS ZERO 22 copyright © 2022 Hiro Mashima
English translation copyright © 2023 Hiro Mashima

All rights reserved.

Published in the United States by Kodansha Comics, an imprint of Kodansha USA Publishing, LLC, New York.

Publication rights for this English edition arranged through Kodansha Ltd., Tokyo.

First published in Japan in 2022 by Kodansha Ltd., Tokyo.

ISBN 978-1-64651-691-9

Printed in the United States of America.

www.kodansha.us

9 8 7 6 5 4 3 2 1
Translation: Alethea Nibley & Athena Nibley
Lettering: AndWorld Design
Editing: David Yoo
Kodansha Comics edition cover design by Phil Balsman

Publisher: Kiichiro Sugawara

Director of publishing services: Ben Applegate
Director of publishing operations: Dave Barrett
Publishing services managing editors: Madison Salters, Alanna Ruse, with Grace Chen
Production manager: Jocelyn O'Dowd